Child's Pay

Acknowledgements

I wish to thank Nicola Van Lennep who has written the computer program and manual, my pupil Emma Crawforth for her patient administrative assistance, Ken Baublis of the D.S.S. and Andy Carter and Mark Webb of the Child Support Agency for keeping me updated on developments, John Dewar of Hertford College, Oxford who has reviewed the text and corrected a number of legal solecisms, Nicholas Wilson Q.C. who has been my mentor in almost all things legal, and, most importantly, my long suffering wife Lucy.

THE FAMILY LAW
BAR ASSOCIATION

FLBA

Child's Pay

The Complete Guide to the Child Support Act 1991 and the Subordinate Legislation

Nicholas Mostyn
LL.B., Barrister-at-law

The right of Nicholas Mostyn to be identified as author of this work has been asserted by him in accordance with the Copyright, Designs and Patents Act 1988

Printing history
First published 1993

A CIP catalogue record for this book is available from the British Library

ISBN 1 872362 12 5

For details of the computer program and manual which accompany this book, please contact the publishers.

Class Publishing, PO Box 1498, London W6 7RS

Designed by Wendy Bann

Edited by Susan Bosanko

Indexed by Elizabeth M. Moys

Production by Landmark Production Consultants Ltd, Princes Risborough

Typesetting by Concept Typesetting, Salisbury, Wilts

Printed in Great Britain
by Short Run Press, Exeter

The structure of the book

Foreword

by NICHOLAS WILSON Q.C.

The old laws relating to child maintenance have not been working well. Too few orders have been made and, where they have been made, they have often been surprisingly divergent, generally too low and frequently disobeyed. One of the major causes of the problem has been the apathy of the Department of Social Security towards pursuing fathers in the Courts for maintenance of children reared on State benefits. So it is ironic that the radical answer given to the problem in the Child Support Act 1991 is to remove child maintenance almost entirely from the ambit of the Courts even in non-benefit cases and to vest the entire administration of the levy in an arm of that Department.

It would be easy for family lawyers to feel sceptical about the removal of the judicial discretion which, so we have been conditioned proudly to believe, provides bespoke justice tailored for each family and about the inconvenient severance of one aspect of the financial consequences of a broken relationship from the others. Nevertheless our response to Parliament's experiment should be generous; and our criticisms constructive.

Even under the new legislation we will have a very active role to play. In every new case the client, whether mother or father, will need to be advised whether to attempt to negotiate a private agreement (and, if so, in what amount) or to apply for an assessment in respect of child maintenance. Such advice will be incompetent unless it includes a prediction of the amount awarded under assessment through application of the statutory formulae to the family's circumstances. Furthermore, where assessment is made, we should anticipate quite frequent dissatisfaction on the part particularly of the absent parent, who may then turn back to lawyers for advice and representation on appeal or on enforcement, to which latter stage that famous discretion appears in part to have been simply shunted forwards. Can you see the unmarried father, after perhaps only one act of intercourse with the mother, tolerating as heavy and as longstanding an inroad into his economy as is decreed by the new legislation? I foresee many fathers, married and unmarried, evading, prevaricating and, where possible, understating their income and overstating the matters which will enlarge their exempt and protected income. One of the most intriguing questions raised by the new Act is whether the Child Support Agency will prove effective in combating such

non-cooperation and specifically in exposing the inaccuracies in data presented to it. We read on a later page of this book that the Agency has
draconian powers to obtain information. But are the powers of Draco vested
in hard-pressed, neutral civil servants a satisfactory substitute for the ferret-
like qualities of the solicitor or counsel specifically engaged by one parent to
probe the veracity of the other's financial presentation by questionnaire and
cross-examination?

It follows that every family lawyer needs a working knowledge of the main
features of this legislation; ready access to its tedious detail; and the facility
to calculate the statutory amount of maintenance assessable on the particular
facts before him. To these ends he almost certainly needs Nicholas Mostyn's
book and his computer disk. Much, arguably too much, of the new law is to
be collected not from the Act itself but from different sets of regulations. To
work one's way through them without the author's guidance would be arduous
indeed. But the actual calculation of an assessment even from these pages will
remain a laborious exercise and I am sure that the vast majority of us will
be quick to pass the burden of it to the computer. Even I, handicapped by a
poor and at times abusive relationship with computers, can work Nicholas
Mostyn's admirable program so the implication behind his title is rightly
there.

Table of Cases

Table of Statutes and Regulations

Note: the Child Support Act 1991 and the Regulations made under it have not been indexed in detail, but citations to other Acts have been included.

Statutes

Statutory Instruments

CHAPTER 1

Introduction

On 5th April 1993 the Child Support Act 1991 ("the Act") and the Regulations made thereunder will come into effect. The Child Support Agency ("the Agency") will begin its operations on that date. The Agency was described by the Lord Chancellor on the second reading of the Child Support Bill in the House of Lords on 25th February 1991 in the following terms:

> "[It] will be established as a next steps agency under the authority of. . .the Secretary of State for Social Security. The agency will trace absent parents, investigate the parents' means and assess, collect and enforce payments of child maintenance. Your Lordships will know that as a next steps agency the agency will have no independent existence in statute. The powers that it will need to do its work are, therefore, expressed as powers of. . .the Secretary of State for Social Security."

The Act revolutionises the principles hitherto applicable to the assessment of child maintenance. It applies to all cases, whether or not social security payments are being made.

The role of the Court will be severely curtailed.

Every family lawyer will need to be familiar with the principles embodied in the Act, for under Section 9(3) of the Act the existence of a maintenance agreement cannot prevent any parent from applying for an assessment under the Act; and by Section 9(4) any provision of any such agreement which purports to restrict that right is void.

Accordingly legal advisers will have to negotiate child maintenance payments by reference to the principles within the Act, for failure so to do will simply expose the client to the risk of a higher or lower assessment by the Agency. Moreover, advisers will undoubtedly be called on to advise aggrieved parents on their rights of review and appeal following an assessment.

In the White Paper *Children Come First* (Cmnd 1264, October 1990) at Paragraph 1.6 the Government stated:

> "In the interests of the children, a single system is needed and that system needs a structure of consistent and rational principles and clearly established priorities."

Although the White Paper speaks in terms of providing a single consistent system for the benefit of all children it is important to recognise that the primary engine for change was that (as stated in its foreword):

> "While many absent parents make regular payments, 70 per cent regrettably do not. The inevitable result is that more and more caring parents and their children have become dependant on Income Support."

The principal underlying policy objective is to recover more money from absent parents for the benefit of parents and children in receipt of Income Support, and hence there is a fundamental dichotomy of treatment within the Act between benefit and non-benefit cases. In a benefit case the Agency can (and by implication usually will) insist on utilisation of the Child Support Act system, whereas in a non-benefit case utilisation of the system is entirely voluntary, in the sense that parents are perfectly entitled to agree levels inconsistent with agency criteria, although, as has been noted, it would generally be unwise for them to do so. Where a parent refuses to co-operate in a benefit case the scheme gives Child Support Officers draconian powers to direct an abatement of the parent's benefit.

The structure that emerged from the White Paper and the consultation process that followed comprises the Act and, so far, 17 sets of subordinate legislation. At the time of writing (February 1993) the D.S.S. is proposing to issue at least one further set of Amendment Regulations in March 1993. The structure that emerges is consistent and rational, but it is certainly not simple. Much of the legislative material is dense and difficult to understand. Accordingly, there is set out below a very attenuated survey of the new scheme identifying the main principles, concepts and philosophies. Chapter 2 lists all the governing statutory material and identifies and explains certain key expressions that are used throughout the legislative material. Most Chapters are prefaced by preliminary paragraphs identifying the basic principles of the subject to be addressed. Where detailed statutory material is analysed and presented use is made of specific comments and examples.

A survey of the scheme

The fundamental principle is that child maintenance will be assessed by reference to a series of algebraic formulae which will be applied by the Child Support Officer to his assessment of the income of the parent in question, which in turn is calculated by reference to a series of further formulae. There is little scope for discretion. The formulae are superficially detailed but are not, in a mathematical sense, of very great complexity.

The first ingredient is the "maintenance requirement". This is the basic sum determined by Parliament to be needed for the support of the children. It is calculated by adding together the Income Support allowances which would be paid for the children and the parent who is responsible for their care, if that family had no other income, and then deducting the basic rate of child benefit payable in respect of the children. Chapter 6 sets out the detailed provisions necessary for calculating the maintenance requirement.

The maintenance requirement is then "paid" by each parent contributing half of his/her "assessable" income until the maintenance requirement is met. In many cases the maintenance requirement will not be met in full as one half of the assessable incomes will not cover it. It is only the absent parent who is actually required to pay money by way of maintenance. The "payment" by the person with care is a notional contribution, the amount of which impacts on the sum to be paid by the absent parent.

Once the maintenance requirement is met, a further liability arises. Paragraph 3.21 of the White Paper stated:

> "The maintenance bill does not fix the maximum amount of child maintenance which should be paid. If the parents have sufficient income, they should pay something over and above that amount so that the children can share in their parents' standard of living. This is, after all, what would happen in ordinary family life."

The White Paper spoke of a contribution of 15% of relevant income from the point that the maintenance bill had been met, although the scheme as ultimately enacted specifies the rate of further contribution at 25%. This is subject to an overall ceiling of 3 times the aggregate of the Income Support allowances for each child and an amount equivalent to the Income Support family premium in respect of each child. The ceiling is set at quite a high level: for example the maximum amount payable in respect of one child under 11 years of age would be £137.70 per week.

Where the ceiling has been reached the parent with care is entitled to apply to the Court for a "top-up". In addition, the Court retains power to make school fees and similar orders. The role of the Court is fully considered in Chapter 19.

Just as with legal aid eligibility, "assessable" income for the purposes of the scheme is calculated in accordance with social security criteria. It amounts to the gross income in question less tax, National Insurance, 50% of pension premiums, housing costs and the amount of the Income Support allowances that would be payable to the parent in question for himself and any natural child of his who is living with him if he was entitled to that benefit. The Regulations are complex and detailed and are set out and analysed in Chapters 7-16.

As under the Attachment of Earnings Act 1971 the scheme provides for an income safety-net for the absent payer. His family's income cannot fall below the "protected income" level, which is assessed by reference to Income Support levels and reasonable housing costs for everyone in his new family.

Not all families will be organised in the common manner with the mother having care of the children and the father having a certain degree of contact. The parents may share the care. A third party may also be caring for the children. The parents may have new partners who in turn have children from previous relationships. The parent and the new partner may have children from that relationship. The parents may have pre-existing maintenance obligations in respect of other children. These are all covered by the ubiquitous "Special Cases" whereby an attempt is made to legislate for every conceivable variety of human existence. These are covered in Chapter 18.

The legislation contains detailed provisions concerning procedure, interim arrangements, disclosure, terminations, reviews, appeals, collection and enforcement. These are comprehensively dealt with in Chapters 20-29.

There is a 4 year phasing-in period during which the role of the Court will be important. This is considered in Chapter 19. During the phasing-in period new "non-benefit" cases can effectively be contracted out of the system and made subject to the conventional discretion of the Court. Advisers will have to consider most carefully whether such a contracting out will be in the interests of the client.

Undertaking the calculation

When undertaking a Child Support Act calculation the adviser must be able to identify which relevant items from an almost infinite array of possible data apply to the case in question, and then to determine which of the many formulae are applicable thereto. With pen, paper and calculator it will inevitably be a tortuous exercise, with much opportunity for error. The procedure is most apt for the assistance of a computer program.

The computer program accompanying this book leads the adviser through every stage of the lengthy path that he must follow, and produces for him the likely result of an assessment. It is written on the explicit premise that an adviser with little or no knowledge of the operation of such a program will be able to use it without any difficulty. It eschews all technical jargon, and is presented in plain language. But for those who prefer to rely on the written word this book endeavours to present all the material relevant to any aspect of assessment or procedure under the Act.

The rates used for Income Support and other social security allowances and for National Insurance are those announced in Parliament on 12th November 1992 for 1993/94, while those used for Income Tax rates and allowances are at 1992/93 levels being those in force at the time of writing. The social security rates for 1993/94 are set out in Appendix 3.

Essential terminology

I THE LEGISLATION

The scheme of the new Child Support system is governed by the following statutory provisions:

The Child Support Act 1991 ("the Act")

Section 62 of the Finance (No 2) Act 1992

The Child Support (Maintenance Assessments and Special Cases) Regulations 1992 (S.I. 1992 No 1815) ("the Assessment Regulations")

The Child Support (Maintenance Assessment Procedure) Regulations 1992 (S.I. 1992 No 1813) ("the Procedure Regulations")

The Child Support (Arrears, Interest and Adjustment of Maintenance Assessments) Regulations 1992 (S.I. 1992 No 1816) ("the Arrears Regulations")

The Child Support (Collection and Enforcement) Regulations 1992 (S.I. 1992 No 1989) ("the Collection Regulations")

The Child Support (Information, Evidence and Disclosure) Regulations 1992 (S.I. 1992 No 1812) ("the Information Regulations")

The Child Support (Collection and Enforcement of other Forms of Maintenance) Regulations 1992 (S.I. 1992 No 2643) ("the Collection of other Forms of Maintenance Regulations")

The Child Support (Maintenance Arrangements and Jurisdiction) Regulations 1992 (S.I. 1992 No 2645) ("the Jurisdiction Regulations")

The Child Support Act 1991 (Commencement No.3 and Transitional Provisions) Order 1992 (S.I. 1992 No 2644) ("the Transitional Provisions Order")

The Child Support Fees Regulations 1992 (S.I. 1992 No 3094) ("the Fees Regulations")

The Child Support Appeal Tribunals (Procedure) Regulations 1992 (S.I. 1992 No 2641) ("the Appeal Tribunals Regulations")

The Child Support Commissioners (Procedure) Regulations 1992(S.I. 1992 No 2640) ("the Commissioners Regulations")

The High Court Distribution of Business Order 1993 (S.I. 1993 No *)

The Children (Allocation of Proceedings) (Amendment) Order 1993 (S.I. 1993 No *)

The Child Support Appeals (Jurisdiction of Courts) Order 1993 (S.I. 1993 No *)

The Child Maintenance (Written Agreements) Order 1993 (S.I. 1993 No *)

The Children (Admissibility of Hearsay Evidence) Order 1993 (S.I. 1993 No *)

The Maintenance Orders (Backdating) Order 1993 (S.I. 1993 No *)

The Family Proceedings (Amendment No. 3) Rules 1993 (S.I. 1993 No *)

All of the above material is reproduced in Appendix 1.

In addition, the following commencement orders have been made:

The Child Support Act 1991 (Commencement No.1) Order 1992 (S.I. 1992 No 1431)

The Child Support Act 1991 (Commencement No.2) Order 1992 (S.I. 1992 No 1938)

The Finance (No 2) Act 1992 Section 62 Commencement Order 1992 (S.I. 1992 No. 2642)

*In draft at time of going to press; number not yet known

II KEY EXPRESSIONS

Certain key expressions appear throughout the statutory provisions.

1. "A person with care"

By Section 3(3) of the Act a person is a person with care if he is a person
  (a) with whom the child has his home, and
  (b) who usually provides day to day care for the child (whether exclusively or in conjunction with any other person), and
  (c) who does not fall within a prescibed category of person.

Regulation 51(1) of the Procedure Regulations provides that the prescribed categories of persons are
  (a) a local authority, or
  (b) a person with whom a child looked after by a local authority (as defined under Section 22 of the Children Act 1989) is placed by that authority under the provisions of the Children Act 1989, or
  (c) in Scotland, a person with whom a child is boarded out by a local authority under the provisions of Section 21 of the Social Work (Scotland) Act 1968.

Regulation 1(2) of the Assessment Regulations defines "day to day care" as care of not less than 2 nights per week on average during
  (a) the 12 month period ending with the relevant week, or
  (b) such other period, ending with the relevant week, as in the opinion of the Child Support Officer is more representative of the current arrangements for the care of the child in question,

and where a child is a boarder at a boarding school or is an in-patient in a hospital, the person who, but for those circumstances, would otherwise provide day to day care of the child, shall be treated as providing day to day care during the periods in question.

Accordingly a parent who has a child to stay overnight on 104 nights each year will qualify as "a person with care", provided that it can properly be said that the child has a "home" with that parent, whereas a parent who has a child to stay 103 days each year will not so qualify.

In determining whether or not a child has a "home" with a parent regard will presumably be had to the basis upon which the child visits that parent. If the child stays with him pursuant to a joint residence order under Section 8 of the Children Act 1989 then it would seem that the existence of a second "home" will be more readily accepted than if the child visits pursuant to a contact order or a voluntary arrangement.

2. "Home"

By Regulation 1(2) of the Assessment Regulations "home" means
  (a) the dwelling in which a person and any family of his normally live, or
  (b) if he or they normally live in more than one home, the principal home of that person and any family of his,

and for the purpose of determining the principal home in which a person normally lives no regard shall be had to residence in a residential care home or a nursing home during a period which does not exceed 52 weeks or, where it appears to the Child Support Officer that the person will return to his principal home after that period has expired, such longer period as that Officer considers reasonable to allow for the return of that person to that home.

3. "An absent parent"

By Section 3(2) of the Act a parent of a child is an absent parent if
   (a) he is not living in the same household as the child, and
   (b) the child has his home with a person who is, in relation to him, a person with care.

By Section 54 of the Act a "parent" means any person who is in law the mother or father of the child. Thus adoptive parents are included, but step-parents are excluded.

It is possible for a parent to be providing "day to day care" for a qualifying child and still to be an absent parent. If a child stays at least 104 nights per annum with a parent, but does not live within his household then that parent will satisfy the test for "day to day care", but will still be "absent". Regulation 18(2)(a)(ii) of the Assessment Regulations expressly contemplates that an absent parent may be providing day to day care for a child.

If an absent parent satisfies the test for "day to day care" there will be a significant impact on the amount of maintenance payable by him for the reasons explained in Chapter 18.

4. "The effective date"

By Regulation 1(2) of the Procedure Regulations "the effective date" means the date on which a maintenance assessment takes effect for the purposes of the Act.

By Regulation 30(2) of the Procedure Regulations the effective date of a new maintenance assessment shall be determined as follows
   (a) where the application for an assessment is made either by a person with care, or by a child in Scotland under Section 7 of the Act, the effective date shall be the date upon which a maintenance enquiry form is given or sent to an absent parent, or
   (b) where the application for an assessment is
      (i)   made by the absent parent, or
      (ii) is made in circumstances where a maintenance assessment has been in force in favour of a person previously with care and that person has been replaced by another person with care, and following such replacement an application for an assessment is made against the person previously with care, or
      (iii) is made in circumstances where a child in Scotland has applied for an assessment under Section 7 of the Act, and that assess-

ment has been cancelled at the request of the child, or that child has ceased to be a child for the purposes of the Act, and following such termination of the assessment an application is made for an assessment of children who were qualifying children for the purpose of the earlier assessment,

the effective date shall be the date upon which an effective maintenance application form is received by the Child Support Agency.

By Regulation 3 of the Procedure Regulations the Child Support Officer shall have the discretion to treat an application made under (b)(ii) or (iii) above as having been received on a date earlier than that on which it was actually received; but such earlier date shall not be more than 8 weeks before the date on which the application was actually received, or (if later) before the first day on which the earlier assessment ceased to have effect.

By Regulation 30(4) of the Procedure Regulations a Child Support Officer may determine in a case under (a) above, where he is satisfied that the absent parent is deliberately avoiding receipt of a maintenance enquiry form, the date upon which the date upon which the form would have been given or sent but for such avoidance.

By Regulation 31 of the Procedure Regulations provisions are made for determining the effective date of a maintenance assessment made following a review under Sections 16-19 of the Act, and these are explained in Chapter 25.

5. "The relevant week"

By Regulation 1(2) of the Assessment Regulations "the relevant week" means

(a) in relation to an application for Child Support maintenance
    (i)   in the case of the person making the application, the period of 7 days immediately preceding the date on which the appropriate maintenance assessment form is submitted to the Agency,
    (ii) in the case of a person to whom a maintenance assessment enquiry form is given or sent as a result of such application, the period of 7 days immediately preceding the date on which that form is to be treated as given or sent under Regulation 1(6)(b) of the Procedure Regulations (i.e. if sent by post, on the second day after posting, excluding Sundays and Bank Holidays),

(b) in relation to a review of a maintenance assessment under Section 16 or Section 17 of the Act, the period of 7 days immediately preceding the date on which a maintenance assessment review enquiry form given or sent to the person in question is to be treated as given or sent under Regulation 1(6)(b) of the Procedure Regulations.

CHAPTER 3

Fundamental principles and jurisdiction

I FUNDAMENTAL PRINCIPLES

Section 1 of the Act provides
  (1) For the purposes of this Act, each parent of a qualifying child is responsible for maintaining him.
  (2) For the purposes of this Act, an absent parent shall be taken to have met his responsibility to maintain any qualifying child of his by making periodical payments of maintenance with respect to the child of such amount, and at such intervals, as may be determined in accordance with the provisions of this Act.
  (3) Where a maintenance assessment made under this Act requires the making of periodical payments, it shall be the duty of the absent parent with respect to whom the assessment was made to make those payments.

Section 2 provides
   Where, in any case which falls to be dealt with under this Act, the Secretary of State or any Child Support Officer is considering the exercise of any discretionary power conferred by this Act, he shall have regard to the welfare of any child likely to be affected by his decision.

II JURISDICTION

By Section 44(1) of the Act a Child Support Officer shall have jurisdiction to make a maintenance assessment with respect to a person who is
   (a) a person with care,
   (b) an absent parent, or
   (c) a qualifying child,
only if that person is habitually resident in the United Kingdom.
   In the event that the person with care is not an individual then the above has effect as if (a) was omitted.
   Accordingly if the qualifying child is in the care of a third party habitually resident in the United Kingdom, and one absent parent only is habitually

resident in the United Kingdom, the Child Support Officer has jurisdiction to make an assessment against that absent parent.

If both absent parents are habitually resident outside the United Kingdom the Child Support Officer has no jurisdiction to make an assessment.

The Court retains its powers to make orders for periodical payments to or for the benefit of the relevant children against parents habitually resident abroad.

In *Shah v Barnet London Borough Council [1983] 2 AC 309* habitual residence was defined as being equivalent for juridiction purposes to ordinary residence. The natural and ordinary meaning of the words is: "the person must be habitually and normally resident here, apart from temporary or occasional absences of long or short duration". For a full exposition of the law appertaining to the meaning of habitual or ordinary residence see *Rayden and Jackson on Divorce and Family Matters* (16th Edition pp 83-87).

CHAPTER 4

Qualifying children

The basic principle

A qualifying child is a child who is
  (a) under 16, or
  (b) under 19 and in full time education, or
  (c) 16 or 17 and has recently left school (and then he only qualifies for a limited period),
and in relation to whom at least one of his parents is absent.

The detail

By Section 3(1) of the Act a child is a qualifying child if
  (a) one of his parents is, in relation to him, an absent parent, or
  (b) both of his parents are, in relation to him, absent parents.
  By Section 55(1) of the Act a person is a child if
  (a) he is under 16, or
  (b) he is under 19 and receiving full time education (which is not advanced education) at
      (i) a recognised educational establishment, or
      (ii) elsewhere, if the education is recognised by the Secretary of State, or
  (c) he does not fall within (a) or (b) above but he is under 18 and certain prescribed conditions are satisfied in respect of him.
  By Section 55(2) of the Act a person is not a child for the purposes of the Act if he is or has been married, or celebrated a marriage which is void, or has celebrated a marriage in respect of which a decree of nullity has been granted.
  By Section 55(5) the Secretary of State is entitled to provide that in prescribed circumstances education may or may not be treated as full time education.

Full time education

Paragraph 3 of Schedule 1 of the Procedure Regulations sets out the circumstances in which education is to be treated as full time education.

For the purposes of Section 55 of the Act education shall be treated as being full time if it is received by a person attending a course of education at a recognised educational establishment and the time spent receiving instruction or tuition, undertaking supervised study, examination or practical work or taking part in any exercise, experiment or project for which provision is made in the curriculum of the course, exceeds 12 hours per week, so however that in calculating the time spent in pursuit of the course no account shall be taken of time occupied by meal breaks or spent on unsupervised study, whether undertaken on or off the premises of the educational establishment.

Tolerated interruptions of full time education

Paragraph 4 of the Schedule sets out the circumstances in which an interruption of full time education will be tolerated.

(1) Subject to sub-paragraph (2), in determining whether a person falls within Section 55(1)(b) of the Act no account shall be taken of a period (whether beginning before or after the person concerned attains age 16) of up to 6 months of any interruption to the extent to which it is accepted that the interruption is attributable to a cause which is reasonable in the particular circumstances of the case; and where the interruption or its continuance is attributable to the illness or disability of mind or body of the person concerned, the period of 6 months may be extended for such further period as a Child Support Officer considers reasonable in the particular circumstances of the case.

(2) The provisions of sub-paragraph (1) shall not apply to any period of interruption of a person's full time education which is likely to be followed immediately or which is followed immediately by a period during which

   (a) provision is made for the training of that person, and for an allowance to be payable to that person, under youth training, or

   (b) he is receiving education by virtue of his employment or of any office held by him.

Paragraph 5 of the Schedule sets out the circumstances in which a person who has ceased to receive full time education is to be treated as continuing to fall within Section 55(1) of the Act.

(1) Subject to sub-paragraphs (2) and (5), a person who has ceased to receive full time education (which is not advanced education) shall, if

   (a) he is under the age of 16 when he so ceases, from the date on which he attains that age, or

   (b) he is 16 or over when he so ceases, from the date on which he so ceases,

be treated as continuing to fall within Section 55(1) of the Act up to and including the week including the terminal date or if he attains the age of 19 on or before that date up to and including the week including the last Monday before he attains that age.

(2) In the case of a person specified in sub-paragraph (1)(a) or (b) who had not attained the upper limit of compulsory school age when he ceased to receive full time education, the terminal date in his case shall be that specified in Paragraph (a), (b) or (c) of sub-paragraph (3), whichever next follows the date on which he would have attained that age.

(3) In this Paragraph the "terminal date" means:
    (a) the first Monday in January, or
    (b) the Monday following Easter Monday, or
    (c) the first Monday in September,
whichever first occurs after the date on which the person's said education ceased.

> **Note:** Easter Monday falls on the following dates
>   12th April 1993
>   4th April 1994
>   17th April 1995
>   8th April 1996
>   31st March 1997
>   13th April 1998
>   5th April 1999
>   24th April 2000

(4) In this Paragraph "compulsory school age" means
    (a) in England and Wales, compulsory school age as determined in accordance with Section 9 of the Education Act 1962,
    (b) in Scotland, school age as determined in accordance with Sections 31 and 33 of the Education (Scotland) Act 1980.

(5) A person shall not be treated as continuing to fall within Section 55(1) of the Act under this Paragraph if he is engaged in remunerative work (for not less than 24 hours per week), other than work of a temporary nature that is due to cease before the terminal date.

(6) Subject to sub-paragraphs (5) and (8), a person whose name was entered as a candidate for any external examination in connection with full time education (which is not advanced education) which he was receiving at that time, shall so long as his name continued to be so entered before ceasing to receive such education be treated as continuing to fall within Section 55(1) of the Act for any week in the period specified in sub-paragraph (7).

(7) Subject to sub-paragraph (8) the period specified for the purposes of sub-paragraph (6) is the period beginning with the date when that person ceased to receive such education ending with
    (a) whichever of the dates in sub-paragraph (3) first occurs after the conclusion of the examination (or the last of them, if there are more than one), or
    (b) the expiry of the week which includes the last Monday before his 19th birthday, whichever is the earlier.

(8) The period specified in sub-paragraph (7) shall, in the case of a person who has not attained the age of 16 when he so ceased, begin with the date on which he attained that age.

The Education Act 1962 (as amended) defines compulsory school age as 5 years to 16 years. By Section 9 of the Act the age is extended so that

(a) if the child attains 16 after 1st September but before 31st January the earliest he can leave school is the end of the spring term following 31st January,

(b) if the child attains 16 after 1st February but before the Friday before the last Monday in May the earliest he can leave school is the Friday before the last Monday in May,

(c) but if the child attains 16 after the Friday before the last Monday in May, but before 1st September he can leave school on his birthday (he is likely to be on his summer vacation so the real effect is that there is no compulsion to return to school).

Advanced education

Advanced education for the purposes of Section 55(1)(b) is defined in Paragraph 2 of Schedule 1 of the Procedure Regulations as follows

For the purposes of Section 55 of the Act "advanced education" means education of the following description

(a) a course in preparation for a degree, a Diploma of Higher Education, a higher national diploma, a higher national diploma or higher national certificate of the Business and Technician Education Council or the Scottish Vocational Education Council or a teaching qualification, or

(b) any other course which is of a standard above that of an ordinary national diploma or national certificate of the Business and Technician Education Council or the Scottish Vocational Education Council, the advanced level of the General Certificate of Education, a Scottish certificate of education (higher level) or a Scottish certificate of sixth year studies.

16 and 17 year olds not receiving education

The prescribed conditions for the purposes of Section 55(1)(c) (16 and 17 year olds) are defined by Paragraph 1 of the Schedule

(1) Subject to sub-paragraph (3), the conditions which must be satisfied for a person to be a child within Section 55(1)(c) of the Act are

(a) the person is registered for work or is registered for training under youth training with

(i) the Department of Employment,

(ii) the Ministry of Defence,

(iii) in England and Wales, a local education authority within the meaning of the Education Acts 1944 to 1992,

      (iv) in Scotland, an education authority within the meaning of Section 135(1) of the Education (Scotland) Act 1980,

      (v) for the purposes of applying Council Regulation (EEC) No 1408/71, any corresponding body in another member State,

  (b) the person is not engaged in remunerative work, other than work of a temporary nature that is due to cease before the end of the extension period which applies in the case of that person,

  (c) the extension period which applies in the case of that person has not expired, and

  (d) immediately before the extension period begins, the person is a child for the purposes of the Act without regard to this Paragraph.

(2) For the purposes of Paragraphs (b) (c) and (d) of sub-paragraph (1), the extension period

  (a) **begins** on the first day of the week in which the person would no longer be a child for the purposes of the Act but for this Paragraph, and

  (b) where a person ceases to fall within Section 55(1)(a) of the Act or within Paragraph 5

      (i) on or after the first Monday in September, but before the first Monday in January of the following year, **ends** on the last day of the week which falls immediately before the week which includes the first Monday in January in that year,

        Example: if the child leaves school on 1st October 1993 then the extension period expires on Sunday 2nd January 1994

      (ii) on or after the first Monday in January but before the Monday following Easter Monday in that year, **ends** on the last day of the week which falls 12 weeks after the week which includes the first Monday in January in that year,

        Example: if the the child leaves school on 5th January 1994, then the extension period ends on Sunday 3rd April 1994

      (iii) at any other time of the year, **ends** on the last day of the week which falls 12 weeks after the week which includes the Monday following Easter Monday in that year.

        Example: if the child leaves school on 13th April 1994 then the extension period expires on Sunday 10th July 1994; and from 10th July 1994 to 4th September 1994 there would be no extension period

(3) A person shall not be a child for the purposes of the Act under this
Paragraph if
   (a) he is engaged in training under youth training, or
   (b) he is entitled to Income Support.

For an exposition of the circumstances in which persons under 18 are
entitled to Income Support see *The National Welfare Benefits Handbook 22nd
Edition* (published by the Child Poverty Action Group) pp 52-53.

CHAPTER 5

The right to apply

The basic principle

A person with care or an absent parent has an unfettered right to apply for an assessment. A child aged 12 or more, living in Scotland, may apply for an assessment where no application therefor has otherwise been made. In a benefit case the Agency can insist on the parent with care authorising it to recover maintenance from an absent parent. If such a parent fails to co-operate the Agency can abate that person's benefit [see Chapter 22].

The detail

Under Section 4 of the Act a person who is, in relation to any qualifying child, either the person with care or the absent parent may apply to the Agency for a maintenance assessment with respect to such child.

Under Section 6 of the Act (as extended by Regulation 34 of the Procedure Regulations) where Income Support, family credit or disability working allowance is claimed by, or paid to, a parent who is a person with care of a qualifying child she shall, if required to do so by the Child Support Agency, authorise the Agency to take action to recover maintenance from the absent parent; but the Agency shall not require such a parent so to authorise it if there are reasonable grounds for believing that if the parent were to be required to give that authorisation, or if she were to give it, there would be a risk of her, or of any child living with her, suffering harm or undue distress as a result.

Under Section 7 of the Act a qualifying child who has attained the age of 12 and who is habitually resident in Scotland may apply to the Agency for a maintenance assessment to be made in respect of him if

(a) no such application has been made by a person who is in respect to him a person with care, or an absent parent, or

(b) the Agency has not been authorised under Section 6 to take action under the Act to recover maintenance from the absent parent (save in a case where the Agency has waived any requirement to be so authorised).

Where such an application is made the Agency shall be authorised to make an assessment of any other children of the absent parent who are in the care of the person with care of the child making the application.

Maintenance agreements

By Section 9 of the Act it remains permissible for any person to enter into an agreement for the making of periodical payments or secured provision to or for the benefit of a child.

However the existence of such an agreement shall not prevent any party to the agreement, or any other person from applying for a maintenance assessment from the Child Support Agency. Moreover any provision within such an agreement which purports to restrict the right of any person to apply for such an assessment shall be void.

This provision mirrors the terms of Section 34 of the Matrimonial Causes Act 1973 which renders void any contractual attempt to oust the jurisdiction of the Divorce Court.

Fees

Under the Fees Regulations, where an assessment is made a fee of £44.00 is payable by the parent with care and the absent parent unless he or she is
  (a) receiving Income Support, family credit, or disability working allowance, or
  (b) under the age of 16, or under the age of 19 and in full time education which is not advanced education, or
  (c) a person whose assessable income is nil, or
  (d) a person whose whose liability to pay maintenance has been adjusted so as to prevent his income falling below the protected level [see Chapter 17].

CHAPTER 6

The maintenance requirement

The basic principle

The maintenance requirement is the basic sum considered by Parliament to be necessary for the support of the children. It is calculated by adding together the Income Support allowances which would be paid for the children and the parent who is responsible for their care, if that family had no other income, and then deducting the basic rate of child benefit payable in respect of the children.

The maintenance requirement is paid by each parent contributing half of his/her "assessable" income until the maintenance requirement is met. In many cases the maintenance requirement will not be met in full as 50% of the assessable incomes will not cover it.

Once the maintenance requirement has been met the parents are required to pay an additional amount. The further contribution rate is 25% of the excess assessable income. This is subject to an overall ceiling of 3 times the aggregate of the Income Support allowances for each child and an amount equivalent to the Income Support family premium in respect of each child.

The detail

By Section 11(2) of the Act the amount of maintenance to be fixed by any maintenance assessment shall be determined in accordance with the provisions of Part I of Schedule 1 to the Act.

By Paragraphs 1(1) and 1(2) of Schedule 1 to the Act and Regulation 3 of the Assessment Regulations the minimum amount necessary for the maintenance of a qualifying child ("the maintenance requirement"), or if there is more than one qualifying child, for all of them, is calculated by reference to the following formula

$$MR = AG - CB$$

Where
MR is the maintenance requirement, and
AG is the aggregate of

(a) for each qualifying child the Income Support personal allowance for a child of that age, viz
child under 11 years: £15.05
11–15 years: £22.15
16–17 years: £26.45
18 years: £34.80
[the aggregate of the sums allowed under (a) shall be called **Q1**]

(b) where a person has care of a qualifying child under 16, the Income Support personal allowance for a single claimant aged not less than 25, viz: £44.00

(c) the Income Support family premium, viz: £9.65
[this figure shall be called **Q2**]

(d) where the person with care has no "partner" (i.e. a spouse or a cohabitee), the Income Support lone parent premium, viz: £4.90, and

CB is the total child benefit payable, excluding any single parent premium, viz: £10.00 for the eldest child and £8.10 for each subsequent child.

By Paragraphs 2-4 of Schedule 1 to the Act a number of steps must be undertaken when calculating how the maintenance requirement is to be met.

The first step is to compute the assessable income of the absent parent. This is called **A**.

The second step is to compute the assessable income of the parent with care. This is called **C**. If the person with care is not a parent, **C** is taken as nil (Regulation 5(a) of the Assessment Regulations).

The lengthy procedures for calculating **A** and **C** are set out in Chapters 7-16.

The third step is to execute the following formula

$$\text{(A + C) x 0.5}$$

If the result is equal to or less than **MR** (as calculated above), then the amount of maintenance to be paid by the absent parent is

$$\text{A x 0.5}$$

The formula is simply the algebraic way of saying that for as long as the sum of one half of each parent's income is less than **MR** then the absent parent pays one half of his income by way of maintenance.

Example: say **MR** for 2 children comes to £65.65 per week calculated as follows

(a) 2 x £15.05 = £30.10 [**Q1**] to which add
(b)   £44.00   to which add
(c)   £ 9.65 [**Q2**]

subtotal: £80.85
less **CB**:   £18.10

TOTAL: £65.65

Say **A** is £100.00
Say **C** is £20.00
then (**A** + **C**) x 0.5 = £60.00
This is less than **MR**
Thus the absent parent pays **A** x 0.5 = £50.00

If the result exceeds **MR** then the absent parent pays maintenance by reference to the following formula

$$BE + AE$$

Where
BE is the basic element, and
AE is the additional element

BE is calculated by reference to the following formula

$$BE = A \times [MR \div (A + C)]$$

The formula is the algebraic way of saying that the absent parent pays a basic element of maintenance which is that proportionate part of **MR** determined by the ratio of the incomes of the two parents.

Mathematical note

The order of calculation is as follows.
  First, perform the calculation in the ordinary rounded brackets. This is (**A** + **C**). Call the result X.
  Second, perform the calculation in the square brackets. This is [**MR** ÷ X].Call the result Z.
  Third, perform the calculation outside the brackets. This is **A** x Y. The result is **BE**.

Example: say **MR** for 2 children under 11 comes to £65.65 per week
Say **A** is £100.00
say **C** is £70.00
then (**A** + **C**) x 0.5 = £85.00.
This is more than **MR**
Thus the absent parent pays a **BE** of
BE = 100 x [65.65 ÷ (100.00 + 70.00)]
    = £38.62

AE is calculated as follows. It is the product that is the **lower** of the following 2 formulae

$$AE =$$
$$\{1- [MR \div ((A + C) \times 0.5)]\}$$
$$\times A \times 0.25$$

or

$$AE =$$
$$3 \times [Q1 + (Q2 \times \text{number of children})]$$
$$\times [A \div (A + C)]$$

where **Q1** and **Q2** were the figures taken in calculating **MR** above

These formulae are the algebraic way of saying that the absent parent pays an additional element of maintenance calculated as 25% of that part of his income from which he did not pay the basic element of maintenance, but subject to a ceiling for each child of 3 times the Income Support family premium and 3 times that child's Income Support personal allowance, reduced by the ratio of the parents' respective incomes.

Mathematical note

For the first formula perform the calculations in the following order.
  First, perform the calculation in the first set of ordinary rounded brackets. This is (**A** + **C**). Call the result W.
  Second, perform the calculation in the second set of rounded brackets. This is (W x 0.5). Call the result X.
  Third, perform the calculation in the square brackets. This is [**MR** ÷ X]. Call the result Y.
  Fourth, perform the calculation in the curly brackets. This is {1 - Y}. Call the result Z.
  Fifth, perform the calculation outside the brackets. This is Z x **A** x 0.25. The result is **AE**.
For the second formula perform the calculations in the following order.
  First, perform the calculation in the first set of ordinary rounded brackets. This is (**Q2** x number of children). Call the result W.
  Second, perform the calculation in the first set of square brackets. This is [**Q1** + W]. Call the result X.
  Third, perform the calculation in the second set of ordinary rounded brackets. This is (**A** + **C**). Call the result Y.
  Fourth, perform the calculation in the second set of square brackets. This is [**A** ÷ Y]. Call the result Z.
  Fifth, perform the calculation outside the brackets. This is 3 x X x Z. The result is **AE**.

Example: say **MR** for 2 children comes to £63.40 per week
Say **A** is £100.00
say **C** is £70.00
then (**A** + **C**) x 0.5 = £85.00
This is more than **MR**
thus the absent parent pays an **AE** of the lower of
AE = {1- [65.65 ÷ ((100.00 + 70.00) x 0.5)]} x 100.00 x 0.25
     = £5.69
or
AE = 3 x [30.10 + (9.65 x 2)] x [100.00 ÷ (100.00 + 70.00)]
     = £87.18
Thus **AE** of £5.69 is taken
Thus the total paid by this parent is
£38.62 + £5.69 = £44.31

Tables of examples

TABLE 1: *Illustrating a sample of different sums payable*

Say the maintenance requirement is calculated as follows
(a)   £30.10 (being the allowances for 2 children under 11),
(b)   £44.00 (being the adult personal allowance), and
(c)   £9.65   (being the family premium)
subtotal: £83.75
less child benefit: £18.10
TOTAL: £65.65

Take A as	100	100	150	200	300	400	500	600	700
Take C as	20	70	80	90	100	110	120	130	140
Is (A+C) x 0.5 more than MR?	no	yes	yes	yes	yes	yes	yes	yes	yes
If no, maintenance is	50	n/a	n/a	n/a	n/a	n/a	n/a	n/a	n/a
if yes, BE is	n/a	38.62	42.82	45.28	49.24	51.49	52.94	53.96	54.71
and AE is the lower of	n/a	5.69	16.09	27.36	50.38	74.25	98.53	123.02	147.65
or the ceiling figure of	n/a	87.18	96.65	102.21	111.15	116.24	119.52	121.81	123.50
Thus total maintenance is	50	44.31	58.91	72.64	99.62	125.74	151.46	175.77	178.21

Where:
A is the absent parent's assessable income,
C is the parent with care's assessable income,
BE is the basic element of maintenance payable, and
AE is the additional element of maintenance payable

TABLE 2: *Illustrating a sample of maximum amounts payable*

Children Aged

under 11	11–15	16–17	18	total	maximum	average
10	0	0	0	10	867.15	86.72
1	0	0	0	1	137.70	137.70
2	0	0	0	2	218.75	109.38
1	1	0	0	2	247.15	123.58
1	2	0	0	3	356.60	118.87
1	1	1	0	3	373.80	124.60
1	1	2	0	4	500.45	125.11
1	1	1	1	4	533.85	133.46
0	1	0	0	1	166.10	166.10
0	2	0	0	2	275.55	137.78
0	1	1	0	2	292.75	146.38
0	1	2	0	3	419.40	139.80
0	1	1	1	3	452.80	150.93
0	0	1	0	1	139.30	139.30
0	0	2	0	2	265.95	132.98
0	0	1	1	2	299.35	149.68
0	0	0	1	1	172.70	172.70

Accordingly the range of per capita maximums is from £86.72 per week per child in the unlikely situation where there are 10 children under the age of 11 to £172.70 per week where there is one 18 year old child.

CHAPTER 7

The assessment of income (general)

The basic principle

The assessable income of a parent is taken as his **net** income less his **exempt** income. In general terms net income is all the parent's income less tax, National Insurance and 50% of pension contributions; while the exempt income comprises the Income Support allowances that would be applicable to the parent's situation, together with his housing costs.

The detail

By Paragraph 5 of Schedule 1 to the Act the assessable income of the absent parent is calculated by reference to the following formula

$$A = N - E$$

where
A is the parent's assessable income
N is the parent's net income calculated in accordance with the provisions set out in Chapters 8-15
E is the parent's exempt income, calculated in accordance with the provisions set out in Chapter 16.

The assessable income of the parent with care is calculated by reference to the following formula

$$C = M - F$$

where
C is the parent's assessable income
M is the parent's net income calculated in accordance with the provisions set out in Chapters 8-15
F is the parent's exempt income, calculated in accordance with the provisions set out in Chapter 16.

Income Support

By Paragraph 5(4) of Schedule 1 to the Act if Income Support is payable to a parent then he is taken as having no assessable income.

However, by Section 43 of the Act such a parent may suffer an automatic abatement of his benefit in certain specified circumstances [see Chapter 18].

CHAPTER 8

The calculation of N & M (general)

The basic principle

By Regulation 7(1) of the Assessment Regulations **N** is the aggregate of the following 5 elements, viz
  (a) the parent's earnings [see Chapters 9 and 10], and
  (b) any benefits paid to him [see Chapter 11], and
  (c) any other income he may have [see Chapter 12], and
  (d) any income of a child of the parent who is a member of his family [see Chapter 13], and
  (e) any sum which is treated as his income [see Chapter 14].
  In computing the aggregated total certain sums are disregarded [see Chapter 15].

Provisos

There are 3 provisos to the basic principle.
  1. By Regulation 7(3), for the purposes of calculating **N** the income of the absent parent shall be disregarded in the following circumstances
      (a) where the income consists only of a youth training allowance, or
      (b) where the income consists of only student grant, parental grant contribution or student loan, or any contribution thereof, or
      (c) where the income consists only of prisoner's pay.
  2. By Regulation 7(4), where the parent and another person are beneficially entitled to any income but it is not possible on the available information to ascertain their respective shares thereof then the income shall be treated as being supplied to the parent and the other person in equal shares.
  3. By Regulation 7(5), if any income normally received at regular intervals has not been received, it shall, if there are reasonable grounds for believing it will be received, be treated as if it had been received.
  By Regulation 8 of the Assessment Regulations **M** is calculated by reference to identical principles to those deployed in the calculation of **N**.

CHAPTER 9

The earnings of the employed parent

The basic principle

The earnings of an employed parent are taken as his gross earnings less Income Tax, National Insurance, and 50% of pension contributions, calculated on a weekly basis.

The detail

By Paragraph 1(1) of Schedule 1 of the Assessment Regulations earnings means in the case of an employed earner **any remuneration or profit** derived from his employment **including (but not limited to)** the following 10 categories of earnings
  (a) any bonus, commission, royalty or fee,
  (b) any holiday pay except any payable more than 4 weeks after termination of the employment,
  (c) any payment by way of a retainer,
  (d) any payment made by the parent's employer in respect of any expenses not wholly, exclusively and necessarily incurred in the performance of the duties of the employment,
  (e) any award of compensation made under Section 68(2) or 71(2)(a) of the Employment Protection (Consolidation) Act 1978 (remedies and compensation for unfair dismissal),
  (f) any such sum as is referred to in Section 112 of the Contributions and Benefits Act (certain sums to be earnings for social security purposes),
  (g) any statutory sick pay under Part I of the Social Security and Housing Benefits Act 1982 or statutory maternity pay under Part V of the Social Security Act 1986,
  (h) any payment in lieu of notice and any compensation in respect of the absence or inadequacy of any such notice but only insofar as such payment or compensation represents loss of income,
  (i) any payment relating to a period of less than a year which is made in respect of the performance of duties as

(i)   an auxiliary coastguard in respect of coast rescue activities,

(ii)   a part-time fireman in a fire brigade maintained in pursuance of the Fire Services Acts 1947 to 1959,

(iii)   a person engaged part-time in the manning or launching of a lifeboat,

(iv)   a member of any territorial or reserve force prescribed in Part I of Schedule 3 to the Social Security (Contributions) Regulations 1979,

(j)   any payment made by a local authority to a member of that authority in respect of the performance of his duties as a member, other than any expenses wholly, exclusively and necessarily incurred in the performance of those duties.

By Paragraph 1(2) of Schedule 1 the following payments are **not** to be included in reckoning the parent's earnings

(a)   any payment in respect of expenses wholly, exclusively and necessarily incurred in the performance of the duties of the employment,

(b)   any occupational pension,

(c)   any payment where

(i)   the employment in respect of which it was made has ceased, and

(ii)   a period of the same length as the period by reference to which it was calculated has expired since that cessation but prior to the effective date (e.g. payments in lieu of notice),

(d)   any advance of earnings or any loan made by an employer to an employee,

(e)   any amount received from an employer during a period when the employee has withdrawn his services by reason of a trade dispute,

(f)   any payment in kind,

(g)   where in any week or other period which falls within the period by reference to which earnings are calculated (as to which see below), earnings are received both in respect of a previous employment and in respect of a subsequent employment, the earnings in respect of the previous employment.

Income Tax, National Insurance and pension contributions

Paragraph 1(3) of Schedule 1 to the Assessment Regulations provides that
The earnings to be taken into account for the purposes of calculating N and M shall be gross earnings less

(a) any amount deducted from those earnings by way of

(i)   Income Tax,

(ii)   primary Class 1 contributions under the Contributions and Benefits Act, and

(b) one half of any sums paid by the parent towards an occupational or personal pension scheme.

The period over which the income is calculated

Paragraph 2(1) of Schedule 1 provides that
  (a) where a person is paid weekly, the amount of those earnings shall be determined by aggregating the amounts received in the 5 weeks ending with the relevant week and dividing by 5,
  (b) where a person is paid monthly, the amount of those earnings shall be determined by aggregating the amounts received in the 2 months ending with the relevant week, multiplying the aggregate by 6 and dividing by 52,
  (c) where a person is paid by reference to some other period, the amount of those earnings shall be determined by aggregating the amount received in the 3 months ending with the relevant week, multiplying the aggregate by 4 and dividing by 52.

Bonuses

Paragraph 2(2) of Schedule 1 provides that
  Where a person's earnings include a bonus or commission which is paid during the period of 52 weeks ending with the relevant week and is paid separately from, or, in relation to a longer period than, the other earnings with which it is paid, the amount of that bonus or commission shall be determined by aggregating such payments received in the 52 weeks ending with the relevant week and dividing by 52.

Students

Paragraph 2(3) of Schedule 1 provides that
  The amount of any earnings of a student shall be determined by aggregating the amount received in the year ending with the relevant week and dividing by 52 or, where the person in question has been a student for less than a year, by aggregating the amount received in the period starting with his becoming a student and ending with the relevant week and dividing by the number of complete weeks in that period.

Proviso

Paragraph 2(4) of Schedule 1 provides that
  Where a calculation would, but for this sub-paragraph, produce an amount which, in the opinion of the Child Support Officer, does not accurately reflect the normal amount of the earnings of the person in question, such earnings, or any part of them, shall be calculated by reference to such other period as may, in the particular case, enable the normal weekly earnings of that person to be determined more accurately and for this purpose the Child Support Officer shall have regard to

(a) the earnings received, or due to be received, from any employment in which the person in question is engaged, has been engaged or is due to be engaged,

(b) the duration and pattern, or the expected duration and pattern, of any employment of that person.

CHAPTER 10

The earnings of the self-employed parent

The basic principle

The earnings of the self-employed parent are taken as his gross receipts less certain expenses (not necessarily all those allowed by the Inland Revenue), Income Tax, Class 2 and 4 National Insurance contributions and 50% of retirement annuity payments or personal pension scheme payments, calculated on a weekly basis.

The detail

By Paragraph 3(1) of Schedule 1 of the Assessment Regulations "earnings" in the case of employment as a self-employed earner means the gross receipts of the employment.

The definition of earnings is accordingly to be contrasted with the definition employed in the taxation legislation where, subject to certain exceptions (e.g. barristers), income for the period in question is computed on the earnings accrued in that period, rather than the cash received in that period.

Special categories of self-employed earnings

1. By Paragraphs 3(1) and 3(2)(a) of the Schedule earnings include, where an allowance in the form of periodic payments is paid under Section 2 of the Employment and Training Act 1973 or Section 2 of the Enterprise and New Towns (Scotland) Act 1990 in respect of the relevant week for the purpose of assisting him in carrying on his business, the total of those payments made during the period by reference to which his earnings are determined under Paragraph 5 of the Schedule (as to which, see below); but do not include any allowance paid under either of those Sections in respect of any part of the period by reference to which his earnings are determined under Paragraph 5 if no part of that allowance is paid in respect of the relevant week.

Accordingly if a training allowance is actually received during the relevant week then all such payments received during the period provided under Paragraph 5 (as to which see below) are taken into account in computing the earnings for the relevant week; but if no such payment is actually received in the relevant week then, even if such payments were otherwise received during the period provided under Paragraph 5, they are not taken into account.

2. Earnings shall not include any income consisting of payments received for the provision of board and lodging accommodation unless such payments form the largest element of the recipient's income (Paragraph 3(2)(b) of the Schedule).

    However, where such income forms the minority part of the parent's income, it will be taken into account as "other income" under Paragraph 10 of the Schedule. The significance of the distinction is that, as is explained below, self-employed earnings and "other income" are reckoned over different periods for the purpose of producing a weekly rate of such income.

    Attention is drawn to the new tax treatment of lodging income introduced by Schedule 10 of the Finance (No 2) Act 1992. Where sums accrue in respect of the provision of accommodation or meals, cleaning and laundry in the individual's only or main residence then the first £3,250 of such income is ignored in computing his tax liability.

3. In a case where a person is self-employed as a childminder the amount of earnings referable to that employment shall be one-third of the gross receipts (Paragraph 4 of the Schedule).

Deductions from gross receipts

In general terms the permitted deductions from the gross receipts are expenses wholly and exclusively incurred for the purpose of the business (but excluding any expense of a capital nature such as depreciation, or capital expenditure, or any sum expended on setting up or expanding the business), together with the notional Income Tax and National Insurance that would be payable on such income at the rates of tax in force on the relevant date, VAT, and 50% of retirement annuity or personal pension premiums.

Accordingly the following differences from the method used for calculating Income tax under Schedule D of the Income and Corporation Taxes Act 1988 should be noted.

(a) Capital expenditure is excluded in computing assessable income. Thus no capital allowances, depreciation or diminution in the value of stock can be deducted, whereas under Schedule D capital allowances are, to the permitted extent, deductible in computing taxable income.

(b) Losses arising in one business cannot be set-off against profits made in another when computing assessable income; and there is no relief given for losses arising prior to the period of assessment.

(c) The cash basis rather than the earnings basis of assessing income is used.

(d) When ascertaining the income upon which notional tax is to be levied the preceding year rule is not used, as would be the case under Schedule D.

(e) When computing the income on which notional tax is to be levied for the purposes of computing the assessable income, no deductions of pension and 50% of Class 4 National Insurance are allowed, as would be the case when computing taxable income under Schedule D.

Permitted and prohibited deductions

By Paragraph 3(3)-(6) of the Schedule, there shall be deducted from the gross receipts

(a) Any expenses which are reasonably incurred and are wholly and exclusively defrayed for the purposes of the earner's business in the period by reference to which his earnings are determined under Paragraph 5(1) (as to which, see below) or, where Paragraph 5(2) applies (see below) any such expenses relevant to the period there mentioned (whether or not defrayed in that period). These expenses include

   (i)   repayment of capital on any loan used for the replacement, in the course of business, of equipment or machinery, or the repair of an existing business asset except to the extent that any sum is payable under an insurance policy for its repair,

   (ii) any income expended in the repair of an existing business asset except to the extent that any sum is payable under an insurance policy for its repair,

   (iii) any payment of interest on a loan taken out for the purposes of the business, **but**

by Paragraph 3(4) such expenses do not include

   (i)   repayment of capital on any other loan taken out for the purposes of the business,

   (ii) any capital expenditure,

   (iii) the depreciation of any capital asset,

   (iv) any sum employed, or intended to be employed, in the setting up or expansion of the business,

   (v)   any loss incurred before the beginning of the period by reference to which earnings are determined,

   (vi) any expenses incurred in providing business entertainment,

   (vii) any loss incurred in any other employment in which he is engaged as a self-employed earner.

(b) Any VAT paid in the period by reference to which earnings are determined in excess of VAT received in that period.

(c) Any amount in respect of Income Tax determined as follows: the amount of Income Tax to be allowed against earnings shall be calculated as if those earnings, less any personal allowance applicable to the earner under Chapter 1 of Part VII of the Income and Corporation Taxes Act 1988 (Personal Relief) (or where the earnings are determined over a period of less than a year, a proportionate part of such relief), were assessable to Income Tax at the rates of tax applicable at the effective date.

Allowances for 1992/93

Personal allowance: £3,445
Married couple's allowance: £1,720
Additional personal relief for children: £1,720
Blind person's relief: £1,080
Age allowance (65 - 74): £4,200
Age allowance (75 and over): £4,370
Widow's bereavement allowance: £1,720

Rates of tax for 1992/93

First £2,000 : 20%
Next £21,700 : 25%
Everything above £23,700 : 40%

By Section 259 Income and Corporation Taxes Act 1988 the additional personal relief for children is available to a single parent where there is resident with him for the whole or part of a year

     (a) a child under 16, or

     (b) a child over 16 in full time education, or

     (c) a child under 18 wholly maintained by the parent in question.

"Residence" is likely to be interpreted in conformity with the definition of "day to day" care, i.e. not less than 104 nights per annum [see Chapter 2].

It would appear that a self-employed earner is required to subtract the personal allowance(s) from his income whatever his tax status. It would be possible that his allowances had been exhausted by earlier or concurrent PAYE employment but this possibility does not appear to be contemplated by the Regulations.

(d) Any amount in respect of National Insurance contributions determined as follows

The amount to be deducted in respect of National Insurance contributions shall be the total of

     (i) the amount of Class 2 contributions (if any) payable under Section 11(1) or, as the case may be, (4) of the Social Security Contributions and Benefits Act 1992, and

     (ii) the amount of Class 4 contributions (if any) payable under Section 15(2) of that Act,

at the rates applicable at the effective date.

Rates of National Insurance contributions for 1993/94

Class 2: £5.55 per week, provided that the earner has earnings in excess of £3,140

Class 4: 6.3% of profits (i.e. after expenses) between £6,340 and £21,840. Exempt if pensionable age (60 for women; 65 for men) reached by 6th April 1992

(e) One half of any premium paid in respect of a retirement annuity contract or a personal pension scheme.

The period over which the income is calculated

Paragraph 5 of the Schedule provides
(1) (a) where a person has been a self-employed earner for 52 weeks or more including the relevant week, the amount of his earnings shall be determined by reference to the average of the earnings which he has received in the 52 weeks ending with the relevant week,
(b) where the person has been a self-employed earner for a period of less than 52 weeks including the relevant week, the amount of his earnings shall be determined by reference to the average of the earnings which he has received during that period.

A different procedure can however be elected by the parent under Paragraph 5(2) of the Schedule.

Where a person who is a self-employed earner provides in respect of the employment a profit and loss account (being a financial statement showing net profit or loss of the employment for the period in question) and, where appropriate, a trading account (being a financial statement showing the revenue from sales, the cost of those sales and the gross profit arising during the period in question) or a balance sheet (being a statement of the financial position of the employment [sic] disclosing its assets, liabilities and capital at the end of the period in question) or both, and the profit and loss account is in respect of a period at least 6 months but not exceeding 15 months and that period terminates within the 12 months immediately preceding the effective date, the amount of his earnings shall be determined by reference to the average of the earnings over the period to which the profit and loss account relates and such earnings shall include receipts relevant to that period (whether or not received in that period).

Accordingly if the parent provides a profit and loss statement which is not more than a year old and which is for a period of at least 6 months and not for more than a period of 15 months then, provided that he can also produce a trading account or a balance sheet (presumably for corroborative purposes), the weekly average from such profit and loss statement may be used if it produces a figure lower than that produced by the calculation for the immediately preceding 52 weeks. It must be noted, however, that the figure for expenses given in the profit and loss statement may fall to be adjusted insofar as they include expenses of the prohibited kinds specified in Paragraph 3(4) of the Schedule (see above).

Proviso

Paragraph 5(3) of Schedule 1 provides that

Where a calculation would, but for this sub-paragraph, produce an amount which, in the opinion of the Child Support Officer, does not accurately reflect the normal amount of the earnings of the person in question, such earnings, or any part of them, shall be calculated by reference to such other period as may, in the particular case, enable the normal weekly earnings of that person to be determined more accurately and for this purpose the Child Support Officer shall have regard to

(a) the earnings received, or due to be received, from any employment in which the person in question is engaged, or has been engaged or is due to be engaged,

(b) the duration and pattern, or the expected duration and pattern, of any employment of that person.

CHAPTER 11

Benefit payments

The basic principle

Any benefit payment received by a parent under the Social Security Contributions and Benefits Act 1992 ("the Contributions and Benefits Act 1992") are intitially taken into account, although certain such payments are then disregarded [see Chapter 15]. Moreover, receipt of certain of the benefits in question will convert the case into a "Special Case" under Regulation 26 of the Assessment Regulations, and in such circumstances child maintenance will not be payable by the recipient of such a benefit, if otherwise that recipient would be liable only to pay the minimum amount of maintenance specified by Regulation 13(1) of the Assessment Regulations [see Chapter 17 for the minimum amount and see Chapter 18 for Special Cases].

Benefit payments are invariably paid on a weekly basis and accordingly the amount of such benefit taken into account will be the weekly rate of such benefit applicable at the effective date.

The detail

Paragraph 6(2)-(3) of Schedule 1 to the Assessment Regulations provides

(2) "Benefit payments" means any benefit payments under the Contributions and Benefits Act except amounts to be disregarded by virtue of Schedule 2.

(3) The amount of any benefit payment to be taken into account shall be determined by reference to the rate of that benefit applicable at the effective date.

The benefits available under the Contributions and Benefits Act are as follows

* attendance allowance (Section 64)
* child benefit (Section 141)
* child's special allowance (Section 56)
* council tax benefit (Section 131)
* disability living allowance (Section 71)
* disabilty working allowance (Section 129)

* disablement pension (Sections 103-105)
* family credit (Section 128)
* graduated retirement benefit (Section 62)
* housing benefit (Section 130)
* Income Support (Section 124)
* industrial injuries benefit (Section 94)
* invalidity allowance (Section 34)
* invalidity pension (Section 33)
* invalidity care allowance (Section 70)
* pensioner's Christmas bonus (Section 148)
* retirement pension (Sections 43-55)
* severe disablement allowance (Section 68)
* sickness benefit (Section 31)
* social fund payments (Section 138)
* state maternity allowance (Section 35)
* statutory sick pay (Section 151)
* statutory maternity pay (Section 164)
* unemployment benefit (Section 25)
* widow's payment (Section 36)
* widow's pension (Section 38)
* widow's invalidity pension (Section 40)
* widowed mother's allowance (Section 37)
* widower's invalidity pension (Section 41)
* workmen's compensation (Section 111)

Income Support

Although included in the general list, it has already been seen that where a parent is in receipt of Income Support he is taken as having no assessable income [see Chapter 7].

Where the benefit includes a dependency increase

Paragraph 7(1) of Schedule 1 provides
(1) Where a benefit payment under the Contributions and Benefits Act includes an adult or child dependency increase
   (a) if that benefit is payable to a parent, the income of that parent shall be calculated or estimated as if it did not include that amount,

   Comment: if the benefit paid to the parent is enhanced because the parent has a dependant child or a dependant adult, then the extent of such enhancement shall be disregarded when reckoning the income of the parent.

   (b) if that benefit is payable to some other person but includes an amount in respect of the parent, the income of the parent shall be calculated or estimated as if it included that amount.

Comment: if a third party receives benefit which includes an amount for the parent then the parent's income shall be reckoned as if it included that sum.

Family credit

This is subject to special treatment. Family credit is a benefit paid to low-paid earners. It is assessed on the earnings of the family unit in question. The question arises as to how family credit should be treated where it has been calculated on the earnings of members of a family, one of whom is being assessed under the Act.

Paragraph 7(2)-(5) of Schedule 1 provides

(2) Subject to sub-paragraph (3), payments to a person by way of family credit shall be treated as the income of the parent who has qualified for them by his engagement in, and normal engagement in, remunerative work.

(3) Subject to sub-paragraphs (4) and (5), where family credit is payable and the amount which is payable has been calculated by reference either to the weekly earnings of the absent parent and another person or the parent with care and another person

   (a) if during the period which is used to calculate his earnings under Paragraph 2 or, as the case may be, Paragraph 5, the weekly earnings of that parent exceed those of the other person, the amount payable by way of family credit shall be treated as the income of that parent,

   Example: if a father being assessed by the Agency and his cohabitee qualified for family credit by virtue of both of their incomes, then if during the period for which earnings are reckoned [see Chapters 9 and 10] the father in fact earned more than the cohabitee, then the entirety of the family credit is treated as his income.

   (b) if during that period the normal weekly earnings of that parent equal those of the other person, half of the amount payable by way of family credit shall be treated as the income of that parent,

   Example: if the above father's income was the same as the cohabitee's during the relevant period, then half of the family credit is treated as his income.

   (c) if during that period the normal weekly earnings of that parent are less than those of that other person, the amount payable by way of family credit shall not be treated as the income of that parent.

Example: if the above father's income was less than the cohabitee's during the relevant period, then none of the family credit is treated as his income.

(4) Where
   (a) family credit (calculated, as the case may be, by reference to the weekly earnings of the absent parent and another person or the parent with care and another person) is in payment, and
   (b) not later than the effective date either or both the persons by reference to whose engagement and normal engagement in remunerative work that payment has been calculated has ceased to be so employed, half of the amount payable by way of family credit shall be treated as the income of the parent in question.

Example: if the above father and his cohabitee qualified for family credit by virtue of both of their incomes, and if prior to the effective date the father becomes unemployed then half of the family credit shall be treated as his income.

(5) Where
   (a) family credit is in payment, and
   (b) not later than the effective date the person or, if more than one, each of the persons by reference to whose engagement, and normal engagement, in remunerative work that payment has been calculated is no longer the partner of the person to whom that payment is made, the payment in question shall only be treated as the income of the parent in question where he is in receipt of it.

Example: if the above father and cohabitee qualified for family credit by virtue of both of their incomes, and if prior to the effective date the father and cohabitee separate and the latter thereafter draws all the family credit, then the benefit is not reckoned as the father's income.

Income Tax

Paragraph 2 of Schedule 2 to the Assessment Regulations provides that an amount in respect of Income Tax applicable to the income in question shall be disregarded when calculating or estimating **N** and **M** where not otherwise allowed for under the Assessment Regulations [see Chapter 15 for the other categories of disregarded income].

Under Section 617(1) Income and Corporation Taxes Act 1988, all payments under the Contributions and Benefits Act are taxable under Schedule E except

* attendance allowance
* child's special allowance
* disability living allowance
* guardian's allowance
* invalidity benefit
* maternity allowance
* severe disablement allowance
* sickness benefit
* widow's payments

By Section 617(2), the following payments shall not be treated as income for any purpose of the Income Tax Acts

* Income Support (save in certain circumstances which are not relevant since where a parent is in receipt of Income Support he has no assessable income [see Chapter 7])
* family credit
* disability working allowance
* housing benefit
* allowances under Paragraph 18 Schedule 7 of the Contributions and Benefits Act
* child benefit
* and any payment excepted under Section 617(1)

Accordingly the relevant list of taxable benefits is as follows

* invalid care allowance
* retirement pension
* unemployment benefit
* widow's benefit

If a parent is in receipt of any such benefit it will be necessary to calculate the tax payable thereon by reference to the allowances and rates of tax set out in Chapter 10. It is understood that the Child Support Agency will calculate Income Tax on the benefits received in the last 52 weeks using current allowances even if (as is likely) some of the 52 week period falls in the previous tax year.

CHAPTER 12

Other income received by the parent

The basic principle

Any other income received by a parent on a periodic basis is taken into account, although different categories of income receive different treatment both as to the amounts to be brought into account and as to the periods over which the receipt of such income is to be reckoned.

The detail

Paragraph 8 of Schedule 1 to the Assessment Regulations provides that the amount of other income to be taken into account in calculating **N** or **M** shall be the aggregate of the following amounts determined in accordance with this Part.

Pension payments

By Paragraph 9 of the Schedule, any periodic payment of pension or other benefit under an occupational or personal pension scheme or a retirement annuity contract or other such scheme for the provision of income in retirement, shall be brought into account.

Board and lodging

By Paragraph 10, any payment received on account of the provision of board and lodging which does not come within Part I of the Schedule, shall be brought into account. (It has already been seen in Chapter 10 that where board and lodging income forms the majority part of a self-employed parent's receipts it shall be taken into account in accordance with the provisions applicable to such a parent; accordingly inclusion here is directed at those parents who provide such a service as a sideline.)

Students

It has already been seen in Chapter 8 that where a student's income derives **only** from student grant or loan (or a combination thereof) then such income shall be disregarded in the calculation of **N** and **M**. If, however, the student has other income, whether earned or unearned, then by Paragraphs 11 and 12 of the Schedule his grant, loan or covenant income will be taken into account as follows

11. Any payment to a student of
    (a) grant,
    (b) an amount in respect of grant contribution,
    (c) gross covenant income except to the extent that it has been taken into account under sub-paragraph (b) above,
    (d) a student loan,
    shall be taken into account.

12. The income of a student shall **not** include any payment
    (a) intended to meet tuition fees or examination fees,
    (b) intended to meet additional expenditure incurred by a disabled student in respect of his attendance on a course,
    (c) intended to meet additional expenditure connected with term time residential study away from the student's educational establishment,
    (d) on account of the student maintaining a home at a place other than that at which he resides during his course,
    (e) intended to meet the cost of books, and equipment (other than special equipment) or, if not so intended, an amount equal to the amount allowed under Regulation 38(2)(f) of the Family Credit (General) Regulations 1987 towards such costs,

    Comment: The allowance is £266.

    (f) intended to meet travel expenses incurred as a result of his attendance on the course.

Interest and allied income

By Paragraph 13, any interest, dividend or other income derived from capital is taken into account.

Maintenance payments to the parent for himself or herself

By Paragraph 14, any maintenance payments in respect of a parent are taken into account.

Any other payments made on a periodic basis

By Paragraph 15, any other payments or other amounts received on a periodic basis which are not otherwise taken into account under Part I, II, IV or V of Schedule 1 are taken into account.

Comment: this represents an encompassing saving provision, bringing into account any other payments made on a regular basis. Thus, for example, if an allowance is received by a mother from her uncle then that will be brought into account. It would seem that irregular ad hoc subventions would not be brought into account.

The period for which such income is to be reckoned

The general rule is that only the income received within the last 26 weeks is taken into account, although there are exceptions for maintenance, for student grants, loans, and covenants, and for interest payments.

Paragraph 16(1) provides

Subject to sub-paragraphs (2) to (6) the amount of any income to which this Part applies shall be calculated or estimated

(a) where it has been received in respect of the whole of the period of 26 weeks which ends at the end of the relevant week, by dividing such income received in that period by 26,

(b) where it has been received in respect of part of the period of 26 weeks which ends at the end of the relevant week, by dividing such income received in that period by the number of complete weeks in respect of which such income is received and for this purpose income shall be treated as received in respect of a week if it is received in respect of any day in the week in question.

Example: if a parent received pension payments totalling £210 during the 6 weeks and 2 days prior to the effective date of the assessment then it is treated as being received at the weekly rate of £30.00.

Maintenance payments

Paragraph 16(2) provides

The amount of maintenance payments made in respect of a parent

(a) where they are payable weekly and have been paid at the same amount in respect of each week in the period of 13 weeks which ends at the end of the relevant week, shall be the amount equal to one of those payments,

(b) in any other case, shall be the amount calculated by aggregating the total amount of those payments received in the period of 13 weeks which ends at the end of the relevant week and dividing by the number of weeks in that period in respect of which maintenance was due.

Student income

Paragraph 16(3) and (4) provides

In the case of a student

(a) the amount of any grant and any amount paid in respect of grant contribution shall be calculated by apportioning it equally between the weeks in respect of which it is payable,

(b) the amount of any covenant income shall be calculated by dividing the amount payable in respect of a year by 52 (or, where such amount is payable in respect of a lesser period, by the number of complete weeks in that period) and deducting £5.00, but not more than £5.00 in total shall be deducted under this sub-paragraph,

Example: if a student receives covenant income from each of 2 grand-parents totalling £1,040 then the weekly rate shall be £1,040 ÷ 52 = £20.00, from which is deducted £5.00 only, producing £15.00.

(c) the amount of any student loan shall be calculated by apportioning the loan equally between the weeks in respect of which it is payable and deducting £10.00, but not more than £10.00 in total shall be deducted under sub-paragraphs (3)(b) and (c).

Example: if the above student additionally receives a student loan amounting to £600 payable for 30 weeks then the weekly rate will be £600 ÷ 30 = £20.00 from which shall be deducted £5.00 only; as a maximum amount of £10.00 only can be deducted under this and the preceding sub-paragraph. Accordingly the weekly rate of the student loan will be taken as £15.00, giving a total weekly income for the student under these sub-paragraphs of £30.00.

Interest and allied income payments

Paragraph 16(5) provides
   Where in respect of the period of 52 weeks which ends at the end of the relevant week a person is in receipt of interest, dividend or other income which has been produced by his capital, the amount of that income shall be calculated by dividing the aggregate of the income so received by 52.

Income Tax

Paragraph 2 of Schedule 2 to the Assessment Regulations provides that an amount in respect of Income Tax applicable to the income in question shall be disregarded (i.e. deducted) when calculating or estimating **N** and **M** where not otherwise allowed for under the Assessment Regulations [see Chapter 15 for the other categories of disregarded income]. Accordingly it will be necessary to identify those items of income paid **gross** and then to calculate the tax thereon by reference to the allowances and rates of tax set out in Chapter 10; similarly it will be necessary to calculate in respect of income paid net of basic rate tax the extent, if any, to which that income would be subjected to higher rate tax. It is understood that the Child Support Agency will calculate Income Tax on interest over the preceding 52 weeks by applying the rates and allowances currently in force notwithstanding that part of the 52 week period will fall in the previous tax year.

Proviso

Paragraph 16(6) provides

Where a calculation would, but for this sub-paragraph, produce an amount which, in the opinion of the Child Support Officer, does not accurately reflect the normal amount of the other income of the person in question, such income, or any part of it, shall be calculated by reference to such other period as may, in the particular case, enable the other income of that person to be determined more accurately and for this purpose the Child Support Officer shall have regard to the nature and pattern of receipt of such income.

CHAPTER 13

The income of a child treated as income of the parent

The basic principle

In certain circumtances the income of a child of a parent may be treated as if it is the income of a parent. If the child in question is **not** the subject of the maintenance assessment then it is included up to the amount allowed for the child when calculating the parent's exempt income [see Chapter 16]. If the child **is** the subject of the maintenance assessment then, if he is the only child the subject of the assessment, his income is brought into account in full; whereas, if he is one of a number of children the subject of the assessment, his income is included to the extent of his rateable share of the maintenance requirement and the maximum additional element [see Chapter 6]. A child's income does not include earnings by the child, maintenance payments to or for the child, certain payments (such as school fees or medical expenses) from a discretionary trust to the child, or any interest payable on arrears of Child Support maintenance for the child.

The detail

Paragraph 18 of Schedule 1 to the Assessment Regulations provides
    Where a child has income which falls within the following Paragraphs of this Part and that child is a member of the family of his parent (whether that child is a qualifying child in relation to that parent or not), the relevant income of that child shall be treated as that of his parent.

Paragraph 19 provides
    Where Child Support maintenance is being assessed for the support of only one qualifying child, the relevant income of that child shall be treated as that of the parent with care.

Comment: thus the entirety of the income of a single child of a parent with whom he lives is included as that parent's income, where that child **is** the subject of a maintenance assessment.

Paragraph 20 provides

Where Child Support maintenance is being assessed to support more than one qualifying child, the relevant income of each of those children shall be treated as that of the parent with care to the extent that it does not exceed the aggregate of

(a) the amount determined under

   (i)   Regulation 3(1)(a) (calculation of **AG**) [see Chapter 6] in relation to the child in question, and

   (ii) the total of any other amounts determined under Regulation 3(1)(b) to (d) which are applicable in the case in question divided by the number of children for whom Child Support maintenance is being calculated, less the basic rate of child benefit (within the meaning of Regulation 4) for the child in question, and

(b) 3 times the total of the amounts calculated under Regulation 3(1)(a) (Income Support personal allowance for child or young person) in respect of that child and Regulation 3(1)(c) (Income Support family premium).

Example: if there are 2 children the subject of a maintenance assessment living with a single parent and one, aged 14, has an income of £40.00 p.w. from a building society then that income will be taken into account as the income of the parent with care provided that it does not exceed

$$\{£22.15 + [(£44.00 + £9.65 + £4.90) \div 2] - £10.00\} +$$
$$\{3 \times (£22.15 + £9.65)\}$$
$$= £136.83$$

which it does not, so it is brought fully into account.

Paragraph 21 provides

Where Child Support maintenance is not being assessed for the support of the child whose income is being calculated or estimated, the relevant income of that child shall be treated as that of his parent to the extent that it does not exceed the amount determined under Regulation 9(1)(g).

Comment: Regulation 9(1)(g) prescibes the amount allowed for a child when calculating the parent's exempt income (E). In general terms the sum allowed corresponds to the child's personal Income Support allowance together with any disability premium; although the allowances can be reduced by 50% in certain circumstances [see Chapter 16].

Paragraph 22 provides

Where a benefit under the Contributions and Benefits Act includes an adult or child dependancy increase in respect of a relevant child, the relevant income of that child shall be calculated or estimated as if it included that amount.

Paragraph 23 provides

For the purposes of this Part, "the relevant income of a child" does not include

(a) any earnings of the child in question,

(b) payments by an absent parent in respect of the child for whom maintenance is being assessed,

(c) where the class of persons who are capable of benefiting from a discretionary trust include the child in question, payments from that trust except in so far as they are made to provide for food, ordinary clothing and footwear, gas, electricity or fuel charges or housing costs, or

(d) any interest payable on arrears of Child Support maintenance for that child.

> **Comment:** the D.S.S. have indicated that maintenance payments made to a child by a step-parent would be included as the relevant income of the child.

Paragraph 24 provides

The amount of the income of a child which is treated as the income of the parent shall be determined in the same way as if such income were the income of the parent.

Comment: accordingly the child's income shall be reckoned over the same periods, and subject to the same qualifications and provisos, as are applicable to "other income" of the parent [see Chapter 12].

CHAPTER 14

Amounts treated as income of the parent

The basic principle

In certain circumstances a notional income will be attributed to a parent. Broadly speaking a Child Support Officer can attribute a notional income to a parent if he is satisfied that that parent has worked for no payment or at an undervalue; that the work in question was done for the benefit of a third party who was able to pay a proper rate for it; and that the principal objective of the parent in undertaking the work was to reduce his assessable income for the purposes of the Act. Similarly, if the Officer is satisfied that a parent, with the same motive, has intentionally deprived himself of income or income producing capital then he may attribute a notional income to that parent.

The Child Support Officer may also attribute a notional income to a parent where payments (other than school fees or from certain trusts established by the Government) are made on behalf of that parent by a third party.

The detail

Paragraph 26 of Schedule 1 to the Assessment Regulations provides
Where a Child Support Officer is satisfied
(a) that a person has performed a service either
  (i)   without receiving any remuneration in respect of it, or
  (ii) for remuneration which is less than that normally paid for that service,
(b) that the service in question was for the benefit of
  (i)   another person who is not a member of the same family as the person in question, or
  (ii) a body which is neither a charity nor a voluntary organisation,
(c) that the service in question was performed for a person who, or as the case may be, a body which was able to pay remuneration at the normal rate for the service in question,
(d) that the principal purpose of the person undertaking the service without receiving any or adequate remuneration is to reduce his assessable income for the purposes of the Act, and

(e) that any remuneration foregone would have fallen to be taken into account as earnings,

the value of the remuneration foregone shall be estimated by a Child Support Officer and an amount equal to the value so estimated shall be treated as income of the person who performed those services.

Paragraph 27 provides

Subject to Paragraphs 28 to 30, where the Child Support Officer is satisified that, otherwise than in the circumstances set out in Paragraph 26, a person has intentionally deprived himself of
(a) any income or capital which would otherwise be a source of income,
(b) any income or capital which it would be reasonable to expect would be secured by him,

with a view to reducing the amount of his assessable income, his net income shall include the amount estimated by a Child Support Officer as representing the income which that person would have had if he had not deprived himself of or failed to secure that income, or as the case may be, that capital.

Paragraph 28 provides

No amount shall be treated as income by virtue of Paragraph 27 in relation to
(a) one parent benefit,
(b) if the parent is a person to, or in respect of, whom Income Support is payable, unemployment benefit,
(c) a payment from a discretionary trust or a trust derived from a payment made in consequence of a personal injury.

Comment: if a person deliberately deprives himself of an amount of one parent benefit; of unemployment benefit (when he is in receipt of Income Support); or of a trust payment, then that amount will not be added back as notional income.

Paragraph 29 provides

Where an amount is included in the income of a person under Paragraph 27 in respect of income which would become available to him on application, the amount included under that Paragraph shall be included from the date on which it could be expected to be acquired.

Paragraph 30 provides

Where a Child Support Officer determines under Paragraph 27 that a person has deprived himself of capital which would otherwise be a source of income, the amount of that capital shall be reduced at intervals of 52 weeks, starting with the week which falls 52 weeks after the first week in respect of which income from it is included in the calculation of the assessment in question, by an amount equal to the amount which the Child Support Officer estimates would represent the income from that source in the immediately preceding period of 52 weeks.

Example: suppose that a parent deliberately alienates the capital sum of £25,000 and that the Child Support Officer attributes a net rate of interest thereto of 6% giving a weekly notional income of £28.84 then after one year the capital sum will be reduced by £1,500 (being 52 x £28.84) to £23,500.

Paragraph 31 provides

Where a payment is made on behalf of a parent or a relevant child in respect of food, ordinary clothing or footwear, gas, electricity or fuel charges, housing costs or council tax, an amount equal to the amount which the Child Support Officer estimates represents the value of that payment shall be treated as the income of the parent in question except to the extent that such amount is

(a) disregarded under Paragraph 38 of Schedule 2 [see Chapter 15],

(b) a payment of school fees paid by or on behalf of someone other than the absent parent.

By Regulation 1(2) of the Assessment Regulations "ordinary clothing or footwear" means clothing or footwear for normal daily use, but does not include school uniforms, or clothing or footwear used solely for sporting activities.

Paragraph 32 provides

Where Paragraph 26 applies the amount to be treated as the income of the parent shall be determined as if it were earnings from employment as an employed earner and in a case to which Paragraph 27 or 31 applies the amount shall be determined as if it were other income to which Part III of this Schedule (i.e. Schedule 1) applies.

CHAPTER 15

Amounts to be disregarded when calculating N & M

The basic principle

By Schedule 2 to the Assessment Regulations certain amounts are to be disregarded when calculating **N** and **M**. They cover a very wide spectrum and it is not possible to generalise about them. The majority of the categories are self-explanatory, but for some of the more opaque items commentary is given below.

The detail

The Schedule provides
1. The amounts referred to in this Schedule are to be disregarded when calculating or estimating **N** and **M** (parent's net income).
2. An amount in respect of Income Tax applicable to the income in question where not otherwise allowed for under these Regulations.

   Comment: in Chapters 11 and 12 reference has already been made to this particular disregard in the context of the treatment of benefit payments to a parent and the other income of a parent. Similarly, in the unlikely event that a child's income is paid gross in a sum in excess of his personal allowance, then allowance must be made for tax. Attention is drawn to the new treatment of lodging income provided for in Schedule 10 of the Finance (No 2) Act 1992 to which reference has been made in Chapter 10.

3. Where a payment is made in a currency other than sterling, an amount equal to any banking charge or commission payable in converting that payment to sterling.
4. Any amount payable in a country outside the United Kingdom where there is a prohibition against the transfer to the United Kingdom of that amount.
5. Any compensation for personal injury and any payments from a trust fund set up for that purpose.

6. Any advance of earnings or any loan made by an employer to an employee.

7. Any payment by way of, or any reduction or discharge of liability resulting from entitlement to, housing benefit or council tax benefit.

   Comment: although housing benefit and certain other benefits (Paragraphs 8-17) are potentially included under Paragraph 6(2) of Schedule 1 to the Assessment Regulations, they are disregarded.

8. Any disability living allowance, mobility supplement or any payment intended to compensate for the non-payment of any such allowance or supplement.

9. Any payment which is
   (a) an attendance allowance under Section 64 of the Contributions and Benefits Act,
   (b) an increase of disablement pension under Section 104 or 105 of that Act (increases where constant attendance needed or for exceptionally severe disablement),
   (c) a payment made under Regulations made in exercise of the power conferred by Schedule 8 to that Act (payments for pre-1948 cases),
   (d) an increase of an allowance payable in respect of constant attendance under that Schedule,
   (e) payable by virtue of articles 14, 15, 16, 43 or 44 of the Personal Injuries (Civilians) Scheme 1983 (allowances for constant attendance and exceptionally severe disablement and severe disablement occupational allowance) or any analogous payment, or
   (f) a payment based on the need for attendance which is paid as part of a war disablement pension.

10. Any payment under Section 148 of the Contributions and Benefits Act (pensioners' Christmas bonus).

11. Any social fund payment within the meaning of Part VIII of the Contributions and Benefits Act.

12. Any payment made by the Secretary of State to compensate for the loss (in whole or in part) of entitlement to housing benefit.

13. Any payment made by the Secretary of State to compensate for loss of housing benefit supplement under Regulation 19 of the Supplementary Benefit (Requirements) Regulations 1983.

14. Any payment made by the Secretary of State to compensate a person who was entitled to supplementary benefit in respect of a period ending immediately before 11th April 1988 but who did not become entitled to Income Support in respect of a period beginning with that day.

15. Any concessionary payment made to compensate for the non-payment of Income Support, disability living allowance, or any payment to which Paragraph 9 applies.

16. Any payments of child benefit to the extent that they do not exceed the basic rate of that benefit as defined in Regulation 4.

    Comment: one parent benefit of £6.05 will not be disregarded.

17. Any payment made under Regulations 9 to 11 or 13 of the Welfare Food Regulations 1988 (payments made in place of milk tokens or the supply of vitamins).

18. Subject to Paragraph 20 and to the extent that it does not exceed £10.00
  (a) war disablement pension or war widow's pension or a payment made to compensate for non-payment of such a pension,
  (b) a pension paid by the government of a country outside Great Britain and which either
    (i) is analogous to a war disablement pension, or
    (ii) is analogous to a war widow's pension.

Comment: unlike the payments made under Paragraphs 7-17, which are wholly disregarded, these payments are disregarded only up to the level of £10.00 p.w. Receipts in excess of £10.00 p.w. are brought into account.

19. (1) Except where sub-paragraph (2) applies and subject to sub-paragraph (3) and Paragraphs 20, 38 and 47, £10.00 of any charitable or voluntary payment made, or due to be made, at regular intervals.
 (2) Subject to sub-paragraph (3) and Paragraphs 38 and 47, any charitable or voluntary payment made or due to be made at regular intervals which is intended and used for an item other than food, ordinary clothing or footwear, gas, electricity or fuel charges, housing costs of any member of the family or the payment of council tax.
 (3) Sub-paragraphs (1) and (2) shall not apply to a payment which is made by a person for the maintenance of any member of his family or of his former partner or of his children.
 (4) For the purposes of sub-paragraph (1) where a number of charitable or voluntary payments fall to be taken into account they shall be treated as though they were one such payment.

Comment: if the parent is in receipt of charitable or other voluntary payments (other than maintenance) then they are ignored up to £10.00 p.w. unless the payments are for purposes other than day to day living costs (e.g. medical expenses or school fees), in which event they are wholly ignored.

20. (1) Where, but for this Paragraph more than £10.00 would be disregarded under Paragraphs 18 and 19(1) in respect of the same week, only £10.00 in aggregate shall be disregarded and where an amount falls to be deducted from the income of a student under Paragraph 16(3)(b) or (c) of Schedule 1 [see Chapter 12], that amount shall count as part of the £10.00 disregard allowed under this Paragraph.

(2) Where any payment which is due to be paid in one week is paid in another week, sub-paragraph (1) and Paragraphs 18 and 19(1) shall have effect as if that payment were received in the week in which it was due.

Comment: only one exempt amount of £10.00 p.w. is permitted. To take an extreme example, if a student is in receipt of a student loan and covenant income (which would, in principle, entitle him to deduct £10.00 p.w. from his weekly income), and is also in receipt of a colonial war disablement pension (from which he can similarly, in principle, deduct £10.00 p.w.), and is further in receipt of charitable payments (from which likewise, in principle, he can deduct £10.00 p.w.), he is not in fact entitled to deduct a total of £30.00 p.w., but only £10.00 p.w.

21. In the case of a person participating in arrangements for training made under Section 2 of the Employment and Training Act 1973 or Section 2 of the Enterprise and New Towns (Scotland) Act 1990 (functions in relation to training for employment etc) or attending a course at an employment rehabilitation centre established under Section 2 of the 1973 Act
    (a) any travelling expenses reimbursed to the person,
    (b) any living away from home allowance under Section 2(2)(d) of the 1973 Act or Section 2(4)(c) of the 1990 Act,
    (c) any training premium,
    but this Paragraph, except insofar as it relates to a payment mentioned in sub-paragraph (a), (b) or (c) does not apply to any part of any allowance under Section 2(2)(d) of the 1973 Act or Section 2(4)(c) of the 1990 Act.

22. Where a parent occupies a dwelling as his home and that dwelling is also occupied by a person, other than a non-dependant or a person who is provided with board and lodging accommodation, and that person is contractually liable to make payments in respect of his occupation of the dwelling to the parent, the amount or, as the case may be, the amounts specified in Paragraph 19 of Schedule 2 to the Family Credit (General) Regulations 1987 which apply in his case, or, if he is not in receipt of family credit, the amounts which would have applied if he had been in receipt of that benefit.

    Paragraph 19 of Schedule 2 to the Family Credit Regulations provides
        Where the claimant occupies a dwelling as his home which is also occupied by a person other than one to whom Paragraph 18 refers or one who is provided with board and lodging accommodation and that person is contractually liable to make payments in respect of his occupation of the dwelling to the claimant
        (a) £4.00 of any payment made by that person, and
        (b) a further £8.60, where that payment is inclusive of an amount for heating.

Comment: if a parent has made a formal agreement to provide accommodation to a tenant or licensee within his home, then that parent is entitled to subtract £4.00 p.w. from the rent (or £8.60 if the rent is inclusive of an amount for heating). This provision does not apply to a letting on a board and lodging basis, which is dealt with under Paragraph 24 below, or to payments made under an informal non-contractual occupation, which are wholly ignored under Paragraph 35 below.

23. Where a parent who is not a self-employed earner is in receipt of rent or any other money in respect of the use and occupation of property other than his home, that rent or other payment to the extent of any sums which that parent is liable to pay by way of
    (a) payments which would be treated as housing costs by Paragraph 3 of Schedule 3 if that property were his home (exempt income: additional provisions relating to housing costs [see Chapter 16]),
    (b) council tax payable in respect of that property,
    (c) water and sewerage charges payable in respect of that property.

Comment: as has been seen in Chapter 10 a self-employed earner is entitled to deduct from his business receipts expenses wholly and exclusively defrayed for the purposes of his business. Thus a self-employed landlord would be entitled to deduct expenses relating to a let property from the gross rents received. No such deductions are permitted to persons who let out property other than as self-employed earners. The rent received is reckoned gross subject only to Income Tax. In order to provide a degree of redress this Paragraph permits certain housing costs to be deducted from the rent received.

24. Where a parent provides board and lodging accommodation in his home otherwise than as a self-employed earner
    (a) £20.00 of any payment for that accommodation made by the person to whom that accommodation is provided, and
    (b) where any such payment exceeds £20.00, 50% of the excess.

Comment: the same point as is made above under Paragraph 23 applies.

25. Any payment made to a person in respect of an adopted child who is a member of his family that is made in accordance with any Regulations made under Section 57A or pursuant to Section 57A(6) of the Adoption Act 1976 (permitted allowances) or, as the case may be, Section 51 of the Adoption (Scotland) Act 1978 (schemes for the payment of allowances to adopters)
    (a) where the child is not a child in respect of whom Child Support maintenance is being assessed, to the extent that it exceeds the amount referred to in Regulation 9(1)(g)(i), reduced, as the case may be, under Regulation 9(4),

(b) in any other case, to the extent that it does not exceed the amount of the income of a child which is treated as that of his parent by virtue of Part IV.

Comment: where an adoption allowance is received for a child who is **not** being assessed then that allowance is ignored to the extent that it exceeds the amounts allowed in respect of the child when calculating the parent's exempt income [see Chapter 16]. If the allowance is received in respect of a child who **is** the subject of the assessment then it is ignored up to the limit set out in Chapter 13 (i.e. for one child all of the allowance will be ignored; if more than one child it will be ignored up to the level determined by the formula within Paragraph 20 of Schedule 1 to the Assessment Regulations).

26. Where a local authority makes a payment in respect of the accommodation and maintenance of a child in pursuance of Paragraph 15 of Schedule 1 to the Children Act 1989 (local authority contribution to child's maintenance) to the extent that it exceeds the amount referred to in Regulation 9(1)(g)(i) (reduced, as the case may be, under Regulation 9(4)).

Comment: where a local authority contributes to the cost of accommodation and maintenance of a child where the child lives or is to live with a person as a result of a residence order then that payment is ignored to the extent that it exceeds the amounts allowed in respect of the child when calculating the parent's exempt income [see Chapter 16].

27. Any payment received under a policy of insurance taken out to insure against the risk of being unable to maintain repayments on a loan taken out to acquire an interest in, or to meet the cost of repairs or improvements to, the parent's home and used to meet such repayments, to the extent that the payment received under that policy does not in any period exceed the total of
(a) any interest payable on that loan,
(b) any capital repayable on that loan, and
(c) any premiums payable on that policy.

Comment: certain mortgage protection policies will meet payments due under a mortgage in the event of illness: such payments will be ignored.

28. In the calculation of the income of the parent with care, any maintenance payments made by the absent parent in respect of his qualifying child.
29. Any payment made by a local authority to a person who is caring for a child under Section 23(2)(a) of the Children Act 1989 (provision of accommodation and maintenance by a local authority for children whom the authority is looking after) or, as the case may be, Section 21 of the Social

Work (Scotland) Act 1968 or by a voluntary organisation under Section 59(1)(a) of the Children Act 1989 (provision of accommodation by voluntary organisations) or by a care authority under Regulation 9 of the Boarding Out and Fostering of Children (Scotland) Regulations 1985 (provision of accommodation and maintenance for children in care).

Comment: if the parent also acts as a foster parent then payments made in respect of such fostering by the local authority will be ignored.

30. Any payment made by a health authority, local authority or voluntary organisation in respect of a person who is not normally a member of the household but is temporarily in the care of a member of it.

31. Any payment made by a local authority under Section 17 or 24 of the Children Act 1989 or, as the case may be, Section 12, 24 or 26 of the Social Work (Scotland) Act 1968 (local authorities' duty to promote welfare of children and powers to grant financial assistance to persons looked after, or in, or formerly in, their care).

Comment: local authorities are empowered to make payments for the support of children who were previously in care: such payments to a parent will be ignored.

32. Any resettlement benefit which is paid to the parent by virtue of Regulation 3 of the Social Security (Hospital In-Patients) Amendment (No. 2) Regulations 1987 (transitional provisions).

33. (1) Any payment or repayment made
    (a) as respects England and Wales, under Regulation 3, 5 or 8 of the National Health Service (Travelling Expenses and Remission of Charges) Regulations 1988 (travelling expenses and health service supplies),
    (b) as respects Scotland, under Regulation 3, 5 or 8 of the National Health Service (Travelling Expenses and Remission of Charges) (Scotland) Regulations 1988 (travelling expenses and health service supplies).
    (2) Any payment or repayment made by the Secretary of State for Health, the Secretary of State for Scotland or the Secretary of State for Wales which is analogous to a payment or repayment mentioned in sub-paragraph (1).

34. Any payment made (other than a training allowance), whether by the Secretary of State or any other person under the Disabled Persons Employment Act 1944 or in accordance with arrangements made under Section 2 of the Employment and Training Act 1973 to assist disabled persons to obtain or retain employment despite their disability.

35. Any contribution to the expenses of maintaining a household which is made by a non-dependant member of that household.

Comment: as stated under Paragraph 22 above payments arising under an informal non-contractual occupation of the property are ignored.

36. Any sum in respect of a course of study attended by a child payable by virtue of Regulations made under Section 81 of the Education Act 1944 (assistance by means of scholarship or otherwise), or by virtue of Section 2(1) of the Education Act 1962 (awards for courses of further education) or Section 49 of the Education (Scotland) Act 1980 (power to assist persons to take advantage of educational facilities).

37. Where a person receives income under an annuity purchased with a loan which satisfies the following conditions

    (a) that loan was made as part of a scheme under which not less than 90% of the proceeds of the loan were applied to the purchase by the person to whom it was made of an annuity ending with his life or with the life of the survivor of 2 or more persons (in this Paragraph referred to as "the annuitants") who include the person to whom the loan was made,

    (b) that the interest on the loan is payable by the person to whom it was made or by one of the annuitants,

    (c) that at the time the loan was made the person to whom it was made or each of the annuitants had attained the age of 65,

    (d) that the loan was secured on a dwelling in Great Britain and the person to whom the loan was made or one of the annuitants owns an estate or interest in that dwelling, and

    (e) that the person to whom the loan was made or one of the annuitants occupies the dwelling on which it was secured as his home at the time the interest is paid, the amount, calculated on a weekly basis equal to

        (i) where, or insofar as, Section 26 of the Finance Act 1982 (deduction of tax from certain loan interest) applies to the payments of interest on the loan, the interest which is payable after the deduction of a sum equal to Income Tax on such payments at the basic rate for the year of assessment in which the payment of interest becomes due,

        (ii) in any other case the interest which is payable on the loan without deduction of such a sum.

    Comment: under certain "home income plans" elderly persons are able to mortgage their homes and to use the proceeds of such a mortgage to buy an annuity, thus retaining their home but liberating otherwise unproductive capital for the generation of income. Such annuity payments can be paid net of tax or gross: in either circumstance they are ignored.

38. Any payment of the description specified in Paragraph 39 of Schedule 9 to the Income Support Regulations (disregard of payments made under certain trusts and disregard of certain other payments) and any income derived from the investment of such payments.

    Comment: the Governement has established certain trusts known as the Macfarlane Trust, the Macfarlane (Special Payments) Trust, the Macfarlane (Special Payments) (No 2) Trust, and the Independent Living Fund.

Such trusts may inter alia make payments to or for the benefit of persons suffering from haemophilia, or their families: such payments are ignored.

39. Any payment made to a juror or witness in respect of attendance at Court other than compensation for loss of earnings or for loss of a benefit payable under the Contributions and Benefits Act.

40. Any special war widows' payment made under
    (a) the Naval and Marine Pay and Pensions (Special War Widows Payment) Order 1990 made under Section 3 of the Naval and Marine Pay and Pensions Act 1865,
    (b) the Royal Warrant dated 19th February 1990 amending the Schedule to the Army Pensions Warrant 1977,
    (c) the Queen's Order dated 26th February 1990 made under Section 2 of the Air Force (Constitution) Act 1917,
    (d) the Home Guard War Widows Special Payments Regulations 1990 made under Section 151 of the Reserve Forces Act 1980,
    (e) the Orders dated 19th February 1990 amending Orders made on 12th December 1980 concerning the Ulster Defence Regiment made in each case under Section 140 of the Reserve Forces Act 1980,
    and any analogous payment by the Secretary of State for Defence to any person who is not a person entitled under the provisions mentioned in sub-paragraphs (a) to (e).

41. Any payment to a person as holder of the Victoria Cross or the George Cross or any analogous payment.

42. Any payment made either by the Secretary of State for the Home Department or by the Secretary of State for Scotland under a scheme established to assist relatives and other persons to visit persons in custody.

43. Any amount by way of a refund of Income Tax deducted from profits or emoluments chargeable to Income Tax under Schedule D or Schedule E.

44. Maintenance payments (whether paid under the Act or otherwise) insofar as they are not treated as income under Part III or IV.

Comment: Paragraph 14 of Schedule 1 includes any maintenance in respect of a parent as "other income" [see Chapter 12]. Paragraph 23 (b) of Schedule 1 excludes maintenance paid to a child by an absent parent as the income of a child treated as the income of a parent, but maintenance paid by a step-parent would be included [see Chapter 13]. Maintenance paid to a parent for the benefit of a child would be disregarded under Paragraph 28 above. It is difficult to conceive of any other forms of maintenance that would fall to be disregarded under this Paragraph.

45. Where following a divorce or separation:
    (a) capital is divided between the parent and the person who was his partner before the divorce or separation; and

    (b) that capital is intended to be used to acquire a new home for that parent or to acquire furnishings for a home of his, income derived from the investment of that capital for one year following the date on which that capital became available to the parent.

46. Payments in kind.

    Comment: it is understood that the proposed Amendment Regulationns will require payments in kind to the self-employed to be taken into account.

47. Any payment made by the Joseph Rowntree Memorial Trust from money provided to it by the Secretary of State for Health for the purpose of maintaining a family fund for the benefit of severely handicapped children.

48. Any payment of expenses to a person who is
    (a) engaged by a charitable or voluntary body, or
    (b) a volunteer,
if he otherwise derives no remuneration or profit from the body or person paying those expenses.

CHAPTER 16

The calculation of E & F

The basic principle

A person's exempt income, broadly speaking, amounts to the aggregate of the Income Support allowances and premiums that would be applicable to him if he was entitled to that benefit together with his housing costs. As has been seen in Chapter 7, where a person is in receipt of Income Support he is taken as having no assessable income. Accordingly in such a case it is not necessary to consider his exempt income.

The detail

I THE GENERAL RULE

Regulation 9 of the Assessment Regulations provides that E shall be the aggregate of the following amounts

- (a) the Income Support personal allowance for a single claimant aged not less than 25 (£44.00),
- (b) the housing costs of the parent calculated in accordance with the provisions set out below at Section IV,
- (c) if the parent has a natural child who is a member of his family, and satisfies the conditions for Income Support lone parent premium, and does not satisfy the conditions for Income Support disability premium, then an amount equivalent to the rate of Income Support lone parent premium (£4.90),
- (d) if the parent satisfies the conditions for Income Support disability premium for applicants aged less than 60, then an amount equivalent to the rate for that benefit (£18.45),
- (e)   (i) if the parent satisfies the conditions for Income Support severe disability premium, then an amount equivalent to the rate for that benefit (£33.70),
  - (ii) if the parent satisfies the conditions for Income Support carer premium, then an amount equivalent to the rate for that benefit (£11.95),

(f) if the parent satisfies the conditions for Income Support family premium (i.e. he has a family of which at least one member is a child or young person), then an amount equivalent to the rate for that benefit (£9.65),

(g) for each natural child of the parent who is a member of his family

    (i) an amount equivalent to the child's Income Support personal allowance (child under 11: £15.05; child 11-15: £22.15; child 16-17: £26.45; child of 18: £34.80), and

    (ii) if the conditions for Income Support disabled child premium are satisfied, then an amount equivalent to the rate for that benefit (£18.45),

(h) fees payable if the parent or his partner lives in N.H.S. accommodation or in a nursing home.

By Regulation 1(2) "family" is defined as

(a) a married or unmarried couple (including the members of a polygamous marriage) and any child or children living with them for whom at least one member of that couple has day to day care (i.e. at least 104 nights each year [see Chapter 2]),

(b) where a person who is not a member of a married or an unmarried couple has day to day care of a child, that person and any such child or children,

and for the purposes of this definition a person shall not be treated as having day to day care of a child who is a member of that person's household where the child in question is being looked after by a local authority within the meaning of Section 22 of the Children Act 1989 or, in Scotland, where the child is boarded out with that person by a local authority under the provisions of Section 21 of the Social Work (Scotland) Act 1968 (i.e. foster children are not included).

II REDUCTION OF THE ALLOWANCES

In certain circumstances some of the amounts allowed above fall to be reduced by virtue of Regulation 9(2)

1. Where the absent parent has a partner and they have a natural child

The existence of the child would have given rise to allowances to augment the parent's exempt income under (f) and (g) above. But Regulation 9(2) contemplates that the partner should contribute to the child's support, provided that she or he can afford to do so. Thus, provided that the partner's income exceeds a certain level then the amount allowed under (f) and (g) is reduced by 50%. That level of income of the partner is calculated as follows.

First her or his net income under **N** principles is calculated [see Chapters 8-15]. It is understood that the proposed Amendment Regulations will provide that when calculating a partner's income under Regulation 7 any income of a child of the partner will **not** be included under Regulation 7(1)(a).

The sums allowed under (f) and (g) will be reduced by 50%, if her or his net income exceeds the aggregate of

(a) the Income Support personal allowance for a single claimant aged 25,
(b) an amount equivalent to half the child's Income Support personal allowance,
(c) an amount equivalent to half of any Income Support disabled child premium payable in respect of that child,
(d) an amount equivalent to half of any Income Support family premium (except when it is payable irrespective of the presence of any joint child of the parent and his partner i.e. there are other children living in the family unit [e.g. step-children of the parent, or children the subject of the assessment in the case of the parent with care, or an absent parent sharing care]),
(e) the amount by which the absent parent's housing costs have been reduced by apportionment (see below at Section IV).

"Partner" is defined by Regulation 1(2) as meaning
(a) in relation to a member of a married or unmarried couple who are living together, the other member of that couple,
(b) in relation to a member of a polygamous marriage, any other member of that marriage with whom he lives.

Comment: this definition would, accordingly, cover a homosexual couple.

2. Where the absent parent has day to day care of his child for less than 7 days each week

By Regulation 9(3), the amounts under (c) and (f) will be reduced if the absent parent does not have day to day care of all the children in question for 7 nights each week, but does have such care of at least one child for less than 7 nights each week. In that event the sums are reduced pro rata. By Regulation 9(4), the amount allowed under (g) will be reduced pro rata if the child in question spends less than 7 nights each week with the absent parent.

III THE INCOME SUPPORT CONDITIONS OF ENTITLEMENT

1. Lone parent premium

The parent will be allowed this premium if he is a lone parent. For as long as the child remains dependant (which can continue until age 19 [see Chapter 4]) the condition is satisfied.

2. Disability premium

This premium will be allowed if the parent
(a) is actually receiving one of the following non-means tested benefits
  (i)   attendance allowance or an equivalent benefit paid to meet attendance needs because of an injury at work or a war injury,
  (ii) disability living allowance,
  (iii) disability working allowance,

(iv) mobility supplement,
(v) invalidity pension,
(vi) severe disablement allowance,
(vii) an extra-statutory payment to compensate for not receiving any of the above, or

(b) is registered as blind with a local authority (if the parent regains his sight he will qualify for a further 28 weeks after he is removed from the register), or

(c) has been provided with an N.H.S. invalid carriage or a private car allowance on account of his disability, or

(d) has been incapable of work for at least 28 weeks and has been accepted as such on account of having received statutory sick pay or has claimed sickness benefit, severe disablement allowance or invalidity benefit and has been accepted as incapable of work.

3. Severe disability premium

This premium will be allowed if the parent
(a) is actually receiving attendance allowance (or the equivalent war pension or industrial injury benefit) or the higher or middle rate care component of disability living allowance (or extra-statutory payments for not receiving any of the aforesaid), and

(b) no non-dependant aged 18 or over is living with him, and

(c) no person is receiving an invalid care allowance in respect of him.

4. Carer premium

This premium will be allowed if the parent or his partner is in receipt of invalid care allowance (or an analogous extra-statutory payment), or would so qualify but for the rule in respect of overlapping benefits (so that, if, for example, a previous recipient of invalid care allowance progresses to a retirement pension which, on account of its quantum, thereby disentitles him to the allowance, the premium will continue to be allowed). If the parent ceases to receive, or is treated as receiving, the allowance, the entitlement to the premium continues for a further 8 weeks.

5. Family premium

This premium will be allowed if the parent's family includes a child.

6. Disabled child premium

This premium will be allowed if a child of the parent living in his family receives disability living allowance or is blind. For the conditions as to blindness see above at Paragraph 2(b). If the child has capital in excess of £3,000 the premium will not be allowed.

Appendix 2 sets out the detailed statutory provisions governing these premiums.

IV HOUSING COSTS

The basic principle

There are 5 steps to be undertaken in calculating the allowed housing costs

1. The first step is to work out which costs qualify as "eligible" housing costs.
2. Once the "eligible" housing costs have been identified and calculated the second step is to identify what proportion of them are taken into account.
3. Following the calculation of the allowable proportion of the eligible housing costs the third step is to consider the position where the parent is living with a spouse or other partner.
4. The fourth step is to consider whether the housing costs are "excessive" and are capped.
5. The fifth and final step is to convert all housing costs to a weekly figure.

The detail

1. "Eligible" housing costs

Regulation 14 of the Assessment Regulations provides that Schedule 3 supplies the criteria therefor.

There are certain pre-conditions as set out in Paragraph 4 of Schedule 3

(1) Subject to the following provisions of this Paragraph the housing costs referred to in this Schedule shall be included as housing costs only where
 (a) they are incurred in relation to the parent's home,
 (b) the parent or, if he is one of a family, he or a member of his family, is responsible for those costs, and
 (c) the liability to meet those costs is to a person other than a member of the same household.
(2) For the purposes of (1)(b) a parent shall be treated as responsible for housing costs where
 (a) because the person liable to meet those costs is not doing so, he has to meet those costs in order to continue to live in the home and either he was formerly the partner of the person liable, or he is some other person whom it is reasonable to treat as liable to meet those costs, or
 (b) he pays a share of those costs in a case where
  (i) he is living in a household with other persons,
  (ii) those other persons include persons who are not close relatives of his or his partner (by Paragraph 7, "close relative" means a parent, parent-in-law, son, son-in-law, daughter,

daughter-in-law, step-parent, step-son, step-daughter, broth-er, sister, or the spouse of any of the preceding persons or, if that person is one of an unmarried couple, the other member of that couple),

(iii) a person who is not such a close relative is responsible for those costs under the preceding provisions of this Paragraph or has an equivalent responsibility for housing expenditure, and

(iv) it is reasonable in the circumstances to treat him as sharing that responsibility.

Examples:

1. The absent father lives in the home of his new wife, but she has recently left him. He has therefore taken up payment of the costs of running that home. He will be treated as responsible for those payments.

2. The absent father lives in a house with a friend. That friend is in fact another absent father, namely the one in Example 1 above. The 2 absent fathers share the costs of that house. They will both be treated as responsible for the payments.

Subject to these pre-conditions Paragraph 1 of Schedule 3 provides that for the purposes of determining exempt income and protected income [see Chapter 17 for protected income] the following payments shall be taken into account as housing costs

(a) payments of, or by way of, rent,

(b) mortgage interest payments,

Comment: mortgage interest is always allowed. As shall be seen below, mortgage principal will be allowed when calculating exempt income, but not when calculating protected income.

(c) interest payments under a hire purchase agreement to buy a home,

(d) interest payments on loans for repairs and improvements to the home,

By Paragraph 2 "repairs and improvements" means major repairs necessary to maintain the fabric of the home and any of the following measures undertaken with a view to improving its fitness for occupation

(i)   installation of a fixed bath, shower, wash basin or lavatory, and necessary associated plumbing,

(ii)   damp proofing measures,

(iii)   provision or improvement of ventilation and natural lighting,

(iv)   provision of electric lighting and sockets,

(v)   provision or improvement of drainage facilities,

(vi)   improvement of the structural condition of the home,

(vii)   improvements to the facilities for the storing, preparation and cooking of food,

(viii) provision of heating, including central heating,

(ix)   provision of storage facilities for fuel and refuse,

(x)   improvements to the insulation of the home,

(xi)   other improvements which the Child Support Officer considers reasonable in the circumstances.

(e) payments by way of ground rent or in Scotland, payments by way of feu duty,

(f) payments under a co-ownership scheme,

(By Paragraph 7, "co-ownership scheme" means a scheme under which the dwelling is let by a housing association and the tenant, or his personal representative, will, under the terms of the tenancy agreement or of the agreement under which he became a member of the association, be entitled, on his ceasing to be a member and subject to any conditions stated in either agreement, to a sum calculated by reference directly or indirectly to the value of the dwelling),

(g) payments in respect of, or in consequence of, the use and occupation of the home,

(h) where the home is a tent, payments in respect of the tent and the site on which it stands,

(i) payments in respect of a licence or permission to occupy the home (whether or not board is provided),

(j) payments by way of mesne profits or, in Scotland, violent profits,

(k) payments of, or by way of, service charges, the payment of which is a condition on which the right to occupy the home depends,

(l) payments under or relating to a tenancy or licence of a Crown tenant,

(m) mooring charges payable for a houseboat,

(n) where the home is a caravan or a mobile home, payments in respect of the site on which it stands,

(o) any contribution payable by a parent resident in an almshouse provided by a housing association which is either a charity of which particulars are entered in the register of charities established under Section 4 of the Charities Act 1960 (register of charities) or an exempt charity within the meaning of that Act which is a contribution towards the cost of maintaining that association's almshouses and essential services in them,

(p) payments under a rental purchase agreement, that is to say an agreement for the purchase of a home under which the whole or part of the purchase price is to be paid in more than one instalment and the completion of the purchase is deferred until the whole or a specified part of the purchase price has been paid,

(q) where in Scotland the home is situated on or pertains to a croft within the meaning of Section 3(1) of the Crofters (Scotland) Act 1955, the payment in respect of the croft land,

(r) where the home is provided by an employer (whether under a condition or term in a contract of service or otherwise), payments to that employer in respect of the home, including payments made by the employer deducting the payment in question from the remuneration of the parent in question,

(s) payments analogous to those mentioned in this Paragraph,
(t) payments in respect of a loan taken out to pay off another loan but only to the extent that it was incurred for that purpose and only to the extent to which the interest on that other loan would have been met under this Paragraph.

Paragraph 3 contains further provisions in relation to the eligibility of housing costs in the calculation of **exempt** income (but not protected income [as to which see Chapter 17])

(2) Subject to sub-paragraph (6), where the home of an absent parent or, as the case may be, a parent with care, is subject to a mortgage or charge and that parent makes periodical payments to reduce the capital secured by that mortgage or charge of an amount provided for in accordance with the terms thereof, the amount of those payments shall be eligible to be taken into account as the housing costs of that parent.

(3) Where the home of an absent parent or, as the case may be, a parent with care, is held under an agreement and certain payments made under that agreement are included as housing costs by virtue of Paragraph 1 of this Schedule the weekly amount of any other payments which are made in accordance with that agreement by the parent in order either

(a) to reduce his liability under that agreement, or
(b) to acquire the home to which it relates,

shall also be eligible to be taken into account as housing costs.

By sub-paragraph (6) for the purposes of sub-paragraphs (2) and (3) above, housing costs shall not include

(a) any payment of arrears or payments in excess of those which are required to be made under or in respect of a mortgage, charge or agreement to which either of those sub-paragraphs relate,
(b) payments under any second or subsequent mortgage on the home to the extent that they are attributable to arrears or would otherwise not be eligible to be taken into account as housing costs,
(c) premiums payable in respect of any policy of insurance against loss caused by the destruction of or damage to any building or land.

(4) Where a policy of insurance has been obtained and retained for the purpose of discharging a mortgage or charge on the home of the parent in question the amount of the premiums paid under that policy shall be eligible to be taken into account as a housing cost.

Comment: the premiums payable under an endowment mortage without profits are allowed in full.

(5) Where a policy of insurance has been obtained and retained for the purpose of discharging a mortgage or charge on the home of the parent

in question and also for the purpose of accruing profits on the maturity of the policy the part of the premiums paid under that policy which are necessarily incurred for the purpose of discharging the mortgage or charge shall be eligible to be taken into account as a housing cost; and, where that part cannot be ascertained, 0.0277% of the amount secured by the mortgage or charge shall be deemed to be the part which is eligible to be taken into account as a housing cost.

Comment: for a with profits or low cost endowment mortgage the premiums will be allowed to the extent that they secure the principal of the mortgage. If, say, there is a £50,000 endowment mortgage and it is impossible to tell what part of the endowment premiums relates to the repayment of the mortgage alone, then £50,000 x 0.0277% = £13.85 p.w. is allowed.

Accommodation also used for other purposes

Paragraph 5 of Schedule 3 provides that

Where amounts are payable in respect of accommodation which consists partly of residential accommodation and partly of other accommodation, only such proportion thereof as is attributable to residential accommodation shall be eligible to be taken into account as housing costs.

Ineligible service and fuel charges

Paragraph 6 of Schedule 3 provides that

Housing costs shall not include

(a) where the costs are inclusive of ineligible service charges within the meaning of Paragraph 1 of Schedule 1 to the Housing Benefit (General) Regulations 1987 (ineligible service charges), the amounts attributable to those ineligible service charges or, where that amount is not separated from or separately identified within the housing costs to be met under this Paragraph, such part of the payments made in respect of the housing costs which are fairly attributable to the provision of those ineligible services having regard to the costs of comparable services.

The ineligible service charges are
  (A) charges in respect of
    (i)   meals (including the preparation of meals or provision of unprepared food),
    (ii) laundry (other than the provision of premises or equipment to enable a person to do his own laundry),
    (iii) leisure items such as sports facilities (except a children's play area), or television rental or licence fees (except television and radio relay charges),

(iv) cleaning of rooms or windows (other than communal areas) except where neither the claimant nor any member of his household is able to clean them himself,

(v) transport,

(B) charges in respect of

(i) the acquisition of furniture or household equipment, and

(ii) the use of such furniture or equipment where that furniture or household equipment will become the property of the claimant by virtue of an agreement with the landlord,

(C) charges in respect of the provision of an emergency alarm system, except where such a system is provided in accommodation which is occupied by elderly, sick or disabled persons and such accommodation, apart from such alarm system, is either

(i) specifically designed or adapted for such persons, or

(ii) otherwise particularly suitable for them, having regard to its size, heating system and other major features or facilities,

(D) charges in respect of medical expenses (including the cost of treatment or counselling related to mental disorder, mental handicap, physical disablement or past or present alcohol or drug dependence),

(E) charges in respect of the provision of nursing care or personal care (including assistance at meal-times or with personal appearance or hygiene),

(F) charges in respect of general counselling or other support services (whether or not provided by social work professionals) except those related to the provision of adequate accommodation or those provided by the landlord in person or someone employed by him who spends the majority of his time providing services for which the charges are not eligible under the terms of this Paragraph,

(G) charges in respect of any services not specified in sub-paragraphs (A) to (F) which are not connected with the provision of adequate accommodation,

(b) where the costs are inclusive of any of the items mentioned in Paragraph 5(2) of Schedule 1 to the Housing Benefit (General) Regulations 1987 (payment in respect of fuel charges) the deductions prescribed in that Paragraph unless the parent provides evidence on which the actual or approximate amount of the service charge for fuel may be estimated, in which case the estimated amount,

The items and the weekly deductions are	
Heating (other than hot water):	£8.60
Hot water:	£1.05
Lighting:	£0.70
Cooking:	£1.05

(c) charges for water, sewerage or allied environmental services and where the amount of such charges is not separately identified, such part of the charges in question as is attributable to those services.

2. The proportion of eligible housing costs taken into account

The general rule is that the housing costs that are allowed are all the eligible housing costs as calculated above (Regulation 15(1) of the Assessment Regulations). There are certain exceptions to this as follows.

A: Housing benefit cases
Regulation 15(2) provides
    Where a local authority has determined that a parent is entitled to housing benefit, the amount of his housing costs shall, subject to Paragraphs (4) to (9), be the weekly amount treated as rent under Regulations 10 and 69 of the Housing Benefit Regulations (rent and calculation of weekly amounts) less the amount of housing benefit.

Comment: this is a Special Case. The elaborate procedure set out above for working out housing cost will not apply where the parent is in receipt of housing benefit. In this case the housing cost is the amount that is treated as rent by the local authority less the amount of housing benefit. So if the rent is £40.00 and the housing benefit is £20.00 then the housing cost is £20.00.

B: Where someone else is liable to make payments towards the home
Regulation 15(3) provides
    Where a parent has eligible housing costs and another person who is not a member of his family is also liable to make payments in respect of the home, the amount of the parent's housing costs shall be his share of those costs.

Example: if a former wife has a Court order which recites that her former husband must pay her mortgage then the the sums paid by way of mortgage are subtracted from her housing costs as computed.

C: Where there are non-dependant members of the household (such as adult children, parents etc, but excluding spouses/partners)
Regulation 15(4) provides
    Where one or more non-dependants are members of the parent's household, there shall be deducted from the amount of any housing costs determined under the preceding Paragraphs of this Regulation any non-dependant amount or amounts determined in accordance with the provisions of Paragraphs (5) to (9).

Regulation 15(5) provides

The non-dependant amount shall be an amount equal to the amount which would be calculated under Paragraph 63 of the Housing Benefit Regulations (non-dependant deductions) for the non-dependant in question if he were a non-dependant in respect of whom a calculation were to be made under that Regulation.

Example: if there is a 25 year old son living in the house of the parent then an amount is deducted from the parent's housing costs. This sum is the amount that would be produced as a non-dependant deduction if the parent applied for housing benefit.

The non-dependant deductions are as follows
Aged 18 or over and in full time work with a weekly gross income of

£70.00–£104.99:	deduct £8.00
£105.00–£134.99:	deduct £12.00
£135.00 or more:	deduct £21.00

Aged 25 or over and in receipt of Income Support: deduct £4.00

All others aged 18 or over (including those in part-time work, on pensions or other benefits but excluding those on Income Support aged between 18 and 24): deduct £4.00

Full time work is paid employment of 16 hours or more each week. In estimating the number of hours worked, any recognised holidays or leave will be ignored. Non-dependants involved in employment training will not be regarded as being in full-time work. Similarly non-dependants on extended sick leave and in receipt of statutory sick pay or on maternity leave and getting statutory maternity pay will not count as being in full-time work.

A non-dependant is defined as any person residing with the parent who does not fall into one of the following categories

1. Any member of the parent's family
2. Any child or young person living with the parent who is not a member of his family (e.g. a foster child)
3. Any person who jointly occupies the accommodation of the parent and who shares liability in respect of occupation (e.g. a co-mortgagor or co-tenant)
4. Any person who occupies the accommodation of the parent who is his tenant, sub-tenant, boarder; or is his landlord or a member of the landlord's family
5. Any carer engaged by a charitable or voluntary body to live in the home and who looks after the parent or his partner and who raises a charge for such services

A non-dependant will be regarded as in residence with the parent if he is not separately liable for his housing costs and shares some accommodation with the parent apart from a bathroom, lavatory or communal areas such as a hall or passage or a common-room in sheltered accommodation. Thus a self-contained annexe occupied by a relation of the parent would not amount to common residence even if that relation shares the use of the bathroom in the property.

Regulation 15(6) provides
For the purposes of Paragraph (5)
(a) in the case of a couple or, as the case may be, the members of a polygamous marriage
    (i)   regard shall be had to their joint weekly income, and
    (ii) only one deduction shall be made at whichever is the higher rate.

Example: the parent's own parents are living with him and have a joint gross income of £110 per week: the deduction made is £12.00.

Regulation 15(7) provides
Where a person is a non-dependant in respect of more than one joint occupier of a dwelling (except where the joint occupiers are a couple or members of a polygamous marriage), the deduction in respect of that non-dependant shall be apportioned between the joint occupiers having regard to the number of joint occupiers and the proportion of the housing costs in respect of the home payable by each of them.

Example: the parent lives in a house with her brother and they share the costs. Their mother also lives with them. She has a gross income of £136 per week. The non-dependant deduction made from the parent's housing costs is £21.00 ÷ 2 = £11.00.

Regulation 15(8) provides
No deduction shall be made in respect of any non-dependants occupying the home of the parent, if the parent or any partner of his is
(a) blind or treated as blind by virtue of Paragraph 12 of the relevant Schedule (Income Support additional condition for the higher pensioner and disability premiums, see above), or
(b) receiving in respect of himself either
    (i)   attendance allowance under Section 64 of the Contributions and Benefits Act, or
    (ii) the care component of disability living allowance.

Comment: no deduction is made if the parent or his partner is registered as blind or has regained eyesight within the last 28 weeks, or if the parent receives attendance allowance, or the care component of the disability allowance.

Regulation 15(9) provides

No deduction shall be made in respect of a non-dependant

(a) if, although he resides with the parent, it appears to the Child Support Officer that his home is normally elsewhere, or

(b) if he is in receipt of a training allowance paid in connection with a youth training programme established under Section 2 of the Employment and Training Act 1973 or Section 2 of the Enterprise and New Towns (Scotland) Act 1990, or

(c) if he is a student, or

(d) if he is aged under 25 and in receipt of Income Support, or

(e) if he is not residing with the parent because he is a prisoner or because he has been a patient for a period, or 2 or more periods separated by not more than 28 days, exceeding 6 weeks.

Regulation 15(10) provides

A parent shall be treated as having no housing costs where

(a) he is a non-dependant member of a household and is not responsible for meeting housing costs except to another member, or other members, of that household, or

(b) but for this Paragraph, his housing costs would be less than nil.

Example: if a wife is living with her parents and pays a contribution to her parents for her board then she is treated as having no housing costs, because she has no formal housing costs. However, her actual costs will be taken into account when computing protected income [see Chapter 17].

Comment: if under the procedure for calculating housing costs a negative figure is produced (say, on account of a substantial non-dependant deduction) then the housing costs are taken as nil.

3. The position where the parent is living with a spouse or other partner

In such circumstances the housing costs are apportioned between the parent and his partner.

Regulation 17 of the Assessment Regulations provides

For the purposes of calculating or estimating exempt income (but not protected income) the amount of the housing costs of a parent shall be

(a) where the parent does not have a partner, the whole amount of the housing costs,

(b) where the parent has a partner, the proportion of the amount of the housing costs calculated by multiplying those costs by

$$[0.75 + (A \times 0.2)] \div [1.00 + (B \times 0.2)]$$

where

A is the number of relevant children (if any)

B is the number of children in that parent's family (if any)

Comment: the Department of Social Security believes that one adult needs to spend on housing about 75% of the amount spent on housing by a married couple. Accordingly, if the absent parent has a new partner and there are no children in his household then 75% of his housing costs are allowed. It is further assumed that a child will require in housing costs 20% of the amount spent by a couple without children.

"Relevant children" are the natural children of the absent parent living in the family unit. The children within B in the formula are all the children in the family i.e. the children of the absent parent and the children of the absent parent's partner, but excluding officially fostered children.

Table of examples

TABLE 3

Family composition	Absent parent's share	Household total	Fractions allowed	Expressed as % of housing costs
Absent parent on own	1	1	1	100%
Absent parent remarried, no children	0.75	1	0.75 ÷ 1	75%
Absent parent remarried, 1 natural child	0.95	1.2	0.95 ÷ 1.2	79.17%
Absent parent remarried, 1 step-child	0.75	1.2	0.75 ÷ 1.2	62.5%
Absent parent remarried, 2 natural children	1.15	1.4	1.15 ÷ 1.4	82.14%
Absent parent remarried, 1 natural child, 1 step-child	0.95	1.4	0.95 ÷ 1.4	67.86%
Absent parent remarried, 2 step-children	0.75	1.4	0.75 ÷ 1.4	53.57%
Absent parent remarried, 2 natural children, 1 step-child	1.15	1.6	1.15 ÷ 1.6	71.88%

(c) where the parent is a member of a polygamous marriage the proportion of the amount of the housing costs calculated by multiplying those costs by

$$[0.75 + (A \times 0.2)] \div [1.00 + (X \times 0.25) + (B \times 0.2)]$$

where

A and B have the same meanings as in sub-paragraph (b), and
X is the number which is one less than the number of partners.

4. Excessive housing costs are capped

Regulation 18 of the Assessment Regulations provides
  (1) Subject to Paragraph (2), the amount of the housing costs of an absent parent which are to be taken into account
      (a) under Regulation 9(1)(b) (i.e. for the purpose of calculating exempt income) shall not exceed the greater of £80.00 or half the amount of **N** as calculated or estimated under Regulation 7,
      (b) under Regulation 11(1)(b) (i.e. for the purpose of calculating protected income [see Chapter 17]) shall not exceed the greater of £80.00 or half of the amount calculated in accordance with Regulation 11(2).
  (2) The restriction imposed by Paragraph (1) shall not apply where
      (a) the absent parent in question
          (i)   has been awarded housing benefit (or is awaiting the outcome of a claim to that benefit), or
          (ii) has the day to day care of any child, or
          (iii) is a person to whom a disability premium under Paragraph 11 of Schedule 2 of the Income Support (General) Regulations 1987 applies in respect of himself or his partner or would so apply if he were entitled to Income Support and were aged less than 60 (i.e. if he or his partner is or would be entitled to Income Support disability premium),
      (b) the absent parent in question, following a divorce from, or the breakdown of his relationship with, his former partner, remains in the home he occupied with his former partner,
      (c) the absent parent in question has paid the housing costs under the mortgage, charge or agreement in question for a period in excess of 52 weeks before the date of the first application for Child Support maintenance in relation to a qualifying child of his and there has been no increase in those costs other than an increase in the interest payable under the mortgage or charge or, as the case may be, in the amount payable under the agreement under which the home is held,

      Comment: if the parent has paid housing costs in excess of the limit at a steady rate for one year with no increases apart from increases in mortgage rates, then the capping restriction will not apply.

      (d) the housing costs in respect of the home in question would not exceed the amount set out in Paragraph (1) but for an increase in the interest payable under a mortgage or charge secured on that home or, as the case may be, in the amount payable under any agreement under which it is held, or

      Comment: if at any time during the existence of a mortgage the interest rate was less than that presently in force, and at the lower rate the capped level would not be exceeded, then the capping restriction will not apply. One is bound to wonder at the workability of this provision, involving, as it does, research into mortgage rates over the life of the mortgage.

(e) the absent parent is responsible for making payments in respect of housing costs which are higher than they would be otherwise by virtue of the unavailability of his share of the equity of the property formerly occupied with his partner and which remains occupied by that former partner.

Comment: This provision is relied on by the D.S.S. to meet the criticism that the effect of the Act will be to deter former husbands from agreeing the transfer of the family home to former wives in circumstances where former wives can no longer wisely agree in return to accept lower than normal child maintenance [see Chapter 30, where the matter is fully discussed]. The removal of the housing cost "cap" for such a former husband is intended to encourage him to cede his share in the equity in the family home; although it must be doubted whether such a concession will, in practical terms, have much of an impact on the problem.

5. Convert all housing costs to a weekly figure

Regulation 16 of the Assessment Regulations provides
   Where a parent pays housing costs
   (a) on a weekly basis, the amount of such housing costs shall be the weekly rate payable at the effective date,
   (b) on a monthly basis, the amount of such housing costs shall be the monthly rate payable at the effective date, multiplied by 12 and divided by 52,
   (c) on any other basis, the amount of such housing costs shall be the rate payable at the effective date, multiplied by the number of payment periods, or the nearest whole number of payment periods (any fraction of one half being rounded up), falling within a period of 365 days and divided by 52.

V THE CALCULATION OF F

By Regulation 10 of the Assessment Regulations **F** is to be calculated or estimated in the same way as **E** is calculated under Regulation 9, but as if references to the absent parent were references to the parent with care.

CHAPTER 17

Protected income and minimum payment

The basic principle

Paragraphs 6 and 7 of Schedule 1 to the Act provide that where a maintenance assessment has been undertaken in respect of an absent parent and the amount payable by him would reduce his income below his "protected income level" then it shall be adjusted so that so far as is reasonably practicable his payment shall not reduce his "disposable" income below that level, but that no such adjustment shall result in him paying less than the "minimum amount".

The detail

I THE MINIMUM AMOUNT

Regulation 13 of the Assessment Regulations provides
   (1) Subject to Regulation 26 (where under Special Case 8 [see Chapter 18] no payments will be made) for the purposes of Paragraph 7(1) of Schedule 1 to the Act the minimum amount shall be 5% of the amount specified in Paragraph 1(1)(e) of the relevant Schedule (Income Support personal allowance for single claimant aged not less than 25 [£44.00]).
   (2) Where an amount calculated under Paragraph (1) results in a sum other than a multiple of 5 pence, it shall be treated as the sum which is the next higher multiple of 5 pence.

Comment: the minimum amount is £44.00 x 5% = £2.20.

II PROTECTED INCOME

Regulation 11 of the Assessment Regulations provides
   The protected income level of an absent parent shall, subject to Paragraphs (3) and (4), be the aggregate of the following amounts
   (1) (a) where
            (i)   the absent parent does not have a partner, an amount equal

to the amount specified in column (2) of Paragraph 1(1)(e) of the relevant Schedule (Income Support personal allowance for a single claimant aged not less than 25 years [£44.00]),

(ii) the absent parent has a partner, an amount equal to the amount specified in column (2) of Paragraph 1(3)(c) of the relevant Schedule (Income Support personal allowance for a couple where both members are aged not less than 18 years [£69.00]),

(iii) the absent parent is a member of a polygamous marriage, an amount in respect of himself and one of his partners, equal to the amount specified in sub-paragraph (ii) and, in respect of each of his other partners, an amount equal to the difference between the amounts specified in sub-paragraph (ii) and sub-paragraph (i),

Example: in the case of a polygamous marriage where the absent parent has 3 wives the amount allowed will be £69.00 + [2 x (£69.00 - £44.00)] = £119.00

(b) an amount in respect of housing costs determined in accordance with Regulations 14, 15, 16 and 18, or, in a case where the absent parent is a non-dependant member of a household who is treated as having no housing costs by Regulation 15(10)(a), the non-dependant amount which would be calculated in respect of him under Regulation 15(5),

Comment: see Chapter 16 for the calculation of housing costs applicable to the protected earnings calculation. The following distinctions from that applied in the calculation of **E** should be noted:

* The payments allowed under Paragraph 3 of Schedule 3 will not be allowed in the calculation of protected income (capital payments towards the acquisition of a home, whether in respect of a mortgage or otherwise);

* where the absent parent is a non-dependant member of a household the amount that would be calculated in respect of him under Regulation 15(5) of the Assessment Regulations will be allowed as housing costs in the calculation of protected income [see Chapter 16 for the amount]. In the calculation of **E** no amount of housing costs are allowed in respect of an absent parent who is a non-dependant member of a household (Regulation 15(10));

* no apportionment of housing costs between an absent parent and his partner is undertaken in the calculation of protected income.

(c) where, if the absent parent were a claimant, the condition in Paragraph 8 of the relevant Schedule (Income Support lone parent premium) would be satisfied but the condition set out in Paragraph 11 of that Schedule (Income Support disability premium) would not be satisfied, an amount equal to the amount specified in column (2) of Paragraph 15(1) of that Schedule (Income Support lone parent premium),

Comment: see Chapter 16 for the conditions for these premiums.

(d) where, if the parent were a claimant, the conditions in Paragraph 11 of the relevant Schedule (Income Support disability premium) would be satisfied, an amount equal to the amount specified in column (2) of Paragraph 15(4) of that Schedule (Income Support disability premium);

Comment: see Chapter 16 for the conditions for this premium.

(e) where, if the parent were a claimant, the conditions in Paragraph 13 or 14ZA of the relevant Schedule (Income Support severe disability and carer premiums) would be satisfied in respect of either or both premiums, an amount equal to the amount or amounts specified in column (2) of Paragraph 15(5) or, as the case may be, (7) of that Schedule in respect of that or those premiums (Income Support premiums),

Comment: see Chapter 16 for the conditions for these premiums.

(f) where, if the parent were a claimant, the conditions in Paragraph 3 of the relevant Schedule (Income Support family premium) would be satisfied, the amount specified in that Paragraph,

Comment: see Chapter 16 for the conditions for this premium.

(g) in respect of each child who is a member of the family of the absent parent
   (i)   an amount equal to the amount of the personal allowance for that child specified in column (2) of Paragraph 2 of the relevant Schedule (Income Support personal allowance),

Comment: see Chapter 6 for the amounts allowable.

   (ii)   if the conditions set out in Paragraphs 14(b) and (c) of the relevant Schedule (Income Support disabled child premium) are satisfied in respect of that child, an amount equal to the amount specified in column (2) of Paragraph 15(6) of the relevant Schedule,

Comment: see Chapter 16 for the conditions for this premium.

(h) where, if the parent were a claimant, the conditions specified in Part III of the relevant Schedule would be satisfied by the absent parent in question or any member of his family in relation to any premium not otherwise included in this Regulation, an amount equal to the amount specified in Part IV of that Schedule (Income Support premiums) in respect of that premium,

Comment: the premiums in question are **pensioner premium** and **higher pensioner premium.**

The **pensioner premium** is paid for persons aged 60 or over. For single persons aged 60-74 the rate is £17.30, for those aged 75-79 the enhanced rate is £19.30. For couples the rate is £26.25 and the enhanced rate is £29.00. The enhanced couple rate will be paid if at least one partner is over 75.

The **higher pensioner premium** is paid to persons aged 80 or over. The rate is £23.55 (single) and £33.70 (couple). This premium will also be paid in the following circumstances

* If the claimant receives severe disablement allowance up to age 60 (female) or 70 (male), then the claimant will be entitled to the allowance for life and will become entitled to this premium. Alternatively, the allowance may cease on account of receipt of a retirement pension of greater quantum: in this circumstance, too, the premium will be payable.
* If the claimant was in receipt of a disability premium as part of his Income Support or housing benefit for at least 8 weeks before age 60 and has continued to claim that benefit after that age, then the higher pensioner premium will be payable.

(i) where the absent parent in question or his partner is living in
    (i) accommodation provided under Part III of the National Assistance Act 1948,
    (ii) accommodation provided under Paragraphs 1 and 2 of Schedule 8 to the National Health Service Act 1977, or
    (iii) a nursing home or residential care home,
the amount of the fees paid in respect of the occupation of that accommodation or, as the case may be, that home.

(j) the amount of council tax which the absent parent in question or his partner is liable to pay in respect of the home for which housing costs are included under sub-paragraph (b) less any council tax benefit,

(k) an amount of £8.00,

(l) where the income of
    (i) the absent parent in question,
    (ii) any partner of his, and
    (iii) any child or children for whom an amount is included under sub-paragraph (g)(i),
exceeds the sum of the amounts to which reference is made in sub-paragraphs (a) to (k), 10% of the excess.

Comment: the D.S.S. have indicated that insofar as the income of a parent includes the income of a child, that income will not be counted again as the income of the child under (iii).

Example: say the net income of the absent parent amounts to £100.00 and that the amount of allowable deductions calculated thus far under sub-paragraphs (a)-(k) amounts to £60.00. He will be entitled to include a further £4.00, being 10% of the difference between £100.00 and £60.00.

(2) For the purposes of sub-paragraph (l) of Paragraph (1) "income" shall be calculated

(a) in respect of the absent parent in question or any partner of his, in the same manner as **N** (net income of absent parent) is calculated under Regulation 7 except

  (i) there shall be taken into account the basic rate of any child benefit and any maintenance which in either case is in payment in respect of any member of the family of the absent parent,

  Comment: the basic rate of child benefit and maintenance paid to children of the family are disregarded in the calculation of **N** [see Chapter 15]. When calculating protected income these payments are included.

  (ii) there shall be deducted the amount of any maintenance under a maintenance order which the absent parent or his partner is paying in respect of a child in circumstances where an application for a maintenance assessment could not be made in accordance with the Act in respect of that child, and

  Comment: see Chapter 18 for the role of the Courts and the ability of the Court to make maintenance orders.

(b) in respect of any child in that family, as being the total of that child's income but only to the extent that such income does not exceed the amount included under sub-paragraph (g) of Paragraph (1) (Income Support personal allowance for a child and Income Support disabled child premium) reduced, as the case may be, under Paragraph (4).

(3) Where an absent parent does not have day to day care of any child (whether or not a relevant child) for 7 nights each week but does have day to day care of one or more such children for fewer than 7 nights each week, any amounts to be taken into account under sub-paragraphs (c) and (f) of Paragraph (1) (Income Support lone parent premium and Income Support family premium) shall be reduced so that they bear the same proportion to the amounts referred to in those sub-paragraphs as the average number of nights each week in respect of which such care is provided has to 7.

(4) Where an absent parent has day to day care of a child (whether or not a relevant child) for fewer than 7 nights each week any amounts in relation to that child to be taken into account under sub-paragraph (g) of Paragraph (1) (Income Support personal allowance for child and Income Support disabled child premium) shall be reduced so that they bear the same proportion to the amounts referred to in that sub-paragraph as the average number of nights in respect of which such care is provided has to 7.

Comment: By Regulation 11(3) the amounts under (c) and (f) will be reduced if the absent parent does not have day to day care of all the children in question for 7 nights each week, but does have such care of at least one child for less than 7 nights each week. In that event the sum(s) are reduced pro rata. By Regulation 11(4) the amount allowed under (g) will be reduced pro rata if the child in question spends less than 7 nights each week with the absent parent. The children in question are not confined to his natural children, as is the case in the calculation of **E**, but extend to all children in the absent parent's family.

(5) The amounts referred to in Paragraph (1) shall be the amounts applicable at the effective date.

Regulation 12(1) provides that the disposable income of a parent shall be the aggregate of his income and the income of any member of his family calculated in like manner as under Regulation 11(2). This will equate to the total income calculation under Regulation 11(1)(l) for the purpose of computing the 10% excess referred to therein. Regulation 12(2) provides that where a maintenance assessment has been made and payment of the amount thereunder by the absent parent would reduce his disposable income below his protected income level, then the assessment shall be adjusted by the minimum amount necessary to prevent his income falling below that level. But, by Regulation 12(3), where the minimum amount of £2.20 p.w. is applicable the amount payable shall not be reduced to less than that amount.

CHAPTER 18

Special cases

By Section 42 of the Act the Secretary of State is empowered to make Regulations modifying any provision made under the Act to specified Special Cases.

Regulations 19 to 28 of the Assessment Regulations set out the specified Special Cases and the modifications to the preceding rules applicable thereto.

The Special Cases are as follows

1. Both parents are absent
2. Persons treated as absent parents
3. One parent is absent and the other is treated as absent
4. Multiple applications relating to an absent parent
5. Person caring for children of more than one absent parent
6. Persons with part time care; not including a person treated as an absent parent
7. Care provided in part by a local authority
8. Cases where Child Support maintenance is not to be payable
9. Child who is a boarder or an in-patient
10. Amount payable where absent parent is in receipt of Income Support or other prescribed benefit

CASE 1: BOTH PARENTS ARE ABSENT

The basic principle

Where each parent is absent an assessment (modified in accordance with the detail below) is undertaken in respect of each [see Chapter 2 for the definition of an absent parent].

The detail

Regulation 19 of the Assessment Regulations provides

(1) Subject to Regulation 27, where the circumstances of a case are that each parent of a qualifying child is an absent parent in relation to that child (neither being a person who is treated as an absent parent by

Regulation 20(2) [see Special Case 2 below]) that case shall be treated as a Special Case for the purposes of the Act.

(2) For the purposes of this case

    (a) where the application is made in relation to both absent parents, separate assessments shall be made under Schedule 1 to the Act in respect of each so as to determine the amount of Child Support maintenance payable by each absent parent,

    (b) subject to Paragraph (3), where the application is made in relation to both absent parents, the value of **C** in each case shall be the assessable income of the other absent parent and where the application is made in relation to only one the value of **C** in the case of the other shall be nil,

    (c) where the person with care is a body of persons corporate or unincorporate, the value of **AG** shall not include any amount mentioned in Regulation 3(1)(d) (Income Support lone parent premium).

(3) Where, for the purposes of Paragraph (2)(b), information regarding the income of the other absent parent has not been submitted to the Secretary of State or to a Child Support Officer within the period specified in Regulation 6(1) of the Maintenance Assessment Procedure Regulations then until such information is acquired the value of **C** shall be nil.

(4) When the information referred to in Paragraph (3) is acquired the Child Support Officer shall make a fresh assessment which shall have effect from the effective date in relation to that other absent parent.

Comment: this case will apply where neither parent has the child living with him or her in his or her household. So, for example, it will apply where a relation cares for the child for 5 nights each week and each parent cares for the child for one night. In such a case a separate assessment is carried out in respect of each parent to determine their respective liability to the person caring for the child. For each such assessment the value of **C** attributed within the formulae set out in Chapter 6 shall be the assessable income of the other parent. If the assessment is made only in relation to one parent, because, for example, the other parent is dead or resides abroad, the value of **C** is nil. Similarly, if the Officer has not received details of the income of one parent within the prescribed time then, in undertaking the assessment of the other parent, the value of **C** will be nil.

CASE 2: PERSONS TREATED AS ABSENT PARENTS

The basic principle

If a parent cares for at least one child for more than 104 nights each year and another person (e.g. the second parent or a third party) cares for that child to a greater extent than the first parent, then that first parent is "treated" as an absent parent. The maintenance payable by the parent treated as absent is rateably reduced with reference to the period the child spends with him.

Such a parent may in fact be absent in any event [see Chapter 2 for the definition of an absent parent] and, accordingly, it seems curious that he should be described in such circumstances as "treated as absent". The D.S.S. pamphlet *Child Support: a new approach* entitles this case as "absent parent shares care of the child" which is more apt, although this description, too, would be inappropriate if the child had a "home" with that parent, for then he would be a "person with care". Perhaps the best description for this case would be simply: "Parent shares care of the child".

The detail

Regulation 20 of the Assessment Regulations provides
(1) Where the circumstances of a case are that
  (a) 2 or more persons who do not live in the same household each provide day to day care for the same qualifying child, and
  (b) at least one of those persons is a parent of that child, that case shall be treated as a Special Case for the purposes of the Act.
(2) For the purposes of this case a parent who provides day to day care for a child of his in the following circumstances is to be treated as an absent parent for the purposes of the Act and these Regulations
  (a) a parent who provides such care to a lesser extent than the other parent, person or persons who provide such care for the child in question,
  (b) where the persons mentioned in Paragraph (1)(a) include both parents and the circumstances are such that care is provided to the same extent by both but each provides care to a greater or equal extent than any other person who provides such care for that child
    (i) the parent who is not in receipt of child benefit for the child in question, or
    (ii) if neither parent is in receipt of child benefit for that child, the parent who, in the opinion of the Child Support Officer, will not be the principal provider of day to day care for that child.
(3) Subject to Paragraphs (5) and (6), where a parent is treated as an absent parent under Paragraph (2) Child Support maintenance shall be payable by that parent in respect of the child in question and the amount of the Child Support maintenance so payable shall be calculated in accordance with the formula set out in Paragraph (4).
(4) The formula for the purposes of Paragraph (3) is

$$T = X - \{(X + Y) \times (J \div [7 \times L])\}$$

where
T is the amount of Child Support maintenance payable
X is the amount of Child Support maintenance which would be payable by the parent who is treated as an absent parent, assessed

under Schedule I to the Act as if Paragraphs 6 and 7 of that Schedule did not apply (i.e. ignoring the provisions relating to protected income and minimum payment), and, where the other parent is an absent parent, as if the value of **C** (the assessable income of the parent with care) was the assessable income of the other parent,

Y is
(i)   the amount of Child Support maintenance assessed under Schedule 1 to the Act payable by the other parent if he is an absent parent or which would be payable if he were an absent parent, and for the purposes of such calculation the value of **C** shall be the assessable income of the parent treated as an absent parent under Paragraph (2), or,

(ii) if there is no such other parent, shall be nil;

J is the total of the weekly average number of nights for which day to day care is provided by the person whois treated as the absent parent in respect of each child included in the maintenance assessment and shall be calculated to 2 decimal places,

L is the number of children who are included in the maintenance assessment in question.

(5) Where the value of T calculated under the provisions of Paragraph (4) is less than zero, no Child Support maintenance shall be payable.

(6) The liability to pay any amount calculated under Paragraph (4) shall be subject to the provision made for protected income and minimum payments under Paragraphs 6 and 7 of Schedule 1 to the Act.

Comment: this case applies where 2 or more persons who live in separate homes provide at least 2 nights care for the child each week and at least one of those persons is a parent of the child. If, for example, a child spends on average 3 nights each week with a relation and 2 nights each week with each of his parents then this case applies. In this case both parents will be "treated" as absent parents (notwithstanding that they may both, in fact, already be absent parents) and their respective maintenance liabilities will be determined in accordance with the formula set out above. The essential principle of the formula is that the absent parent who cares for a child for more than 2 nights each week is relieved from contributing that rateable proportion of the joint maintenance obligation that is referable to the period that the child spends with him.

Example: assume again that there is one child only who spends 2 nights each week with each of his parents and that X (the maintenance that would have been payable by the mother) is £20.00 and Y (the maintenance that would have been payable by the father) is £50.00.

The maintenance payable by the father is
£50 − {(£50 + £20) x 2 ÷ (7 x 1)} = £30.00.
The maintenance payable by the mother is
£20 − {(£20 + £50) x 2 ÷ (7 x 1)} = nil.

It should be noted that the Child Support Officer has complete discretion under Regulation 2 of the Collection Regulations to determine to whom such maintenance should be paid [see Chapter 27].

CASE 3:   ONE PARENT IS ABSENT AND THE OTHER IS TREATED AS ABSENT

The basic principle

Where one parent is absent, and the other is treated as absent under Special Case 2, then the assessment against the absent parent is calculated as if **C** within the formula [see Chapter 6] is the income of the parent treated as absent.

The detail

Regulation 21 of the Assessment Regulations provides
  (1) Where the circumstances of a case are that one parent is an absent parent and the other parent is treated as an absent parent by Regulation 20(2), that case shall be treated as a Special Case for the purposes of the Act.
  (2) For the purpose of assessing the Child Support maintenance payable by an absent parent where this case applies, each reference in Schedule 1 to the Act to a parent who is a person with care shall be treated as a reference to a person who is treated as an absent parent by Regulation 20(2).

Example: assume that a child is cared for 4 nights each week by a relation, for 2 nights by his mother and for one night by his father. In such circumstances the mother is treated as absent under Regulation 20(2), as she provides less "day to day care" (as defined) than the relation. The father is an absent parent under the definition set out in Chapter 2. In such a case the maintenance payable by the father will be calculated as if **C** was the mother's income in the formulae set out in Chapter 6. The mother's liability to pay maintenance will be determined under Special Case 2.

CASE 4:   MULTIPLE APPLICATIONS RELATING TO AN ABSENT PARENT

The basic principle

Where an absent parent has to pay maintenance to more than one set of children then his assessable income is apportioned between the 2 sets by reference to their respective maintenance requirements.

The detail

Regulation 22 of the Assessment Regulations provides
 (1) Where the circumstances of a case are that
   (a) 2 or more applications for a maintenance assessment have been made which relate to the same absent parent (or to a person who is treated as an absent parent by Regulation 20(2)), and
   (b) those applications relate to different children,
  that case shall be treated as a Special Case for the purposes of the Act.
 (2) For the purposes of assessing the amount of Child Support maintenance payable in respect of each application where Paragraph (1) applies, for references to the assessable income of an absent parent in the Act and in these Regulations there shall be substituted references to the amount calculated by the formula

$$A \times [B \div D]$$

where
A is the assessable income of the absent parent,
B is the maintenance requirement calculated in respect of the application in question,
D is the sum of the maintenance requirements as calculated for the purposes of each application relating to the absent parent in question.

Comment: this case deals with the not uncommon situation where a parent has children living in more than one household and is absent in relation to all of them. A father, for example, may have suffered 2 failed marriages leaving children in the care of each of his former wives. In such circumstances, for the purposes of the formula, his assessable income is apportioned between the 2 sets of children in proportion to their respective maintenance requirements.

Example: a father has 2 children by his first wife and their maintenance requirement is £70.00. He has one child by his second wife and that child's maintenance requirement is £50.00. The father's assessable income is £200.

His apportioned assessable income in relation to the 2 children by his first marriage is
  £200 x £70 ÷ (£70 + £50) = £116.66

His apportioned assessable income in relation to the child by his second marriage is
  £200 x £50 ÷ (£70 + £50) = £83.33

 (3) Where more than one maintenance assessment has been made with respect to the absent parent and payment by him of the aggregate of the amounts of those assessments would reduce his disposable income below

his protected income level, the aggregate amount of those assessments shall be reduced (each being reduced by reference to the same proportion as those assessments bear to each other) by the minimum amount necessary to prevent his disposable income being reduced below his protected income level provided that the aggregate amount payable under those assessments shall not be reduced to less than the minimum amount prescribed in Regulation 13(1).

Example: the father above has been assessed to pay maintenance for the children of his first marriage of £58.33 and to the child of his second marriage of £41.67, aggregating £100.00. His actual net income is £300, and his protected income is £220. He can thus only pay £80.00. The maintenance is therefore rateably reduced as follows:

For the 2 children by his first marriage to:
£58.33 x £80 ÷ £100 = £46.66
For the child by his second marriage to:
£41.67 x £80 ÷ £100 = £33.34

(4) Where the aggregate of the Child Support maintenance payable by the absent parent is less than the minimum amount prescribed in Regulation 13(1), the Child Support maintenance payable shall be that prescribed minimum amount apportioned between the 2 or more applications in the same ratio as the maintenance requirements in question bear to each other.

Example: the minimum payment is £2.20 [see Chapter 17]. If the maintenance requirements are as above then the minimum payment will be apportioned as follows:

For the 2 children by his first marriage
£2.20 x £70 ÷ (£70 + £50) = £1.28
For the child by his second marriage
£2.20 x £50 ÷ (£70 + £50) = £0.92.

(5) Payment of each of the maintenance assessments calculated under this Regulation shall satisfy the liability of the absent parent (or a person treated as such) to pay Child Support maintenance.

CASE 5: PERSON CARING FOR CHILDREN OF MORE THAN ONE ABSENT PARENT

The basic principle

Where a person with care receives or is entitled to receive maintenance from more than one parent for different children within her family then for the purposes of an assessment the Income Support adult personal allowance, family and lone parent premiums are divided by the number of absent parents in question. Only one set of such allowances/premiums is allowed for each family.

The detail

Regulation 23 of the Assessment Regulations provides
    (1) Where the circumstances of a case are that
        (a) a person is a person with care in relation to 2 or more qualifying children, and
        (b) in relation to at least 2 of those children there are different persons who are absent parents or persons treated as absent parents by Regulation 20(2),
    that case shall be treated as a Special Case for the purposes of the Act.

    Comment: this case deals with the equally common situation where a parent with care has a number of children living in her household deriving from different absent parents. A mother, for example, may have suffered 2 failed marriages and is now living alone with children from each of those marriages.

    (2) In calculating the maintenance requirements for the purposes of this case, for any amount which (but for this Paragraph) would have been included under Regulation 3(1)(b), (c) or (d) (amounts included in the calculation of **AG**) there shall be substituted an amount calculated by dividing the amount which would have been so included by the relevant number.
    (3) In Paragraph (2) "the relevant number" means the number equal to the total number of persons who, in relation to those children, are either absent parents or persons treated as absent parents by Regulation 20(2) except that, where in respect of the same child both parents are persons who are either absent parents or persons who are treated as absent parents under that Regulation, they shall count as one person.

    Comment: when calculating **MR** in relation to each absent parent the amounts allowed within **AG** at (b) (Income Support personal allowance), at (c) (family premium), and at (d) (lone parent premium) are all divided by the number of absent parents in question. The principle is simply that there shall be allowed only one set of such premiums per family [see Chapter 6 for the calculation of **MR**].

    (4)   Where the circumstances of a case fall within this Regulation and the person with care is the parent of any of the children, for **C** in Paragraph 2(1) of Schedule 1 to the Act (the assessable income of that person) there shall be substituted the amount which would be calculated under

Regulation 22(2) if the references therein to an absent parent were references to a parent with care in the manner prescribed under Special Case 4 above.

Comment: the assessable income of a parent with care in such circumstances is apportioned between the sets of children for the purposes of the formulae in Chapter 6.

CASE 6: PERSONS WITH PART-TIME CARE – NOT INCLUDING A PERSON TREATED AS AN ABSENT PARENT

The basic principle

Where a person with care shares the care of the children with another person who is not a parent then the person with care should agree privately with that person to share proportionately maintenance received by her, but in default of agreement the Agency will direct a fair, proportionate sharing.

The detail

Regulation 24 of the Assessment Regulations provides
  (1) Where the circumstances of a case are that
      (a) 2 or more persons who do not live in the same household each provide day to day care for the same qualifying child, and
      (b) those persons do not include any parent who is treated as an absent parent of that child by Regulation 20(2),
  that case shall be treated as a Special Case for the purposes of the Act.

Comment: this case deals with the common situation where a parent with care is predominantly caring for her children but is sharing the care with another person. A mother, for example, may share the care of her children with her own mother.

  (2) For the purposes of this case
      (a) the person whose application for a maintenance assessment is being proceeded with shall, subject to Paragraph (b), be entitled to receive all of the Child Support maintenance payable under the Act in respect of the child in question,
      (b) on request being made to the Secretary of State by
          (i) that person, or
          (ii) any other person who is providing day to day care for that child and who intends to continue to provide that care,
      the Secretary of State may make arrangements for the payment of any Child Support maintenance payable under the Act to the persons who provide such care in the same ratio as that in which it appears to the Secretary of State, that each is to provide such care for the child in question,

(c) before making an arrangement under sub-paragraph (b), the Secretary of State shall consider all of the circumstances of the case and in particular the interests of the child, the present arrangements for the day to day care of the child in question and any representations or proposals made by the persons who provide such care for that child.

Comment: if, for example, a mother cares for her children for 5 nights each week and her own mother cares for the children for 2 nights each week the Officer may, upon request being made by either the mother or the grandmother, apportion the maintenance recovered from the absent father five-sevenths to the mother and two-sevenths to the grandmother. In the first instance, however, the mother and the grandmother will be expected to try and agree the division between themselves.

CASE 7: CARE PROVIDED IN PART BY A LOCAL AUTHORITY
The basic principle

Where a local authority shares care of a child with a person with care the maintenance payable by the absent parent is rateably reduced in proportion to the amount of time that the child lives with the person with care.

The detail

Regulation 25 of the Assessment Regulations provides
(1) Where the circumstances of a case are that a local authority and a person each provide day to day care for the same qualifying child, that case shall be treated as a Special Case for the purposes of the Act.
(2) In a case where this Regulation applies
    (a) Child Support maintenance shall be calculated in respect of that child as if this Regulation did not apply,
    (b) the amount so calculated shall be divided by 7 so as to produce a daily amount,
    (c) in respect of each night for which day to day care for that child is provided by a person other than the local authority, the daily amount relating to that period shall be payable by the absent parent (or, as the case may be, by the person treated as an absent parent under Regulation 20(2)),
    (d) Child Support maintenance shall not be payable in respect of any night for which the local authority provides day to day care for that qualifying child.

Comment: it has already been seen in Chapter 2 that a local authority cannot qualify as a person with care. The rights of the local authority to recover contributions for a child in care are set out in the Children Act 1989.

CASE 8: CASES WHERE CHILD SUPPORT MAINTENANCE IS NOT TO BE PAYABLE

The basic principle

Where an absent parent is in specified impoverished circumstances he is exempted from having to pay even the minimum payment of £2.20 p.w.

The detail

Regulation 26 of the Assessment Regulations provides
  (1) Where the circumstances of a case are that
      (a) but for this Regulation the minimum amount prescribed in Regulation 13(1) would apply, and
      (b) any of the following conditions are satisfied
          (i) the income of the absent parent includes one or more of the payments or awards specified in Schedule 4 or would include such a payment but for a provision preventing the receipt of that payment by reason of it overlapping with some other benefit payment or would, in the case of the payments referred to in Paragraph (a)(i) or (iv) of that Schedule (sickness benefit or maternity allowance), include such a payment if the relevant contribution conditions for entitlement had been satisfied,
          (ii) an amount to which Regulation 11(1)(f) applies (protected income: Income Support family premium) is taken into account in calculating or estimating the protected income of the absent parent,
          (iii) the absent parent is a child within the meaning of Section 55 of the Act,
          (iv) the absent parent is a prisoner, or
          (v) the absent parent is a person in respect of whom **N** (as calculated or estimated under Regulation 7(1)) is less than the minimum amount prescribed by Regulation 13(1),
      the case shall be treated as a Special Case for the purposes of the Act.
  (2) For the purposes of this case
      (a) the requirement in Paragraph 7(2) of Schedule 1 to the Act (minimum amount of Child Support maintenance fixed by an assessment to be the prescribed minimum amount) shall not apply,
      (b) the amount of the Child Support maintenance to be fixed by the assessment shall be nil.

Schedule 4 to the Assessment Regulations provides
  The payments and awards specified for the purposes of Regulation 26(1)(b)(i) are

(a) the following payments under the Contributions and Benefits Act
    (i)   sickness benefit under Section 31,
    (ii)   invalidity pension under Section 33,
    (iii)   invalidity pension for widowers under Section 34,
    (iv)   maternity allowance under Section 35,
    (v)   invalidity pension for widows under Section 40,
    (vi)   attendance allowance under Section 64,
    (vii) severe disablement allowance under Section 68,
    (viii) invalid care allowance under Section 70,
    (ix)   disability living allowance under Section 71,
    (x)   disablement benefit under Section 103,
    (xi)   disability working allowance under Section 129,
    (xii) statutory sick pay within the meaning of Section 151,
    (xiii) statutory maternity pay within the meaning of Section 164,
(b) awards in respect of disablement made under (or under provisions analogous to)
    (i)   the War Pensions (Coastguards) Scheme 1944,
    (ii)   the War Pensions (Naval Auxiliary Personnel) Scheme 1964,
    (iii)   the Pensions (Polish Forces) Scheme 1964,
    (iv)   the War Pensions (Mercantile Marine) Scheme 1964,
    (v)   the Royal Warrant of 21st December 1964 (service in the Home Guard before 1945),
    (vi)   the Order by Her Majesty of 22nd December 1964 concerning pensions and other grants in respect of disablement or death due to service in the Home Guard after 27th April 1952,
    (vii) the Order by Her Majesty (Ulster Defence Regiment) of 4th January 1971,
    (viii) the Personal Injuries (Civilians) Scheme 1983,
    (ix)   the Naval, Military and Air Forces Etc. (Disablement and Death) Service Pensions Order 1983, and
(c) payments from the Independent Living Fund.

Comment: where any of the above conditions is satisfied the minimum of £2.20 will not be payable and the absent parent will be wholly acquitted of liability to pay maintenance.

CASE 9: CHILD WHO IS A BOARDER OR AN IN-PATIENT

The basic principle

Where a parent provides the main home of a child who is at boarding school or who is an in-patient in a hospital then he is deemed to be a person with care.

The detail

Regulation 27 of the Assessment Regulations provides
  (1) Where the circumstances of a case are that

(a) a qualifying child is a boarder at a boarding school or is an in-patient in a hospital, and

(b) by reason of those circumstances, the person who would otherwise provide day to day care is not doing so,

that case shall be treated as a Special Case for the purposes of the Act.

(2) For the purposes of this case, Section 3(3)(b) of the Act shall be modified so for the reference to the person who usually provides day to day care for the child there shall be substituted a reference to the person who would usually be providing such care for that child but for the circumstances specified in Paragraph (1).

CASE 10: AMOUNT PAYABLE WHERE ABSENT PARENT IS IN RECEIPT OF INCOME SUPPORT OR OTHER PRESCRIBED BENEFIT

The basic principle

It has been seen in Chapter 7 that a parent in receipt of Income Support has no assessable income for the purposes of the formula. If the parent is over 18, does not have a child within his family, and does not satisfy the conditions of entitlement for any of the benefits within Schedule 4, then his Income Support will be abated by £2.20 p.w.

The detail

Regulation 28 of the Assessment Regulations provides

(1) Where the condition specified in Section 43(1)(a) of the Act is satisfied in relation to an absent parent (assessable income to be nil where Income Support or other prescribed benefit is paid), the prescribed conditions for the purposes of Section 43(1)(b) of the Act are that

(a) the absent parent is aged 18 or over,

(b) he does not satisfy the conditions in Paragraph 3 of the relevant Schedule (Income Support family premium), and

(c) he does not satisfy the conditions for entitlement to one or more of the payments or awards specified in Schedule 4 (other than by reason of a provision preventing receipt of overlapping benefits or by reason of a failure to satisfy the relevant contribution conditions).

(2) For the purposes of Section 43(2)(a) of the Act, the prescribed amount shall be equal to the minimum amount prescribed in Regulation 13(1) for the purposes of Paragraph 7(1) of Schedule 1 to the Act.

CHAPTER 19

The role of the court

The basic principles

The Court's powers in relation to the making of maintenance orders for children are severely attenuated by the provisions of the Act.

In general terms, in any case where a Child Support Officer would have jurisdiction to make a maintenance assessment, no Court shall exercise any power which it would otherwise have to make, vary or revive any maintenance order in relation to the child and the absent parent in question.

There are, however, certain exceptions to this general rule. The exceptions fall into 2 categories. In the first the Court will retain power to make an order in a non-benefit case that conforms to a prior written agreement between the parties for maintenance.

The second category of exception applies only to the transitional period which runs from 5th April 1993 to 6th April 1997. Within that period the Court will have power to vary any maintenance order or written maintenance agreement in force. The Court will only be empowered to make a maintenance order de novo during the transitional period under the circumstances specified in the first category; but there will be many orders which predate the coming into force of the Act (5th April 1993) which will also fall within this latter exception. The Court will at all times retain power to revoke a maintenance order.

During the transitional period, where there is in force a maintenance order or a maintenance agreement in respect of a qualifying child, or where there is pending before any Court an application for such a maintenance order, no application may be made by either the absent parent or the person with care for a maintenance assessment.

Accordingly, it will be necessary, if a parent wishes to seek an assessment from the Agency, to procure the revocation of any such maintenance order or agreement so as to revive the right to seek an assessment from the agency. Advisers are likely to face difficult tactical decisions in relation to new cases arising within the transitional period. If they advise their client to enter into a written agreement, which is then made into an order of the Court, then neither parent will, for as long as that order is in force, have the right to seek a maintenance assessment. The Court will, however, be empowered to vary such an order. Thus advisers will have to consider carefully whether their client's interests are more likely better to be served by making an agreement which will ultimately be the subject of the Court's discretionary powers, or by not making an agreement and directing their clients to seek an assessment from the Agency. It can be reasonably anticipated, however, that the Court, in exercising its discretionary powers, will be influenced by the principles of the Act and the Regulations made thereunder.

The detail

I THE GENERAL POWERS OF THE COURT

Section 8 of the Act provides
1. This subsection applies where a Child Support Officer would have jurisdiction to make a maintenance assessment with respect to a qualifying child and an absent parent of his on an application duly made by a person entitled to apply for such an assessment with respect to that child.
2. Subsection (1) applies even though the circumstances of the case are such that a Child Support Officer would not make an assessment if it were applied for.
3. In any case where subsection (1) applies no Court shall exercise any power which it would otherwise have to make, vary or revive any maintenance order in relation to the child and absent parent concerned.
4. Subsection (3) does not prevent a Court from revoking a maintenance order.

    Comment: the general rule is, therefore, that where a Child Support Officer has jurisdiction to make a maintenance assessment the Court is wholly prevented from either making a fresh maintenance order, from varying an existing maintenance order or from reviving a maintenance order which has been suspended under Section 31 of the Matrimonial Causes Act 1973. The Court however retains full power to revoke a maintenance order. It will be seen, when considering the transitional provisions, that this power to revoke a maintenance order may be of great significance.

5. The Lord Chancellor or, in relation to Scotland, the Lord Advocate may by order provide that in such circumstances as may be specified by the order, this Section shall not prevent a Court from exercising any power which it has to make a maintenance order in relation to a child if
    (a) a written agreement (whether or not enforceable) provides for the making, or securing, by an absent parent of the child of periodical payments to or for the benefit of the child, and
    (b) the maintenance order which the Court makes is, in all material respects, in the same terms as that agreement.

Comment: the Lord Chancellor has, pursuant to his powers under this provision, made the Child Maintenance (Written Agreements) Order 1993. This provides that the Court may make an order in the circumstances specified in (a) and (b) above. The phraseology of the Section would permit the Court to make such an order even if one party had signified following the making of the agreement that he was not content for the Court to make such an order. It is to be emphasised that the power of the Court to make such an order can be exercised on a non-consensual basis provided that the order conforms to the content of a pre-existing written agreement made by an absent parent for the making of periodical payments or secured provision to or for the benefit of a child. This provision will not enable people on benefit to agree a lesser amount than would obtain under an Agency assessment. In benefit cases assessments will be mandatory.

6. This Section shall not prevent a Court from exercising any power which it has to make a maintenance order in relation to a child if
    (a) a maintenance assessment is in force with respect to the child,
    (b) the amount of the Child Support maintenance payable in accordance with the assessment was determined by reference to the alternative formula mentioned in Paragraph 4(3) of Schedule 1, and
    (c) the Court is satisfied that the circumstances of the case make it appropriate for the absent parent to make or secure the making of periodical payments under a maintenance order in addition to the Child Support maintenance payable by him in accordance with the maintenance assessment.

Comment: this Section permits a parent to seek from the Court a "top-up" to a maintenance assessment. The right to apply for such a "top-up" is only available where the agency has used the second method for calculating **AE** (i.e. the additional liability has been limited by the pre-scribed ceiling). Reference should be made to Chapter 6 for the alternative bases of calculating **AE**. It can be seen from Table 1 within Chapter 6 that the right to seek a "top-up" will only be relevant where the assessable income of the absent parent is of a significant amount.

7. This Section shall not prevent a Court from exercising any power which it has to make a maintenance order in relation to a child if
    (a) the child is, will be, or (if the order were to be made) would be receiving instruction at an educational establishment or undergoing training for a trade, profession or vocation (whether or not while in gainful employment), and
    (b) the order is made solely for the purposes of making or securing the making of periodical payments fixed by the order to meet some or all of the expenses incurred in connection with the provision of the instruction or training.

Comment: the Court retains power to make a maintenance order to cover school fees or training expenses.

8. This Section shall not prevent a Court from exercising any power which it has to make a maintenance order in relation to a child if
    (a) a disability living allowance is paid to or in respect of him, or
    (b) no such allowance is paid but he is disabled,
    and the order is made solely for the purpose of requiring the person making or securing the making of periodical payments fixed by the order to meet some or all of any expenses attributable to the child's disability.

9. For the purposes of subsection 8, a child is disabled if he is blind, deaf or dumb or is substantially and permanently handicapped by illness, injury, mental disorder or congenital deformity or such other disability as may be prescribed.

    Comment: a maintenance order may be made by the Court to cover expenses attributable to a child's disability of a specified sort. No other disability has, as yet, been prescribed under subsection 9.

10. This Section shall not prevent a Court from exercising any power which it has to make a maintenance order in relation to a child if the order is made against a person with care of the child.

    Comment: it is possible to conceive of circumstances where a child in the care of a parent seeks to apply to the Court for a maintenance order for himself against that parent. Where there has been a divorce between the parents of the child he will require leave to intervene in the cause of the purpose of applying for such an order (Rule 2.54(1)(f) Family Proceeding Rules 1991). Similarly a parent with care might seek an order against herself to take advantage of the very limited tax relief available on maintenance payments.

11. In this Act "maintenance order", in relation to any child, means an order which requires the making or securing of periodical payments to or for the benefit of the child and which is made under
    (a) Part II of the Matrimonial Causes Act 1973,
    (b) The Domestic Proceedings and Magistrates' Courts Act 1978,
    (c) Part III of the Matrimonial and Family Proceedings Act 1984,
    (d) The Family Law (Scotland) Act 1985,
    (e) Schedule 1 to the Children Act 1989,
    (f) Any other prescribed enactment,
    and includes any order varying or reviving such an order.
        By Regulation 2 of the Jurisdiction Regulations the Affiliation Proceedings Act 1957 has been prescribed for the purposes of sub-paragraph (f) above.

    An equivalent bar on the insertion by the Court of child maintenance provisions within a maintenance agreement, or on upwards variation of pre-existing child maintenance provisions in a maintenance agreement, is imposed by Section 9(5) of the Act where it is provided that where Section 8 would prevent any Court from making a maintenance order in relation to a child and an absent parent of his, no Court shall exercise any power that it has to vary any agreement so as

> (a) to insert a provision requiring that absent parent to make or secure the making of periodical payments by way of maintenance, or in Scotland aliment, to or for the benefit of that child, or
> (b) to increase the amount payable under such a provision

Section 10 of the Act provides that where a maintenance order or maintenance agreement is in force with respect to any qualifying child with respect to whom a maintenance assessment is made the order or agreement shall cease to have effect to the extent provided for in the Regulations, or shall have effect subject to such modifications as the Regulations may provide.

The Regulations in question are made within the Jurisdiction Regulations.

Regulation 3(2) and (3) provides

> (2) Subject to Paragraphs (3) and (4), where a maintenance assessment is made with respect to
>> (a) all of the children with respect to whom an order falling within Paragraph (1) is in force, or
>> (b) one or more but not all of the children with respect to whom an order falling within Paragraph (1) is in force and where the amount payable under the order to or for the benefit of each child is separately specified,
>
> that order shall, so far as it relates to the making or securing of periodical payments to or for the benefit of the children with respect to whom the maintenance assessment has been made, cease to have effect.
>
> (3) The provisions of Paragraph (2) shall not apply where a maintenance order has been made in accordance with Section 8(7) or (8) of the Act.

> **Comment:** Paragraph (1) repeats the list of the enactments set out under Section 8 (11) of the Act as modified by the Jurisdiction Regulations. The effect of Paragraph (2) is to bring any order made under any such enactment, insofar as it relates to maintenance for the children, to an end. In the event that a maintenance assessment is made in respect of only some of the children in question, but the pre-existing order does not separately identify the amounts payable to each child, then such an order is not brought to an end. Such orders are, of course, exceedingly rare. Orders for school fees, training expenses, or for meeting the expenses of a disabled child are not affected by a maintenance assessment.

By Regulation 3(4), in Scotland, where an order has ceased to have effect by virtue of the provisions of Paragraph (2) above and a Child Support Officer no longer has jurisdiction to make a maintenance assessment in respect of a child with respect to whom the order has ceased to have effect, then the order shall automatically revive from the date that the Child Support Officer loses his jurisdiction to make a maintenance assessment (for example, where the absent parent ceases to be habitually resident within the United Kingdom).

By virtue of Regulation 3(5) and (6) the meaning of "the effective date" is modified where there is an order in force. In such circumstances the effective date is 2 days after the maintenance assessment is made. The maintenance order ceases to have effect from the modified effective date of the maintenance assessment.

Similar provisions are made under Regulation 4 in respect of maintenance agreements. A maintenance agreement is defined under Section 9(1) of the Act as any agreement for the making or securing the making of periodical payments to or for the benefit of any child. Such an agreement may be made orally, or in writing.

Regulation 4(2) provides

Where a maintenance assessment with respect to
- (a) all of the children with respect to whom a (maintenance) agreement . . . is in force, or
- (b) one or more but not all of the children with respect to whom a (maintenance) agreement . . . is in force and where the amount payable under the agreement to or for the benefit of each child is separately specified,

that agreement shall so far as it relates to the making or securing of periodical payments to or for the benefit of the children with respect to whom the maintenance assessment has been made, become unenforceable from the effective date of the assessment.

Comment: the same principles apply in relation to pre-existing maintenance agreements as apply to Court orders. The maintenance agreement ceases to have effect and becomes unenforceable from the modified effective date of the maintenance assessment.

By Regulation 4(3) the agreement remains unenforceable until such date as the Child Support Officer no longer has jurisdiction to make a maintenance assessment with respect to that child.

Regulation 5 provides that where a Child Support Officer is aware that an order of the kind described is in force and considers that the making of the maintenance assessment has affected or is likely to affect that order he shall notify the person with care, any absent parent, and any person who is treated as an absent parent, and any child in Scotland who has made an application under Section 7 of the Act, together with the Court that made the order.

Similarly, under Regulation 6, where the Court becomes aware that a maintenance assessment is in force and makes an order under any of the enactments mentioned which it considers has affected or is likely to affect that assessment then the Court shall notify the Child Support Agency to that effect. It has been seen in Chapter 12 that maintenance paid to or for the benefit of a parent will be taken into account as "other income" of the parent in the calculation of a maintenance assessment. When a Court makes an order for such maintenance it is obliged to notify the Agency. Similarly, any interest or other income derived from capital belonging to a parent is taken into account as "other income" received by the parent; and if the Court makes an order for a lump sum intended to provide unearned income for the parent then it will be obliged to notify the Agency accordingly.

II TRANSITIONAL PROVISIONS

By Paragraph 1 of the Transitional Provisions Order the transitional period is defined as the period beginning with 5th April 1993 and ending with 6 April 1997.

Paragraphs 2-5 of the Order provide

2. Subject to Paragraph 4 below, during the transitional period no application under Section 4 of the Act (applications for Child Support maintenance) in relation to a qualifying child or any qualifying children may be made at any time when

    (a) there is in force a maintenance order or maintenance agreement in respect of that qualifying child or those qualifying children of the absent parent, or there is pending before any Court an application for such a maintenance order, or

    (b) benefit is being paid to a parent of that child or those children.

3. Subject to Paragraph 4 below, during the transitional period no application under Section 7 of the Act (right of child in Scotland to apply for assessment) may be made by a qualifying child at any time when there is in force a maintenance order or maintenance agreement in respect of that child and the absent parent, or there is pending before any Court an application for such a maintenance order.

4. (1) Paragraphs 2 and 3 do not apply to an application made

    (a) in that part of the transitional period beginning with 5th April 1996, if the surname of the person with care begins with any of the letters A-D inclusive,

    (b) in that part of the transitional period beginning with 1st July 1996, if the surname of the person with care begins with any of the letters E-K inclusive,

    (c) in that part of the transitional period beginning with 7th October 1996, if the surname of the person with care begins with any of the letters L-R inclusive, and

    (d) in that part of the transitional period beginning with 6th January 1997, if the surname of the person with care begins with any of the letters S-Z inclusive.

    (2) Where Paragraph 2 or 3 applies to a case because there is pending before a Court an application for a maintenance order, and that application was made before 5th April 1993, those Paragraphs shall not prevent the making of an application for a maintenance assessment under Section 4 or, as the case may be, Section 7 of the Act; but in such a case Section 8(3) of the Act shall not have effect until such an application is actually made.

5. For as long as Paragraph 2 or 3 above operates in a case so as to prevent an application being made under Section 4 of the Act or, as the case may be, Section 7 of the Act, and no application has been made under Section 6 of the Act, then in relation to that case Section 8(3) of the Act (role of the Courts with respect to maintenance orders) shall be modified so as to have effect as if the word "vary" was omitted.

Comment: during the transitional period no application for an assessment may be made where there is an order or maintenance agreement in force or where benefit is being paid to a parent of that child or of those children. While an order is in force the Court will retain its full discretionary powers to vary it; but if the Court should revoke the order the parents will be at liberty to seek an assessment. Benefit cases will be dealt with under Section 6, where the parent can be required to authorise the Agency to seek an assessment against the absent parent and to recover maintenance from him. The existence of an order in a benefit case will not prevent the Agency from forcing a parent to make an assessment under Section 6; and once the assessment is made any such order will cease to have effect. It is understood that the proposed Amendment Regulations will limit the maintenance agreements in question to those in writing. Such agreements, if made between the parties to a marriage, will be variable under Section 35 Matrimonial Causes Act 1973, and the Amendment Regulations will preserve such power to vary.

III SUMMARY OF THE POWERS OF THE COURT

(a) Orders in force on 5th April 1993

While such an order is in force no person shall be entitled to apply to the Agency until the date determined in Paragraph 4 ("the relevant date"). The order is fully variable while it remains in force. If, however, the Court revokes the order then either parent or a person with care (if not a parent) can apply to the Agency for a maintenance assessment.

(b) Agreements in force on 5th April 1993

While a written maintenance agreement is in force no person may apply to the Agency until the relevant date. Such an agreement between the parties to a marriage will be variable, but an agreement between an unmarried couple will not be variable. However, the Court will be able to make an order mirroring the agreement under Section 8(5) of the Act and such an order would thereafter be variable. The Court has power to revoke an agreement between the parties to a marriage under Section 35(2) Matrimonial Causes Act 1973; that power not being prohibited by Section 9(5) of the Act.

(c) **Applications for orders pending on 5th April 1993**

Prior to the adjudication of the application the parent or a person with care may apply for a maintenance assessment. Once the application has been **made** to the Agency the Court will be prevented from making any order on the pending application. However, the Court will be empowered to adjudicate a pending application prior to any application to the Agency; and any order made upon such adjudication will be variable. While such an order is in force the principles in (a) above will apply.

(d) **No order or agreement in force and no application for order pending on 5th April 1993**

In such a case (which comprises any new case arising after 5th April 1993) the parents will have to make a choice. Such a parent will either
(i) decide not to make a maintenance agreement with the other parent. In such an event the parent can seek a maintenance assessment from the agency, or
(ii) make an agreement. Once the agreement is in force no parent may seek an assessment until the relevant date and the provisions of (b) above will apply

(e) **Benefit Cases**

During the transitional period a parent in receipt of benefit for himself or any child cannot apply for an assessment under Section 4. But the Agency can require a parent to make such an application under Section 6, whether or not there is in force an order. Upon the making of an assessment any order for child maintenance in force will cease to have effect.

The legal adviser will have to give careful consideration to the best advantages of his clients during the transitional period. In particular he will have to consider
(a) in relation to orders in force, whether his client should apply to vary the order or, alternatively, to apply to revoke the order and then to seek an assessment from the Agency,
(b) in relation to agreements in force, whether his client should apply for an order mirroring the agreement under Section 8(5) of the Act and thereafter to seek to vary such order; or, alternatively, should apply to revoke the agreement and seek an assessment from the Agency,
(c) in relation to new cases, whether his client should make a maintenance agreement with the other party and thereafter obtain an order mirroring such agreement under Section 8(5) of the Act, thus placing their client within the discretionary regime of the Court, or should apply directly to the Agency for a maintenance assessment.
It should be borne in mind that Agency assessments will tend to be higher than conventional awards presently made by the Court; although it can be reasonably anticipated that the Court will begin to adopt the principles underlying the Act when varying orders.

Consequential changes

The Court's residual powers to make orders under Section 8(6), (7) and (8) of the Act have been enlarged by the Maintenance Orders (Backdating) Order 1993. This Order is made under Section 58(7) of the Act whereby the Lord Chancellor may by order make such amendments or repeals in, or such modifications of, such enactments as may be specified, as appear to him to be necessary or expedient in consequence of any provision made by or under the Act.

The Order seeks to enlarge the Court's backdating powers in 4 categories of cases.

1. "Top-up" applications under Section 8(6) of the Act

There will inevitably be a delay between the date of a maintenance assessment and the date of the making of an application of a parent for a "top-up" order under Section 8(6) of the Act. At present the Court cannot backdate an original order beyond the date of the application therefor (Section 29(2) Matrimonial Causes Act 1973, Section 5(2) Domestic Proceedings and Magistrates' Courts Act 1978, and Schedule 1 Paragraph 3(1) Children Act 1989). The Backdating Order therefore provides that where a maintenance assessment is in force in respect to a child the top-up order may be backdated to the date on which the maintenance assessment took effect, provided that the application for a top-up order was made within 6 months of the date of the maintenance assessment.

2. Supersession of unduly high child maintenance orders

It is not uncommon for an unduly high child maintenance order to be made coupled with an unduly low orders for periodical payments in favour of a wife. Some husbands find such orders easier to accept than those in conventional amounts. In such a case there is a latent element of wife support within the child order. Upon the making of an Agency assessment the child order will cease. The Backdating Order provides that in such circumstances the Court may retroactively exercise its powers of variation of the spousal order so that it takes effect from the date of the Agency assessment. It is considered that this provision is unnecessary in circumstances where it is well established in law that the Court has the fullest power retroactively to exercise its powers of variation beyond the date of the application therefor (see *Warden v Warden [1982] Fam 10, Morley-Clarke v Jones [1986] Ch 311 @ 316H–317G and 330H, S v S [1987] 2 All ER 312 @ 318h)*

3. Termination of assessment

In certain circumstances an assessment will be automatically terminated or be cancelled by a Child Support Officer [see Chapter 24]. In such circumstances there will be a lapse of time between the termination of the assessment and the application for a fresh order. The Backdating Order therefore provides that payments under a fresh order may be backdated to the date of the termination of the assessments.

4.   Orders remaining in force following a maintenance assessment

It has been seen, by virtue of Regulation 3(2)(b) of the Jurisdiction Regulations, that where there is in force an order in respect of the children of the family, but where the amount payable under the order to or for the benefit of each child is not separately specified, such an order will remain in force where there is an assessment in respect of one or more, but not all, of the children in question. In such circumstances the paying parent will undoubtedly wish to vary the order. The Backdating Order provides that in such circumstances the Court can antedate the order for variation back to the date of the Agency assessment. Again, it is considered that such a provision is unnecessary in circumstances where the Court has unrestricted power to exercise its variation powers retroactively beyond the date of an application for variation.

Certain other consequential Orders, Regulations and Rules have been made and these can be summarised as follows.

The High Court (Distribution of Business) Order 1993

This instrument provides that any proceedings under the Child Support Act which are heard in the High Court will be assigned to the Family Division.

The Children (Allocation of Proceedings) (Amendment) Order 1993

This instrument provides that proceedings that go to Court under Section 27 of the Act (reference to the Court for a declaration of parentage) or under Section 45 of the Act (appeals involving questions of parentage) will be allocated, generally speaking, in the way that public law cases are allocated in the Children Act (Allocation of Proceedings) Order 1991. Such proceedings will be commenced in the Magistrates' Courts and can be transferred either to another Magistrates' Court, to a County Court or to the High Court in accordance with the criteria set out in the 1991 Order.

The Child Support Appeals (Jurisdiction of Courts) Order 1993

Where a Child Support Officer makes a decision upon a review as to whether a particular person is a parent of child, any appeal therefrom will be directed to the Court rather than to a Child Support Appeal Tribunal.

The Children (Admissibility of Hearsay Evidence) Order 1993

This instrument amends the earlier Order of the same name so as to permit evidence given in connection with the upbringing, maintenance or welfare of a child to be admissible in Child Support Act proceedings despite the fact that it is hearsay evidence. In particular, this instrument will render admissible computer evidence adduced by the Agency in enforcement proceedings in the Magistrates' Court.

The Family Proceedings (Amendment No 3) Rules 1993

This promulgates new rules as follows.

New Rules 3.21 and 3.22	These cover applications for a declaration of parentage under Section 27 of the Act, and appeals from an Officer upon an issue of parentage. The Court is given a wide discretion to give directions in such proceedings
New Rule 3.23	This governs appeals to the Court of Appeal from Child Support Commissioners. The same procedure is applied as that governing social security appeals under R.S.C. Ord. 59 r 21.
New Rules 10.24-26	These rules govern the procedure to deal with cases where there is a dispute as to whether the Court or the Agency has jurisdiction. The Court staff will filter out those cases where the Agency obviously has jurisdiction. In doubtful cases the District Judge will deal with the matter on paper and an appeal will lie from such a decision to the Judge in chambers.

Chapter 25 deals with appeals and Chapter 26 deals with disputes about parentage.

CHAPTER 20

Assessment procedure

General procedure

An application for a maintenance assessment shall be an effective application only if it is made on a duly prescribed maintenance application form and that form has been completed in accordance with the Agency's instructions (Regulation 2(4) of the Procedure Regulations). Where, however, an application does not comply with these requirements, and is not, therefore, effective, the Agency may ask the applicant fully to comply with the formalities and, provided that he does so within 14 days of being so requested by the Agency, his application shall be treated as having been made on the date on which he submitted his earlier defective application (Regulation 2(5)). [For the definition of the "effective date" see Chapter 2.]

Once a person has made an effective application he may, at any time before a maintenance assessment is made, amend his application by giving notice in writing to the Agency. However, he may not amend his application so as to include any change in circumstances arising after the effective date (Regulations 2(6) and (7)).

Where an effective application for a maintenance assessment has been made, the Agency shall as soon as is reasonably practicable give written notice of that application to the relevant persons other than the applicant. For these purposes the relevant persons include the person with care, any absent parent, or any parent who is treated as an absent parent. Where such notice is given, the Agency shall supply to any such person to whom notice has been given a maintenance enquiry form together with a request that the form be completed and returned for the purposes of enabling the maintenance assessment application to be proceed. Where the person to whom notice is given is an absent parent the notice shall specify the effective date and set out, in general terms, the provisions relating to interim assessments [see chapter 21] (Regulation 5).

Where any person has received a maintenance enquiry form supplied in the above circumstances then he is obliged to complete that form in accordance with the Agency's instructions and return it to the Agency within 14 days of its having been supplied. A person returning such a maintenance enquiry form may amend the information he has provided at any time before the assessment is made by notifying the Agency in writing of the amendment. However, as in the case of an application for a maintenance assessment, no amendment shall relate to any change of circumstances that arises after the effective date (Regulation 6).

In the melancholy circumstances where a qualifying child dies before the determination of an application for a maintenance assessment then the Child Support Officer shall proceed with the application as if it had not included that child; or if the assessment has been made, but the parent or person with care has not been notified of the result of that assessment, he shall undertake a fresh assessment as if the application had not included that child. If all the qualifying children with respect to whom an application had been made have died then the Child Support Officer shall treat the application as not having been made (Regulation 7).

Where a Child Support Officer makes a new or fresh maintenance assessment following an application duly made under the Act, then he shall immediately notify the parents, or the person with care (if not a parent), or the child (if the application is made under Section 7 of the Act in Scotland), of the amount of the Child Support maintenance payable under the assessment.

The notification shall set out

(a) the maintenance requirement,

(b) the effective date,

(c) the absent parent's assessable income and, where relevant, his protected income level,

(d) the assessable income of the parent with care,

(e) the minimum amount payable [see Chapter 17],

(f) details as to apportionment where the case is a Special Case.

(Regulation 10)

Multiple applications

Schedule 2 of the Procedure Regulations sets out the procedure to be followed by the Child Support Officer where more than one application is made for a maintenance assessment.

1. Where a person makes an effective application for an assessment under Section 4 or 6 of the Act and, before that assessment is made, he makes a subsequent effective application with respect to the same absent parent or person with care then those applications shall be treated as a single application (Paragraph 1 of Schedule 2).

2. Where a parent with care makes an effective application for a maintenance assessment under Section 4 and, before the assessment is made, makes a subsequent effective application under Section 6 with respect to the same absent parent, then those applications shall, if the parent with care does not cease to fall within Section 6 of the Act (i.e. she continues to be in receipt of benefit for herself or any child) be treated as a single application under Section 6 of the Act (Paragraph 1(2)(a) and (c)).

3. Where a parent with care makes an effective application for a maintenance assessment under Section 6 of the Act and, before that assessment is made, makes a subsequent effective application under Section 4 of the Act with respect to the same absent parent, then those applications shall, if the parent with care has ceased to fall within Section 6 of the Act (i.e. has ceased to be in receipt of benefit), be treated as a single application under Section 4 of the Act (Paragraph 1(2)(b) and (d)).

4. Where a child in Scotland makes an application under Section 7 and before the assessment is made, makes a subsequent effective application under that same Section with respect to the same person with care and the same absent parent, then both applications shall be treated as a single application for an assessment (Paragraph 2).

5. Where an application is made by a person with care under Section 4 or 6 of the Act and an application is also made by an absent parent under Section 4 of the Act, then the Child Support Officer shall proceed with the application of the person with care (Paragraph 3(2)).

6. (a) Where a child makes an application in Scotland under Section 7 of the Act and a subsequent application is made with respect to that child by a person with care or an absent parent, then the Child Support Officer shall proceed with the application of the parent (Paragraph 3(3)).

   (b) Where, in a case falling within (a) above there is more than one subsequent application by a parent, then the Child Support Officer shall apply the provisions of category 5 above or categories 9 or 10 below (as appropriate) to determine which application shall be proceeded with (Paragraph 3(4)).

   (c) Where there is an application by more than one qualifying child in Scotland under Section 7 of the Act in relation to the same person with care and absent parent the Child Support Officer shall proceed with the application of the eldest of the qualifying children (Paragraph 3(5)).

7. Where Special Case 1 applies [see Chapter 18], and an application is received from each absent parent, then the Child Support Officer shall proceed with both applications, treating them as a single application (Paragraph 3(6)).

8. Where Special Case 2 applies [see Chapter 18], and 2 persons are to be treated as absent parents, and an effective application is received from each such person, then the Child Support Officer shall proceed with both applications, treating them as a single application (Paragraph 3(7)).

9. Where a parent with care makes an application under Section 6 (i.e. the parent with care is in receipt of benefit and is required to make the application by the Agency), and there is a further application under Section 4 of the Act made by another person with care who has parental responsibility (for example, a step-father who has obtained a residence order under Section 8 of the Children Act 1989), then the Child Support Officer shall proceed with the application under Section 6 made by the parent with care (Paragraph 3(8)).

10. Where more than one person with care makes an application for an

assessment under Section 4 and each such person has parental responsibility for the children in question, and under Special Case 2 [see Chapter 18] one of the persons is to be treated as an absent parent, then the Child Support Officer shall proceed with the application of the person who does not fall to be treated as an absent parent under Special Case 2. If there is more than one person who does not fall to be treated as an absent parent then the Child Support Officer shall apply the provisions of category 11 below to determine with which application he shall proceed (Paragraph 3(9) and (10)).

11. Where more than one person with care makes an application for a maintenance assessment under Section 4 and none of those persons has parental responsibility in respect of the children in question; or where all of the persons have parental responsibility but the Child Support Officer has not been able to determine with which application he is to proceed, then he shall proceed with the application of the principal provider of day to day care (Paragraph 3(11) and (12)).

12. Where a maintenance assessment is in force and a subsequent application is made under the same Section of the Act for an assessment with respect of the same person with care, absent parent, and qualifying child as those with respect to whom the assessment in force has been made, then that application shall not be proceeded with unless the Agency treats the application as an application for a review under Section 17 [see Chapter 25] (Paragraph 4).

13. Where a maintenance assessment is in force following an application under Section 4 or 7 of the Act and the person with care makes an application under Section 6 of the Act (i.e. if she has become in receipt of benefit and has been required by the Agency to make an application), then any assessment made following that application shall replace the assessment in force (Paragraph 5).

14. Where a maintenance assessment has been made following an application by an absent parent under Section 4, but that assessment is not in respect of all of his children who are in the care of the person with care with respect to whom that assessment has been made, then any assessment made in response to a later application by the person with care under Section 4 of the Act with respect to any children in respect of whom the assessment currently in force was made, and any additional children in that person's care who are the children of that absent parent, shall replace the assessment currently in force (Paragraph 6(1)).

15. Where a maintenance assessment has been made following an application by an absent parent or a person with care under Section 4, and that assessment is not in respect of all of the children of the absent parent who are in the care of the person with respect to whom that application was made, and the absent parent makes a subsequent application in respect of any additional children of his in the care of the person with care, then that later application shall be treated as an application for a maintenance assessment in respect of all of the relevant children, and the assessment made thereon shall replace the earlier assessment (Paragraph 6(2)).

16. Where an assessment has been made following an application by a child under Section 7 and the person with care of that child makes a later application for an assessment under Section 4 in respect of that child and other children of the absent parent who are in her care, then the assessment made thereon shall replace the earlier assessment (Paragraph 6(3)).

CHAPTER 21

Interim Assessments

The basic principles

By Section 12 of the Act a Child Support Officer may make an interim assessment where he does not have sufficient information to enable him to make a full maintenance assessment. The objective of the legislation is, where possible, to make a full maintenance assessment. Although it is nowhere explicitly stated in the Act or in the Procedure Regulations, it is the intention that interim assessment should generally be limited to cases where information is being deliberately withheld by an absent parent. In the Consultation Document issued by the Department of Social Security in November 1991 it is stated (at Paragraph 2.7.2)

> "The threat of an interim maintenance assessment, rigorously enforced, should be a strong incentive to absent parents to provide the information necessary to lead to the calculation of an assessment under the formula."

By Section 12(4) of the Act a Child Support Officer shall, before making any interim assessment, and provided it is reasonably practicable to do so, give written notice of his intention to make such an assessment to the absent parent concerned, the person with care concerned, and, where the application is made under Section 7, to the child concerned. Where such notice is served, the Child Support Officer is not permitted to make the proposed interim assessment before the expiration of such period as may be prescribed. This period has been set at 14 days.

The Act therefore provides for a warning period before an interim assessment is made. During this warning period the absent parent will be able to rectify the deficiencies in his disclosure so as to permit the maintenance application to proceed normally.

The procedure is to be contrasted with that obtaining in conventional litigation. There, deliberate non-disclosure is dealt with by the drawing of adverse inferences; and it is rare that the Court will decline to deal with the matter substantively simply on account of inadequate disclosure. By contrast, the Child Support scheme gives the Child Support Officer a wide discretion to decline to make a full maintenance assessment should he believe that he does not have sufficient information. In that event he is able, after the expiration of the warning period, to impose a punitive interim assessment.

The detail

The provisions governing interim assessments are made in Regulations 8 and 9 of the Procedure Regulations. By Regulation 8(1) the warning period is set at 14 days commencing with the date that notice is given under Section 12(4) of the Act.

The amount of maintenance fixed by an interim assessment is simply calculated. It is one and a half times the amount of **MR** calculated in respect of the qualifying child or children concerned [see Chapter 6 for the calculation of **MR**]. None of the other procedures for determining the amount of maintenance payable under a full maintenance assessment applies.

Originally the Government proposed that the interim rate should be twice the amount of **MR** but there were strong protests that this was absurdly penal.

The effective date of an interim assessment, where Regulation 30(2)(a) or (4) applies [see Chapter 2] shall be the date not earlier than the first day, and not later than the seventh day, following the expiration of the 14 day warning period as falls on the same day of the week as the date specified in Regulation 30(2)(a) (which is the date upon which a maintenance enquiry form is given or sent to the absent parent).

By Regulation 8(6) a Child Support Officer has the discretion to cancel an interim assessment where he is satisfied that there was an unavoidable delay by the absent parent in completing and returning a maintenance enquiry form or in providing the information or evidence that is required by the Agency for the determination of an application for a full assessment; but an interim assessment shall not be cancelled with effect from a date earlier than 14 days after the supply of a maintenance enquiry form to any person.

Subject to the power to cancel as stated above, it is provided by Regulation 8(8) that where a full maintenance assessment is made it shall not be adjusted in respect of any period in respect of which an interim maintenance assessment was in force. Accordingly, if the maintenance assessment is at a lower rate than the interim assessment the absent parent will not be able to recover the over-payments made by him during the period of the interim assessment. Conversely, under Regulation 8(10), in the event that the amount of the full assessment exceeds the amount of the interim assessment, then the full amount of the assessment will be payable for the period during which the interim assessment was in force with credits being given for the amounts paid under the interim assessment. Similarly, under Regulation 8(4) and (5), if a full maintenance assessment provides for payments for a period prior to the effective date of an interim assessment then maintenance will be payable in respect of that period irrespective of the making of the interim assessment.

As described, the intention of the interim assessment scheme is to impose punitive rates of maintenance upon parents who default in their obligation to give a full disclosure. The scheme envisages that a parent who repents of his default, or who otherwise is in a position to complete his disclosure, should be in a position to apply for any interim assessment made to be cancelled. Accordingly by Regulation 9 it is provided that an absent parent who has had an interim maintenance assessment made against him may apply in writing, giving grounds, for that interim assessment to be cancelled. Upon receipt of such an application for cancellation the Child Support Officer shall decide whether the assessment is to be cancelled and, if so, the date with effect from which it is to be cancelled. Where he does cancel the interim assessment the Child Support Officer shall then go on to decide whether it is appropriate for a full assessment to be made; and if he so decides he shall proceed to make that assessment. The Child Support Officer is required to give immediate notification to the applicant in writing of the reasons for his decision.

It is not open to a parent to seek a review of a decision of the Child Support Officer to impose an interim assessment. However he is entitled, by Regulation 9(6), to seek a review of a Child Support Officer's decision following an an application by a parent for a cancellation of such an assessment [see Chapter 25 for reviews and appeals].

CHAPTER 22

The requirement to co-operate in benefit cases

The basic principle

No provision within the Child Support Bill caused greater political controversy during its passage through Parliament than the imposition on a parent with care of a child and in receipt of benefit of a duty to co-operate and to supply information as to the identity and whereabouts of the absent parent, coupled with the sanction of a reduction of social security benefits in the event of a refusal to do so. So well-publicised was the debate on this topic that even now it is widely believed, quite erroneously, that the ambit of the Act is confined to benefit cases where the absent parent is not contributing properly to the maintenance of his children.

As has been seen in Chapter 5, Section 6 of the Act (as extended by Regulation 34 of the Procedure Regulations) provides that where Income Support, family credit or disability working allowance is claimed by, or paid to, a parent with care of a qualifying child, she shall, if required to do so by the Agency, authorise the Agency to take action to recover maintenance from the absent parent. The Agency shall not, however, require such a parent so to authorise it if there are reasonable grounds for believing that, if the parent were required to give that authorisation, or if she were to give it, there would be a risk of her, or of any child living with her, suffering harm or undue distress as a result.

The detail

By Section 6(9) a parent with care who is under such a duty shall, so far as she reasonably can, comply with such Regulations as may be made with a view to the Agency being provided with the information which is required to enable the absent parent to be traced; for the amount of Child Support maintenance payable by the absent parent to be assessed; and for that amount to be recovered from the absent parent.

By Section 46(1) and (2) of the Act, where any parent with care fails to comply with her duty to authorise the recovery of maintenance from the absent parent, or her duty to supply information so as to facilitate the tracing of the absent parent, then a Child Support Officer may serve written notice on that parent requiring her, before the end of the specified period (set at 6 weeks: see Regulation 35(2) of the Procedure Regulations), either to comply or to give him reasons for failing so to do.

At the expiration of the 6 week period the Child Support Officer must consider, pursuant to Section 46(3) of the Act, whether, having regard to any reasons given by the parent, there are reasonable grounds for believing that, if she were to be required to comply, there would be a risk of her or if any children living with her suffering harm or undue distress as a result of complying.

If the Child Support Officer considers that there are such reasonable grounds he shall take no further action (Section 46(4)); but if he considers that there are no such reasonable grounds, he may give a "reduced benefit direction" with respect to the parent (Section 46(5)).

The amount of the reduced benefit direction is set by Regulation 36 of the Procedure Regulations at 20% of the Income Support personal allowance (the allowance is £44.00 per week so 20% is £8.80 per week) for the first 26 weeks following the issue of the direction and then 10% of the allowance for the next 52 weeks (i.e. £4.40 per week) (Regulation 36(2) and (3)).

If an additional qualifying child is born within the aggregate 78 week period and the person with care refuses to co-operate in furnishing details concerning the father of that new child, then the 18 month period recommences de novo (Regulation 47).

If a parent subjected to a direction moves from one benefit to another then she takes with her the balance of the weeks applicable under the direction (Regulation 39).

Suspension and modification of the direction

(a) A reduced benefit direction will be modified so that the minimum amount of benefit payable under the relevant social security Regulations is maintained (Regulation 37).

(b) A reduced benefit direction will be suspended where the benefit ceases to be payable. It goes into abeyance for 52 weeks and if the benefit does not revive during that period the reduced benefit direction will be extinguished. If, however, the benefit does revive during the period then the balance of the period of the direction revives with it (Regulation 38).

(c) If Income Support is calculated and paid to persons in residential care or nursing homes, or to patients, or to persons in residential accommodation then the reduced benefit direction will be suspended for as long as the Income Support is calculated on that basis (Regulation 40).

(d) Where a sole qualifying child ceases to be a child for the purposes of the Act, or the parent ceases to be a parent with care, then the reduced benefit direction is suspended for 52 weeks, and if these conditions do not revive during that period then it is extinguished; but if the conditions do revive within that period then the balance of the period of the direction revives therewith (Regulation 48).

Termination

(a) Where a child applies in Scotland under Section 7 of the Act, and an assessment is made thereon, then a reduced benefit direction will cease to have effect (Regulation 43). Similarly, where an absent parent comes onto the scene and applies under Section 4 of the Act, and an assessment is made thereon, then the reduced benefit direction ceases (Regulation 44). But it should be noted that no such application can be made under Section 4 during the transitional period while a parent is in receipt of benefit [see Chapter 19].

(b) Where a parent complies with the obligations imposed on her (either to authorise a maintenance application against an absent parent, or to reveal his whereabouts) then any reduced benefit direction issued will be terminated (Regulation 41).

(c) Where a parent supplies further information as to why there should not be a reduced benefit direction under Section 46(3) (i.e. she supplies further grounds as to why there would be a risk of her or any children living with her suffering harm or undue distress as a result of complying) then a review will be held by a different Child Support Officer, and if he considers the reasons to be valid then the reduced benefit direction will be terminated (Regulation 42).

By virtue of Section 46(7) of the Act any person who is aggrieved by a decision of a Child Support Officer to give a reduced benefit direction may appeal to a Child Support Appeal Tribunal against that decision [see Chapter 25 for appeals].

Policy guidelines

On 12th January 1993 the Parliamentary Secretary for Social Security (Mr Alistair Burt M.P.) made public the guidance to staff of the Child Support Agency concerning the handling of cases where mothers do not wish to name their child's father.

In a written answer to a Parliamentary question Mr Burt stated

"Mothers will be told... that the Child Support Agency will act as a buffer between the parents so that, if they do not wish to do so, they will not have to see the child's father, and he will not be told where the mother and her children live. However, if the mother continues to believe, in spite of this, that there is a risk to her or the children, then the guidelines will be applied."

In summary the guidelines provide

(a) the welfare of any children living with the parent with care must be considered,

(b) the parent with care has a right to be believed unless what she says is inherently contradictory or implausible,

(c) a reduced benefit direction is a strong sanction and will have an important impact on the income of a parent with care.

Where the parent refuses to co-operate she will be made aware of the following points

(a) the Agency exists to help her obtain maintenance,

(b) she need not see the absent parent,

(c) the absent parent will not be given her address, or even information about the town in which she lives,

(d) the Agency will collect maintenance for her,

(e) paying maintenance does not give the absent parent the right to contact with the child,

(f) she may want more flexibility in her life in future, and maintenance will help give her that flexibility,

(g) getting maintenance should increase her income if she starts work and gets family credit or disability working allowance or moves off benefit altogether,

(h) £15.00 of maintenance is ignored when family credit, disability working allowance, housing benefit and council tax benefit are claimed.

If, after having the above spelled out, the parent with care still declines to co-operate, the Child Support Officer will go on to consider whether or not the case falls into one of the following categories where it will be prima facie reasonable to conclude that the parent with care has good cause not to co-operate. The guidelines emphasise that the list is not intended to be exhaustive, but only amount to "indicative circumstances".

(a) The parent with care fears violence. In such a case a decision of "good cause" may be easier to reach if there is a history of violence; but the fear of violence may be reasonable even when there is no history of it.

(b) The parent with care is a rape victim.

(c) The absent parent has sexually abused the child of the parent with care.

(d) The child was conceived as a result of incest or other sexual abuse.

The guidelines then set out a list of circumstances which may be raised by a parent with care which will not, on their own, normally suffice to establish good cause. Again, the guidelines emphasise that the list is not exhaustive.

(a) The parent with care fears that the absent parent will want to see the child.

(b) The parent with care wishes to sever links with the absent parent.

(c) The parent with care wishes to protect the absent parent from a claim.

(d) The absent parent is under 16.

(e) The parent with care says that she deliberately set out to conceive the child with no intention of involving the father.

(f) The parent with care says that a satisfactory voluntary agreement exists.

The guidelines then set out a list of special circumstances where special treatment will be applied.

(a) The parent with care is under 16, or is over 16 and still at school, and features in a benefit claim of another person, such as her parents. In such a case the requirement to co-operate will be waived until and unless the parent with care makes her own application for benefit.

(b) The child was conceived by anonymous sperm donation. In such circumstances no further action should be taken.

The guidelines also set out circumstances where good concrete evidence should be provided before any further action is taken, such as the case where the parent with care names a person as the father, but on the balance of probabilities it appears unlikely that the person is in fact the father.

The guidelines are reproduced in full in Appendix 4.

CHAPTER 23

The duty to provide and the powers to obtain information

The basic principle

The Act imposes a duty upon parents (or persons with care if not parents) to supply the necessary information to enable the absent parent to be traced where that is necessary, for the amount of Child Support maintenance payable by the absent parent to be assessed, and for that amount to be recovered from the absent parent.

The duty is imposed in respect of applications made by a person with care or an absent parent by Section 4(4), in respect of applications made in benefit cases by Section 6(9) [as has been seen in Chapter 22] and, in respect of applications by a child in Scotland, by Section 7(5).

The detail

By Section 14 of the Act the Secretary of State is empowered to make Regulations requiring any information or evidence needed for the determination of any application made under the Act, or any question arising in connection with such an application, or needed in connection with the collection or enforcement of Child Support or other maintenance under the Act, to be furnished in accordance with Regulations to be made. The detail is to be found in the Information Regulations.

Regulation 2 of the Information Regulations imposes an obligation on listed categories of persons to provide specified information or evidence. If the person in question has such information or evidence in his possession, or could reasonably be expected to acquire it, then he is obliged to provide it. By Regulation 5, such information must be provided as soon as is reasonably practicable.

A person with care, an absent parent, a parent who is treated as an absent parent under Special Case 2 [see Chapter 18] or a child where the application is made in Scotland under Section 7 have the obligation to provide information to enable a decision to be made in relation to the following matters

    (a) whether in relation to an application for a maintenance assessment, there exists a qualifying child, an absent parent and a person with care,

(b) whether a Child Support Officer has jurisdiction to make a maintenance assessment,

(c) where more than one application has been made, as to which application is to be proceeded with,

(d) to enable an absent parent to be identified,

(e) to enable an absent parent to be traced,

(f) to enable the amount of Child Support maintenance payable by an absent parent to be assessed,

(g) to enable the amount payable under a relevant Court order to be ascertained (a relevant Court order is an order for income or capital provision or adjustment of property rights made under any of the enactments specified in Chapter 19, or an order under Part II of the Children Act 1989 or the equivalent legislation in Scotland),

(h) to enable the amounts of child maintenance payable by an absent parent or payable under a relevant Court order to be recovered from an absent parent,

(i) to enable the amount of interest payable with respect to arrears to be determined,

(j) to enable the interest as determined to be recovered from an absent parent,

(k) to enable any related proceedings to be identified (related proceedings are proceedings in which a Court order as described above was or is being sought).

A person alleged to be a parent of a qualifying child but who denies the allegation (e.g. a putative father or a husband seeking to deny the presumption of legitimacy) is obliged to supply information only in relation to items (b) and (d) above.

A current or recent employer of the absent parent or the parent with care is obliged to supply information in relation to items (d), (e), (f), (h) and (j) above.

The local authority in whose area a person with care, an absent parent, a parent treated as an absent parent under Special Case 2, a child where the application is made under Section 7, or a putative father, lives is obliged to supply the information in item (a) above.

Where a Court has made an order of the nature described in item (g) above, or where there have been proceedings where such an order was sought, or where there are proceedings pending in which such an order is sought, then the Court is obliged to provide the information set out in (g), (h) and (k) above.

By Regulation 3(2) the information or evidence to be furnished in accordance with Regulation 2 may in particular include (but not necessarily be limited to) information and evidence as to

(a) the habitual residence of the person with care, the absent parent and any child in respect of whom an application for a maintenance assessment has been made,

(b) the name and address of the person with care and of the absent parent, their marital status, and the relationship of the person with care to any child in respect of whom the application for a maintenance assessment has been made,

(c) the name, address and date of birth of any such child, that child's marital status, and any education that child is undergoing,

(d) the persons who have parental responsibility for (or, in Scotland, parental rights over) any qualifying child where there is more than one person with care,

(e) the time spent by a qualifying child in respect of whom an application for a maintenance assessment has been made with each person with care, where there is more than one such person,

(f) the matters relevant for determining, in a case falling within Section 26 of the Act (disputes about parentage), whether that case falls within one of the cases set out in subsection 2 of that Section, and if it does not, the matters relevant for determining the parentage of a child whose parentage is in dispute [see Chapter 26],

(g) the name and address of any current or recent employer of an absent parent or a parent with care, and the gross earnings and the deduction from those earnings deriving from each employment,

(h) the address from which an absent parent or parent with care who is self-employed carries on his trade or business, the trading name, and the gross receipts and expenses and other outgoings of the trade or business,

(i) any other income of an absent parent and a parent with care,

(j) any income, other than earnings, of a qualifying child,

(k) amounts payable and paid under a relevant Court order or a maintenance agreement,

(l) the persons living in the same household as the absent parent or living in the same household as the parent with care, their relationship to the absent parent or the parent with care, as the case may be, and to each other, and, in the case of the children of any such parent, the dates of birth of those children,

(m) the matters set out in sub-paragraphs (g) and (h) in relation to the person specified in sub-paragraph (l) other than any children living in the same household as the absent parent or the parent with care, as the case may be,

(n) income other than earnings of the persons living in the same household of the absent parent or the person with care,

(o) benefits related to disability that the absent parent, parent with care and other persons living in the same household as the absent parent or the parent with care are entitled to or would be entitled to if certain conditions were satisfied,

(p) the housing costs to be taken into account for the purposes of determining assessable or disposable income,

(q) the identifying details of any bank, building society or similar account held in the name of the absent parent or the person with care, and statements relating to any such account,

(r) the matters relevant for determining whether
  (i) a maintenance assessment has ceased to have effect or should be cancelled under the provisions of Paragraph 16 of Schedule 1 to the Act [see Chapter 24], or
  (ii) a person is a child within the meaning of Section 55 of the Act.

The Inland Revenue

Where the Agency requires information for the purpose of tracing either the current address of an absent parent, or the current employer of an absent parent then, by Paragraph 1 of Schedule 2 to the Act no obligation as to secrecy shall prevent disclosure of any information obtained or held in connection with the assessment or collection of Income Tax from being disclosed to the Agency.   Such disclosure shall be confined only for the purposes above stated or for the purposes of any proceedings, civil or criminal, in connection with the operation of the Act.

Local authority data

Similarly, under Paragraph 2 of Schedule 2 to the Act, where the Agency requires "relevant information" in connection with the discharge by it or by any Child Support Officer of functions under the Act then a local authority may be required to provide such relevant information in connection with any housing benefit or council tax to which an absent parent or a person with care is entitled to the extent that the Agency considers it necessary in connection with the determination of
  (a) that person's income of any kind,
  (b) the amount of housing costs to be taken into account in determining that person's income of any kind,
  (c) the amount of that person's protected income.
  By Regulation 4 of the Regulations, "relevant information" means either information as to the amount of housing costs of an absent parent or a person with care which are treated as eligible rent for housing benefit purposes [see Chapter 16] and the entitlement to housing benefit as at the date that the information is sought; or information as to the amount of council tax payable by an absent parent or person with care and as to the entitlement to council tax benefit as at the date that the information is sought.

By virtue of Regulation 6 of the Regulations where a person with care with respect to whom a maintenance assessment has been made believes that the assessment has either ceased to have effect or should be cancelled then there is a duty imposed upon her, as soon as is reasonably practicable, to inform the Agency of that belief, and of the reasons for it, and to provide such other information as the Agency may reasonably require with a view to assisting it or a Child Support Officer in determining whether the assessment has ceased to have effect, or should be cancelled.

By Section 15 of the Act the Agency is vested with draconian powers to obtain information which has not become available under the above procedures. The Secretary of State may, where he considers it appropriate to do so for the purpose of acquiring information which the Agency or any Child Support Officer requires for the purposes of the Act, appoint a person to act as an inspector for a particular case (the appointment of inspector is always ad hoc). Each inspector shall be furnished with a certificate of appointment. An inspector shall have power to enter at all reasonable times any premises specified in his certificate of appointment, other than premises used solely as a dwelling house, and any premises which are not specified in the certificate but which are used by any person specified in the certificate for the purpose of carrying on any trade, profession, vocation or business, and to make such examination and enquiry there as he considers appropriate. An inspector exercising his powers may question any person aged 18 or over whom he finds on the premises. When exercising his powers an inspector may require any person who has been an occupier of the premises in question, or an employer or employee working at or from the premises in question, or any person carrying on at or from the premises in question any trade, profession, vocation or business, or any employee or agent of any such person mentioned, to furnish to the inspector all such information and documents as the inspector may reasonably require. If any person intentionally delays or obstructs any inspector exercising his powers or, without reasonable excuse, refuses or neglects to answer any question or furnish any information or to produce any document when required to do so under the Section, then he shall be guilty of a criminal offence. However, no person shall be required under Section 15 to answer any question or give any evidence tending to incriminate himself or, in the case of a person who is married, his or her spouse. By virtue of Regulation 7 of the Information Regulations an inspector may enter any Crown premises for the purposes of exercising any powers conferred to him by that Section (subject to the Queen not being in actual residence).

Disclosure of information by the Agency

By virtue of Section 14(2) the Secretary of State is empowered to make Regulations authorising the disclosure by him or by Child Support Officers, in such circumstances as may be prescribed, of such information held by them for the purposes of the Act as may be prescribed. By Regulation 8 of the Information Regulations the Agency or a Child Support Officer may disclose any information held for the purposes of the Act to a Court, or to any tribunal or other body or person mentioned in the Act, or to any tribunal established under the Social Security Benefit Acts, where such disclosure is made for the purposes of any proceedings before any of those bodies relating to the Act or the Social Security Benefit Acts.

The Agency or a Child Support Officer may disclose information held for the purposes of the Act to an appropriate local authority for the use in the exercise of its functions relating to housing benefit or council tax benefit (Regulation 9).

The Child Support Officer is permitted to disclose any information held by him for the purposes of the Act to the Secretary of State for use in connection with the functions of the Secretary of State under any of the Social Security Benefit Acts.

By Section 50 of the Act, as extended by Regulation 11 of the Information Regulations, if any person is employed as

(a) the Chief Child Support Officer,

(b) any other Child Support Officer,

(c) any Clerk to, or other officer of, a Child Support Appeal Tribunal,

(d) any member of staff of such a tribunal,

(e) a civil servant in connection with the carrying out of any functions under the Act,

(f) the Comptroller and Auditor General,

(g) the Parliamentary Commissioner for Administration,

(h) the Health Service Commissioner for England,

(i) the Health Service Commissioner for Wales,

(j) the Health Service Commissioner for Scotland,

(k) any member of the staff of the National Audit Office,

(l) any other person who carries out the administrative work of that office, or who provides, or is employed in the provision of, services to it,

(m) any officer of any of the Commissioners referred to above,

(n) any person who provides, or is employed in the provision of, services to the Department of Social Security,

he shall be guilty of an offence if, without lawful authority, he discloses any information which was acquired by him in the course of that employment and which relates to a particular person. There are defences to such an offence set out in Section 50(2) and (6) to (8) to which reference should be made.

CHAPTER 24

Termination of assessments

A maintenance assessment *shall* be terminated, cancelled or otherwise cease to have effect in the following circumstances

1. On the death of the absent parent, or the person with care (Paragraph 16(1)(a) of Schedule 1 to the Act).
2. On there no longer being a qualifying child on account of age or death (Paragraph 16(1)(b)).
3. On the absent parent ceasing to be the parent of all of the qualifying children (the only circumstance would be adoption of the child(ren)) (Paragraph 16(1)(c)).
4. On the absent parent and person with care living together for a continuous period of 6 months (Paragraph 16(1)(d)).

   Regulation 52 of the Procedure Regulations provides that where a question arises under any of the above categories the matter shall be referred for decision to a Child Support Officer. He must give reasons for his decision, which shall be susceptible to a review [see Chapter 25].
5. Where a new maintenance assessment is made (Paragraph 16(1)(e)).
6. Where an application has been made under Section 4 or Section 7, and the applicant asks that the assessment be cancelled (Paragraph 16(2)).

   Similarly, where an application is made under these Sections then, by Section 4(5) and Section 7(5) of the Act, the applicant can require the Agency to discontinue it prior to determination (save that by Regulation 52(8) of the Procedure Regulations, in Special Case 1 [see Chapter 18], where both absent parents have applied, both must ask the Agency to discontinue the application).
7. Where an application has been made under Section 6, and the applicant asks that the assessment be cancelled and the Officer is satisfied that the applicant is no longer in receipt of Income Support, family credit or disability working allowance (Paragraph 16(3)).

   By Regulation 32 of the Procedure Regulations where an assessment is cancelled in the circumstances described in Paragraphs 6 and 7 above it shall cease to have effect from the date of receipt of the request for cancellation, or such later date as the Officer may determine.

8. Where a person with care, or an absent parent, or a qualifying child with respect to whom an assessment is in force ceases to be habitually resident within the United Kingdom (Section 44 of the Act and Regulation 7 of the Jurisdiction Regulations).

A maintenance assessment *may* be cancelled by a Child Support Officer in the following circumstances

1. Where both the absent parent and the person with care ask that the assessment be cancelled, provided that the Officer is satisfied that they are living together (Paragraph 16(6)).
2. Where the Officer is satisfied that the person with care has ceased to be the person with care of any of the qualifying children (Paragraph 16(4)).

   Comment: the Officer may cancel the assessment with effect from the date upon which, in his opinion, the change of circumstances took place.

3. Where the assessment is in force but an Officer would no longer have jurisdiction to make an original assessment it may be cancelled in prescribed circumstances (Paragraph 16(5)).

   Comment: no Regulations have as yet been made under this Paragraph; although it is understood that the D.S.S. propose to procure the making of Regulations in February or March 1993 to cover the position where a child in Scotland has obtained an assessment under Section 7 of the Act, and has subsequently moved to England.

Regulations 13-15 of the Procedure Regulations require a Child Support Officer to give reasons in writing when cancelling an assessment under Paragraph 16 of Schedule 1 to the Act, or when refusing to cancel such an assessment.

CHAPTER 25

Reviews of assessments, and appeals

Reviews
The basic principles

Reviews fall into 2 categories. In the first a review may be sought after the expiration of a fixed period (set at 52 weeks) or upon a change of circumstances. Such a review can be likened to an application to vary a maintenance order under Section 31 Matrimonial Causes Act 1973.

The second category of review is more akin to an appeal. An aggrieved parent may seek a review by another Child Support Officer of a maintenance assessment, or of a refusal to make a maintenance assessment, or of a refusal to review by way of "variation" a maintenance assessment, or of a refusal of an application for the cancellation of a maintenance assessment. Such a review can only proceed where there are reasonable grounds for supposing that the refusal, assessment or cancellation in question was made in ignorance of a material fact, or was based on a mistake as to a material fact, or was wrong in law.

The detail
I REVIEWS BY WAY OF VARIATION

(a) Periodical reviews

Section 16 of the Act provides that the Secretary of State shall make such arrangements as he considers necessary to secure that, where any assessment has been in force for a prescribed period, the amount of maintenance fixed by that assessment is reviewed by a Child Support Officer as soon as is reasonably practicable after the end of that prescribed period. By Regulation 17(1) of the Procedure Regulations the prescribed period is set at 52 weeks.

Section 16(2) of the Act as supplemented by Regulation 17(4) of the Procedure Regulations provides that before any such review is conducted the Child Support Officer shall give 14 days notice of the proposed review to the person with care, to any absent parent, to any parent who is treated as an absent parent, and to the child where the application is made under Section 7 of the Act.

By Section 16(3) of the Act it is provided that a review shall be conducted as if a fresh application for an assessment had been made by the person in whose favour the original assessment was made. Upon completing his review the Child Support Officer is obliged to make a fresh assessment, unless he is satisfied that the original assessment has ceased to have effect and should be brought to an end (Section 16(4)). However, the Child Support Officer is entitled to decline to conduct a review if a fresh maintenance assessment following such a review would cease to have effect within 28 days of the effective date of that fresh assessment (Regulation 17(3)).

Where a fresh assessment is made it takes effect from the day immediately following the end of the 52 week period mentioned above.

Where a Child Support Officer gives notice to any person of a proposed review he is entitled to seek disclosure of that information specified in Regulations 2 and 3 of the Information Regulations [see Chapter 23]. However such a disclosure requirement does not apply to any person to whom or in respect of whom Income Support is payable or to a person with care where Income Support is payable to or in respect of the absent parent (Regulations 17(5) and (6)). Similarly, the disclosure obligation does not apply where Special Case 4 or 5 applies [see Chapter 18], and where there has been a previous review in relation to another assessment in force relating to the person in question, and where the Child Support Officer has no reason to believe that there has been a change in that person's circumstances (Regulation 17(7)).

(b) Reviews on a change of circumstances

By Section 17 of the Act where a maintenance assessment is in force then either the absent parent or the person with care (or where the application is made in Scotland under Section 7, the child) may apply for a review on the ground that by reason of a change of circumstances since the original assessment was made, the amount of Child Support maintenance payable by the absent parent would be **significantly different** if it were to be fixed by an assessment made by reference to the circumstances of the case as at the date of the application (Section 17(2)).

The Child Support Officer shall, by virtue of Section 17(4) as supplemented by Regulations 19(1) and (2), give 14 days notice to the same persons as mentioned above in respect of reviews under Section 16 and such persons shall be subject to the same requirements of disclosure as set out above (Regulations 19(1), (2) and (3)). Again, a review under this Section shall be conducted as if a fresh application for a maintenance assessment had been made by the person in whose favour the original assessment was made (Section 17(5)).

The Child Support Officer to whom an application has been referred shall not proceed with it unless he considers that it is likely that he will be required by Section 17(6) to make a fresh assessment if he conducts the review applied for. Section 17(6) provides that on completing any review a Child Support Officer shall make a fresh assessment unless he is satisfied that the original assessment has ceased to have effect or should be brought to an end, or that the difference between the amount of maintenance fixed by the original assessment and the amount that would be fixed if a fresh assessment were to be made is less than such an amount as may be prescribed.

By Regulation 20 of the Procedure Regulations it is provided that a Child Support Officer shall not make a fresh assessment if the difference between the amount of maintenance fixed by the assessment currently in force and the amount that would be fixed if a fresh assessment were to be made is less than £10.00 per week; however, if the Child Support Officer determines that were the fresh assessment to be made as a result of the review the circumstances of the absent parent would be such that the level of his protected income would affect the amount of that assessment, then the £10.00 figure is reduced to £1.00. Similarly, where a Child Support Officer determines that were a fresh assessment to be made the children referable to that latter assessment would not be the same children in respect of whom the original assessment were made, then, again, the £10.00 figure is reduced to £1.00 (Regulation 20(2) and (3)).

Under Special Case 4 [see Chapter 18], where a review is applied for under Section 17 where there is a change in the circumstances of the absent parent, then the Child Support Officer shall not make a fresh assessment if the difference between the total amount of maintenance fixed by the assessments currently in force and the total amount that would be fixed if fresh assessment were to be made is less than £10.00 per week, unless the provisions relating to the absent parent's protected income apply, in which event the figure is £1.00 per week (Regulation 21).

Where Special Case 5 applies, then by Regulation 22 the provisions of Regulation 20 above will apply where there is a change in circumstances of the person with care or one or more absent parent.

II REVIEWS BY WAY OF APPEAL

By Section 18(1) of the Act, where an application for a maintenance assessment is refused, or where an application for a review of an assessment made under Section 17 above (change of circumstances) is refused then the applicant may seek a review of that decision.

Where a maintenance assessment is in force then the absent parent, or the person with care, or the child (where the application is made in Scotland under Section 7) may seek a review (Section 18(2)).

Where an assessment is cancelled a review may be sought (Section 18(3)).

Similarly, where an application for a cancellation of an assessment is refused a review may be sought (Section 18(4)).

An application for such a review shall be supported by grounds in writing (Section 18(5)).

The Child Support Officer conducting the review shall proceed therewith unless in his opinion there are no reasonable grounds for supposing that the refusal, assessment or cancellation in question was made in ignorance of a material fact, or was based on a mistake as to a material fact, or was wrong in law (Section 18(6)). If, however, he is satisfied that a fresh assessment should be made, he shall proceed accordingly (Section 18(9)). The Child Support Officer is obliged by virtue of Section 18(10) to take into account any change of circumstances since the decision being reviewed was taken.

It goes without saying that the review must be undertaken by a Child Support Officer who played no part in taking the original decision (Section 18(7)).

Where the review is in respect of a refusal of an application for a maintenance assessment, or a refusal of an application for a review under Section 17 of a maintenance assessment on account of a change of circumstances, or in respect of the cancellation of an assessment, or in respect of the refusal of the cancellation of a maintenance assessment, then the application for a review must be made within 28 days of notification of the decision in respect of which review is sought (Regulation 24). However, the period of 28 days may be extended by the Secretary of State if he is satisfied that there was unavoidable delay in making the application (Regulation 24(2)).

Where a Child Support Officer proposes to conduct such a review he is obliged to give 14 days notice to the same persons mentioned above in respect of reviews under Section 16 and shall send to them the applicant's reasons for making the application for the review, and certain further information, and shall invite representations either orally or in writing from such persons. If such persons fail to keep their appointments or to supply their reasons in writing, the Child Support Officer may proceed to complete his review in the absence of representations (Regulation 25).

There is no time limit in respect of an application to seek a review under Section 18(2) of a maintenance assessment in force. By Regulation 29 the jurisdiction to seek a review will be preserved notwithstanding that an assessment has ceased to be in force prior to the determination of the review, provided that the application for review was received by the Agency within 28 days of the date of notification to the applicant of the original maintenance assessment. The Secretary of State can extend the 28 day period if he is satisfied that there was unavoidable delay in lodging the application.

III REVIEWS AT THE INSTIGATION OF CHILD SUPPORT OFFICERS

By Section 19(1) of the Act where a Child Support Officer is satisfied that an assessment is defective by reason of having been made in ignorance of a material fact, or having been based on a mistake as to a material fact, or being wrong in law then he may make a fresh assessment even though no application for a review has been made. Similarly, by Section 19(2), if a Child Support Officer is satisfied that if an application were to be made under Section 17 (change of circumstances) or Section 18 (application for review by way of appeal) it would be appropriate to make a fresh assessment, then he may make of his own motion a fresh assessment. By Regulation 23 of the Procedure Regulations the provisions of Regulations 20, 21 and 22 (see above) shall apply to a review made under Section 19 of the Act. Similarly, by virtue of Regulation 27 a review instigated by a Child Support Officer under Section 19 which had been conducted as if an application for review under Section 18(1)(b) applied (review of a refusal to review on account of change of circumstances a maintenance assessment) then Regulation 27 (see above) shall apply.

IV EFFECTIVE DATES OF ASSESSMENTS FOLLOWING A REVIEW

Regulation 31 of the Procedure Regulations sets out detailed provisions in respect of the effective date of assessments following a review.

Where the review was made under Section 16 of the Act (review after 52 weeks) then the effective date of the new assessment is 52 weeks after the effective date of the previous assessment.

Where the application is made for a review following a change of circumstances the effective date is set within a week of the date of receipt of the application (reference should be made to the definition of "the first day of the maintenance period" within Regulations 31 and 33).

Where a review by way of appeal results in a maintenance assessment following a refusal to make a maintenance assessment the effective date shall be the effective date of the assessment that would have been made had the original assessment not been refused.

Where an application is made for a review of a maintenance assessment in force under Section 18(2) the effective date of any fresh assessment made shall be, generally speaking, the date which the Child Support Officer shall determine.

There are further provisions for determining the effective date in the event of the death of a qualifying child, or in the event of reinstatement of a cancelled assessment, or in the event of error, misrepresentation and such like. Reference should be made to the provisions of Regulation 31.

Appeals

By Section 20 of the Act any person who is aggrieved by the decision of a Child Support Officer on a review under Section 18 (review by way of appeal) or where an application for such a review has been refused, may appeal to a Child Support Appeal Tribunal against that decision. By Section 46(7) where a reduced benefit direction has been made [see Chapter 22] an aggrieved person may appeal to a Child Support Appeal Tribunal. Any such appeal must be made within 28 days of the notification of the decision, but such a period may be extended with the leave of the chairman of the Child Support Appeal Tribunal. Where an appeal is allowed by the Tribunal then the case shall be remitted to the Agency who shall arrange for it to be dealt with by a different Child Support Officer. By Section 45 of the Act the Lord Chancellor may by order make such provision to secure that appeals may, in such circumstances as he may specify, be made to a Court instead of a Child Support Appeal Tribunal. The Lord Chancellor has made the Child Support Appeals (Jurisdiction of Courts) Order 1993. This provides for appeals to go to a Court instead of a tribunal where the issue involved is whether a particular person is a parent of a child in question. By the Children (Allocation of Proceedings) (Amendment) Order 1993 such an appeal will be allocated initially to the Magistrates' Court although it may be transferred therefrom either to the County Court or to the High Court [see Chapter 19].

The Appeal Tribunals Regulations 1992 set out the procedure for the determination of appeals to Child Support Appeal Tribunals. They provide that at any stage of the proceedings the Chairman of the Tribunal may give directions for the efficient conduct of the proceedings and may direct any party to give further particulars or to produce such documents as may be reasonably required. The Chairman may order that proceedings be struck out for failure to comply with procedure, or make provision for the withdrawal of appeals or the postponement of appeals. The Regulations provide that a party to the proceedings may be represented by another person whether such person be professionally qualified or not. The Appeal Tribunals are given the power to summon witnesses. Appeal hearings must be heard orally and in private unless the Chairman otherwise directs. The Regulations make provision for the giving of evidence and the making of decisions. Reference should be made to the Regulations. In a letter to *The Times* dated 17th February 1993, the President of the Independent Tribunal Service (His Honour Judge Thorpe) stated that the Tribunal would not make orders for costs and that appellants' expenses for appearing would be met from public funds. The D.S.S. has indicated that it would be permissible for a parent who believes that the other parent has made a false presentation of his resources to the Child Support Officer to utilise the Appeal Tribunal as a court of first instance and, in particular, by means of the powers of discovery and the summoning of witnesses, to seek to obtain findings of fact as to the true state of the other parent's resources.

By Section 24 of the Act any person who is aggrieved by a decision of a Child Support Officer or of a Child Support Appeal Tribunal may appeal to a Child Support Commissioner on a question of law. Where a Child Support Commissioner holds that the decision was wrong he shall set it aside, and may either give his own decision, if he can do so without making fresh or further findings of fact, or, alternatively, may refer the case to a Child Support Officer or to a Child Support Appeal Tribunal. Section 24(6) provides that appeals to a Commissioner must be with leave. The Commissioners Regulations 1992 set out the procedure for such appeals and reference should be made thereto.

By Section 25 of the Act an appeal lies to the Court of Appeal from any decision of a Child Support Commissioner. Leave to appeal is required from the Commissioner, or in the event of refusal of leave by him, by the Court of Appeal. (See Rule 3.23 of the Family Proceedings Rules, as amended by the Family Proceedings (Amendment No. 3) Rules, as to the procedure obtaining on such an appeal.)

CHAPTER 26

Disputes about parentage

The basic principle

By Section 26 of the Act a Child Support Officer shall not make an assessment on the assumption that a person is the parent of a qualifying child where that person denies that he is the parent of the child unless the case falls within one of those cases set out within Section 26(2) of the Act.

The detail

Section 26(2) sets out 6 cases where the Child Support Officer may make an assessment against a person on the assumption that he is the parent, even if that person denies that he is. They are as follows.

CASE A

Where the alleged parent is the parent of the child in question by virtue of having adopted him.

CASE B

Where the alleged parent is a parent of the child in question by virtue of an order under Section 30 of the Human Fertilisation and Embryology Act 1990. Under Section 30 the Court may order, subject to certain conditions, that a child is to be treated as a child in law of the parties to a marriage where that child was created by the gametes of the parties notwithstanding that he was carried in the womb of a surrogate mother.

CASE C

Where
(a) either
     (i)   a declaration that the alleged parent is a parent of the child in question (or a declaration which has that effect) is in force under

Section 56 of the Family Law Act 1986, or

    (ii) a declarator by a Court in Scotland that the alleged parent of the child in question (or a declarator which has that effect) is in force, and

(b) the child has not subsequently been adopted.

CASE D

Where

(a) a declaration to the effect that the alleged parent is one of the parents of the child in question has been made under Section 27 of the Act, and

(b) the child has not been adopted.

   Reference is made below to applications made under Section 27 of the Act.

CASE E

Where

(a) the child is habitually resident in Scotland,

(b) the Child Support Officer is satisfied that one or other of the presumptions set out in Section 5(1) of the Law Reform (Parent and Child) (Scotland) Act 1986 applies, and

(c) the child has not subsequently been adopted.

CASE F

Where

(a) the alleged parent has been found, or adjudged, to be the father of the child in question

    (i) in proceedings before any Court in England and Wales which are relevant proceedings for the purposes of Section 12 of the Civil Evidence Act 1968, or

    (ii) in affiliation proceedings before any Court in the United Kingdom,

(whether or not he offered any defence to the allegation of paternity) and that finding or adjudication still subsists, and

(b) the child has not subsequently been adopted.

Under Section 27 of the Act where a person denies that he is a parent of a child in question and the Child Support Officer is not satisfied that the case falls within any of the cases set out above, then either the Secretary of State or the person with care may apply to the Court for a declaration that the person is the parent of the child. As has been seen in Chapter 19 such an application will be initially allocated to the Magistrates' Court, but may be transferred therefrom pursuant to the criteria within the Children Act (Allocation of Proceedings) Order 1991. The Secretary of State may initiate similar proceedings for a declaration of parentage in Scotland under Section 28 of the Act.

Where a Child Support Officer is satisfied that the circumstances do fall within one of the cases set out above then he may make an assessment on the assumption that the person concerned is the parent of the child in question. A parent aggrieved by the making of such an assessment may seek a review in the usual way [see Chapter 25] and may appeal the result of such a review under Section 20 of the Act. By virtue of The Child Support Appeals (Jurisdiction of Courts) Order 1993 (made under Section 45 of the Act) such an appeal will, exceptionally, be initially allocated to the Magistrates' Court, and may be transferred therefrom pursuant to the criteria within the Children Act (Allocation of Proceedings) Order 1991. It is possible to contemplate the slightly curious scenario whereby a declaration of parentage is made in the Magistrates' Court under Section 27 of the Act; the Child Support Officer makes an assessment against the person found to be the parent; the person seeks a review of that decision which is refused; and the person then appeals to the same Magistrates' Court against that decision. This is likely only to be of theoretical interest for, undoubtedly, the original finding would amount to res judicata or issue estoppel in the later appeal.

A person alleged to be a parent of a child is under a limited obligation to provide information and evidence under Regulation 2 of the Information Regulations [see Chapter 23].

CHAPTER 27

Collection, payment and enforcement

I COLLECTION AND PAYMENT

The basic principles

By Section 4(2) and Section 7(3) of the Act the person with care, the absent parent, or in a case proceeding under Section 7, the child, may, in a non-benefit case, apply to the Agency for
(a) the collection of Child Support maintenance payable in accordance with a maintenance assessment, and/or
(b) the enforcement of the obligation to pay such maintenance in accordance with the assessment.

The Agency has a complete discretion as to whether it accepts an application for collection or enforcement.

In a benefit case proceeding under Section 6 of the Act the Agency will automatically assume responsibility for collection and enforcement.

The detail

By Section 29(1) of the Act the Secretary of State is entitled to make arrangements for the collection of maintenance in those cases where the Agency has agreed to undertake collection and/or enforcement, or in those benefit cases proceeding under Section 6 of the Act.

By Section 29(2) where a maintenance assessment is made under the Act payments of maintenance under the assessment shall be made in accordance with Regulations made by the Secretary of State.

Unlike Section 29(1) the phraseology of Section 29(2) suggests that it is within the power of the Secretary of State to make Regulations governing the payment of maintenance even in those cases where no application has been made for a collection and/or enforcement service pursuant to Section 4(2) or Section 7(3) of the Act.

This possible ambiguity is perpetuated in the Collection Regulations. By Regulation 2 it is provided that the Secretary of State is entitled to specify as to how maintenance is to be paid in a case **to which Section 29 of the Act applies**.

As has been seen, Section 29(1) of the Act provides that the Secretary of State is entitled to make arrangements for the collection of maintenance where the case proceeds under Section 6 or where a request has been made under Section 4(2) or Section 7(3) for a collection service. It has also been seen however that Section 29(2) is of general application to all maintenance assessments.

The question that therefore arises is this: do the Collection Regulations have a general application or are they confined to benefit cases and those cases where a collection and/or enforcement service has been requested?

In the D.S.S. handbook *Child Support: a new approach* it would appear that the narrower interpretation is favoured. It is stated at Paragraph 92:

> "If neither of these criteria applies, the timing, form and method of payment will be a private matter between the parties themselves, though either party may request a collection service at any time."

By contrast, Paragraph 6.2.1 of the D.S.S. consultation document published in November 1991 suggests that the Regulations are of general application.

The issue is probably only of theoretical interest, for it is plain that if a private arrangement between the parties is not working satisfactorily then either party may seek a collection and/or enforcement service in which event, incontrovertibly, the Collection Regulations would apply.

Regulation 2 of the Collection Regulations provides that the Secretary of State may specify that payments of Child Support maintenance shall be made by the person liable to make payments of maintenance either to the person caring for the child; or to the child himself where an application has been made under Section 7; or to, or through, the Secretary of State; or to, or through, such other person as the Secretary of State may specify. This latter provision enabling payment to be made to a third party is, according to Paragraph 6.2.4.1 of the Consultation Document, intended to enable payments to be received by the partner of an incapacitated person with care, or to facilitate payments where the person with care does not want any contact with the absent parent but does not want the Agency to collect on her behalf.

By Regulation 3 the Secretary of State is empowered to specify that maintenance is payable either by standing order, or by any like arrangement, or by cheque or postal order, or by cash. The Secretary of State is also entitled to direct that a person liable to make payments of maintenance is to take all reasonable steps to open an account from which payments under the assessment should be made in accordance with such method of payment as he may specify. These provisions closely mirror the provisions of the Maintenance Enforcement Act 1991 which governs all Court orders for maintenance.

The Secretary of State is entitled to specify the day and interval by reference to which payments are to be made and may vary such day or interval. In specifying the day and interval the Secretary of State is required to have regard all the circumstances, and in particular to the needs of the payee, the day and interval by reference to which the income of the person making the payments is normally received, and to such period as is necessary to enable cheques to clear (Regulation 4). Similarly, the Secretary of State is entitled to specify the method by which payments are made by him to a person with care in circumstances where the payments are made through the Secretary of State (Regulation 5).

The Collection Regulations do not specify the sanction that any absent parent may face in the event that he fails to comply with a direction as to the method of payment. As will be seen, there are robust sanctions applicable to parents who fail to make payments. It is unclear, however, what sanction, if any, a parent faces in the event that he deliberately defies a direction that he makes his payments in a certain way (e.g. by standing order) and persists in making payments in another way (e.g. in cash). His defiance would not amount to a contempt of Court and does not amount to an offence under the Act or the Regulations.

Fees

Under the Fees Regulations there is a fee of £34.00 for the collection service although this is not payable by certain persons who are taken as not being in a position to pay. Reference should be made to the Regulations.

II ENFORCEMENT

The basic principles

The powers of the Agency to enforce assessments against defaulting parents are wide and far reaching. Remarkably, the Agency has the power to make an attachment of earnings order against a defaulting parent without the intervention of a Court. In this respect the legislation goes one step further even than the Community Charge Enforcement Regulations whereunder a local authority can of its own motion make an attachment of earnings order against a defaulter, but only after a Court has made a "liability order" against that defaulter (see *R v Leicester Justices ex parte Barrow [1991] 2 Q.B. 260*).

Where the Agency decides that it is inappropriate to make an attachment of earnings order, or has concluded that such an order is not effective as a means for securing payment, then it may apply to a Magistrates' Court for a "liability order" against the defaulting party. Once a liability order has been made the Agency may enforce the arrears of maintenance by distress and sale of the defaulting person's goods. Alternatively, the arrears may be enforced in County Court proceedings by means of a garnishee or charging order. Where these methods of enforcement have not resulted in discharge of the arrears then the Magistrates' Court may commit the defaulting person to prison provided that it is proved that the failure to pay arises from the defaulter's wilful refusal or culpable neglect. As in proceedings by way of Judgment Summons under Section 5 of the Debtors Act 1848 the maximum term of imprisonment is 6 weeks. In the decision of *Woodley v Woodley [1992] 2 FLR 417* it was held that proof of such wilful refusal or culpable neglect had to be demonstrated to the criminal standard, namely beyond a reasonable doubt.

The detail

1. Deduction from earnings

By Section 31 of the Act the Agency is entitled to make a "deduction from earnings order" against a liable person. By Section 31(3) the order may be made to secure payment of arrears, or future payments, or a combination of these. It is not necessary for the liable person to be in default before the power to make such an order arises. The principles applicable in determining the amount to be deducted are very similar to those applicable under the Attachment of Earnings Act 1972.

By Regulations 8 and 10 of the Collection Regulations the Agency may prescribe the rate at which deductions are to be made from the liable person's net earnings; and the period by reference to which that rate is set; but in any event shall not provide that the amount so deducted shall reduce a person's disposable income below his protected income level less the prescribed minimum amount [see Chapter 17].

By Regulation 17 the Secretary of State shall review a deduction from earnings order where there is a change in the amount of the maintenance assessment, or where any arrears or interest on arrears payable under the order are paid off.

By Regulation 18 the Secretary of State may, whether on a review under Regulation 17 or otherwise, vary a deduction of earnings order so as to include any amount which may be included in such an order, or to exclude or decrease any such amount, or to make directions as to the substitution of a different employer of the person in question.

A liable person in respect of whom a deduction from earnings order has been made may appeal to the Magistrates' Court on the grounds that the order is defective, or that the payments in question do not constitute earnings. The Court hearing such an appeal may, where it is satisfied that the appeal should be allowed, quash the order, or specify which, if any, of the payments in question do not constitute earnings (Regulation 22).

There are detailed provisions as to the obligations of employers when presented with a deduction from earnings order and reference should be made to the Regulations.

By Section 32(8) and Regulations 15, 16, 19 and 25, if a liable person fails to provide the necessary information as to his employment, or if an employer fails to comply with the provisions of a deduction from earnings order then the person or the employer, as the case may be, shall be guilty of an offence.

2. Liability orders

By Section 33 of the Act where a person who is liable to make payments of maintenance fails to make such payments and it appears to the Agency that it is inappropriate to make a deduction from earnings order against that person because, for example, he is not employed, or, although such a deduction from earnings order has been made against him, it has proved ineffective as a means of securing that payments are made in accordance with the assessment, then the Secretary of State may apply to a Magistrates' Court for a liability order against the liable person. On an application for a liability order the Court shall not question the maintenance assessment under which there was default in payment of the maintenance. By Regulation 27 the liable person must be given at least 7 days notice of the Agency's intention to apply for a liability order. The notice must set out the amount of the arrears and of any interest payable in respect of those arrears.

By Regulation 28(2) there is a limitation period of 6 years in respect of arrears.

In *R v Leicester Justices ex parte Barrow [ibid]* Lord Donaldson of Lymington M.R. said in respect of liability orders sought under the community charge legislation:

"Mr and Mrs Barrow live at 57, Alenson Close, Leicester and each was admittedly liable to pay a Community Charge of £405 for the year 1990/91, the charge being payable by 10 instalments. They fell into arrears and the Leicester City Council issued a summons seeking what is known as a liability order: See Regulation 29 of the Community Charges (Administration and Enforcement) Regulations 1989. The beauty of a liability order from the point of view of local authorities is that (a) it subjects the community charge payer to an obligation, if asked, to provide the local authority with information as to the identity of his employer and his sources of income and (b) entitles the local authority of its own motion and without the intervention of a Court to make an Attachment of Earnings Order."

Under the Child Support Act the beauty of the liability order is that it enables the Agency to enforce arrears of Child Support maintenance by distress without further intervention of the Court, or to proceed directly to garnishee or charging order proceedings, or to institute proceedings for committal to prison.

By Regulation 29 of the Collection Regulations a liability order made by the Sheriff in Scotland, or a corresponding order made by a Court in Northern Ireland, shall not be enforced in England or Wales unless it has been registered in England or Wales in accordance with the provisions of part I of the Maintenance Orders Act 1950.

3. Distress

By Section 35 of the Act where a liability order has been made against a person in default the Agency may levy the appropriate amount by distress and sale of the defaulting person's goods. As in proceedings for distress under the County Courts Act 1981, or by way of fieri facias in the High Court, goods necessary for the use of the person in his employment business or vocation, or clothing, bedding, furniture, household equipment and provisions necessary for satisfying basic domestic needs are exempt. Money or similar securities are likewise exempt.

By Regulation 30 of the Collection Regulations distress may be made anywhere in England or Wales and shall not be deemed unlawful on account of any defect or want of form in the order. By Regulation 30(4) if, before any goods are seized, the arrears and any charges arising from the distress are paid or tendered to the Agency then the Agency shall accept the amount and the levy shall not proceed. Similarly, if payment is made after seizure, but before sale, then the payment shall be accepted and the goods shall not be sold. By Regulation 31 any person aggrieved by such a distress may appeal to the Magistrates' Court. If the Court is satisfied that the distress was irregular then it may order the goods to be returned, or may order compensation, or may order the Agency to desist from proceeding with the distress in the manner giving rise to the irregularity.

4. Imprisonment

By Section 40 of the Act, where the Secretary of State has sought to levy by means of distress or to enforce by means of garnishee proceedings in the County Court pursuant to Section 36 of the Act, and the amount remains unpaid, then he may apply for a committal to prison of the person in default. By Section 40(2) on any such application the Court shall in the presence of the person in default enquire as to his means and as to whether the failure to pay arises from his wilful refusal or culpable neglect. The Court **may** only sentence him to imprisonment provided that it is of the opinion that there has been such wilful refusal or culpable neglect. The Court is empowered to issue a suspended sentence. Regulations 33 to 34 set out the provisions in relation to the form of application and the form of the warrant of commitment. As has been stated, it is incumbent on the Agency, when prosecuting such an application, to demonstrate to the criminal standard of proof that there has been wilful refusal or culpable neglect on the part of the defaulting party (*Woodley v Woodley (ibid)*).

It is interesting to observe that while the Child Support scheme strives to eliminate judicial discretion wherever possible, such discretion is retained when consideration is being given to the imposition of the ultimate sanction.

III COLLECTION AND ENFORCEMENT OF OTHER FORMS OF MAINTENANCE

By Section 30 of the Act, where the Secretary of State is arranging for the collection of any payments under Section 29 or under Section 30(2), he may also arrange for the collection of any periodical payments or secured periodical payments of a prescribed kind which are payable to or for the benefit of any person who falls within a prescribed category.

Section 30(2) provides that the Secretary of State may arrange for the collection of any periodical payments or secured periodical payments of a prescribed kind which are payable for the benefit of the child even though he is not arranging for the collection of Child Support maintenance with respect to that child. However, by the Transitional Provisions Order 1992 this Section will not be brought into force on 5th April 1993, unlike the vast majority of the Act, and there is no date appointed for its coming into force. It is understood that there are no proposals for bringing this subsection into force.

Under the Collection and Enforcement of Other Forms of Maintenance Regulations it is provided, by Regulation 2, that where

(a) any payments are made under a maintenance order made under Section 8(6) (an order by way of "top-up"), or under Section 8(7) (an order providing for school or training fees) or under Section 8(8) (orders providing for the provisions of expenses relating to disability), or

(b) any periodical payments are made under a maintenance order which are payable to or for the benefit of a spouse or former spouse who is the person with care of the child in respect of whom a child maintenance assessment is in force and of which the Agency has arranged a collection service, or

(c) any periodical payments are made under a maintenance order payable to or for the benefit of a former child of the family of the person against whom the order is made, that child having his home with the person with care (e.g. orders against step-fathers),

then the Agency may deploy the full array of its collection and enforcement powers to enforce such other forms of maintenance.

Accordingly if a parent has sought a collection service in relation to child maintenance payable pursuant to an assessment then she may seek collection and enforcement of her own personal order for periodical payments from her former husband; and this will be undertaken by the Agency without the necessity of further intervention by a Court.

Indeed, it would appear that it is open to the Agency to insist on enforcing by means of its own procedures a personal periodical payments order in favour of a former wife in circumstances where it is collecting Child Support maintenance whether or not the payee of such an order seeks such enforcement facilities.

The opportunity to invoke the assistance of the Agency in enforcing orders for payments between former spouses will require advisers to consider most carefully whether or not, during the transitional period, they should be making agreements followed by consent orders for child maintenance, or whether they should be invoking the assessment procedure offered by the Agency.

CHAPTER 28

Arrears and interest

The basic principle

Where a parent falls into arrears then he will be liable to pay interest thereon at 1% over bank base rate.

The detail

By Section 41 of the Act, where the Agency has been authorised to collect maintenance under Section 4(2) or Section 7(3) of the Act, or is collecting maintenance in a benefit case under Section 6 of the Act, and the absent parent has failed to make one or more payments of maintenance, then the absent parent shall be liable to make payment of interest with respect to the arrears.

By Section 41(2) where the Secretary of State recovers arrears he may retain them to such extent as may be prescribed if he is satisfied that the amount of any benefit paid to the person with care of any child in question would have been less had the absent parent not been in arrear. In other words, if the benefit was augmented to reflect the default in payment by the absent parent then, not surprisingly, the Secretary of State may retain those arrears pro tanto.

The provisions of the Act with respect to the collection and enforcement of maintenance as set out in Chapter 27 apply equally to the collection and enforcement of interest.

The Arrears Regulations set out the provisions for regulating the recovery of arrears and interest. Regulation 2 provides that, before taking action with regard to arrears, the Agency shall serve an arrears notice on the absent parent setting out the amounts of maintenance due and not paid and, in general terms, the legislative provisions as to arrears and interest.

By Regulation 3 interest is payable on arrears arising after the payment date and shall be payable until the date when the arrears are discharged.

However, by Regulation 4 an absent parent is acquitted of liability to pay interest if he did not know, and could not reasonably have been expected to know, of the existence of the arrears, or where the arrears have arisen solely in consequence of an operational or administrative error on the part of the Secretary of State or a Child Support Officer.

By Regulation 6 the rate of interest is set at 1% above the median bank base rate prevailing from time to time calculated on a daily basis. It is simple, not compound interest (i.e. there is no interest charged on outstanding interest).

By Regulation 7 the arrears shall be paid to the person specified under Regulation 2 of the Collection Regulations as though they were payments of child maintenance. However, where the Agency has been authorised to recover maintenance in a benefit case under Section 6 and Income Support is paid to or in respect of the parent with care then the interest may be retained by the Agency, but with discretion to advance the interest to the parent with care if the Secretary of State considers that had the defaulting absent parent made payments of child maintenance then the parent with care would not have been entitled to Income Support.

By Regulation 9 where a maintenance assessment is or has been in force, and where there are arrears of Child Support maintenance, the Agency may attribute any payment of Child Support maintenance made by an absent parent to Child Support maintenance due as it thinks fit. Accordingly it is open to the Agency, where there are arrears, to attribute payments that are made either to the satisfaction of those arrears or to the satisfaction of current sums falling due, as the Agency thinks appropriate. In the light of its decision it may then proceed to enforce accordingly.

CHAPTER 29

Adjustment and modification of assessments

I ADJUSTMENT

The basic principle

A Child Support Officer may adjust an assessment having retrospective effect so as to take into account, and to provide for payment of, arrears thereby created.

The detail

By Regulation 10 of the Arrears Regulations where a new or fresh assessment has retrospective effect the amount payable under that new or fresh assessment may be adjusted by a Child Support Officer in order to take account of the retrospective effect of the assessment.

The Child Support Officer may make such adjustment as he considers appropriate in the circumstances of the case, but, in the case of a new (i.e. original) assessment the Child Support Officer shall not increase the amount payable by an amount more than one-and-a-half times the amount of that original assessment; and similarly, in the case of a fresh assessment (i.e. replacing an earlier assessment) he shall not adjust the amount payable by an amount more than one-and-a-half times the difference between the amount payable under the earlier assessment and the amount payable under the fresh assessment.

In a case

(a) which does not fall within Section 41 of the Act, (i.e. where it is not a benefit case nor a case where a collection service has been authorised), and

(b) where there has been a failure of a parent fully to make at least one payment of maintenance due, and

(c) where the payments of maintenance have involved over-payment or under-payment, but

(d) there has been no total failure to make any individual payment,

then the amount payable under an assessment may, by virtue of Regulation 10(2), be adjusted for the purpose of taking into account such over-payments or under-payments by such amount as the Child Support Officer thinks appropriate.

The Child Support Officer shall not, in such circumstances, adjust the amount payable under the assessment by more than one-and-a-half times greater than the mean over-payment or under-payment.

The mean over-payment or under-payment is defined by Regulation 10(6) as the total excess or deficit divided by the number of occasions on which there have been over-payments or under-payments made.

Example: if over 10 weeks a parent underpays by a total of £100.00 then the mean under-payment is £10.00. The Child Support Officer is, accordingly, entitled to augment the assessment by not more than £15.00 per week to take account of such mean under-payment.

II MODIFICATION OF ASSESSMENTS DURING THE TRANSITIONAL PERIOD

The basic principle

Where in a benefit case
(a) there is already in existence prior to 5th April 1993 an arrangement for the payment of maintenance,
(b) the absent parent has a second family,
(c) the formula amount is £60.00 p.w. or less, and
(d) the formula amount exceeds the existing arrangement by at least £20.00,
then for a period of one year the parent will only be obliged to pay at a rate of the existing arrangement plus £20.00.

The underlying principle is that where an absent parent has established a second family it will, generally, be necessary to mitigate the effect of the increase occasioned by an assessment over existing arrangements for a period of one year, so that the absent parent has time to adjust to the new maintenance regime and to arrange his finances accordingly.

The detail

By Paragraph 7 of the Transitional Provisions Order, where there is in force on 4th April 1993 in respect of all the qualifying children in respect of whom an application for a maintenance assessment is made, one or more maintenance orders or agreements; and the absent parent is responsible for maintaining at least one child residing with him other than the children in respect of whom the application is made; and the formula amount is not more than £60.00; and the formula amount exceeds the amounts payable under the orders or agreements by more than £20.00 per week; then the assessment will be modified.

As has been explained in Chapter 19, it is only in a benefit case that during the transitional period a maintenance assessment can be made by the Agency where there is in force a maintenance order; for by virtue of Paragraph 2 of the Transitional Provisions Order no application under Section 4 of the Act or Section 7 of the Act may be made during the transitional period while there is in force a maintenance order in respect of a qualifying child.

The modified amount payable where the above criteria are satisfied is, by virtue of Paragraph 6, the amount which is £20.00 greater than the aggregate weekly amount payable under the order or agreement. The modified amount shall be paid, by virtue of Paragraph 8, for a period of one year beginning with the date upon which the original assessment takes effect.

The above provisions do not apply to an interim assessment made under Section 12 of the Act (Paragraph 7(2)) [see Chapter 21].

CHAPTER 30

The impact on the wider issue of ancillary relief

It is the opinion of the Government that assessments under the Act will generally produce higher awards of child maintenance than have conventionally been awarded by the Courts.

Even where an assessment is not sought, and an agreement is made between the parties, it is likely, for the reasons set out in Chapter 19, that the quantum of maintenance agreed will be arrived at by reference to the principles underlying the Act.

The Child Support Act will therefore have some impact on the wider ancillary relief issue.

Where, as usual following the breakdown of marriage, resources are stretched, the increase in periodical provision for the children will be likely to lead to adjustments to the other limbs of an ancillary relief settlement.

Conventional periodical payment orders to wives

Where the former wife is to be in receipt of periodical payments for herself then probably there will be a reduction of the sum that she would have otherwise have received for herself. In such cases settlement is usually reached on the basis of a global family budget, which is then apportioned between the constituent members of the family. Unless the higher figures for child maintenance lead the Court to embrace a higher figure for the global family budget, the result will be to lower the figure for the former wife in inverse ratio to the increase for the children.

Hanlon orders

A more difficult scenario is where a wife seeks to accept a low level of child maintenance, or even no maintenance (as happened in *Hanlon v Hanlon [1978] 1 WLR 592*) in order to secure the outright transfer of the family home to her on a clean break basis.

It has to be said at once that even prior to the passage of the Act, where a wife entered into such an arrangement in circumstances where she was in receipt of benefit, or following the agreement went on to benefit, then such an arrangement did not bind the D.S.S. (see *Hully v Thompson [1981] 2 FLR 53*). The D.S.S. was entitled to pursue the father as a liable relative for a contribution to that benefit notwithstanding the terms of the agreement.

Accordingly the passage of the Act changes nothing in benefit cases.

In non-benefit cases it remains open to the parties to agree a lower rate of maintenance than the formula would produce, and to incorporate such an agreement within a consent order under Section 8(5) of the Act [see Chapter 19]. During the transitional period the existence of such an order would prevent access to the Agency.

If the parties want to agree that no maintenance will be sought, then such an agreement will be void under Section 9(4) of the Act. There will be nothing to stop a parent from making such an agreement, receiving the house, and then proceeding to the Agency for an assessment. In such a case consideration would have to be given to appealing the original order on the grounds of mistake, fraud, non-disclosure, or a supervening fundamental change of circumstances. But the problem is not new. Where such an agreement was made under the old regime, as happened in *Hanlon (ibid)*, it was, as the judgment of Ormrod LJ makes clear, non-binding, being void under Section 34 of the Matrimonial Causes Act 1973. Moreover, it is and was trite law that a child maintenance claim can never be dismissed by order of the Court (see *Dipper v Dipper [1981] Fam 31*).

It is plain that if entered into such an agreement would violate the principle of joint responsibility for maintenance of children set out in Section 1(1) of the Act. To suggest that the provision of absolute ownership of a dwelling to a mother (as opposed to part ownership where occupation is assured) meets such a responsibility would be an argument of considerable sophistry. Such an argument was, in effect, rejected in *Hully v Thompson (ibid)* where it was held that the obligation to maintain imposed by Section 17 of the Supplementary Benefits Act 1976 could not be displaced by a consent arrangement between the parties. It would be unwise for advisers to suggest that any such agreement should be made in the future.

It has been suggested by certain writers (e.g. David Burrows at *(1992) Fam Law 342*) that in order to mitigate the loss of the opportunity to make such an agreement parties may care to consider making an arrangement whereby the amounts of any Child Support maintenance paid by the absent parent are refundable to him by the parent with care, are charged on the property on a *Mesher* or *Martin* basis and are ultimately repaid to him. While there is no doubt that this would be jurisdictionally possible, it is suggested that any such arrangement would be inapt and unduly complex if only for the reason that if it is appropriate for a husband to retain an interest in a property then that should be achieved on the conventional fractional basis. The retention of such an interest on a *Martin* basis does not offend against the principle of the clean break (see *Clutton v Clutton [1991] 1 WLR 359*). It also has to be asked whether such an arrangement offends public policy as enshrined in the Act in circumstances where it is plain that the Child Support scheme does not envisage child maintenance being refundable to the payer.

Tax relief

By virtue of Section 62 Finance (No 2) Act 1992 payments made under an assessment in a non-benefit case will attract tax relief. If the assessment is the first legal obligation to pay maintenance then relief will be given under the "new" rules as enshrined in Section 347B Income and Corporation Taxes Act 1988 (i.e. up to £1,720). If the assessment replaces an existing order or agreement which attracted relief under the "old" rules as enshrined in Section 39 Finance Act 1988 (i.e. relief up to the amount paid in the tax year 1988-89), then such relief will continue to be given to the payments made pursuant to the assessment.

In a benefit case, where the Agency collects and retains the payments under Section 6 of the Act, the payments made pursuant to the assessment will not attract relief under the principle established in *McBurnie v Tacey [1984] STC 347*.

APPENDIX 1:

Child Support statutory material

Note: The text follows the statutory material obtained from Her Majesty's Stationery Office. Where the material is only available in draft form at the time of printing this book, this draft material has been included.

CONTENTS

The Child Support Commissioners (Procedure) Regulations 1992 (S.I. 1992 No. 2640)

The High Court Distribution of Business Order 1993 (S.I. 1993 DRAFT)

The Children (Allocation of Proceedings) (Amendment) Order 1993 (S.I. 1993 DRAFT)

The Chi}d Support Appeals (Jurisdiction of Courts Order 1993 (S.I. 1993 DRAFT)

The Child Maintenance (Written Agreements) Order 1993 (S.I. 1993 DRAFT)

The Children (Admissibility of Hearsay Evidence) Order 1993 (S.I. 1993 DRAFT)

The Maintenance Orders (Backdating) Order 1993 (S.I. 1993 DRAFT)

The Family Proceedings (Amendment No. 3) Rules 1993 (S.I. 1993 DRAFT)

Child Support Act 1991

ARRANGEMENT OF SECTIONS

Collection and enforcement

Special cases

Jurisdiction

Miscellaneous and supplemental

Child Support Act 1991

1991 CHAPTER 48

An Act to make provision for the assessment, collection and enforcement of periodical maintenance payable by certain parents with respect to children of theirs who are not in their care; for the collection and enforcement of certain other kinds of maintenance; and for connected purposes. [25th July 1991]

B E IT ENACTED by the Queen's most Excellent Majesty, by and with the advice and consent of the Lords Spiritual and Temporal, and Commons, in this present Parliament assembled, and by the authority of the same, as follows:—

The basic principles

1.—(1)   For the purposes of this Act, each parent of a qualifying child is responsible for maintaining him.

(2) For the purposes of this Act, an absent parent shall be taken to have met his responsibility to maintain any qualifying child of his by making periodical payments of maintenance with respect to the child of such amount, and at such intervals, as may be determined in accordance with the provisions of this Act.

(3) Where a maintenance assessment made under this Act requires the making of periodical payments, it shall be the duty of the absent parent with respect to whom the assessment was made to make those payments.

2   Where, in any case which falls to be dealt with under this Act, the Secretary of State or any child support officer is considering the exercise of any discretionary power conferred by this Act, he shall have regard to the welfare of any child likely to be affected by his decision.

3.—(1) A child is a "qualifying child" if—

(a) one of his parents is, in relation to him, an absent parent; or

(b) both of his parents are, in relation to him, absent parents.

(2) The parent of any child is an "absent parent", in relation to him, if—

(a) that parent is not living in the same household with the child; and

(b) the child has his home with a person who is, in relation to him, a person with care.

(3) person is a "person with care", in relation to any child, if he is a person—

    (a) with whom the child has his home;

    (b) who usually provides day to day care for the child (whether exclusively or in conjunction with any other person); and

    (c) who does not fall within a prescribed category of person.

(4) The Secretary of State shall not, under subsection (3)(c), prescribe as a category—

    (a) parents;

    (b) guardians;

    (c) persons in whose favour residence orders under section 8 of the Children Act 1989 are in force;

    (d) in Scotland, persons having the right to custody of a child.

(5) For the purposes of this Act there may be more than one person with care in relation to the same qualifying child.

(6) Periodical payments which are required to be paid in accordance with a maintenance assessment are referred to in this Act as "child support maintenance".

(7) Expressions are defined in this section only for the purposes of this Act.

4.—(1) A person who is, in relation to any qualifying child or any qualifying children, either the person with care or the absent parent may apply to the Secretary of State for a maintenance assessment to be made under this Act with respect to that child, or any of those children.

(2) Where a maintenance assessment has been made in response to an application under this section the Secretary of State may, if the person with care or absent parent with respect to whom the assessment was made applies to him under this subsection, arrange for—

    (a) the collection of the child support maintenance payable in accordance with the assessment;

    (b) the enforcement of the obligation to pay child support maintenance in accordance with the assessment.

(3) Where an application under subsection (2) for the enforcement of the obligation mentioned in subsection (2)(b) authorises the Secretary of State to take steps to enforce that obligation whenever he considers it necessary to do so, the Secretary of State may act accordingly.

(4) A person who applies to the Secretary of State under this section shall, so far as that person reasonably can, comply with such regulations as may be made by the Secretary of State with a view to the Secretary of State or the child support officer being provided with the information which is required to enable—

    (a) the absent parent to be traced (where that is necessary);

    (b) the amount of child support maintenance payable by the absent parent to be assessed; and

    (c) that amount to be recovered from the absent parent.

(5) Any person who has applied to the Secretary of State under this section may at any time request him to cease acting under this section.

(6) It shall be the duty of the Secretary of State to comply with any request made under subsection (5) (but subject to any regulations made under

subsection (8)).

(7) The obligation to provide information which is imposed by subsection (4)—

    (a) shall not apply in such circumstances as may be prescribed; and

    (b) may, in such circumstances as may be prescribed, be waived by the Secretary of State.

(8) The Secretary of State may by regulations make such incidental, supplemental or transitional provision as he thinks appropriate with respect to cases in which he is requested to cease to act under this section.

(9) No application may be made under this section if there is in force with respect to the person with care and absent parent in question a maintenance assessment made in response to an application under section 6.

5.—(1) Where—

    (a) there is more than one person with care of a qualifying child; and

    (b) one or more, but not all, of them have parental responsibility for provisions. (or, in Scotland, parental rights over) the child;

no application may be made for a maintenance assessment with respect to the child by any of those persons who do not have parental responsibility for (or, in Scotland, parental rights over) the child.

(2) Where more than one application for a maintenance assessment is made with respect to the child concerned, only one of them may be proceeded with.

(3) The Secretary of State may by regulations make provision as to which of two or more applications for a maintenance assessment with respect to the same child is to be proceeded with.

6.—(1) Where income support, family credit or any other benefit of a prescribed kind is claimed by or in respect of, or paid to or in respect of, the parent of a qualifying child she shall, if—

    (a) she is a person with care of the child; and

    (b) she is required to do so by the Secretary of State,

authorise the Secretary of State to take action under this Act to recover child support maintenance from the absent parent.

(2) The Secretary of State shall not require a person ("the parent") to give him the authorisation mentioned in subsection (1) if he considers that there are reasonable grounds for believing that—

    (a) if the parent were to be required to give that authorisation; or

    (b) if she were to give it,

        there would be a risk of her, or of any child living with her, suffering harm or undue distress as a result.

(3) Subsection (2) shall not apply if the parent requests the Secretary of State to disregard it.

(4) The authorisation mentioned in subsection (1) shall extend to all children of the absent parent in relation to whom the parent first mentioned in subsection (1) is a person with care.

(5) That authorisation shall be given, without unreasonable delay, by completing and returning to the Secretary of State an application—

    (a) for the making of a maintenance assessment with respect to the qualifying child or qualifying children; and

(b) for the Secretary of State to take action under this Act to recover, on her behalf, the amount of child support maintenance so assessed.

(6) Such an application shall be made on a form ("a maintenance application form") provided by the Secretary of State.

(7) A maintenance application form shall indicate in general terms the effect of completing and returning it.

(8) Subsection (1) has effect regardless of whether any of the benefits mentioned there is payable with respect to any qualifying child.

(9) A person who is under the duty imposed by subsection (1) shall, so far as she reasonably can, comply with such regulations as may be made by the Secretary of State with a view to the Secretary of State or the child support officer being provided with the information which is required to enable—

(a) the absent parent to be traced;

(b) the amount of child support maintenance payable by the absent parent to be assessed; and

(c) that amount to be recovered from the absent parent.

(10) The obligation to provide information which is imposed by subsection (9)—

(a) shall not apply in such circumstances as may be prescribed; and

(b) may, in such circumstances as may be prescribed, be waived by the Secretary of State.

(11) A person with care who has authorised the Secretary of State under subsection (1) but who subsequently ceases to fall within that subsection may request the Secretary of State to cease acting under this section.

(12) It shall be the duty of the Secretary of State to comply with any request made under subsection (11) (but subject to any regulations made under subsection (13)).

(13) The Secretary of State may by regulations make such incidental or transitional provision as he thinks appropriate with respect to cases in which he is requested under subsection (11) to cease to act under this section.

(14) The fact that a maintenance assessment is in force with respect to a person with care shall not prevent the making of a new maintenance assessment with respect to her in response to an application under this section.

7.—(1) A qualifying child who has attained the age of 12 years and who is habitually resident in Scotland may apply to the Secretary of State for a maintenance assessment to be made with respect to him if—

(a) no such application has been made by a person who is, with respect to that child, a person with care or an absent parent; or

(b) the Secretary of State has not been authorised under section 6 to take action under this Act to recover child support maintenance from the absent parent (other than in a case where he has waived any requirement that he should be so authorised).

(2) An application made under subsection (1) shall authorise the Secretary of State to make a maintenance assessment with respect to any other children of the absent parent who are qualifying children in the care of the same

person as the child making the application.

(3) Where a maintenance assessment has been made in response to an application under this section the Secretary of State may, if the person with care, the absent parent with respect to whom the assessment was made or the child concerned applies to him under this subsection, arrange for—

(a) the collection of the child support maintenance payable in accordance with the assessment;

(b) the enforcement of the obligation to pay child support maintenance in accordance with the assessment.

(4) Where an application under subsection (3) for the enforcement of the obligation mentioned in subsection (3)(b) authorises the Secretary of State to take steps to enforce that obligation whenever he considers it necessary to do so, the Secretary of State may act accordingly.

(5) Where a child has asked the Secretary of State to proceed under this section, the person with care of the child, the absent parent and the child concerned shall, so far as they reasonably can, comply with such regulations as may be made by the Secretary of State with a view to the Secretary of State or the child support officer being provided with the information which is required to enable—

(a) the absent parent to be traced (where that is necessary);

(b) the amount of child support maintenance payable by the absent parent to be assessed; and

(c) that amount to be recovered from the absent parent.

(6) The child who has made the application (but not the person having care of him) may at any time request the Secretary of State to cease acting under this section.

(7) It shall be the duty of the Secretary of State to comply with any request made under subsection (6) (but subject to any regulations made under subsection (9)).

(8) The obligation to provide information which is imposed by subsection (5)—

(a) shall not apply in such circumstances as may be prescribed by the Secretary of State; and

(b) may, in such circumstances as may be so prescribed, be waived by the Secretary of State.

(9) The Secretary of State may by regulations make such incidental, supplemental or transitional provision as he thinks appropriate with respect to cases in which he is requested to cease to act under this section.

8.—(1) This subsection applies in any case where a child support officer would have jurisdiction to make a maintenance assessment with respect to a qualifying child and an absent parent of his on an application duly made by a person entitled to apply for such an assessment with respect to that child.

(2) Subsection (1) applies even though the circumstances of the case are such that a child support officer would not make an assessment if it were applied for.

(3) In any case where subsection (1) applies, no court shall exercise any power which it would otherwise have to make, vary or revive any maintenance

order in relation to the child and absent parent concerned.

(4) Subsection (3) does not prevent a court from revoking a maintenance order.

(5) The Lord Chancellor or in relation to Scotland the Lord Advocate may by order provide that, in such circumstances as may be specified by the order, this section shall not prevent a court from exercising any power which it has to make a maintenance order in relation to a child if—

  (a) a written agreement (whether or not enforceable) provides for the making, or securing, by an absent parent of the child of periodical payments to or for the benefit of the child; and

  (b) the maintenance order which the court makes is, in all material respects, in the same terms as that agreement.

(6) This section shall not prevent a court from exercising any power which it has to make a maintenance order in relation to a child if—

  (a) a maintenance assessment is in force with respect to the child;

  (b) the amount of the child support maintenance payable in accordance with the assessment was determined by reference to the alternative formula mentioned in paragraph 4(3) of Schedule 1; and

  (c) the court is satisfied that the circumstances of the case make it appropriate for the absent parent to make or secure the making of periodical payments under a maintenance order in addition to the child support maintenance payable by him in accordance with the maintenance assessment.

(7) This section shall not prevent a court from exercising any power which it has to make a maintenance order in relation to a child if—

  (a) the child is, will be or (if the order were to be made) would be receiving instruction at an educational establishment or undergoing training for a trade, profession or vocation (whether or not while in gainful employment); and

  (b) the order is made solely for the purposes of requiring the person making or securing the making of periodical payments fixed by the order to meet some or all of the expenses incurred in connection with the provision of the instruction or training.

(8) This section shall not prevent a court from exercising any power which it has to make a maintenance order in relation to a child if—

  (a) a disability living allowance is paid to or in respect of him; or

  (b) no such allowance is paid but he is disabled,

and the order is made solely for the purpose of requiring the person making or securing the making of periodical payments fixed by the order to meet some or all of any expenses attributable to the child's disability.

(9) For the purposes of subsection (8), a child is disabled if he is blind, deaf or dumb or is substantially and permanently handicapped by illness, injury, mental disorder or congenital deformity or such other disability as may be prescribed.

(10) This section shall not prevent a court from exercising any power which it has to make a maintenance order in relation to a child if the order is made against a person with care of the child.

(11) In this Act "maintenance order", in relation to any child, means an order which requires the making or securing of periodical payments to or for the benefit of the child and which is made under—

(a) Part II of the Matrimonial Causes Act 1973;

(b) the Domestic Proceedings and Magistrates' Courts Act 1978;

(c) Part III of the Matrimonial and Family Proceedings Act 1984;

(d) the Family Law (Scotland) Act 1985;

(e) Schedule 1 to the Children Act 1989; or

(f) any other prescribed enactment,

and includes any order varying or reviving such an order.

9.—(1) In this section "maintenance agreement" means any agreement for the making, or for securing the making, of periodical payments by way of maintenance, or in Scotland aliment, to or for the benefit of any child.

(2) Nothing in this Act shall be taken to prevent any person from entering into a maintenance agreement.

(3) The existence of a maintenance agreement shall not prevent any party to the agreement, or any other person, from applying for a maintenance assessment with respect to any child to or for whose benefit periodical payments are to be made or secured under the agreement.

(4) Where any agreement contains a provision which purports to restrict the right of any person to apply for a maintenance assessment, that provision shall be void.

(5) Where section 8 would prevent any court from making a maintenance order in relation to a child and an absent parent of his, no court shall exercise any power that it has to vary any agreement so as—

(a) to insert a provision requiring that absent parent to make or secure the making of periodical payments by way of maintenance, or in Scotland aliment, to or for the benefit of that child; or

(b) to increase the amount payable under such a provision.

10.—(1) Where an order of a kind prescribed for the purposes of this subsection is in force with respect to any qualifying child with respect to whom a maintenance assessment is made, the order—

(a) shall, so far as it relates to the making or securing of periodical payments, cease to have effect to such extent as may be determined in accordance with regulations made by the Secretary of State; or

(b) where the regulations so provide, shall, so far as it so relates, have effect subject to such modifications as may be so determined.

(2) Where an agreement of a kind prescribed for the purposes of this subsection is in force with respect to any qualifying child with respect to whom a maintenance assessment is made, the agreement—

(a) shall, so far as it relates to the making or securing of periodical payments, be unenforceable to such extent as may be determined in accordance with regulations made by the Secretary of State; or

(b) where the regulations so provide, shall, so far as it so relates, have effect subject to such modifications as may be so determined.

(3) Any regulations under this section may, in particular, make such

provision with respect to—

(a) any case where any person with respect to whom an order or agreement of a kind prescribed for the purposes of subsection (1) or (2) has effect applies to the prescribed court, before the end of the prescribed period, for the order or agreement to be varied in the light of the maintenance assessment and of the provisions of this Act;

(b) the recovery of any arrears under the order or agreement which fell due before the coming into force of the maintenance assessment,

as the Secretary of State considers appropriate and may provide that, in prescribed circumstances, an application to any court which is made with respect to an order of a prescribed kind relating to the making or securing of periodical payments to or for the benefit of a child shall be treated by the court as an application for the order to be revoked.

(4) The Secretary of State may by regulations make provision for—

(a) notification to be given by the child support officer concerned to the prescribed person in any case where that officer considers that the making of a maintenance assessment has affected, or is likely to affect, any order of a kind prescribed for the purposes of this subsection;

(b) notification to be given by the prescribed person to the Secretary of State in any case where a court makes an order which it considers has affected, or is likely to affect, a maintenance assessment.

(5) Rules may be made under section 144 of the Magistrates' Courts Act 1980 (rules of procedure) requiring any person who, in prescribed circumstances, makes an application to a magistrates' court for a maintenance order to furnish the court with a statement in a prescribed form, and signed by a child support officer, as to whether or not, at the time when the statement is made, there is a maintenance assessment in force with respect to that person or the child concerned.

In this subsection—

"maintenance order" means an order of a prescribed kind for the making or securing of periodical payments to or for the benefit of a child; and

"prescribed" means prescribed by the rules.

Maintenance assessments

11.—(1) Any application for a maintenance assessment made to the Secretary of State shall be referred by him to a child support officer whose duty it shall be to deal with the application in accordance with the provision made by or under this Act.

(2) The amount of child support maintenance to be fixed by any maintenance assessment shall be determined in accordance with the provisions of Part I of Schedule 1.

(3) Part II of Schedule 1 makes further provision with respect to maintenance assessments.

12.—(1) Where it appears to a child support officer who is required to make a maintenance assessment that he does not have sufficient information to enable him to make an assessment in accordance with the provision made by or under this Act, he may make an interim maintenance assessment.

(2) The Secretary of State may by regulations make provision as to interim maintenance assessments.

(3) The regulations may, in particular, make provision as to—

    (a) the procedure to be followed in making an interim maintenance assessment; and

    (b) the basis on which the amount of child support maintenance fixed by an interim assessment is to be calculated.

(4) Before making any interim assessment a child support officer shall, if it is reasonably practicable to do so, give written notice of his intention to make such an assessment to—

    (a) the absent parent concerned;

    (b) the person with care concerned; and

    (c) where the application for a maintenance assessment was made under section 7, the child concerned.

(5) Where a child support officer serves notice under subsection (4), he shall not make the proposed interim assessment before the end of such period as may be prescribed.

Child support officers

13.—(1) The Secretary of State shall appoint persons (to be known as child support officers) for the purpose of exercising functions—

    (a) conferred on them by this Act, or by any other enactment; or

    (b) assigned to them by the Secretary of State.

(2) A child support officer may be appointed to perform only such functions as may be specified in his instrument of appointment.

(3) The Secretary of State shall appoint a Chief Child Support Officer.

(4) It shall be the duty of the Chief Child Support Officer to—

    (a) advise child support officers on the discharge of their functions in relation to making, reviewing or cancelling maintenance assessments;

    (b) keep under review the operation of the provision made by or under this Act with respect to making, reviewing or cancelling maintenance assessments; and

    (c) report to the Secretary of State annually, in writing, on the matters with which the Chief Child Support Officer is concerned.

(5) The Secretary of State shall publish, in such manner as he considers appropriate, any report which he receives under subsection (4)(c).

(6) Any proceedings (other than for an offence) in respect of any act or omission of a child support officer which, apart from this subsection, would fall to be brought against a child support officer resident in Northern Ireland may instead be brought against the Chief Child Support Officer.

(7) For the purposes of any proceedings brought by virtue of subsection (6), the acts or omissions of the child support officer shall be treated as the acts or omissions of the Chief Child Support Officer.

Information

14.—(1) The Secretary of State may make regulations requiring any information or evidence needed for the determination of any application under this Act, or any question arising in connection with such an application, or needed in connection with the collection or enforcement of child support or other maintenance under this Act, to be furnished—

    (a) by such persons as may be determined in accordance with regulations made by the Secretary of State; and

    (b) in accordance with the regulations.

(2) Where the Secretary of State has in his possession any information acquired by him in connection with his functions under any of the benefit Acts, he may—

    (a) make use of that information for purposes of this Act; or

    (b) disclose it to the Department of Health and Social Services for Northern Ireland for purposes of any enactment corresponding to this Act and having effect with respect to Northern Ireland.

(3) The Secretary of State may by regulations make provision authorising the disclosure by him or by child support officers, in such circumstances as may be prescribed, of such information held by them for purposes of this Act as may be prescribed.

(4) The provisions of Schedule 2 (which relate to information which is held for purposes other than those of this Act but which is required by the Secretary of State) shall have effect.

15.—(1) Where, in a particular case, the Secretary of State considers it appropriate to do so for the purpose of acquiring information which he or any child support officer requires for purposes of this Act, he may appoint a person to act as an inspector under this section.

(2) Every inspector shall be furnished with a certificate of his appointment.

(3) Without prejudice to his being appointed to act in relation to any other case, or being appointed to act for a further period in relation to the case in question, an inspector's appointment shall cease at the end of such period as may be specified.

(4) An inspector shall have power—

    (a) to enter at all reasonable times—

        (i) any specified premises, other than premises used solely as a dwelling-house; and

        (ii) any premises which are not specified but which are used by any specified person for the purpose of carrying on any trade, profession, vocation or business; and

    (b) to make such examination and enquiry there as he considers appropriate.

(5) An inspector exercising his powers may question any person aged 18 or over whom he finds on the premises.

(6) If required to do so by an inspector exercising his powers, any person who is or has been—

   (a) an occupier of the premises in question;

   (b) an employer or an employee working at or from those premises;

   (c) carrying on at or from those premises any trade, profession, vocation or business;

   (d) an employee or agent of any person mentioned in paragraphs (a) to (c),

shall furnish to the inspector all such information and documents as the inspector may reasonably require.

(7) No person shall be required under this section to answer any question or to give any evidence tending to incriminate himself or, in the case of a person who is married, his or her spouse.

(8) On applying for admission to any premises in the exercise of his powers, an inspector shall, if so required, produce his certificate.

(9) If any person—

   (a) intentionally delays or obstructs any inspector exercising his powers; or

   (b) without reasonable excuse, refuses or neglects to answer any question or furnish any information or to produce any document when required to do so under this section,

he shall be guilty of an offence and liable on summary conviction to a fine not exceeding level 3 on the standard scale.

(10) In this section—

"certificate" means a certificate of appointment issued under this section;

"inspector" means an inspector appointed under this section;

"powers" means powers conferred by this section; and

"specified" means specified in the certificate in question.

Reviews and appeals

16.—(1) The Secretary of State shall make such arrangements as he considers necessary to secure that, where any maintenance assessment has been in force for a prescribed period, the amount of child support maintenance fixed by that assessment ("the original assessment") is reviewed by a child support officer under this section as soon as is reasonably practicable after the end of that prescribed period.

(2) Before conducting any review under this section, the child support officer concerned shall give, to such persons as may be prescribed, such notice of the proposed review as may be prescribed.

(3) A review shall be conducted under this section as if a fresh application for a maintenance assessment had been made by the person in whose favour the original assessment was made.

(4) On completing any review under this section, the child support officer concerned shall make a fresh maintenance assessment, unless he is satisfied that the original assessment has ceased to have effect or should be brought to an end.

(5) Where a fresh maintenance assessment is made under subsection (4), it shall take effect—

(a) on the day immediately after the end of the prescribed period mentioned in subsection (1); or

(b) in such circumstances as may be prescribed, on such later date as may be determined in accordance with regulations made by the Secretary of State.

(6) The Secretary of State may by regulations prescribe circumstances (for example, where the maintenance assessment is about to terminate) in which a child support officer may decide not to conduct a review under this section.

17.—(1) Where a maintenance assessment is in force—

(a) the absent parent or person with care with respect to whom it was made; or

(b) where the application for the assessment was made under section 7, either of them or the child concerned,

may apply to the Secretary of State for the amount of child support maintenance fixed by that assessment ("the original assessment") to be reviewed under this section.

(2) An application under this section may be made only on the ground that, by reason of a change of circumstance since the original assessment was made, the amount of child support maintenance payable by the absent parent would be significantly different if it were to be fixed by a maintenance assessment made by reference to the circumstances of the case as at the date of the application.

(3) The child support officer to whom an application under this section has been referred shall not proceed unless, on the information before him, he considers that it is likely that he will be required by subsection (6) to make a fresh maintenance assessment if he conducts the review applied for.

(4) Before conducting any review under this section, the child support officer concerned shall give to such persons as may be prescribed, such notice of the proposed review as may be prescribed.

(5) A review shall be conducted under this section as if a fresh application for a maintenance assessment had been made by the person in whose favour the original assessment was made.

(6) On completing any review under this section, the child support officer concerned shall make a fresh maintenance assessment, unless—

(a) he is satisfied that the original assessment has ceased to have effect or should be brought to an end; or

(b) the difference between the amount of child support maintenance fixed by the original assessment and the amount that would be fixed if a fresh assessment were to be made as a result of the review is less than such amount as may be prescribed.

18.—(1) Where—

(a) an application for a maintenance assessment is refused; or

(b) an application, under section 17, for the review of a maintenance assessment which is in force is refused, the person who made that application may apply to the Secretary of State for the refusal to be reviewed.

(2) Where a maintenance assessment is in force—

(a) the absent parent or person with care with respect to whom it was made; or

(b) where the application for the assessment was made under section 7, either of them or the child concerned,

may apply to the Secretary of State for the assessment to be reviewed.

(3) Where a maintenance assessment is cancelled the appropriate person may apply to the Secretary of State for the cancellation to be reviewed.

(4) Where an application for the cancellation of a maintenance assessment is refused, the appropriate person may apply to the Secretary of State for the refusal to be reviewed.

(5) An application under this section shall give the applicant's reasons (in writing) for making it.

(6) The Secretary of State shall refer to a child support officer any application under this section which is duly made; and the child support officer shall conduct the review applied for unless in his opinion there are no reasonable grounds for supposing that the refusal, assessment or cancellation in question—

(a) was made in ignorance of a material fact;

(b) was based on a mistake as to a material fact;

(c) was wrong in law.

(7) The Secretary of State shall arrange for a review under this section to be conducted by a child support officer who played no part in taking the decision which is to be reviewed.

(8) Before conducting any review under this section, the child support officer concerned shall give to such persons as may be prescribed, such notice of the proposed review as may be prescribed.

(9) If a child support officer conducting a review under this section is satisfied that a maintenance assessment or (as the case may be) a fresh maintenance assessment should be made, he shall proceed accordingly.

(10) In making a maintenance assessment by virtue of subsection (9), a child support officer shall, if he is aware of any material change of circumstance since the decision being reviewed was taken, take account of that change of circumstance in making the assessment.

(11) The Secretary of State may make regulations—

(a) as to the manner in which applications under this section are to be made;

(b) as to the procedure to be followed with respect to such applications; and

(c) with respect to reviews conducted under this section.

(12) In this section "appropriate person" means—

(a) the absent parent or person with care with respect to whom the maintenance assessment in question was, or remains, in force; or

(b) where the application for that assessment was made under section 7, either of those persons or the child concerned.

19.—(1) Where a child support officer is not conducting a review under section 16, 17 or 18 but is nevertheless satisfied that a maintenance assessment which is in force is defective by reason of—

(a) having been made in ignorance of a material fact;

(b) having been based on a mistake as to a material fact; or

(c) being wrong in law,

he may make a fresh maintenance assessment on the assumption that the person in whose favour the original assessment was made has made a fresh application for a maintenance assessment.

(2) Where a child support officer is not conducting such a review but is nevertheless satisfied that if an application were to be made under section 17 or 18 it would be appropriate to make a fresh maintenance assessment, he may do so.

(3) Before making a fresh maintenance assessment under this section, a child support officer shall give to such persons as may be prescribed such notice of his proposal to make a fresh assessment as may be prescribed.

20.—(1) Any person who is aggrieved by the decision of a child support officer—

(a) on a review under section 18;

(b) to refuse an application for such a review,

may appeal to a child support appeal tribunal against that decision.

(2) Except with leave of the chairman of a child support appeal tribunal, no appeal under this section shall be brought after the end of the period of 28 days beginning with the date on which notification was given of the decision in question.

(3) Where an appeal under this section is allowed, the tribunal shall remit the case to the Secretary of State, who shall arrange for it to be dealt with by a child support officer.

(4) The tribunal may, in remitting any case under this section, give such directions as it considers appropriate.

21.—(1) There shall be tribunals to be known as child support appeal tribunals which shall, subject to any order made under section 45, hear and determine appeals under section 20.

(2) The Secretary of State may make such regulations with respect to proceedings before child support appeal tribunals as he considers appropriate.

(3) The regulations may in particular make provision—

(a) as to procedure;

(b) for the striking out of appeals for want of prosecution;

(c) as to the persons entitled to appear and be heard on behalf of any of the parties;

(d) requiring persons to attend and give evidence or to produce documents;

(e) about evidence;

(f) for authorising the administration of oaths;

(g) as to confidentiality;

(h) for notification of the result of an appeal to be given to such persons as may be prescribed.

(4) Schedule 3 shall have effect with respect to child support appeal tribunals.

22.—(1)   Her Majesty may from time to time appoint a Chief Child Support Commissioner and such number of other Child Support Commissioners as she may think fit.

(2) The Chief Child Support Commissioner and the other Child Support Commissioners shall be appointed from among persons who—

(a) have a 10 year general qualification; or

(b) are advocates or solicitors in Scotland of 10 years' standing.

(3) The Lord Chancellor, after consulting the Lord Advocate, may make such regulations with respect to proceedings before Child Support Commissioners as he considers appropriate.

(4) The regulations—

(a) may, in particular, make any provision of a kind mentioned in section 21(3); and

(b) shall provide that any hearing before a Child Support Commissioner shall be in public except in so far as the Commissioner for special reasons directs otherwise.

(5) Schedule 4 shall have effect with respect to Child Support Commissioners.

23.—(1)   Her Majesty may from time to time appoint a Chief Child Support Commissioner for Northern Ireland and such number of other Child Support Commissioners for Northern Ireland as she may think fit.

(2) The Chief Child Support Commissioner for Northern Ireland and the other Child Support Commissioners for Northern Ireland shall be appointed from among persons who are barristers or solicitors of not less than 10 years' standing.

(3) Schedule 4 shall have effect with respect to Child Support Commissioners for Northern Ireland, subject to the modifications set out in paragraph 8.

(4) Subject to any Order made after the passing of this Act by virtue of subsection (1)(a) of section 3 of the Northern Ireland Constitution Act 1973, the matters to which this subsection applies shall not be transferred matters for the purposes of that Act but shall for the purposes of subsection (2) of that section be treated as specified in Schedule 3 to that Act.

(5) Subsection (4) applies to all matters relating to Child Support Commissioners, including procedure and appeals, other than those specified in paragraph 9 of Schedule 2 to the Northern Ireland Constitution Act 1973.

24.—(1)   Any person who is aggrieved by a decision of a child support appeal tribunal, and any child support officer, may appeal to a Child Support Commissioner on a question of law.

(2) Where, on an appeal under this section, a Child Support Commissioner holds that the decision appealed against was wrong in law he shall set it aside.

(3) Where a decision is set aside under subsection (2), the Child Support Commissioner may—

(a) if he can do so without making fresh or further findings of fact, give the decision which he considers should have been given by the child support appeal tribunal;

(b) if he considers it expedient, make such findings and give such decision as he considers appropriate in the light of those findings; or

(c) refer the case, with directions for its determination, to a child support officer or, if he considers it appropriate, to a child support appeal tribunal.

(4) Any reference under subsection (3) to a child support officer shall, subject to any direction of the Child Support Commissioner, be to a child support officer who has taken no part in the decision originally appealed against.

(5) On a reference under subsection (3) to a child support appeal tribunal, the tribunal shall, subject to any direction of the Child Support Commissioner, consist of persons who were not members of the tribunal which gave the decision which has been appealed against.

(6) No appeal lies under this section without the leave—

(a) of the person who was the chairman of the child support appeal tribunal when the decision appealed against was given or of such other chairman of a child support appeal tribunal as may be determined in accordance with regulations made by the Lord Chancellor; or

(b) subject to and in accordance with regulations so made, of a Child Support Commissioner.

(7) The Lord Chancellor may by regulations make provision as to the manner in which, and the time within which, appeals under this section are to be brought and applications for leave under this section are to be made.

(8) Where a question which would otherwise fall to be determined by a child support officer first arises in the course of an appeal to a Child Support Commissioner, he may, if he thinks fit, determine it even though it has not been considered by a child support officer.

(9) Before making any regulations under subsection (6) or (7), the Lord Chancellor shall consult the Lord Advocate.

25.—(1) An appeal on a question of law shall lie to the appropriate court from any decision of a Child Support Commissioner.

(2) No such appeal may be brought except—

(a) with leave of the Child Support Commissioner who gave the decision or, where regulations made by the Lord Chancellor so provide, of a Child Support Commissioner selected in accordance with the regulations; or

(b) if the Child Support Commissioner refuses leave, with the leave of the appropriate court.

(3) An application for leave to appeal under this section against a decision of a Child Support Commissioner ("the appeal decision") may only be made by—

(a) a person who was a party to the proceedings in which the original decision, or appeal decision, was given;

(b) the Secretary of State; or

(c) any other person who is authorised to do so by regulations made by the Lord Chancellor.

(4) In this section—

"appropriate court" means the Court of Appeal unless in a particular case the Child Support Commissioner to whom the application for leave is made directs that, having regard to the circumstances of the case, and in particular the convenience of the persons who may be parties to the appeal, the appropriate court is the Court of Session; and

"original decision" means the decision to which the appeal decision in question relates.

(5) The Lord Chancellor may by regulations make provision with respect to—

(a) the manner in which and the time within which applications must be made to a Child Support Commissioner for leave under this section; and

(b) the procedure for dealing with such applications.

(6) Before making any regulations under subsection (2), (3) or (5), the Lord Chancellor shall consult the Lord Advocate.

26.—(1)   Where a person who is alleged to be a parent of the child with respect to whom an application for a maintenance assessment has been made ("the alleged parent") denies that he is one of the child's parents, the child support officer concerned shall not make a maintenance assessment on the assumption that the alleged parent is one of the child's parents unless the case falls within one of those set out in subsection (2).

(2) The Cases are—

CASE A

Where the alleged parent is a parent of the child in question by virtue of having adopted him.

CASE B

Where the alleged parent is a parent of the child in question by virtue of an order under section 30 of the Human Fertilisation and Embryology Act 1990 (parental orders in favour of gamete donors).

Case C

Where—
  (a) either—
    (i)   a declaration that the alleged parent is a parent of the child in question (or a declaration which has that effect) is in force under section 56 of the Family Law Act 1986 (declarations of parentage); or
    (ii) a declarator by a court in Scotland that the alleged parent is a parent of the child in question (or a declarator which has that effect) is in force; and
  (b) the child has not subsequently been adopted.

Case D

Where—
  (a) a declaration to the effect that the alleged parent is one of the parents of the child in question has been made under section 27; and
  (b) the child has not subsequently been adopted.

Case E

Where—
  (a) the child is habitually resident in Scotland;
  (b) the child support officer is satisfied that one or other of the presumptions set out in section 5(1) of the Law Reform (Parent and Child) (Scotland) Act 1986 applies; and
  (c) the child has not subsequently been adopted.

Case F

Where—
  (a) the alleged parent has been found, or adjudged, to be the father of the child in question—
    (i)   in proceedings before any court in England and Wales which are relevant proceedings for the purposes of section 12 of the Civil Evidence Act 1968; or
    (ii) in affiliation proceedings before any court in the United Kingdom, (whether or not he offered any defence to the allegation of paternity) and that finding or adjudication still subsists; and
  (b) the child has not subsequently been adopted.
  (3) In this section—
    "adopted" means adopted within the meaning of Part IV of the Adoption Act 1976 or, in relation to Scotland, Part IV of the Adoption (Scotland) Act 1978; and
    "affiliation proceeding", in relation to Scotland, means any action of affiliation and aliment.

27.—(1) Where—

(a) a child support officer is considering whether to make a maintenance assessment with respect to a person who is alleged to be a parent of the child, or one of the children, in question ("the alleged parent");

(b) the alleged parent denies that he is one of the child's parents; and

(c) the child support officer is not satisfied that the case falls within one of those set out in section 26(2),

the Secretary of State or the person with care may apply to the court for a declaration as to whether or not the alleged parent is one of the child's parents.

(2) If, on hearing any application under subsection (1), the court is satisfied that the alleged parent is, or is not, a parent of the child in question it shall make a declaration to that effect.

(3) A declaration under this section shall have effect only for the purposes of this Act.

(4) In this section "court" means, subject to any provision made under Schedule 11 to the Children Act 1989 (jurisdiction of courts with respect to certain proceedings relating to children) the High Court, a county court or a magistrates' court.

(5) In the definition of "relevant proceedings" in section 12(5) of the Civil Evidence Act 1968 (findings of paternity etc. as evidence in civil proceedings) the following paragraph shall be added at the end—

   "(d) section 27 of the Child Support Act 1991."

(6) This section does not apply to Scotland.

28.—(1) Where—

(a) a child support officer is considering whether to make a maintenance assessment with respect to a person who is alleged to be a parent of the child, or one of the children, in question ("the alleged parent");

(b) the alleged parent denies that he is a parent of the child in question; and

(c) the child support officer is not satisfied that the case falls within one of those set out in section 26(2),

the Secretary of State may bring an action for declarator of parentage under section 7 of the Law Reform (Parent and Child) (Scotland) Act 1986.

(2) The Secretary of State may defend an action for declarator of non-parentage or illegitimacy brought by a person named as the alleged parent in an application for a maintenance assessment.

(3) This section applies to Scotland only.

Collection and enforcement

29.—(1) The Secretary of State may arrange for the collection of any child support maintenance payable in accordance with a maintenance assessment where—

(a) the assessment is made by virtue of section 6; or

(b) an application has been made to the Secretary of State under section 4(2) or 7(3) for him to arrange for its collection.

(2) Where a maintenance assessment is made under this Act, payments of child support maintenance under the assessment shall be made in accordance with regulations made by the Secretary of State.

(3) The regulations may, in particular, make provision—

(a) for payments of child support maintenance to be made—

(i)   to the person caring for the child or children in question;

(ii) to, or through, the Secretary of State; or

(iii) to, or through, such other person as the Secretary of State may, from time to time, specify;

(b) as to the method by which payments of child support maintenance are to be made;

(c) as to the intervals at which such payments are to be made;

(d) as to the method and timing of the transmission of payments which are made, to or through the Secretary of State or any other person, in accordance with the regulations;

(e) empowering the Secretary of State to direct any person liable to make payments in accordance with the assessment—

(i)   to make them by standing order or by any other method which requires one person to give his authority for payments to be made from an account of his to an account of another's on specific dates during the period for which the authority is in force and without the need for any further authority from him;

(ii) to open an account from which payments under the assessment may be made in accordance with the method of payment which that person is obliged to adopt;

(f) providing for the making of representations with respect to matters with which the regulations are concerned.

30.—(1)   Where the Secretary of State is arranging for the collection of any payments under section 29 or subsection (2), he may also arrange for the collection of any periodical payments, or secured periodical payments, of a prescribed kind which are payable to or for the benefit of any person who falls within a prescribed category.

(2) The Secretary of State may arrange for the collection of any periodical payments or secured periodical payments of a prescribed kind which are payable for the benefit of a child even though he is not arranging for the collection of child support maintenance with respect to that child.

(3) Where—

(a) the Secretary of State is arranging, under this Act, for the collection of different payments ("the payments") from the same absent parent;

(b) an amount is collected by the Secretary of State from the absent parent which is less than the total amount due in respect of the payments; and

(c) the absent parent has not stipulated how that amount is to be allocated by the Secretary of State as between the payments,

the Secretary of State may allocate that amount as he sees fit.

(4) In relation to England and Wales, the Secretary of State may by regulations make provision for sections 29 and 31 to 40 to apply, with such modifications (if any) as he considers necessary or expedient, for the purpose of enabling him to enforce any obligation to pay any amount which he is authorised to collect under this section.

(5) In relation to Scotland, the Secretary of State may by regulations make provision for the purpose of enabling him to enforce any obligation to pay any amount which he is authorised to collect under this section—

  (a) empowering him to bring any proceedings or take any other steps (other than diligence against earnings) which could have been brought or taken by or on behalf of the person to whom the periodical payments are payable;

  (b) applying sections 29, 31 and 32 with such modifications (if any) as he considers necessary or expedient.

31.—(1) This section applies where any person ("the liable person") is liable to make payments of child support maintenance.

(2) The Secretary of State may make an order ("a deduction from earnings order") against a liable person to secure the payment of any amount due under the maintenance assessment in question.

(3) A deduction from earnings order may be made so as to secure the payment of—

  (a) arrears of child support maintenance payable under the assessment;

  (b) amounts of child support maintenance which will become due under the assessment; or

  (c) both such arrears and such future amounts.

(4) A deduction from earnings order—

  (a) shall be expressed to be directed at a person ("the employer") who has the liable person in his employment; and

  (b) shall have effect from such date as may be specified in the order.

(5) A deduction from earnings order shall operate as an instruction to the employer to—

  (a) make deductions from the liable person's earnings; and

  (b) pay the amounts deducted to the Secretary of State.

(6) The Secretary of State shall serve a copy of any deduction from earnings order which he makes under this section on—

  (a) the person who appears to the Secretary of State to have the liable person in question in his employment; and

  (b) the liable person.

(7) Where—

  (a) a deduction from earnings order has been made; and

  (b) a copy of the order has been served on the liable person's employer,

it shall be the duty of that employer to comply with the order; but he shall not be under any liability for non-compliance before the end of the period of 7 days beginning with the date on which the copy was served on him.

(8) In this section and in section 32 "earnings" has such meaning as may be prescribed.

32.—(1) The Secretary of State may by regulations make provision with respect to deduction from earnings orders.

(2) The regulations may, in particular, make provision—

(a) as to the circumstances in which one person is to be treated as employed by another;

(b) requiring any deduction from earnings under an order to be made in the prescribed manner;

(c) requiring an order to specify the amount or amounts to which the order relates and the amount or amounts which are to be deducted from the liable person's earnings in order to meet his liabilities under the maintenance assessment in question;

(d) requiring the intervals between deductions to be made under an order to be specified in the order;

(e) as to the payment of sums deducted under an order to the Secretary of State;

(f) allowing the person who deducts and pays any amount under an order to deduct from the liable person's earnings a prescribed sum towards his administrative costs;

(g) with respect to the notification to be given to the liable person of amounts deducted, and amounts paid, under the order;

(h) requiring any person on whom a copy of an order is served to notify the Secretary of State in the prescribed manner and within a prescribed period if he does not have the liable person in his employment or if the liable person ceases to be in his employment;

(i) as to the operation of an order where the liable person is in the employment of the Crown;

(j) for the variation of orders;

(k) similar to that made by section 31(7), in relation to any variation of an order;

(l) for an order to lapse when the employer concerned ceases to have the liable person in his employment;

(m) as to the revival of an order in such circumstances as may be prescribed;

(n) allowing or requiring an order to be discharged;

(o) as to the giving of notice by the Secretary of State to the employer concerned that an order has lapsed or has ceased to have effect.

(3) The regulations may include provision that while a deduction from earnings order is in force—

(a) the liable person shall from time to time notify the Secretary of State, in the prescribed manner and within a prescribed period, of each occasion on which he leaves any employment or becomes employed, or re-employed, and shall include in such a notification a statement of his earnings and expected earnings from the employment concerned and of such other matters as may be prescribed;

(b) any person who becomes the liable person's employer and knows that the order is in force shall notify the Secretary of State, in the prescribed manner and within a prescribed period, that he is the liable person's employer, and shall include in such a notification a statement of the liable person's earnings and expected earnings from the employment concerned and of such other matters as may be prescribed.

(4) The regulations may include provision with respect to the priority as between a deduction from earnings order and—

(a) any other deduction from earnings order;

(b) any order under any other enactment relating to England and Wales which provides for deductions from the liable person's earnings;

(c) any diligence against earnings.

(5) The regulations may include a provision that a liable person may appeal to a magistrates' court (or in Scotland to the sheriff) if he is aggrieved by the making of a deduction from earnings order against him, or by the terms of any such order, or there is a dispute as to whether payments constitute earnings or as to any other prescribed matter relating to the order.

(6) On an appeal under subsection (5) the court or (as the case may be) the sheriff shall not question the maintenance assessment by reference to which the deduction from earnings order was made.

(7) Regulations made by virtue of subsection (5) may include provision as to the powers of a magistrates' court, or in Scotland of the sheriff, in relation to an appeal (which may include provision as to the quashing of a deduction from earnings order or the variation of the terms of such an order).

(8) If any person fails to comply with the requirements of a deduction from earnings order, or with any regulation under this section which is designated for the purposes of this subsection, he shall be guilty of an offence.

(9) In subsection (8) "designated" means designated by the regulations.

(10) It shall be a defence for a person charged with an offence under subsection (8) to prove that he took all reasonable steps to comply with the requirements in question.

(11) Any person guilty of an offence under subsection (8) shall be liable on summary conviction to a fine not exceeding level two on the standard scale.

33.—(1) This section applies where—

(a) a person who is liable to make payments of child support maintenance ("the liable person") fails to make one or more of those payments; and

(b) it appears to the Secretary of State that—

(i)   it is inappropriate to make a deduction from earnings order against him (because, for example, he is not employed); or

(ii) although such an order has been made against him, it has proved ineffective as a means of securing that payments are made in accordance with the maintenance assessment in question.

(2) The Secretary of State may apply to a magistrates' court or, in Scotland, to the sheriff for an order ("a liability order") against the liable person.

(3) Where the Secretary of State applies for a liability order, the magistrates' court or (as the case may be) sheriff shall make the order if satisfied that the payments in question have become payable by the liable person and have not been paid.

(4) On an application under subsection (2), the court or (as the case may be) the sheriff shall not question the maintenance assessment under which the payments of child support maintenance fell to be made.

34.—(1) The Secretary of State may make regulations in relation to England and Wales—

(a) prescribing the procedure to be followed in dealing with an application by the Secretary of State for a liability order;

(b) prescribing the form and contents of a liability order; and

(c) providing that where a magistrates' court has made a liability order, the person against whom it is made shall, during such time as the amount in respect of which the order was made remains wholly or partly unpaid, be under a duty to supply relevant information to the Secretary of State.

(2) In subsection (1) "relevant information" means any information of a prescribed description which is in the possession of the liable person and which the Secretary of State has asked him to supply.

35.—(1) Where a liability order has been made against a person ("the liable person"), the Secretary of State may levy the appropriate amount by distress and sale of the liable person's goods.

(2) In subsection (1), "the appropriate amount" means the aggregate of—

(a) the amount in respect of which the order was made, to the extent that it remains unpaid; and

(b) an amount, determined in such manner as may be prescribed, in respect of the charges connected with the distress.

(3) The Secretary of State may, in exercising his powers under subsection (1) against the liable person's goods, seize—

(a) any of the liable person's goods except—

(i) such tools, books, vehicles and other items of equipment as are necessary to him for use personally by him in his employment, business or vocation;

(ii) such clothing, bedding, furniture, household equipment and provisions as are necessary for satisfying his basic domestic needs; and

(b) any money, banknotes, bills of exchange, promissory notes, bonds, specialties or securities for money belonging to the liable person.

(4) For the purposes of subsection (3), the liable person's domestic needs shall be taken to include those of any member of his family with whom he resides.

(5) No person levying a distress under this section shall be taken to be a trespasser—

    (a) on that account; or

    (b) from the beginning, on account of any subsequent irregularity in levying the distress.

(6) A person sustaining special damage by reason of any irregularity in levying a distress under this section may recover full satisfaction for the damage (and no more) by proceedings in trespass or otherwise.

(7) The Secretary of State may make regulations supplementing the provisions of this section.

(8) The regulations may, in particular—

    (a) provide that a distress under this section may be levied anywhere in England and Wales;

    (b) provide that such a distress shall not be deemed unlawful on account of any defect or want of form in the liability order;

    (c) provide for an appeal to a magistrates' court by any person aggrieved by the levying of, or an attempt to levy, a distress under this section;

    (d) make provision as to the powers of the court on an appeal (which may include provision as to the discharge of goods distrained or the payment of compensation in respect of goods distrained and sold).

36.—(1)   Where a liability order has been made against a person, the amount in respect of which the order was made, to the extent that it remains unpaid, shall, if a county court so orders, be recoverable by means of garnishee proceedings or a charging order, as if it were payable under a county court order.

(2) In subsection (1) "charging order" has the same meaning as in section 1 of the Charging Orders Act 1979.

37.—(1)   Section 34(1) does not apply to Scotland.

(2) In Scotland, the Secretary of State may make regulations providing that where the sheriff made a liability order, the person against whom it is made shall, during such time as the amount in respect of which the order was made remains wholly or partly unpaid, be under a duty to supply relevant information to the Secretary of State.

(3) In this section "relevant information" has the same meaning as in section 34(2).

38.—(1)   In Scotland, where a liability order has been made against a person, the order shall be warrant anywhere in Scotland—

    (a) for the Secretary of State to charge the person to pay the appropriate amount and to recover that amount by a poinding and sale under Part II of the Debtors (Scotland) Act 1987 and, in connection therewith, for the opening of shut and lockfast places;

(b) for an arrestment (other than an arrestment of the person's earnings in the hands of his employers) and action of furthcoming or sale,

and shall be apt to found a Bill of Inhibition or an action of adjudication at the instance of the Secretary of State.

(2) In subsection (1) the "appropriate amount" means the amount in respect of which the order was made, to the extent that it remains unpaid.

39.—(1) The Secretary of State may by regulations provide for—

(a) any liability order made by a court in England and Wales; or

(b) any corresponding order made by a court in Northern Ireland,

to be enforced in Scotland as if it had been made by the sheriff.

(2) The power conferred on the Court of Session by section 32 of the Sheriff Courts (Scotland Act 1971 (power of Court of Session to regulate civil procedure in the sheriff court) shall extend to making provision for the registration in the sheriff court for enforcement of any such order as is referred to in subsection (1).

(3) The Secretary of State may by regulations make provision for, or in connection with, the enforcement in England and Wales of—

(a) any liability order made by the sheriff in Scotland; or

(b) any corresponding order made by a court in Northern Ireland,

as if it had been made by a magistrates' court in England and Wales.

(4) Regulations under subsection (3) may, in particular, make provision for the registration of any such order as is referred to in that subsection in connection with its enforcement in England and Wales.

40.—(1) Where the Secretary of State has sought—

(a) to levy an amount by distress under this Act; or

(b) to recover an amount by virtue of section 36,

and that amount, or any portion of it, remains unpaid he may apply to a magistrates' court for the issue of a warrant committing the liable person to prison.

(2) On any such application the court shall (in the presence of the liable person) inquire as to—

(a) the liable person's means; and

(b) whether there has been wilful refusal or culpable neglect on his part.

(3) If, but only if, the court is of the opinion that there has been wilful refusal or culpable neglect on the part of the liable person it may—

(a) issue a warrant of commitment against him; or

(b) fix a term of imprisonment and postpone the issue of the warrant until such time and on such conditions (if any) as it thinks just.

(4) Any such warrant—

(a) shall be made in respect of an amount equal to the aggregate of—

  (i) the amount mentioned in section 35(1) or so much of it as remains outstanding; and

(ii) an amount (determined in accordance with regulations made by the Secretary of State) in respect of the costs of commitment; and

(b) shall state that amount.

(5) No warrant may be issued under this section against a person who is under the age of 18.

(6) A warrant issued under this section shall order the liable person—

(a) to be imprisoned for a specified period; but

(b) to be released (unless he is in custody for some other reason) on payment of the amount stated in the warrant.

(7) The maximum period of imprisonment which may be imposed by virtue of subsection (6) shall be calculated in accordance with Schedule 4 to the Magistrates' Courts Act 1980 (maximum periods of imprisonment in default of payment) but shall not exceed six weeks.

(8) The Secretary of State may by regulations make provision for the period of imprisonment specified in any warrant issued under this section to be reduced where there is part payment of the amount in respect of which the warrant was issued.

(9) A warrant issued under this section may be directed to such person or persons as the court issuing it thinks fit.

(10) Section 80 of the Magistrates' Courts Act 1980 (application of money found on defaulter) shall apply in relation to a warrant issued under this section against a liable person as it applies in relation to the enforcement of a sum mentioned in subsection (1) of that section.

(11) The Secretary of State may by regulations make provision—

(a) as to the form of any warrant issued under this section;

(b) allowing an application under this section to be renewed where no warrant is issued or term of imprisonment is fixed;

(c) that a statement in writing to the effect that wages of any amount have been paid to the liable person during any period, purporting to be signed by or on behalf of his employer, shall be evidence of the facts stated;

(d) that, for the purposes of enabling an inquiry to be made as to the liable person's conduct and means, a justice of the peace may issue a summons to him to appear before a magistrates' court and (if he does not obey) may issue a warrant for his arrest;

(e) that for the purpose of enabling such an inquiry, a justice of the peace may issue a warrant for the liable person's arrest without issuing a summons;

(f) as to the execution of a warrant for arrest.

(12) Subsections (1) to (11) do not apply to Scotland.

(13) For the avoidance of doubt, it is declared that a sum payable under a liability order is a sum decerned for aliment for the purposes of the Debtors (Scotland) Act 1880 and the Civil Imprisonment (Scotland) Act 1882.

(14) Where a liability order has been made, the Secretary of State (and he alone) shall be regarded as, and may exercise all the powers of, the creditor for the purposes of section 4 (imprisonment for failure to obey decree for alimentary debt) of the Civil Imprisonment (Scotland) Act 1882.

41.—(1)   This section applies where—
(a) the Secretary of State is authorised under section 4, 6 or 7 to recover child support maintenance payable by an absent parent in accordance with a maintenance assessment; and
(b) the absent parent has failed to make one or more payments of child support maintenance due from him in accordance with that assessment.

(2) Where the Secretary of State recovers any such arrears he may, in such circumstances as may be prescribed and to such extent as may be prescribed, retain them if he is satisfied that the amount of any benefit paid to the person with care of the child or children in question would have been less had the absent parent not been in arrears with his payments of child support maintenance.

(3) In such circumstances as may be prescribed, the absent parent shall be liable to make such payments of interest with respect to the arrears of child support maintenance as may be prescribed.

(4) The Secretary of State may by regulations make provision—
(a) as to the rate of interest payable by virtue of subsection (3);
(b) as to the time at which, and person to whom, any such interest shall be payable;
(c) as to the circumstances in which, in a case where the Secretary of State has been acting under section 6, any such interest may be retained by him;
(d) for the Secretary of State, in a case where he has been acting under section 6 and in such circumstances as may be prescribed, to waive any such interest (or part of any such interest).

(5) The provisions of this Act with respect to—
(a) the collection of child support maintenance;
(b) the enforcement of any obligation to pay child support maintenance,
shall apply equally to interest payable by virtue of this section.

(6) any sums retained by the Secretary of State by virtue of this section shall be paid by him into the Consolidated Fund.

Special cases

42.—(1)   The Secretary of State may by regulations provide that in prescribed circumstances a case is to be treated as a special case for the purposes of this Act.

(2) Those regulations may, for example, provide for the following to be special cases—
(a) each parent of a child is an absent parent in relation to the child;
(b) there is more than one person who is a person with care in relation to the same child;
(c) there is more than one qualifying child in relation to the same absent parent but the person who is the person with care in relation to one of those children is not the person who is the person with care in relation to all of them;

    (d) a person is an absent parent in relation to more than one child and the other parent of each of those children is not the same person;

    (e) the person with care has care of more than one qualifying child and there is more than one absent parent in relation to those children;

    (f) a qualifying child has his home in two or more separate households.

  (3) The Secretary of State may by regulations make provision with respect to special cases.

  (4) made under subsection (3) may, in particular—

    (a) modify any provision made by or under this Act, in its application to any special case or any special case falling within a prescribed category;

    (b) make new provision for any such case; or

    (c) provide for any prescribed provision made by or under this Act not to apply to any such case.

  43.—(1) This section applies where—

    (a) by virtue of paragraph 5(4) of Schedule 1, an absent parent taken for the purposes of that Schedule to have no assessable income; and

    (b) such conditions as may be prescribed for the purposes of this section are satisfied.

  (2) The power of the Secretary of State to make regulations under section 51 of the Social Security Act 1986 by virtue of subsection (1)(r), (deductions from benefits) may be exercised in relation to cases to which this section applies with a view to securing that—

    (a) payments of prescribed amounts are made with respect to qualifying children in place of payments of child support maintenance; and

    (b) arrears of child support maintenance are recovered.

Jurisdiction

  44.—(1) A child support officer shall have jurisdiction to make a maintenance assessment with respect to a person who is—

    (a) a person with care;

    (b) an absent parent; or

    (c) a qualifying child,

only if that person is habitually resident in the United Kingdom.

  (2) Where the person with care is not an individual, subsection (1) shall have effect as if paragraph (a) were omitted.

  (3) The Secretary of State may by regulations make provision for the cancellation of any maintenance assessment where—

    (a) the person with care, absent parent or qualifying child with respect to whom it was made ceases to be habitually resident in the United Kingdom;

    (b) in a case falling within subsection (2), the absent parent or qualifying child with respect to whom it was made ceases to be habitually resident in the United Kingdom; or

(c) in such circumstances as may be prescribed, a maintenance order of a prescribed kind is made with respect to any qualifying child with respect to whom the maintenance assessment was made.

45.—(1)   The Lord Chancellor or, in relation to Scotland, the Lord Advocate may by order make such provision as he considers necessary to secure that appeals, or such class of appeals as may be specified in the order—
(a) shall be made to a court instead of being made to a child support appeal tribunal; or
(b) shall be so made in such circumstances as may be so specified.

(2) In subsection (1), "court" means—
(a) in relation to England and Wales and subject to any provision made under Schedule 11 to the Children Act 1989 (Jurisdiction of courts with respect to certain proceedings relating to children) the High Court, a county court or a magistrates' court; and
(b) in relation to Scotland, the Court of Session or the sheriff.

(3) Schedule 11 to the Act of 1989 shall be amended in accordance with subsections (4) and (5).

(4) The following sub-paragraph shall be inserted in paragraph 1, after sub-paragraph 2
"(2A) Sub-paragraphs (1) and (2) shall also apply in relation to proceedings—
(a) under section 27 of the Child Support Act 1991 (reference to court for declaration of parentage); or
(b) which are to be dealt with in accordance with an order made under section 45 of that Act (jurisdiction of courts in certain proceedings under that Act)".

(5) In paragraphs 1(3) and 2(3), the following shall be inserted after "Act 1976"—
"(bb)   section 20 (appeals) or 27 (reference to court for declaration of parentage) of the Child Support Act 1991;".

(6) Where the effect of any order under subsection (1) is that there are no longer any appeals which fall to be dealt with by child support appeal tribunals, the Lord Chancellor after consultation with the Lord Advocate may by order provide for the abolition of those tribunals.

(7) Any order under subsection (1) or (6) may make—
(a) such modifications of any provision of this Act or of any other enactment; and
(b) such transitional provision,
as the Minister making the order considers appropriate in consequence of any provision made by the order.

Miscellaneous and supplemental

46.—(1)   This section applies where any person ("the parent")—
(a) fails to comply with a requirement imposed on her by the Secretary of State under section 6(1); or

(b) fails to comply with any regulation made under section 6(9).

(2) A child support officer may serve written notice on the parent requiring her, before the end of the specified period, either to comply or to give him her reasons for failing to do so.

(3) When the specified period has expired, the child support officer shall consider whether, having regard to any reasons given by the parent, there are reasonable grounds for believing that, if she were to be required to comply, there would be a risk of her or of any children living with her suffering harm or undue distress as a result of complying.

(4) If the child support officer considers that there are such reasonable grounds, he shall—

    (a) take no further action under this section in relation to the failure in question; and

    (b) notify the parent, in writing, accordingly.

(5) If the child support officer considers that there are no such reasonable grounds, he may give a reduced benefit direction with respect to the parent.

(6) Where the child support officer gives a reduced benefit direction he shall send a copy of it to the parent.

(7) Any person who is aggrieved by a decision of a child support officer to give a reduced benefit direction may appeal to a child support appeal tribunal against that decision.

(8) Sections 20(2) to (4) and 21 shall apply in relation to appeals under subsection (7) as they apply in relation to appeals under section 20.

(9) A reduced benefit direction shall take effect on such date as may be specified in the direction.

(10) Reasons given in response to a notice under subsection (2) may be given either in writing or orally.

(11) In this section—

    "comply" means to comply with the requirement or with the regulation in question; and "complied" and "complying" shall be construed accordingly;

    "reduced benefit direction" means a direction, binding on the adjudication officer, that the amount payable by way of any relevant benefit to, or in respect of, the parent concerned be reduced by such amount, and for such period, as may be prescribed;

    "relevant benefit" means income support, family credit or any other benefit of a kind prescribed for the purposes of section 6; and

    "specified", in relation to any notice served under this section, means specified in the notice; and the period to be specified shall be determined in accordance with regulations made by the Secretary of State.

47.—(1) The Secretary of State may by regulations provide for the payment, by the absent parent or the person with care (or by both), of such fees as may be prescribed in cases where the Secretary of State takes any action under section 4 or 6.

(2) The Secretary of State may by regulations provide for the payment, by

the absent parent, the person with care or the child concerned (or by any or all of them), of such fees as may be prescribed in cases where the Secretary of State takes any action under section 7.

(3) Regulations made under this section—

(a) may require any information which is needed for the purpose of determining the amount of any such fee to be furnished, in accordance with the regulations, by such person as may be prescribed;

(b) shall provide that no such fees shall be payable by any person to or in respect of whom income support, family credit or any other benefit of a prescribed kind is paid; and

(c) may, in particular, make provision with respect to the recovery by the Secretary of State of any fees payable under the regulations.

48.—(1)   Any person authorised by the Secretary of State for the purposes of this section shall have, in relation to any proceedings under this Act before a magistrates' court, a right of audience and the right to conduct litigation.

(2) In this section "right of audience" and "right to conduct litigation" have the same meaning as in section 119 of the Courts and Legal Services Act 1990.

49.   In relation to any proceedings before the sheriff under any provision of this Act, the power conferred on the Court of Session by section 32 of the Sheriff Courts (Scotland) Act 1971 (power of Court of Session to regulate civil procedure in sheriff court) shall extend to the making of rules permitting a party to such proceedings, in such circumstances as may be specified in the rules, to be represented by a person who is neither an advocate nor a solicitor.

50.—(1)   Any person who is, or has been, employed in employment to which this section applies is guilty of an offence if, without lawful authority, he discloses any information which—

(a) was acquired by him in the course of that employment; and

(b) relates to a particular person.

(2) It is not an offence under this section—

(a) to disclose information in the form of a summary or collection of information so framed as not to enable information relating to any particular person to be ascertained from it; or

(b) to disclose information which has previously been disclosed to the public with lawful authority.

(3) It is a defence for a person charged with an offence under this section to prove that at the time of the alleged offence—

(a) he believed that he was making the disclosure in question with lawful authority and had no reasonable cause to believe otherwise; or

(b) he believed that the information in question had previously been disclosed to the public with lawful authority and had no reasonable cause to believe otherwise.

(4) A person guilty of an offence under this section shall be liable—
  (a) on conviction on indictment, to imprisonment for a term not exceeding two years or a fine or both; or
  (b) on summary conviction, to imprisonment for a term not exceeding six months or a fine not exceeding the statutory maximum or both.

(5) This section applies to employment as—
  (a) the Chief Child Support Officer;
  (b) any other child support officer;
  (c) any clerk to, or other officer of, a child support appeal tribunal;
  (d) any member of the staff of such a tribunal;
  (e) a civil servant in connection with the carrying out of any functions under this Act,

and to employment of any other kind which is prescribed for the purposes of this section.

(6) For the purposes of this section a disclosure is to be regarded as made with lawful authority if, and only if, it is made—
  (a) by a civil servant in accordance with his official duty; or
  (b) by any other person either—
      (i) for the purposes of the function in the exercise of which he holds the information and without contravening any restriction duly imposed by the responsible person; or
      (ii) to, or in accordance with an authorisation duly given by, the responsible person;
  (c) in accordance with any enactment or order of a court;
  (d) for the purpose of instituting, or otherwise for the purposes of, any proceedings before a court or before any tribunal or other body or person mentioned in this Act; or
  (c) with the consent of the appropriate person.

(7) "The responsible person" means—
  (a) the Lord Chancellor;
  (b) the Secretary of State;
  (c) any person authorised by the Lord Chancellor, or Secretary of State, for the purposes of this subsection; or
  (d) any other prescribed person, or person falling within a prescribed category.

(8) "The appropriate person" means the person to whom the information in question relates, except that if the affairs of that person are being dealt with—
  (a) under a power of attorney;
  (b) by a receiver appointed under section 99 of the Mental Health Act 1983;
  (c) by a Scottish mental health custodian, that is to say—
      (i) a curator bonis, tutor or judicial factor; or
      (ii) the managers of a hospital acting on behalf of that person under section 94 of the Mental Health (Scotland) Act 1984; or
  (d) by a mental health appointee, that is to say—
      (i) a person directed or authorised as mentioned in sub- paragraph (a) of rule 41(1) of the Court of Protection Rules 1984; or

(ii) a receiver ad interim appointed under sub-paragraph (b) of that
         rule;

the appropriate person is the attorney, receiver, custodian or appointee (as the
case may be) or, in a case falling within paragraph (a), the person to whom
the information relates.

51.—(1) The Secretary of State may by regulations make such incidental,
supplemental and transitional provision as he considers appropriate in connection with any provision made by or under this Act.

(2) The regulations may, in particular, make provision—
  (a) as to the procedure to be followed with respect to
      (i)   the making of applications for maintenance assessments;
      (ii) the making, cancellation or refusal to make maintenance
            assessments;
      (iii) reviews under sections 16 to 19;
  (b) extending the categories of case to which section 18 or 19 applies;
  (c) as to the date on which an application for a maintenance assessment
      is to be treated as having been made;
  (d) for attributing payments made under maintenance assessments to the
      payment of arrears;
  (e) for the adjustment, for the purpose of taking account of the retro-
      spective effect of a maintenance assessment, of amounts payable
      under the assessment;
  (f) for the adjustment, for the purpose of taking account of overpayments
      or under-payments of child support maintenance, of amounts payable
      under a maintenance assessment;
  (g) as to the evidence which is to be required in connection with such
      matters as may be prescribed;
  (h) as to the circumstances in which any official record or certificate is to
      be conclusive (or in Scotland, sufficient) evidence;
  (i) with respect to the giving of notices or other documents;
  (j) for the rounding up or down of any amounts calculated, estimated or
      otherwise arrived at in applying any provision made by or under this
      Act.

(3) No power to make regulations conferred by any other provision of this
Act shall be taken to limit the powers given to the Secretary of State by this
section.

52.—(1) Any power conferred on the Lord Chancellor, the Lord Advocate
or the Secretary of State by this Act to make regulations or orders (other than
a deduction from earnings order) shall be exercisable by statutory
instrument.

(2) No statutory instrument containing (whether alone or with other provisions) regulations made under section 4(7), 5(3), 6(1), (9) or (10), 7(8), 12(2),
41(2), (3) or (4), 42, 43(1), 46 or 47 or under Part I of Schedule 1, or an order

made under section 45(1) or (6), shall be made unless a draft of the instrument has been laid before Parliament and approved by a resolution of each House of Parliament.

(3) Any other statutory instrument made under this Act (except an order made under section 58(2)) shall be subject to annulment in pursuance of a resolution of either House of Parliament.

(4) Any power of a kind mentioned in subsection (1) may be exercised—

(a) in relation to all cases to which it extends, in relation to those cases but subject to specified exceptions or in relation to any specified cases or classes of case;

(b) so as to make, as respects the cases in relation to which it is exercised—

(i) the full provision to which it extends or any lesser provision (whether by way of exception or otherwise);

(ii) the same provision for all cases, different provision for different cases or classes of case or different provision as respects the same case or class of case but for different purposes of this Act;

(iii) provision which is either unconditional or is subject to any specified condition;

(c) so to provide for a person to exercise a discretion in dealing with any matter.

53. Any expenses of the Lord Chancellor or the Secretary of State under this Act shall be payable out of money provided by Parliament.

54. In this Act—

"absent parent", has the meaning given in section 3(2);

"adjudication officer" has the same meaning as in the benefit Acts;

"assessable income" has the meaning given in paragraph 5 of Schedule 1;

"benefit Acts" means the Social Security Acts 1975 to 1991;

"Chief Adjudication Officer" has the same meaning as in the benefit Acts;

"Chief Child Support Officer" has the meaning given in section 13

"child benefit" has the same meaning as in the Child Benefit 1975;

"child support appeal tribunal" means a tribunal appointed under section 21;

"child support maintenance" has the meaning given in section 3(6);

"child support officer" has the meaning given in section 13;

"deduction from earnings order" has the meaning given in section 31(2);

"disability living allowance" has the same meaning as in the Social Security Act 1975;

"family credit" has the same meaning as in the benefit Acts;

"general qualification" shall be construed in accordance with section 71 of the Courts and Legal Services Act 1990 (qualification for judicial appointments);

"income support" has the same meaning as in the benefit Acts;

"interim maintenance assessment" has the meaning given in section 12;

"liability order" has the meaning given in section 33(2);

"maintenance agreement" has the meaning given in section 9(1);

"maintenance assessment" means an assessment of maintenance made under this Act and, except in prescribed circumstances, includes an interim maintenance assessment;

"maintenance order" has the meaning given in section 8(11);

"maintenance requirement" means the amount calculated in accordance with paragraph 1 of Schedule 1;

"parent", in relation to any child, means any person who is in law the mother or father of the child;

"parental responsibility" has the same meaning as in the Children Act 1989;

"parental rights" has the same meaning as in the Law Reform (Parent and Child) (Scotland) Act 1986;

"person with care" has the meaning given in section 3(3);

"prescribed" means prescribed by regulations made by the Secretary of State;

"qualifying child" has the meaning given in section 3(1);

55.—(1) For the purposes of this Act a person is a child if—

(a) he is under the age of 16;

(b) he is under the age of 19 and receiving full-time education (which is not advanced education)—

   (i) by attendance at a recognised educational establishment; or

   (ii) elsewhere, if the education is recognised by the Secretary of State; or

(c) he does not fall within paragraph (a) or (b) but—

   (i) he is under the age of 18, and

   (ii) prescribed conditions are satisfied with respect to him.

(2) A person is not a child for the purposes of this Act if he—

(a) is or has been married;

(b) has celebrated a marriage which is void; or

(c) has celebrated a marriage in respect of which a decree of nullity has been granted.

(3) In this section—

"advanced education" means education of a prescribed description; and

"recognised educational establishment" means an establishment recognised by the Secretary of State for the purposes of this section as being, or as comparable to, a university, college or school.

(4) Where a person has reached the age of 16, the Secretary of State may recognise education provided for him otherwise than at a recognised educational establishment only if the Secretary of State is satisfied that education was being so provided for him immediately before he reached the age of 16.

(5) The Secretary of State may provide that in prescribed circumstances education is or is not to be treated for the purposes of this section as being full-time.

(6) In determining whether a person falls within subsection (1)(b), no account shall be taken of such interruptions in his education as may be prescribed.

(7) The Secretary of State may by regulations provide that a person who ceases to fall within subsection (1) shall be treated as continuing to fall within that subsection for a prescribed period.

(8) No person shall be treated as continuing to fall within subsection (1) by virtue of regulations made under subsection (7) after the end of the week in which he reaches the age of 19.

56.—(1)   An Order in Council made under paragraph 1(1)(b) of Schedule 1 to the Northern Ireland Act 1974 which contains a statement that it is made only for purposes corresponding to those of the provisions of this Act, other than provisions which relate to the appointment Child Support Commissioners for Northern Ireland—

    (a) shall not be subject to sub-paragraphs (4) and (5) of paragraph 1 of that Schedule (affirmative resolution of both Houses of Parliament); but

    (b) shall be subject to annulment in pursuance of a resolution of either House of Parliament.

(2) The Secretary of State may make arrangements with the Department of Health and Social Services for Northern Ireland with a view to securing, to the extent allowed for in the arrangements, that—

    (a) the provision made by or under this Act ("the provision made for Great Britain"); and

    (b) the provision made by or under any corresponding enactment having effect with respect to Northern Ireland ("the provision made for Northern Ireland"),

provide for a single system within the United Kingdom.

(3) The Secretary of State may make regulations for giving effect to any such arrangements.

(4) The regulations may, in particular—

    (a) adapt legislation (including subordinate legislation) for the time being in force in Great Britain so as to secure its reciprocal operation with the provision made for Northern Ireland; and

    (b) make provision to secure that acts, omissions and events which have any effect for the purposes of the provision made for Northern Ireland have a corresponding effect for the purposes of the provision made for Great Britain.

57.—(1)   The power of the Secretary of State to make regulations under section 14 requiring prescribed persons to furnish information may be exercised so as to require information to be furnished by persons employed in the service of the Crown or otherwise in the discharge of Crown functions.

(2) In such circumstances, and subject to such conditions, as may be prescribed, an inspector appointed under section 15 may enter any Crown premises for the purpose of exercising any powers conferred on him by that section.

(3) Where such an inspector duly enters any Crown premises for those purposes, section 15 shall apply in relation to persons employed in the service of the Crown or otherwise in the discharge of Crown functions as it applies in relation to other persons.

(4) Where a liable person is in the employment of the Crown, a deduction from earnings order may be made under section 31 in relation to that person; but in such a case subsection (8) of section 32 shall apply only in relation to the failure of that person to comply with any requirement imposed on him by regulations made under section 32.

58.—(1)   This Act may be cited as the Child Support Act 1991.

(2) Section 56(1) and subsections (1) to (11) and (14) of this section shall come into force on the passing of this Act but otherwise this Act shall come into force on such date as may be appointed by order made by the Lord Chancellor, the Secretary of State or Lord Advocate, or by any of them acting jointly.

(3) Different dates may be appointed for different provisions of this Act and for different purposes (including, in particular, for different cases or categories of case).

(4) An order under subsection (2) may make such supplemental, incidental or transitional provision as appears to the person making the order to be necessary or expedient in connection with the provisions brought into force by the order, including such adaptations or modifications of—

    (a) the provisions so brought into force;

    (b) any provisions of this Act then in force; or

    (c) any provision of any other enactment,

as appear to him to be necessary or expedient.

(5) Different provision may be made by virtue of subsection (4) with respect to different periods.

(6) Any provision made by virtue of subsection (4) may, in particular, include provision for—

    (a) the enforcement of a maintenance assessment (including the collection of sums payable under the assessment) as if the assessment were a court order of a prescribed kind;

    (b) the registration of maintenance assessments with the appropriate court in connection with any provision of a kind mentioned in paragraph (a);

    (c) the variation, on application made to a court, of the provisions of a maintenance assessment relating to the method of making payments fixed by the assessment or the intervals at which such payments are to be made;

    (d) a maintenance assessment, or an order of a prescribed kind relating to one or more children, to be deemed, in prescribed circumstances, to have been validly made for all purposes or for such purposes as may be prescribed.

In paragraph (c) "court" includes a single justice.

(7) The Lord Chancellor, the Secretary of State or the Lord Advocate may by order make such amendments or repeals in, or such modifications of, such enactments as may be specified in the order, as appear to him to be necessary or expedient in consequence of any provision made by or under this Act (including any provision made by virtue of subsection (4)).

(8) This Act shall, in its application to the Isles of Scilly, have effect subject to such exceptions, adaptations and modifications as the Secretary of State may by order prescribe.

(9 Sections 27, 35 and 48 and paragraph 7 of Schedule 5 do not extend to Scotland.

(10) Sections 7, 28 and 49 extend only to Scotland.

(11) With the exception of sections 23 and 56(1), subsections (1) to (3) of this section and Schedules 2 and 4, and (in so far as it amends any enactment extending to Northern Ireland) Schedule 5, this Act does not extend to Northern Ireland.

(12) Until Schedule 1 to the Disability Living Allowance and Disability Working Allowance Act 1991 comes into force, paragraph 1(1) of Schedule 3 shall have effect with the omission of the words "and disability appeal tribunals" and the insertion, after "social security appeal tribunals", of the word "and".

(13) The consequential amendments set out in Schedule 5 shall have effect.

(14) In Schedule 1 to the Children Act 1989 (financial provision for children), paragraph 2(6)(b) (which is spent) is hereby repealed.

SCHEDULES

Section 11.

SCHEDULE 1

MAINTENANCE ASSESSMENTS

PART I

CALCULATION OF CHILD SUPPORT MAINTENANCE

The maintenance requirement

1.—(1) In this Schedule "the maintenance requirement" means the amount, calculated in accordance with the formula set out in sub-paragraph (2), which is to be taken as the minimum amount necessary for the maintenance of the qualifying child or, where there is more than one qualifying child, all of them.

(2) The formula is—

$$MR = AG - CB$$

where—

　　MR is the amount of the maintenance requirement;

　　AG is the aggregate of the amounts to be taken into account under subparagraph (3); and

　　CB is the amount payable by way of child benefit (or which would be so payable if the person with care of the qualifying child were an individual) or, where there is more than one qualifying child, the aggregate of the amounts so payable with respect to each of them.

(3) The amounts to be taken into account for the purpose of calculating AG are—

　　(a) such amount or amounts (if any), with respect to each qualifying child, as may be prescribed;

　　(b) such amount or amounts (if any), with respect to the person with care of the qualifying child or qualifying children, as may be prescribed; and

　　(c) such further amount or amounts (if any) as may be prescribed.

(4) For the purposes of calculating CB it shall be assumed that child benefit is payable with respect to any qualifying child at the basic rate.

(5) In sub-paragraph (4) "basic rate" has the meaning for the time being prescribed.

The general rule

2.—(1) In order to determine the amount of any maintenance assessment, first calculate—

$$(A + C) \ x \ P$$

where—

　　A is the absent parent's assessable income;

　　C is the assessable income of the other parent, where that parent is the person with care, and otherwise has such value (if any) as may be prescribed; and

P is such number greater than zero but less than 1 as may be prescribed.

(2) Where the result of the calculation made under sub-paragraph (1) is an amount which is equal to, or less than, the amount of the maintenance requirement for the qualifying child or qualifying children, the amount of maintenance payable by the absent parent for that child or those children shall be an amount equal to—

$$A \times P$$

where A and P have the same values as in the calculation made under subparagraph (1).

(3) Where the result of the calculation made under sub-paragraph (1) is an amount which exceeds the amount of the maintenance requirement for the qualifying child or qualifying children, the amount of maintenance payable by the absent parent for that child or those children shall consist of—

(a) a basic element calculated in accordance with the provisions of paragraph 3; and

(b) an additional element calculated in accordance with the provisions of paragraph 4.

The basic element

3.—(1)   The basic element shall be calculated by applying the formula—

$$BE = A \times G \times P$$

where—

BE is the amount of the basic element;

A and P have the same values as in the calculation made under paragraph 2(1); and

G has the value determined under sub-paragraph (2).

(2) The value of G shall be determined by applying the formula—

$$G = \frac{MR}{(A + C) \times P}$$

where—

MR is the amount of the maintenance requirement for the qualifying child or qualifying children; and

A, C and P have the same values as in the calculation made under paragraph 2(1).

The additional element

4.—(1)   Subject to sub-paragraph (2), the additional element shall be calculated by applying the formula—

$$AE = (1 - G) \times A \times R$$

where—
   AE is the amount of the additional element;
   A has the same value as in the calculation made under paragraph 2(1);
   G has the value determined under paragraph 3(2); and
   R is such number greater than zero but less than 1 as may be prescribed.

(2) Where applying the alternative formula set out in sub-paragraph (3) would result in a lower amount for the additional element, that formula shall be applied in place of the formula set out in sub-paragraph (1).

(3) The alternative formula is—

$$AE = Z \times Q \times \left(\frac{A}{A + C} \right)$$

where—
   A and C have the same values as in the calculation made under paragraph 2(1);
   Z is such number as may be prescribed; and
   Q is the aggregate of—
   (a) any amount taken into account by virtue of paragraph 1(3)(a) in calculating the maintenance requirement; and
   (b) any amount which is both taken into account by virtue of paragraph 1(3)(c) in making that calculation and is an amount prescribed for the purposes of this paragraph.

Assessable income

5.—(1)   The assessable income of an absent parent shall be calculated by applying the formula—

$$A = N - E$$

where—
   A is the amount of that parent's assessable income;
   N is the amount of that parent's net income, calculated or estimated in accordance with regulations made by the Secretary of State for the purposes of this sub-paragraph; and
   E is the amount of that parent's exempt income, calculated or estimated in accordance with regulations made by the Secretary of State for those purposes.

(2) The assessable income of a parent who is a person with care of the qualifying child or children shall be calculated by applying the formula—

$$C = M - F$$

where—

C is the amount of that parent's assessable income;

M is the amount of that parent's net income, calculated or estimated in accordance with regulations made by the Secretary of State for the purposes of this sub-paragraph; and

F is the amount of that parent's exempt income, calculated or estimated in accordance with regulations made by the Secretary of State for those purposes.

(3) Where the preceding provisions of this paragraph would otherwise result in a person's assessable income being taken to be a negative amount his assessable income shall be taken to be nil.

(4) Where income support or any other benefit of a prescribed kind is paid to or in respect of a parent who is an absent parent or a person with care that parent shall, for the purposes of this Schedule, be taken to have no assessable income.

Protected income

6.—(1) This paragraph applies where—

(a) one or more maintenance assessments have been made with respect to an absent parent; and

(b) payment by him of the amount, or the aggregate of the amounts, so assessed would otherwise reduce his disposable income below his protected income level.

(2) The amount of the assessment, or (as the case may be) of each assessment, shall be adjusted in accordance with such provisions as may be prescribed with a view to securing so far as is reasonably practicable that payment by the absent parent of the amount, or (as the case may be) aggregate of the amounts, so assessed will not reduce his disposable income below his protected income level.

(3) Regulations made under sub-paragraph (2) shall secure that, where the prescribed minimum amount fixed by regulations made under paragraph 7 applies, no maintenance assessment is adjusted so as to provide for the amount payable by an absent parent in accordance with that assessment to be less than that amount.

(4) The amount which is to be taken for the purposes of this paragraph as an absent parent's disposable income shall be calculated, or estimated, in accordance with regulations made by the Secretary of State.

(5) Regulations made under sub-paragraph (4) may, in particular, provide that, in such circumstances and to such extent as may be prescribed—

(a) income of any child who is living in the same household with the absent parent; and

(b) where the absent parent is living together in the same household with another adult of the opposite sex (regardless of whether or not they are married), income of that other adult,

is to be treated as the absent parent's income for the purposes of calculating his disposable income.

(6) In this paragraph the "protected income level" of a particular absent parent means an amount of income calculated, by reference to the circumstances of that parent, in accordance with regulations made by the Secretary of State.

The minimum amount of child support maintenance

7.—(1)   The Secretary of State may prescribe a minimum amount for the purposes of this paragraph.

(2) Where the amount of child support maintenance which would be fixed by a maintenance assessment but for this paragraph is nil, or less than the prescribed minimum amount, the amount to be fixed by the assessment shall be the prescribed minimum amount.

(3) In any case to which section 43 applies, and in such other cases (if any) as may be prescribed, sub-paragraph (2) shall not apply.

Housing costs

8.   Where regulations under this Schedule require a child support officer to take account of the housing costs of any person in calculating, or estimating, his assessable income or disposable income, those regulations may make provision—

(a) as to the costs which are to be treated as housing costs for the purpose of the regulations;

(b) for the apportionment of housing costs; and

(c) for the amount of housing costs to be taken into account for prescribed purposes not to exceed such amount (if any) as may be prescribed by, or determined in accordance with, the regulations.

Regulations about income and capital

9. The Secretary of State may by regulations provide that, in such circumstances and to such extent as may be prescribed—

(a) income of a child shall be treated as income of a parent of his;

(b) where the child support officer concerned is satisfied that a person has intentionally deprived himself of a source of income with a view to reducing the amount of his assessable income, his net income shall be taken to include income from that source of an amount estimated by the child support officer;

(c) a person is to be treated as possessing capital or income which he does not possess;

(d) capital or income which a person does possess is to be disregarded;

(e) income is to be treated as capital;

(f) capital is to be treated as income.

References to qualifying children

10. References in this Part of this Schedule to "qualifying children" are to those qualifying children with respect to whom the maintenance assessment falls to be made.

PART II

GENERAL PROVISIONS ABOUT MAINTENANCE ASSESSMENTS

Effective date of assessment

11.—(1) A maintenance assessment shall take effect on such date as may be determined in accordance with regulations made by the Secretary of State.

(2) That date may be earlier than the date on which the assessment is made.

Form of assessment

12. Every maintenance assessment shall be made in such form and contain such information as the Secretary of State may direct.

Assessments where amount of child support is nil

13. A child support officer shall not decline to make a maintenance assessment only on the ground that the amount of the assessment is nil.

Consolidated applications and assessments

14. The Secretary of State may by regulations provide—
  (a) for two or more applications for maintenance assessments to be treated, in prescribed circumstances, as a single application; and
  (b) for the replacement, in prescribed circumstances, of a maintenance assessment made on the application of one person by a later maintenance assessment made on the application of that or any other person.

Separate assessments for different periods

15. Where a child support officer is satisfied that the circumstances of a case require different amounts of child support maintenance to be assessed in respect of different periods, he may make separate maintenance assessments each expressed to have effect in relation to a different specified period.

Termination of assessments

16.—(1) A maintenance assessment shall cease to have effect—

(a) on the death of the absent parent, or of the person with care, with respect to whom it was made;

(b) on there no longer being any qualifying child with respect to whom it would have effect;

(c) on the absent parent with respect to whom it was made ceasing to be a parent of—

    (i)   the qualifying child with respect to whom it was made; or

    (ii) where it was made with respect to more than one qualifying child, all of the qualifying children with respect to whom it was made;

(d) where the absent parent and the person with care with respect to whom it was made have been living together for a continuous period of six months;

(e) where a new maintenance assessment is made with respect to any qualifying child with respect to whom the assessment in question was in force immediately before the making of the new assessment.

(2) A maintenance assessment made in response to an application under section 4 or 7 shall be cancelled by a child support officer if the person on whose application the assessment was made asks him to do so.

(3) A maintenance assessment made in response to an application under section 6 shall be cancelled by a child support officer if—

(a) the person on whose application the assessment was made ("the applicant") asks him to do so; and

(b) he is satisfied that the applicant has ceased to fall within subsection (1) of that section.

(4) Where a child support officer is satisfied that the person with care with respect to whom a maintenance assessment was made has ceased to be a person with care in relation to the qualifying child, or any of the qualifying children, with respect to whom the assessment was made, he may cancel the assessment with effect from the date on which, in his opinion, the change of circumstances took place.

(5) Where—

(a) at any time a maintenance assessment is in force but a child support officer would no longer have jurisdiction to make it if it were to be applied for at that time; and

(b) the assessment has not been cancelled, or has not ceased to have effect, under or by virtue of any other provision made by or under this Act,

it shall be taken to have continuing effect unless cancelled by a child support officer in accordance with such prescribed provision (including provision as to the effective date of cancellation) as the Secretary of State considers it appropriate to make.

(6) Where both the absent parent and the person with care with respect to whom a maintenance assessment was made request a child support officer to

cancel the assessment, he may do so if he is satisfied that they are living together.

(7) Any cancellation of a maintenance assessment under sub-paragraph (5) or (6) shall have effect from such date as may be determined by the child support officer.

(8) Where a child support officer cancels a maintenance assessment, he shall immediately notify the absent parent and person with care, so far as that is reasonably practicable.

(9) Any notice under sub-paragraph (8) shall specify the date with effect from which the cancellation took effect.

(10) A person with care with respect to whom a maintenance assessment is in force shall provide the Secretary of State with such information, in such circumstances, as may be prescribed, with a view to assisting the Secretary of State or a child support officer in determining whether the assessment has ceased to have effect, or should be cancelled.

(11) The Secretary of State may by regulations make such supplemental, incidental or transitional provision as he thinks necessary or expedient in consequence of the provisions of this paragraph.

SCHEDULE 2

PROVISION OF INFORMATION TO SECRETARY OF STATE

Inland Revenue records

1 .—(1) This paragraph applies where the Secretary of State or the Department of Health and Social Services for Northern Ireland requires information for the purpose of tracing—

  (a) the current address of an absent parent; or

  (b) the current employer of an absent parent.

(2) In such a case, no obligation as to secrecy imposed by statute or otherwise on a person employed in relation to the Inland Revenue shall prevent any information obtained or held in connection with the assessment or collection of income tax from being disclosed to—

  (a) the Secretary of State;

  (b) the Department of Health and Social Services for Northern Ireland; or

  (c) an officer of either of them authorised to receive such information in connection with the operation of this Act or of any corresponding Northern Ireland legislation.

(3) This paragraph extends only to disclosure by or under the authority of the Commissioners of Inland Revenue.

(4) Information which is the subject of disclosure to any person by virtue of this paragraph shall not be further disclosed to any person except where the further disclosure is made—

(a) to a person to whom disclosure could be made by virtue of subparagraph (2); or

(b) for the purposes of any proceedings (civil or criminal) in connection with the operation of this Act or of any corresponding Northern Ireland legislation.

Local authority records

2.—(1) This paragraph applies where—

(a) the Secretary of State requires relevant information in connection with the discharge by him, or by any child support officer, of functions under this Act; or

(b) the Department of Health and Social Services for Northern Ireland requires relevant information in connection with the discharge of any functions under any corresponding Northern Ireland legislation.

(2) The Secretary of State may give a direction to the appropriate authority requiring them to give him such relevant information in connection with any housing benefit or community charge benefit to which an absent parent or person with care is entitled as the Secretary of State considers necessary in connection with his determination of—

(a) that person's income of any kind;

(b) the amount of housing costs to be taken into account in determining that person's income of any kind; or

(c) the amount of that person's protected income.

(3) The Secretary of State may give a similar direction for the purposes of enabling the Department of Health and Social Services for Northern Ireland to obtain such information for the purposes of any corresponding Northern Ireland legislation.

(4) In this paragraph—

"appropriate authority" means—

(a) in relation to housing benefit, the housing or local authority concerned; and

(b) in relation to community charge benefit, the charging authority or, in Scotland, the levying authority; and

"relevant information" means information of such a description as may be prescribed.

SCHEDULE 3

CHILD SUPPORT APPEAL TRIBUNALS

The President

1.—(1) The person appointed under Schedule 10 to the Social Security Act 1975 as President of the social security appeal tribunals, medical appeal tribunals and disability appeal tribunals shall, by virtue of that appointment, also be President of the child support appeal tribunals.

(2) It shall be the duty of the President to arrange such meetings of the chairmen and members of child support appeal tribunals, and such training for them, as he considers appropriate.

(3) The President may, with the consent of the Secretary of State as to numbers, remuneration and other terms and conditions of service, appoint such officers and staff as he thinks fit for the child support appeal tribunals and their full-time chairmen.

Membership of child support appeal tribunals

2.—(1) A child support appeal tribunal shall consist of a chairman and two other persons.

(2) The chairman and the other members of the tribunal must not all be of the same sex.

(3) Sub-paragraph (2) shall not apply to any proceedings before a child support appeal tribunal if the chairman of the tribunal rules that it is not reasonably practicable to comply with that sub-paragraph in those proceedings.

The chairmen

3.—(1) The chairman of a child support appeal tribunal shall be nominated by the President.

(2) The President may nominate himself or a person drawn—
  (a) from the appropriate panel appointed by the Lord Chancellor, or (as the case may be) the Lord President of the Court of Session, under section 7 of the Tribunals and Inquiries Act 1971;
  (b) from among those appointed under paragraph 4; or
  (c) from among those appointed under paragraph 1A of Schedule 10 to the Social Security Act 1975 to act as full-time chairmen of social security appeal tribunals.

(3) Subject to any regulations made by the Lord Chancellor, no person shall be nominated as a chairman of a child support appeal tribunal by virtue of subparagraph (2)(a) unless he has a 5 year general qualification or is an advocate or solicitor in Scotland of 5 years' standing.

4.—(1) The Lord Chancellor may appoint regional and other full-time chairmen for child support appeal tribunals.

(2) A person is qualified to be appointed as a full-time chairman if he has a 7 year general qualification or is an advocate or solicitor in Scotland of 7 years' standing.

(3) A person appointed to act as a full-time chairman shall hold and vacate office in accordance with the terms of his appointment, except that he must

vacate his office at the end of the completed year of service in which he reaches the age of 72 unless his appointment is continued under sub-paragraph (4).

(4) Where the Lord Chancellor considers it desirable in the public interest to retain a full-time chairman in office after the end of the completed year of service in which he reaches the age of 72, he may from time to time authorise the continuance of that person in office until any date not later than that on which that person reaches the age of 75.

(5) A person appointed as a full-time chairman may be removed from office by the Lord Chancellor, on the ground of misbehaviour or incapacity.

(6) Section 75 of the Courts and Legal Services Act 1990 (judges etc. barred from legal practice) shall apply to any person appointed as a full-time chairman under this Schedule as it applies to any person holding as a full-time appointment any of the offices listed in Schedule 11 to that Act.

(7) The Secretary of State may pay, or make such payments towards the provision of, such remuneration, pensions, allowances or gratuities to or in respect of persons appointed as full-time chairmen under this paragraph as, with the consent of the Treasury, he may determine.

Other members of child support appeal tribunals

5.—(1) The members of a child support appeal tribunal other than the chairman shall be drawn from the appropriate panel constituted under this paragraph.

(2) The panels shall be constituted by the President for the whole of Great Britain, and shall—
  (a) act for such areas; and
  (b) be composed of such persons,
as the President thinks fit.

(3) The panel for an area shall be composed of persons appearing to the President to have knowledge or experience of conditions in the area and to be representative of persons living or working in the area.

(4) Before appointing members of a panel, the President shall take into consideration any recommendations from such organisations or persons as he considers appropriate.

(5) The members of the panels shall hold office for such period as the President may direct.

(6) The President may at any time terminate the appointment of any member of a panel.

Clerks of tribunals

6.—(1) Each child support appeal tribunal shall be serviced by a clerk appointed by the President.

(2) The duty of summoning members of a panel to serve on a child support appeal tribunal shall be performed by the clerk to the tribunal.

Expenses of tribunal members and others

7.—(1) The Secretary of State may pay—

    (a) to any member of a child support appeal tribunal, such remuneration and travelling and other allowances as the Secretary of State may determine with the consent of the Treasury;

    (b) to any person required to attend at any proceedings before a child support appeal tribunal, such travelling and other allowances as may be so determined; and

    (c) such other expenses in connection with the work of any child support appeal tribunal as may be so determined.

(2) In sub-paragraph (1), references to travelling and other allowances include references to compensation for loss of remunerative time.

(3) No compensation for loss of remunerative time shall be paid to any person under this paragraph in respect of any time during which he is in receipt of other remuneration so paid.

Consultation with Lord Advocate

8. Before exercising any of his powers under paragraph 3(3) or 4(1), (4) or (5), the Lord Chancellor shall consult the Lord Advocate.

SCHEDULE 4

CHILD SUPPORT COMMISSIONERS

Tenure of office

1.—(1) Every Child Support Commissioner shall vacate his office at the end of the completed year of service in which he reaches the age of 72.

(2) Where the Lord Chancellor considers it desirable in the public interest to retain a Child Support Commissioner in office after the end of the completed year of service in which he reaches the age of 72, he may from time to time authorise the continuance of that Commissioner in office until any date not later than that on which he reaches the age of 75.

(3) A Child Support Commissioner may be removed from office by the Lord Chancellor on the ground of misbehaviour or incapacity.

Commissioners' remuneration and their pensions

2.—(1) The Lord Chancellor may pay, or make such payments towards the provision of such remuneration, pensions, allowances or gratuities to or in respect of persons appointed as Child Support Commissioners as, with the consent of the Treasury, he may determine.

(2) The Lord Chancellor shall pay to a Child Support Commissioner such expenses incurred in connection with his work as such a Commissioner as may be determined by the Treasury.

Commissioners barred from legal practice

3. Section 75 of the Courts and Legal Services Act 1990 (judges etc. barred from legal practice) shall apply to any person appointed as a Child Support Commissioner as it applies to any person holding as a full-time appointment any of the offices listed in Schedule 11 to that Act.

Deputy Child Support Commissioners

4.—(1) The Lord Chancellor may appoint persons to act as Child Support Commissioners (but to be known as deputy Child Support Commissioners) in order to facilitate the disposal of the business of Child Support Commissioners.

(2) A deputy Child Support Commissioner shall be appointed—
  (a) from among persons who have a 10 year general qualification or are advocates or solicitors in Scotland of 10 years' standing; and
  (b) for such period or on such occasions as the Lord Chancellor thinks fit.

(3) Paragraph 2 applies to deputy Child Support Commissioners as if the reference to pensions were omitted and paragraph 3 does not apply to them.

Tribunals of Commissioners

5.—(1) If it appears to the Chief Child Support Commissioner (or, in the case of his inability to act, to such other of the Child Support Commissioners as he may have nominated to act for the purpose) that an appeal falling to be heard by one of the Child Support Commissioners involves a question of law of special difficulty, he may direct that the appeal be dealt with by a tribunal consisting of any three of the Child Support Commissioners.

(2) If the decision of such a tribunal is not unanimous, the decision of the majority shall be the decision of the tribunal.

Finality of decisions

6.—(1) Subject to section 25, the decision of any Child Support Commissioner shall be final.

(2) Sub-paragraph (1) shall not be taken to make any finding of fact or other determination embodied in, or necessary to, a decision, or on which it is based, conclusive for the purposes of any further decision.

Consultation with Lord Advocate

7. Before exercising any of his powers under paragraph 1(2) or (3), or 4(1) or (2)(b), the Lord Chancellor shall consult the Lord Advocate.

Northern Ireland

8. In its application to Northern Ireland this Schedule shall have effect as if—

(a) for any reference to a Child Support Commissioner (however expressed) there were substituted a corresponding reference to a Child Support Commissioner for Northern Ireland;

(b) in paragraph 2(1), the word "pensions" were omitted;

(c) for paragraph 3, there were substituted—

"3.   A Child Support Commissioner for Northern Ireland, so long as he holds office as such, shall not practise as a barrister or act for any remuneration to himself as arbitrator or referee or be directly or indirectly concerned in any matter as a conveyancer, notary public or solicitor.";

(d) in paragraph 4—

(i)   for paragraph (a) of sub-paragraph (2) there were substituted—

"(a)   from among persons who are barristers or solicitors of not less than 10 years standing; and";

(ii)   for sub-paragraph (3) there were substituted—

"(3)   Paragraph 2 applies to deputy Child Support Commissioners for Northern Ireland, but paragraph 3 does not apply to them."; and

(e) paragraphs 5 to 7 were omitted.

SCHEDULE 5

CONSEQUENTIAL AMENDMENTS

The Tribunals and Inquiries Act 1971 (c.62)

1.—(1) In section 7(3) of the Tribunals and Inquiries Act 1971 (chairmen of certain tribunals to be drawn from panels) after "paragraph" there shall be inserted "4A".

(2) In Schedule 1 to that Act (tribunals under the general supervision of the Council on Tribunals) the following entry shall be inserted at the appropriate place—

| "Child support maintenance | 4A.—(a)   The child support appeal tribunals established under section 21 of the Child Support Act 1991. |
| | (b)   A Child Support Commissioner appointed under section 22 of the Child Support Act 1991 and any tribunal presided over by such a Commissioner." |

The Northern Ireland Constitution Act 1973 (c. 36)

2. In paragraph 9 of Schedule 2 to the Northern Ireland Constitution Act 1973 (certain judicial appointments to be an excepted matter), after the words "for Northern Ireland", where they first occur, there shall be inserted "the Chief and other Child Support Commissioners for Northern Ireland".

The House of Commons Disqualification Act 1975 (c.24)

3.—(1) The House of Commons Disqualification Act 1975 shall be amended as follows.

(2) In Part I (disqualifying judicial offices), the following entries shall be inserted at the appropriate places—

"Chief or other Child Support Commissioner (excluding a person appointed under paragraph 4 of Schedule 4 to the Child Support Act 1991)."

"Chief or other Child Support Commissioner for Northern Ireland (excluding a person appointed under paragraph 4 of Schedule 4 to the Child Support Act 1991)."

(3) In Part III (other disqualifying offices), the following entry shall be inserted at the appropriate place—

"Regional or other full-time chairman of a child support appeal tribunal established under section 21 of the Child Support Act 1991".

The Northern Ireland Assembly Disqualification Act 1975 (c.25)

4.—(1) In Part I of the Northern Ireland Assembly Disqualification Act 1975 (disqualifying judicial offices), the following entries shall be inserted at the appropriate places—

"Chief or other Child Support Commissioner (excluding a person appointed under paragraph 4 of Schedule 4 to the Child Support Act 1991)."

"Chief or other Child Support Commissioner for Northern Ireland (excluding a person appointed under paragraph 4 of Schedule 4 to the Child Support Act 1991)."

The Family Law (Scotland) Act 1985 (c.37)

5. In section 4 (amount of aliment) of the Family Law (Scotland) Act 1985, at the end there shall be added—

"(4)   Where a court makes an award of aliment in an action brought by or on behalf of a child under the age of 16 years, it may include in that award such provision as it considers to be in all the circumstances reasonable in respect of the expenses incurred wholly or partly by the person having care of the child for the purpose of caring for the child."

Bankruptcy (Scotland) Act 1985 (c.66)

6.—(1) The Bankruptcy (Scotland) Act 1985 shall be amended as follows.

(2) In section 32 (vesting of estate and dealings of debtor after sequestration)—

(a) in subsection (3)—

(i) after paragraph (b) there shall be inserted—

"(c) any obligation of his to pay child support maintenance under the Child Support Act 1991,";

(ii) after "relevant obligations" where second occurring there shall be inserted "referred to in paragraphs (a) and (b) above";

(b) in subsection (5) after "Diligence" there shall be inserted "(which, for the purposes of this section, includes the making of a deduction from earnings order under the Child Support Act 1991)".

(3) In section 37 (effect of sequestration on diligence), in subsection (5A) for "or a conjoined arrestment order" there is substituted ", a conjoined arrestment order or a deduction from earnings order under the Child Support Act 1991".

(4) In section 55 (effect of discharge under section 54), in subsection (2)(d)—

(a) after "being" there shall be inserted "(i)";

(b) at the end there shall be inserted—

"or

(ii) child support maintenance within the meaning of the Child Support Act 1991 which was unpaid in respect of any period before the date of sequestration of—

(aa) any person by whom it was due to be paid; or

(bb) any employer by whom it was, or was due to be, deducted under section 31(5) of that Act.".

The Insolvency Act 1986 (c.45)

7. In section 281(5)(b) of the Insolvency Act 1986 (effect of discharge of bankrupt), after "family proceedings" there shall be inserted "or under a maintenance assessment made under the Child Support Act 1991".

The Debtors (Scotland) Act 1987 (c.18)

8.—(1) The Debtors (Scotland) Act 1987 shall be amended as follows.

(2) In section 1(5) (time to pay directions not competent in certain cases) after paragraph (c) there shall be inserted—

"(cc) in connection with a liability order within the meaning of the Child Support Act 1991;".

(3) In section 15(3) (interpretation of Part I), in the definition of "decree or other document", after "maintenance order" there shall be inserted ", a liability order within the meaning of the Child Support Act 1991".

(4) In section 54(1) (maintenance arrestment to be preceded by default) in paragraph (c) for "the aggregate of 3 instalments" there shall be substituted "one instalment".

(5) In section 72 (effect of sequestration on diligence against earnings)—

(a) in subsection (2) after "order" there shall be inserted "or deduction from earnings order under the Child Support Act 1991";

(b) after subsection (3) there shall be inserted—

"(3A)   Any sum deducted by the employer under such a deduction from earnings order made before the date of sequestration shall be paid to the Secretary of State, notwithstanding that the date of payment will be after the date of sequestration.";

(c) after subsection (4) there shall be inserted—

"(4A)   A deduction from earnings order under the said Act shall not be competent after the date of sequestration to secure the payment of any amount due by the debtor under a maintenance assessment within the meaning of that Act in respect of which a claim could be made in the sequestration.".

(6) In section 73(1) (interpretation of Part III), in the definition of "net earnings",

(a) in paragraph (c) for "within the meaning of the Wages Councils Act 1979" there shall be substituted ", namely any enactment, rules, deed or other instrument providing for the payment of annuities or lump sums—

(i) to the persons with respect to whom the instrument has effect on their retirement at a specified age or on becoming incapacitated at some earlier age, or

(ii) to the personal representatives or the widows, relatives or dependants of such persons on their death or otherwise,

whether with or without any further or other benefit;"; and

(b) at the end there shall be added—

"(d)   any amount deductible by virtue of a deduction from earnings order which, in terms of regulations made under section 32(4)(c) of the Child Support Act 1991, is to have priority over diligences against earnings."

(7) In section 106 (interpretation) in the definition of "maintenance order"—

(a) the word "or" where it appears after paragraph (g), shall be omitted; and

(b) at the end there shall be inserted "or

(j)   a maintenance assessment within the meaning of the Child Support Act 1991.".

Finance (No. 2) Act 1992

62. Qualifying maintenance payments: maintenance assessments etc.

(1) In section 347B of the Taxes Act 1988 (qualifying maintenance payments), the following subsections shall be added at the end—

"(8) In subsections (1)(a) and (5)(a) above, the reference to an order made by a court in the United Kingdom includes a reference to a maintenance assessment.

(9) Where—

(a) any periodical payment is made under a maintenance assessment by one of the parties to a marriage (including a marriage which has been dissolved or annulled),

(b) the other party to the marriage is, for the purpose of the Child Support Act 1991 or (as the case may be) the Child Support (Northern Ireland) Order 1991, a parent of the child or children with respect to whom the assessment has effect,

(c) the assessment was not made under section 7 of the Child Support Act 1991 (right of child in Scotland to apply for maintenance assessment, and

(d) any of the conditions mentioned in subsection (10) below is satisfied, this section shall have effect as if the payment had been made to the other party for the maintenance by that other party of that child or (as the case may be) those children.

(10) The conditions are that—

(a) the payment is made to the Secretary of State in accordance with regulations made under section 29 of the Child Support Act 1991, by virtue of subsection (3)(a)(ii) of that section;

(b) the payment is made to the Department of Health and Social Services for Northern Ireland in accordance with regulations made under Article 29 of the Child Support (Northern Ireland) Order 1991, by virtue of paragraph (3)(a)(ii) of that Article;

(c) the payment is retained by the Secretary of State in accordance with regulations made under section 41 of that Act;

(d) the payment is retained by the Department of Health and Social Services for Northern Ireland in accordance with regulations made under Article 38 of that Order.

(11) In this section "maintenance assessment" means a maintenance assessment made under the Child Support Act 1991 or the Child Support (Northern Ireland) Order 1991.

(12) Where any periodical payment is made to the Secretary of State or to the Department of Health and Social Services for Northern Ireland—

(a) by one of the parties to a marriage (including a marriage which has been dissolved or annulled), and

(b) under an order made under section 106 of the Social Security Administration Act 1992 or section 101 of the Social Security Administration
   (Northern Ireland) Act 1992 (recovery of expenditure on benefit from
   person liable for maintenance) in respect of income support claimed by
   the other party to the marriage,

this section shall have effect as if the payment had been made to the other
party to the marriage to or for the benefit, and for the maintenance, of that
other party or (as the case may be) to that other party for the maintenance
of the child or children concerned."

(2) In section 36 of the Finance Act 1988 (annual payments), the following
subsection shall be inserted after subsection (5)—

   "(5A) The reference in subsection (4)(d) above to an order made by a court,
   and the reference in subsection (5)(b) above to an order, in each case
   includes a reference to a maintenance assessment made under the Child
   Support Act 1991 or the Child Support (Northern Ireland) Order 1991."

(3) In section 38 of the Finance Act 1988 (maintenance payments under
existing obligations), the following subsections shall be inserted after subsection (8)—

   "(8A) The reference in subsection (1)(a) above to an order made by a court
   includes a reference to a maintenance assessment made under the Child
   Support Act 1991 or under the Child Support (Northern Ireland) Order
   1991"

(4) This section shall come into force on such date as the Secretary of State
may by order provide.

(5) The power conferred by subsection (4) above shall be exercisable by
statutory instrument.

(6) The provision made by this section shall have effect, so far as it concerns
orders under section 106 of the Social Security Administration Act 1992 or
section 101 of the Social Security Adminstration (Northern Ireland) Act 1992,
only in relation to payments which fall due after the coming into force of this
section.

S.I. 1992 No. 1815

The Child Support (Maintenance Assessments and Special Cases) Regulations 1992

Made – – – –	*20th July 1992*
Coming into force	*5th April 1993*

ARRANGEMENT OF REGULATIONS

PART I

General

PART II

Calculation or estimation of child support maintenance

PART III

Special cases

25. Care provided in part by a local authority
26. Cases where child support maintenance is not to be payable
27. Child who is a boarder or an in-patient
28. Amount payable where absent parent is in receipt of income support or other prescribed benefit

SCHEDULES

SCHEDULE 1—Calculation of N and M

SCHEDULE 2—Amounts to be disregarded when calculating or estimating N and M

SCHEDULE 3—Eligible housing costs

SCHEDULE 4—Cases where child support maintenance is not to be payable

Whereas a draft of this instrument was laid before Parliament in accordance with section 52(2) of the Child Support Act 1991 and approved by a resolution of each House of Parliament:

Now, therefore, the Secretary of State for Social Security, in exercise of the powers conferred by sections 42, 43, 51, 52(4) and 54 of, and paragraphs 1, 2 and 4 to 9 of Schedule 1 to, the Child Support Act 1991 and of all other powers enabling him in that behalf hereby makes the following Regulations:

PART I

GENERAL

Citation, commencement and interpretation

1.—(1) These Regulations may be cited as the Child Support (Maintenance Assessments and Special Cases) Regulations 1992 and shall come into force on 5th April 1993.

(2) In these Regulations unless the context otherwise requires—

"the Act" means the Child Support Act 1991;

"claimant " means a claimant for income support;

"Contributions and Benefits Act" means the Social Security Contributions and Benefits Act 1992;

"council tax benefit " has the same meaning as in the Local Government Finance Act 1992;

"course of advanced education" means

(a) a full-time course leading to a postgraduate degree or comparable qualification, a first degree or comparable qualification, a Diploma of Higher Education, a higher national diploma, a higher national diploma or higher national certificate of the Business and Technician Education Council or the Scottish Vocational Education Council or a teaching qualification; or

    (b) any other full-time course which is a course of a standard above that of an ordinary national diploma, a national diploma or national certificate of the Business and Technician Education Council or the Scottish Vocational Education Council, the advanced level of the General Certificate of Education, a Scottish certificate of education (higher level) or a Scottish certificate of sixth year studies;

"covenant income" means the gross income payable to a student under a Deed of Covenant by a parent;

"day " includes any part of a day;

"day to day care" means care of not less than 2 nights per week on average during—

    (a) the 12 month period ending with the relevant week; or

    (b) such other period, ending with the relevant week, as in the opinion of the child support officer is more representative of the current arrangements for the care of the child in question;

and for the purposes of this definition, where a child is a boarder at a boarding school or is an in-patient in a hospital, the person who, but for those circumstances, would otherwise provide day to day care of the child, shall be treated as providing day to day care during the periods in question.

"disability working allowance" has the same meaning as in section 129 of the Contributions and Benefits Act;

"earnings" has the meaning assigned to it by paragraph 1 or 3, as the case may be, of Schedule 1;

"effective date" means the date on which a maintenance assessment takes effect for the purposes of the Act;

"eligible housing costs" shall be construed in accordance with Schedule 3;

"employed earner" has the same meaning as in section 2(1)(a) of the Contributions and Benefits Act;

"family" means—

    (a) a married or unmarried couple (including the members of a polygamous marriage) and any child or children living with them for whom at least one member of that couple has day to day care;

    (b) where a person who is not a member of a married or unmarried couple has day to day care of a child, that person and any such child or children;

and for the purposes of this definition a person shall not be treated as having day to day care of a child who is a member of that person's household where the child in question is being looked after by a local authority within the meaning of section 22 of the Children Act 1989 or, in Scotland, where the child is boarded out with that person by a local authority under the provisions of section 21 of the Social Work (Scotland) Act 1968;

"grant" means any kind of educational grant or award and includes any scholarship, exhibition, allowance or bursary but does not include a payment made under section 100 of the Education Act 1944 or section 73 of the Education (Scotland) Act 1980;

"grant contribution" means any amount which a Minister of the Crown or an education authority treats as properly payable by another person when assessing the amount of a student's grant and by which that amount is, as a consequence, reduced;

"home" means—

(a) the dwelling in which a person and any family of his normally live; or

(b) if he or they normally live in more than one home, the principal home of that person and any family of his,

and for the purpose of determining the principal home in which a person normally lives no regard shall be had to residence in a residential care home or a nursing home during a period which does not exceed 52 weeks or, where it appears to the child support officer that the person will return to his principal home after that period has expired, such longer period as that officer considers reasonable to allow for the return of that person to that home;

"housing benefit" has the same meaning as in section 130 of the Contributions and Benefits Act;

"Housing Benefit Regulations" means the Housing Benefit (General) Regulations 1987;

"Income Support Regulations" means the Income Support (General) Regulations 1987;

"Maintenance Assessment Procedure Regulations" means the Child Support (Maintenance Assessment Procedure) Regulations 1992;

"married couple" means a man and a woman who are married to each other and are members of the same household;

"non-dependant" means a person who is a non-dependant for the purposes of either—

(a) regulation 3 of the Income Support Regulations; or

(b) regulation 3 of the Housing Benefit Regulations,

or who would be a non-dependant for those purposes if another member of the household in which he is living were entitled to income support or housing benefit as the case may be;

"nursing home" has the same meaning as in regulation 19(3) of the Income Support Regulations;

"occupational pension scheme" has the same meaning as in section 66(1) of the Social Security Pensions Act 1975;

"ordinary clothing or footwear" means clothing or footwear for normal daily use, but does not include school uniforms, or clothing or footwear used solely for sporting activities;

"parent with care" means a person who, in respect of the same child or children, is both a parent and a person with care;

"partner" means—

(a) in relation to a member of a married or unmarried couple who are living together, the other member of that couple;

(b) in relation to a member of a polygamous marriage, any other member of that marriage with whom he lives;

"patient" means a person (other than a person who is serving a sentence of imprisonment or detention in a young offender institution within the meaning of the Criminal Justice Act 1982 as amended by the Criminal Justice Act 1988) who is regarded as receiving free in-patient treatment within the meaning of the Social Security (Hospital In-Patients) Regulations 1975;

"person" does not include a local authority;

"personal pension scheme" has the same meaning as in section 84(1) of the Social Security Act 1986 and, in the case of a self-employed earner, includes a scheme approved by the Inland Revenue under Chapter IV of Part XIV of the Income and Corporation Taxes Act 1988;

"polygamous marriage" means any marriage during the subsistence of which a party to it is married to more than one person and in respect of which any ceremony of marriage took place under the law of a country which at the time of that ceremony permitted polygamy;

"prisoner" means a person who is detained in custody pending trial or sentence upon conviction or under a sentence imposed by a court other than a person whose detention is under the Mental Health Act 1983 or the Mental Health (Scotland) Act 1984;

"relevant child" means a child of an absent parent or a parent with care who is a member of the same family as that parent;

"relevant Schedule" means Schedule 2 to the Income Support Regulations (income support applicable amounts);

"relevant week" means—

    (a) in relation to an application for child support maintenance—

        (i)   in the case of the person making the application, the period of 7 days immediately preceding the date on which the appropriate maintenance assessment application form is submitted to the Secretary of State;

        (ii) in the case of a person to whom a maintenance assessment enquiry form is given or sent as a result of such application, the period of 7 days immediately preceding the date on which that form is to be treated as given or sent under regulation 1(6)(b) of the Maintenance Assessment Procedure Regulations;

    (b) in relation to a review of a maintenance assessment under section 16 or 17 of the Act, the period of 7 days immediately preceding the date on which a maintenance assessment review enquiry form given or sent to the person in question is to be treated as having been given or sent under regulation 1(6)(b) of the Maintenance Assessment Procedure Regulations;

"residential care home" has the same meaning as in regulation 19(3) of the Income Support Regulations;

"retirement annuity contract" means an annuity contract for the time being approved by the Board of Inland Revenue as having for its main object the provision of a life annuity in old age or the provision of an annuity for a partner or dependant and in respect of which relief from income tax may be given on any premium;

"self-employed earner" has the same meaning as in section 2(1)(b) of the Contributions and Benefits Act;

"student" means a person, other than a person in receipt of a training allowance, who is aged less than 19 and attending a full-time course of advanced education or who is aged 19 or over and attending a full-time course of study at an educational establishment; and for the purposes of this definition—

    (a) a person who has started on such a course shall be treated as attending it throughout any period of term or vacation within it, until the last day of the course or such earlier date as he abandons it or is dismissed from it;

    (b) a person on a sandwich course (within the meaning of paragraph 1(1) of Schedule 5 to the Education (Mandatory Awards) Regulations 1988) shall be treated as attending a full-time course of advanced education or, as the case may be, of study;

"student loan" means a loan which is made to a student pursuant to arrangements made under section 1 of the Education (Student Loans) Act 1990;

"the Independent Living Fund" means the charitable trust of that name established out of funds provided by the Secretary of State for the purpose of providing financial assistance to those persons incapacitated by or otherwise suffering from very severe disablement who are in need of such assistance to enable them to live independently;

"training allowance" has the same meaning as in regulation 2 of the Income Support Regulations;

"unmarried couple" means a man and a woman who are not married to each other but are living together as husband and wife;

"weekly council tax" means the annual amount of the council tax in question payable in respect of the year in which the effective date falls, divided by 52;

"year" means a period of 52 weeks;

"youth training" means—

    (a) arrangements made under section 2 of the Employment and Training Act 1973 or section 2 of the Enterprise and New Towns (Scotland) Act 1990; or

    (b) arrangements made by the Secretary of State for persons enlisted in Her Majesty's forces for any special term of service specified in regulations made under section 2 of the Armed Forces Act 1966 (power of Defence Council to make regulations as to engagement of persons in regular forces);

for purposes which include the training of persons who, at the beginning of their training, are under the age of 18.

    (3) In these Regulations, unless the context otherwise requires, a reference—

    (a) to a numbered Part is to the Part of these Regulations bearing that number;

    (b) to a numbered Schedule is to the Schedule to these Regulations bearing that number;

    (c) to a numbered regulation is to the regulation in these Regulations bearing that number;

(d) in a regulation or Schedule to a numbered paragraph is to the paragraph in that regulation or Schedule bearing that number;

(e) in a paragraph to a lettered or numbered sub-paragraph is to the sub-paragraph in that paragraph bearing that letter or number.

(4) The regulations in Part II and the provisions of the Schedules to these Regulations are subject to the regulations relating to special cases in Part III.

PART II
CALCULATION OR ESTIMATION OF CHILD SUPPORT MAINTENANCE

Calculation or estimation of amounts

2.—(1) Where any amount falls to be taken into account for the purposes of these Regulations, it shall be calculated or estimated as a weekly amount and, except where the context otherwise requires, any reference to such an amount shall be construed accordingly.

(2) Subject to regulation 13(2), where any calculation made under these Regulations results in a fraction of a penny that fraction shall be treated as a penny if it is either one half or exceeds one half, otherwise it shall be disregarded.

(3) A child support officer shall calculate the amounts to be taken into account for the purposes of these Regulations by reference, as the case may be, to the dates, weeks, months or other periods specified herein provided that if he becomes aware of a material change of circumstances occurring after such date, week, month or other period but before the effective date, he shall take that change of circumstances into account.

Calculation of AG

3.—(1) The amounts to be taken into account for the purposes of calculating AG in the formula set out in paragraph 1(2) of Schedule 1 to the Act are—

(a) with respect to each qualifying child, an amount equal to the amount specified in column (2) of paragraph 2 of the relevant Schedule for a person of the same age (income support personal allowance for child or young person);

(b) with respect to a person with care of a qualifying child aged less than 16, an amount equal to the amount specified in column (2) of paragraph 1(1)(e) of the relevant Schedule (income support personal allowance for a single claimant aged not less than 25);

(c) an amount equal to the amount specified in paragraph 3 of the relevant Schedule (income support family premium);

(d) where the person with care of the qualifying child or children has no partner, an amount equal to the amount specified in paragraph 15(1) of the relevant Schedule (income support lone parent premium).

(2) The amounts referred to in paragraph (1) shall be the amounts applicable at the effective date.

Basic rate of child benefit

4. For the purposes of paragraph 1(4) of Schedule 1 to the Act "basic rate" means the rate of child benefit which is specified in regulation 2(1) of the Child Benefit and Social Security (Fixing and Adjustment of Rates) Regulations 1976 (rates of child benefit) applicable to the child in question at the effective date.

The general rule

5. For the purposes of paragraph 2(1) of Schedule 1 to the Act—
   (a) the value of C, otherwise than in a case where the other parent is the person with care, is nil; and
   (b) the value of P is 0.5.

The additional element

6.—(1) For the purposes of the formula in paragraph 4(1) of Schedule 1 to the Act, the value of R is 0.25.
   (2) For the purposes of the alternative formula in paragraph 4(3) of Schedule 1 to the Act—
   (a) the value of Z is 3;
   (b) the amount for the purposes of paragraph (b) of the definition of Q is the same as the amount specified in regulation 3(1)(c) (income support family premium) in respect of each qualifying child.

Net income: calculation or estimation of N

7.—(1)   Subject to the following provisions of this regulation, for the purposes of the formula in paragraph 5(1) of Schedule 1 to the Act, the amount of N (net income of absent parent) shall be the aggregate of the following amounts—
   (a) the amount, determined in accordance with Part I of Schedule 1, of any earnings of the absent parent;
   (b) the amount, determined in accordance with Part II of Schedule 1, of any benefit payments under the Contributions and Benefits Act paid to or in respect of the absent parent;
   (c) the amount, determined in accordance with Part III of Schedule 1, of any other income of the absent parent;
   (d) the amount, determined in accordance with Part IV of Schedule 1, of any income of a relevant child which is treated as the income of the absent parent;
   (e) any amount, determined in accordance with Part V of Schedule 1, which is treated as the income of the absent parent.
   (2)   Any amounts referred to in Schedule 2 shall be disregarded.
   (3)   Where an absent parent's income consists—
   (a) only of a youth training allowance; or

   (b) in the case of a student, only of grant, an amount paid in respect of grant contribution or student loan or any combination thereof; or

   (c) only of prisoner's pay,

then for the purposes of determining N such income shall be disregarded.

(4) Where a parent and any other person are beneficially entitled to any income but the shares of their respective entitlements are not ascertainable the child support officer shall estimate their respective entitlements having regard to such information as is available but where sufficient information on which to base an estimate is not available the parent and that other person shall be treated as entitled to that income in equal shares.

(5) Where any income normally received at regular intervals has not been received it shall, if it is due to be paid and there are reasonable grounds for believing it will be received, be treated as if it had been received.

Net income: calculation or estimation of M

8. For the purposes of paragraph 5(2) of Schedule 1 to the Act, the amount of M (net income of the parent with care) shall be calculated in the same way as N is calculated under regulation 7 but as if references to the absent parent were references to the parent with care.

Exempt income: calculation or estimation of E

9.—(1) For the purposes of paragraph 5(1) of Schedule 1 to the Act, the amount of E (exempt income of absent parent) shall, subject to paragraphs (3) and (4), be the aggregate of the following amounts—

   (a) an amount equal to the amount specified in column (2) of paragraph 1(1)(e) of the relevant Schedule (income support personal allowance for a single claimant aged not less than 25);

   (b) an amount in respect of housing costs determined in accordance with regulations 14 to 18;

   (c) where—

      (i)   the absent parent is the parent of a relevant child; and

      (ii) if he were a claimant, the condition in paragraph 8 of the relevant Schedule (income support lone parent premium) would be satisfied but the conditions referred to in sub-paragraph (1)(d) would not be satisfied;

   an amount equal to the amount specified in column (2) of paragraph 15(1) of that Schedule (income support lone parent premium);

   (d) where, if the parent were a claimant aged less than 60, the conditions in paragraph 11 of the relevant Schedule (income support disability premium) would be satisfied in respect of him, an amount equal to the amount specified in column (2) of paragraph 15(4)(a) of that Schedule (income support disability premium);

   (e) where—

      (i)   if the parent were a claimant, the conditions in paragraph 13 of the relevant Schedule (income support severe disability premium) would be satisfied, an amount equal to the amount specified in column (2) of paragraph 15(5)(a) of that Schedule (except that no such amount shall be taken into account in the case of an absent parent in respect of whom an invalid care allowance under section 70 of the Contributions and Benefits Act is payable to some other person);

(ii) if the parent were a claimant, the conditions in paragraph 14ZA of the relevant Schedule (income support carer premium) would be satisfied in respect of him, an amount equal to the amount specified in column (2) of paragraph 15(7) of that Schedule;

(f) where, if the parent were a claimant, the conditions in paragraph 3 of the relevant Schedule (income support family premium) would be satisfied in respect of a relevant child of that parent, the amount specified in that paragraph or, where those conditions would be satisfied only by virtue of the case being one to which paragraph (2) applies, half that amount;

(g) in respect of each relevant child—
    (i) an amount equal to the amount of the personal allowance for that child, specified in column (2) of paragraph 2 of the relevant Schedule (income support personal allowance) or, where paragraph (2) applies, half that amount;

    (ii) if the conditions set out in paragraph 14(b) and (c) of the relevant Schedule (income support disabled child premium) are satisfied in respect of that child, an amount equal to the amount specified in column (2) of paragraph 15(6) of the relevant Schedule or, where paragraph (2) applies, half that amount;

(h) where the absent parent in question or his partner is living in—
    (i) accommodation provided under Part III of the National Assistance Act 1 1948;

    (ii) accommodation provided under paragraphs 1 and 2 of Schedule 8 to the National Health Service Act 1977; or

    (iii) a nursing home or residential care home,

the amount of the fees paid in respect of the occupation of that accommodation or, as the case may be, that home.

(2) This paragraph applies where—

(a) the absent parent has a partner;

(b) the absent parent and the partner are parents of the same relevant child; and

(c) the income of the partner, calculated under regulation 7(1) as if that partner were an absent parent to whom that regulation applied, exceeds the aggregate of—
    (i) the amount specified in column 2 of paragraph 1(1)(e) of the relevant Schedule (income support personal allowance for a single claimant aged not less than 25);

    (ii) half the amount of the personal allowance for that child specified in column (2) of paragraph 2 of the relevant Schedule (income support personal allowance);

(iii) half the amount of any income support disabled child premium specified in column (2) of paragraph 15(6) of that Schedule in respect of that child;

(iv) half the amount of any income support family premium specified in paragraph 3 of the Schedule except where such premium is payable irrespective of that child; and

(v) the amount by which the housing costs of the absent parent, calculated in accordance with these Regulations, have been reduced by an apportionment under regulation 17.

(3) Where an absent parent does not have day to day care of any relevant child for 7 nights each week but does have day to day care of one or more such children for fewer than 7 nights each week, any amounts to be taken into account under sub-paragraphs (1)(c) and (f) shall be reduced so that they bear the same proportion to the amounts referred to in those sub-paragraphs as the average number of nights each week in respect of which such care is provided has to 7.

(4) Where an absent parent has day to day care of a relevant child for fewer than 7 nights each week, any amounts to be taken into account under sub-paragraph (1)(g) in respect of such a child shall be reduced so that they bear the same proportion to the amounts referred to in that sub-paragraph as the average number of nights each week in respect of which such care is provided has to 7.

(5) The amounts referred to in paragraph (1) are the amounts applicable at the effective date.

Exempt income: calculation or estimation of F

10. For the purposes of paragraph 5(2) of Schedule 1 to the Act, the amount of F (exempt income of parent with care) shall be calculated in the same way as E is calculated under regulation 9 but as if references to the absent parent were references to the parent with care.

Protected income

11.—(1) For the purposes of paragraph 6 of Schedule 1 to the Act the protected income level of an absent parent shall, subject to paragraphs (3) and (4), be the aggregate of the following amounts—

(a) where—

(i) the absent parent does not have a partner, an amount equal to the amount specified in column (2) of paragraph 1(1)(e) of the relevant Schedule (income support personal allowance for a single claimant aged not less than 25 years);

(ii) the absent parent has a partner, an amount equal to the amount specified in column (2) of paragraph 1(3)(c) of the relevant Schedule (income support personal allowance for a couple where both members are aged not less than 18 years);

(iii) the absent parent is a member of a polygamous marriage, an amount in respect of himself and one of his partners, equal to the amount specified in sub-paragraph (ii) and, in respect of each of his other partners, an amount equal to the difference between the amounts specified in sub-paragraph (ii) and sub-paragraph (i);

(b) an amount in respect of housing costs determined in accordance with regulations 14, 15, 16 and 18, or, in a case where the absent parent is a non-dependant member of a household who is treated as having no housing costs by regulation 15(10)(a), the non-dependant amount which would be calculated in respect of him under regulation 15(5);

(c) where, if the absent parent were a claimant, the condition in paragraph 8 of the relevant Schedule (income support lone parent premium) would be satisfied but the condition set out in paragraph 11 of that Schedule (income support disability premium) would not be satisfied, an amount equal to the amount specified in column (2) of paragraph 15(1) of that Schedule (income support lone parent premium);

(d) where, if the parent were a claimant, the conditions in paragraph 11 of the relevant Schedule (income support disability premium) would be satisfied, an amount equal to the amount specified in column (2) of paragraph 15(4) of that Schedule (income support disability premium);

(e) where, if the parent were a claimant, the conditions in paragraph 13 or 14ZA of the relevant Schedule (income support severe disability and carer premiums) would be satisfied in respect of either or both premiums, an amount equal to the amount or amounts specified in column (2) of paragraph 15(5) or, as the case may be, (7) of that Schedule in respect of that or those premiums (income support premiums);

(f) where, if the parent were a claimant, the conditions in paragraph 3 of the relevant Schedule (income support family premium) would be satisfied, the amount specified in that paragraph;

(g) in respect of each child who is a member of the family of the absent parent—
   (i) an amount equal to the amount of the personal allowance for that child, specified in column (2) of paragraph 2 of the relevant Schedule (income support personal allowance);
   (ii) if the conditions set out in paragraphs 14(b) and (c) of the relevant Schedule (income support disabled child premium) are satisfied in respect of that child, an amount equal to the amount specified in column (2) of paragraph 15(6) of the relevant Schedule;

(h) where, if the parent were a claimant, the conditions specified in Part III of the relevant Schedule would be satisfied by the absent parent in question or any member of his family in relation to any premium not otherwise included in this regulation, an amount equal to the amount specified in Part IV of that Schedule (income support premiums) in respect of that premium;

(i) where the absent parent in question or his partner is living in—
   (i) accommodation provided under Part III of the National Assistance Act 1948;

(ii)   accommodation provided under paragraphs 1 and 2 of Schedule 8 to the National Health Service Act 1977; or

(iii) a nursing home or residential care home,

the amount of the fees paid in respect of the occupation of that accommodation or, as the case may be, that home.

(j)   the amount of council tax which the absent parent in question or his partner is liable to pay in respect of the home for which housing costs are included under sub-paragraph (b) less any council tax benefit;

(k)   an amount of £8·00;

(l)   where the income of—

(i)   the absent parent in question;

(ii)   any partner of his; and

(iii) any child or children for whom an amount is included under sub-paragraph (g)(i);

exceeds the sum of the amounts to which reference is made in sub-paragraphs (a) to (k), 10 per centum of the excess.

(2) For the purposes of sub-paragraph (1) of paragraph (1) "income" shall be calculated—

(a)   in respect of the absent parent in question or any partner of his, in the same manner as N (net income of absent parent) is calculated under regulation 7 except—

(i)   there shall be taken into account the basic rate of any child benefit and any maintenance which in either case is in payment in respect of any member of the family of the absent parent;

(ii)   there shall be deducted the amount of any maintenance under a maintenance order which the absent parent or his partner is paying in respect of a child in circumstances where an application for a maintenance assessment could not be made in accordance with the Act in respect of that child; and

(b)   in respect of any child in that family, as being the total of that child's income but only to the extent that such income does not exceed the amount included under sub-paragraph (g) of paragraph (1) (income support personal allowance for a child and income support disabled child premium) reduced, as the case may be, under paragraph (4).

(3) Where an absent parent does not have day to day care of any child (whether or not a relevant child) for 7 nights each week but does have day to day care of one or more such children for fewer than 7 nights each week, any amounts to be taken into account under sub-paragraphs (c) and (f) of paragraph (1) (income support lone parent premium and income support family premium) shall be reduced so that they bear the same proportion to the amounts referred to in those sub-paragraphs as the average number of nights each week in respect of which such care is provided has to 7.

(4) Where an absent parent has day to day care of a child (whether or not a relevant child) for fewer than 7 nights each week any amounts in relation to that child to be taken into account under sub-paragraph (g) of paragraph (1) (income support personal allowance for child and income support disabled

child premium) shall be reduced so that they bear the same proportion to the amounts referred to in that sub-paragraph as the average number of nights in respect of which such care is provided has to 7.

(5) The amounts referred to in paragraph (1) shall be the amounts applicable at the effective date.

Disposable income

12.—(1) For the purposes of paragraph 6(4) of Schedule 1 to the Act (protected income), the disposable income of an absent parent shall be the aggregate of his income and any income of any member of his family calculated in like manner as under regulation 11(2)

(2) Subject to paragraph (3), where a maintenance assessment has been made with respect to the absent parent and payment of the amount of that assessment would reduce his disposable income below his protected income level the amount of the assessment shall be reduced by the minimum amount necessary to prevent his disposable income being reduced below his protected income level.

(3) Where the prescribed minimum amount fixed by regulations under paragraph 7 of Schedule 1 to the Act is applicable (such amount being specified in regulation 13) the amount payable under the assessment shall not be reduced to less than the prescribed minimum amount.

The minimum amount

13.—(1) Subject to regulation 26, for the purposes of paragraph 7(1) of Schedule 1 to the Act the minimum amount shall be 5 per centum of the amount specified in paragraph 1(1)(e) of the relevant Schedule (income support personal allowance for single claimant aged not less than 25).

(2) Where an amount calculated under paragraph (1) results in a sum other than a multiple of 5 pence, it shall be treated as the sum which is the next higher multiple of 5 pence.

Eligible housing costs

14. Schedule 3 shall have effect for the purpose of determining the costs which are eligible to be taken into account as housing costs for the purposes of these Regulations.

Amount of housing costs

15.—(1) Subject to the provisions of this regulation and regulations 16 to 18, a parent's housing costs shall be the aggregate of the eligible housing costs payable in respect of his home.

(2) Where a local authority has determined that a parent is entitled to housing benefit, the amount of his housing costs shall, subject to paragraphs (4) to (9), be the weekly amount treated as rent under regulations 10 and 69 of the Housing Benefit Regulations (rent and calculation of weekly amounts) less the amount of housing benefit.

(3) Where a parent has eligible housing costs and another person who is not

a member of his family is also liable to make payments in respect of the home, the amount of the parent's housing costs shall be his share of those costs.

(4) Where one or more non-dependants are members of the parent's household, there shall be deducted from the amount of any housing costs determined under the preceding paragraphs of this regulation any non-dependant amount or amounts determined in accordance with the provisions of paragraphs (5) to (9).

(5) The non-dependant amount shall be an amount equal to the amount which would be calculated under paragraph 63 of the Housing Benefit Regulations (non-dependant deductions) for the non-dependant in question if he were a non-dependant in respect of whom a calculation were to be made under that regulation.

(6) For the purposes of paragraph (5)—
  (a) in the case of a couple or, as the case may be, the members of a polygamous marrlage—
    (i)   regard shall be had to their joint weekly income; and
    (ii) only one deduction shall be made at whichever is the higher rate.

(7) Where a person is a non-dependant in respect of more than one joint occupier of a dwelling (except where the joint occupiers are a couple or members of a polygamous marriage), the deduction in respect of that non-dependant shall be apportioned between the joint occupiers having regard to the number of joint occupiers and the proportion of the housing costs in respect of the home payable by each of them.

(8) No deduction shall be made in respect of any non-dependants occupying the home of the parent, if the parent or any partner of his is—
  (a) blind or treated as blind by virtue of paragraph 12 of the relevant Schedule (income support additional condition for the higher pensioner and disability premiums); or
  (b) receiving in respect of himself either—
    (i)   attendance allowance under section 64 of the Contributions and Benefits Act; or
    (ii) the care component of disability living allowance.

(9) No deduction shall be made in respect of a non-dependant—
  (a) if, although he resides with the parent, it appears to the child support officer that his home is normally elsewhere; or
  (b) if he is in receipt of a training allowance paid in connection with a Youth Training Programme established under section 2 of the Employment and Training Act 1973 or section 2 of the Enterprise and New Towns (Scotland) Act 1990; or
  (c) if he is a student; or
  (d) if he is aged under 25 and in receipt of income support; or
  (e) if he is not residing with the parent because he is a prisoner or because he has been a patient for a period, or two or more periods separated by not more than 28 days, exceeding 6 weeks.

(10) A parent shall be treated as having no housing costs where—
  (a) he is a non-dependant member of a household and is not responsible

for meeting housing costs except to another member, or other members, of that household; or

(b) but for this paragraph, his housing costs would be less than nil.

Weekly amount of housing costs

16. Where a parent pays housing costs—

(a) on a weekly basis, the amount of such housing costs shall be the weekly rate payable at the effective date;

(b) on a monthly basis, the amount of such housing costs shall be the monthly rate payable at the effective date, multiplied by 12 and divided by 52;

(c) on any other basis, the amount of such housing costs shall be the rate payable at the effective date, multiplied by the number of payment periods, or the nearest whole number of payment periods (any fraction of one half being rounded up), falling within a period of 365 days and divided by 52.

Apportionment of housing costs: exempt income

17. For the purposes of calculating or estimating exempt income the amount of the housing costs of a parent shall be—

(a) where the parent does not have a partner, the whole amount of the housing costs;

(b) where the parent has a partner, the proportion of the amount of the housing costs calculated by multiplying those costs by—

$$\frac{0.75 + (A \times 0.2)}{1.00 + (B \times 0.2)}$$

where—

A   is the number of relevant children (if any);

B   is the number of children in that parent's family (if any);

(c) where the parent is a member of a polygamous marriage the proportion of the amount of the housing costs calculated by multiplying those costs by—

$$\frac{0.75 + (A \times 0.2)}{1.00 + (X \times 0.25) + (B \times 0.2)}$$

where—

A and B have the same meanings as in sub-paragraph (b); and

X   is the number which is one less than the number of partners.

Excessive housing costs

18.—(1) Subject to paragraph (2), the amount of the housing costs of an absent parent which are to be taken into account—

(a) under regulation 9(1)(b) shall not exceed the greater of £80·00 or half the amount of N as calculated or estimated under regulation 7;

(b) under regulation 11(1)(b) shall not exceed the greater of £80·00 or half of the amount calculated in accordance with regulation 11(2).

(2) The restriction imposed by paragraph (1) shall not apply where—
  (a) the absent parent in question—
    (i)   has been awarded housing benefit (or is awaiting the outcome of a claim to that benefit);
    (ii) has the day to day care of any child; or
    (iii) is a person to whom a disability premium under paragraph 11 of the relevant Schedule applies in respect of himself or his partner or would so apply if he were entitled to income support and were aged less than 60;
  (b) the absent parent in question, following a divorce from, or the breakdown of his relationship with, his former partner, remains in the home he occupied with his former partner;
  (c) the absent parent in question has paid the housing costs under the mortgage, charge or agreement in question for a period in excess of 52 weeks before the date of the first application for child support maintenance in relation to a qualifying child of his and there has been no increase in those costs other than an increase in the interest payable under the mortgage or charge or, as the case may be, in the amount payable under the agreement under which the home is held;
  (d) the housing costs in respect of the home in question would not exceed the amount set out in paragraph (1) but for an increase in the interest payable under a mortgage or charge secured on that home or, as the case may be. in the amount payable under any agreement under which it is held; or
  (e) the absent parent is responsible for making payments in respect of housing costs which are higher than they would be otherwise by virtue of the unavailability of his share of the equity of the property formerly occupied with his partner and which remains occupied by that former partner.

PART III
SPECIAL CASES

Both parents are absent
19.—(1) Subject to regulation 27, where the circumstances of a case are that each parent of a qualifying child is an absent parent in relation to that child (neither being a person who is treated as an absent parent by regulation 20(2)) that case shall be treated as a special case for the purposes of the Act.

(2) For the purposes of this case—
  (a) where the application is made in relation to both absent parents, separate assessments shall be made under Schedule 1 to the Act in respect of each so as to determine the amount of child support maintenance payable by each absent parent;
  (b) subject to paragraph (3), where the application is made in relation to both absent parents, the value of C in each case shall be the assessable income of the other absent parent and where the application is made

in relation to only one the value of C in the case of the other shall be nil;

(c) where the person with care is a body of persons corporate or unincorporate, the value of AG shall not include any amount mentioned in regulation 3(1)(d) (income support lone parent premium).

(3) Where, for the purposes of paragraph (2)(b), information regarding the income of the other absent parent has not been submitted to the Secretary of State or to a child support officer within the period specified in regulation 6(1) of the Maintenance Assessment Procedure Regulations then until such information is acquired the value of C shall be nil.

(4) When the information referred to in paragraph (3) is acquired the child support officer shall make a fresh assessment which shall have effect from the effective date in relation to that other absent parent.

Persons treated as absent parents
20.—(1) Where the circumstances of a case are that—

(a) two or more persons who do not live in the same household each provide day to day care for the same qualifying child; and

(b) at least one of those persons is a parent of that child,

that case shall be treated as a special case for the purposes of the Act.

(2) For the purposes of this case a parent who provides day to day care for a child of his in the following circumstances is to be treated as an absent parent for the purposes of the Act and these Regulations—

(a) a parent who provides such care to a lesser extent than the other parent, person or persons who provide such care for the child in question;

(b) where the persons mentioned in paragraph (1)(a) include both parents and the circumstances are such that care is provided to the same extent by both but each provides care to a greater or equal extent than any other person who provides such care for that child—

(i)   the parent who is not in receipt of child benefit for the child in question; or

(ii) if neither parent is in receipt of child benefit for that child, the parent who, in the opinion of the child support officer, will not be the principal provider of day to day care for that child.

(3) Subject to paragraphs (5) and (6), where a parent is treated as an absent parent under paragraph (2) child support maintenance shall be payable by that parent in respect of the child in question and the amount of the child support maintenance so payable shall be calculated in accordance with the formula set out in paragraph (4).

(4) The formula for the purposes of paragraph (3) is—

$$T = X - \left\{ (X + Y) \ \times \frac{J}{7 \ \times \ L} \right\}$$

where—

T   is the amount of child support maintenance payable;

X   is the amount of child support maintenance which would be payable by the parent who is treated as an absent parent, assessed under Schedule 1 to the Act as if paragraphs 6 and 7 of that Schedule did not apply, and, where the other parent is an absent parent, as if the value of C was the assessable income of the other parent;

Y   is—

(i)   the amount of child support maintenance assessed under Schedule 1 to the Act payable by the other parent if he is an absent parent or which would be payable if he were an absent parent, and for the purposes of such calculation the value of C shall be the assessable income of the parent treated as an absent parent under paragraph (2); or,

(ii)   if there is no such other parent, shall be nil;

J   is the total of the weekly average number of nights for which day to day care is provided by the person who is treated as the absent parent in respect of each child included in the maintenance assessment and shall be calculated to 2 decimal places;

L   is the number of children who are included in the maintenance assessment in question.

(5) Where the value of T calculated under the provisions of paragraph (4) is less than zero, no child support maintenance shall be payable.

(6) The liability to pay any amount calculated under paragraph (4) shall be subject to the provision made for protected income and minimum payments under paragraphs 6 and 7 of Schedule 1 to the Act.

One parent is absent and the other is treated as absent

21.—(1) Where the circumstances of a case are that one parent is an absent parent and the other parent is treated as an absent parent by regulation 20(2), that case shall be treated as a special case for the purposes of the Act.

(2) For the purpose of assessing the child support maintenance payable by an absent parent where this case applies, each reference in Schedule 1 to the Act to a parent who is a person with care shall be treated as a reference to a person who is treated as an absent parent by regulation 20(2).

Multiple applications relating to an absent parent

22.—(1) Where the circumstances of a case are that—

(a)   two or more applications for a maintenance assessment have been made which relate to the same absent parent (or to a person who is treated as an absent parent by regulation 20(2)); and

(b)   those applications relate to different children,

that case shall be treated as a special case for the purposes of the Act.

(2) For the purposes of assessing the amount of child support maintenance payable in respect of each application where paragraph (1) applies, for references to the assessable income of an absent parent in the Act and in these

Regulations there shall be substituted references to the amount calculated by the formula—

$$A \times \frac{B}{D}$$

where—

A   is the assessable income of the absent parent;

B   is the maintenance requirement calculated in respect of the application in question;

D   is the sum of the maintenance requirements as calculated for the purposes of each application relating to the absent parent in question.

(3) Where more than one maintenance assessment has been made with respect to the absent parent and payment by him of the aggregate of the amounts of those assessments would reduce his disposable income below his protected income level, the aggregate amount of those assessments shall be reduced (each being reduced by reference to the same proportion as those assessments bear to each other) by the minimum amount necessary to prevent his disposable income being reduced below his protected income level provided that the aggregate amount payable under those assessments shall not be reduced to less than the minimum amount prescribed in regulation 13(1).

(4) Where the aggregate of the child support maintenance payable by the absent parent is less than the minimum amount prescribed in regulation 13(1), the child support maintenance payable shall be that prescribed minimum amount apportioned between the two or more applications in the same ratio as the maintenance requirements in question bear to each other.

(5) Payment of each of the maintenance assessments calculated under this regulation shall satisfy the liability of the absent parent (or a person treated as such) to pay child support maintenance.

Person caring for children of more than one absent parent

23.—(1) Where the circumstances of a case are that—

(a) a person is a person with care in relation to two or more qualifying children; and

(b) in relation to at least two of those children there are different persons who are absent parents or persons treated as absent parents by regulation 20(2);

that case shall be treated as a special case for the purposes of the Act.

(2) In calculating the maintenance requirements for the purposes of this case, for any amount which (but for this paragraph) would have been included under regulation 3(1)(b), (c) or (d) (amounts included in the calculation of AG) there shall be substituted an amount calculated by dividing the amount which would have been so included by the relevant number.

(3) In paragraph (2) "the relevant number" means the number equal to the total number of persons who, in relation to those children, are either absent parents or persons treated as absent parents by regulation 20(2) except that

where in respect of the same child both parents are persons who are either absent parents or persons who are treated as absent parents under that regulation, they shall count as one person.

(4) Where the circumstances of a case fall within this regulation and the person with care is the parent of any of the children, for C in paragraph 2(1) of Schedule 1 to the Act (the assessable income of that person) there shall be substituted the amount which would be calculated under regulation 22(2) if the references therein to an absent parent were references to a parent with care.

Persons with part-time care – not including a person treated as an absent parent

24.—(1) Where the circumstances of a case are that—

(a) two or more persons who do not live in the same household each provide day to day care for the same qualifying child; and

(b) those persons do not include any parent who is treated as an absent parent of that child by regulation 20(2),

that case shall be treated as a special case for the purposes of the Act.

(2) For the purposes of this case—

(a) the person whose application for a maintenance assessment is being proceeded with shall, subject to paragraph (b), be entitled to receive all of the child support maintenance payable under the Act in respect of the child in question;

(b) on request being made to the Secretary of State by—

(i)   that person; or

(ii) any other person who is providing day to day care for that child and who intends to continue to provide that care,

the Secretary of State may make arrangements for the payment of any child support maintenance payable under the Act to the persons who provide such care in the same ratio as that in which it appears to the Secretary of State, that each is to provide such care for the child in question;

(c) before making an arrangement under sub-paragraph (b), the Secretary of State shall consider all of the circumstances of the case and in particular the interests of the child, the present arrangements for the day to day care of the child in question and any representations or proposals made by the persons who provide such care for that child.

Care provided in part by a local authority

25.—(1) Where the circumstances of a case are that a local authority and a person each provide day to day care for the same qualifying child, that case shall be treated as a special case for the purposes of the Act.

(2) In a case where this regulation applies—

(a) child support maintenance shall be calculated in respect of that child as if this regulation did not apply;

(b) the amount so calculated shall be divided by 7 so as to produce a daily amount;

(c) in respect of each night for which day to day care for that child is provided by a person other than the local authority, the daily amount relating to that period shall be payable by the absent parent (or, as the case may be, by the person treated as an absent parent under regulation 20(2));

(d) child support maintenance shall not be payable in respect of any night for which the local authority provides day to day care for that qualifying child.

Cases where child support maintenance is not to be payable

26.—(1) Where the circumstances of a case are that—

(a) but for this regulation the minimum amount prescribed in regulation 13(1) would apply; and

(b) any of the following conditions are satisfied—

(i)   the income of the absent parent includes one or more of the payments or awards specified in Schedule 4 or would include such a payment but for a provision preventing the receipt of that payment by reason of it overlapping with some other benefit payment or would, in the case of the payments referred to in paragraph (a)(i) or (iv) of that Schedule, include such a payment if the relevant contribution conditions for entitlement had been satisfied;

(ii) an amount to which regulation 11(1)(f) applies (protected income: income support family premium) is taken into account in calculating or estimating the protected income of the absent parent;

(iii) the absent parent is a child within the meaning of section 55 of the Act;

(iv) the absent parent is a prisoner; or

(v)   the absent parent is a person in respect of whom N (as calculated or estimated under regulation 7(1)) is less than the minimum amount prescribed by regulation 13(1),

the case shall be treated as a special case for the purposes of the Act.

(2) For the purposes of this case—

(a) the requirement in paragraph 7(2) of Schedule 1 to the Act (minimum amount of child support maintenance fixed by an assessment to be the prescribed minimum amount) shall not apply;

(b) the amount of the child support maintenance to be fixed by the assessment shall be nil.

Child who is a boarder or an in-patient

27.—(1) Where the circumstances of a case are that—

(a) a qualifying child is a boarder at a boarding school or is an in-patient in a hospital; and

(b) by reason of those circumstances, the person who would otherwise provide day to day care is not doing so,

that case shall be treated as a special case for the purposes of the Act.

(2) For the purposes of this case, section 3(3)(b) of the Act shall be modified so for the reference to the person who usually provides day to day care for the child there shall be substituted a reference to the person who would usually be providing such care for that child but for the circumstances specified in paragraph (1).

Amount payable where absent parent is in receipt of income support or other prescribed benefit

28.—(1) Where the condition specified in section 43(1)(a) of the Act is satisfied in relation to an absent parent (assessable income to be nil where income support or other prescribed benefit is paid), the prescribed conditions for the purposes of section 43(1)(b) of the Act are that—

    (a) the absent parent is aged 18 or over;

    (b) he does not satisfy the conditions in paragraph 3 of the relevant Schedule (income support family premium); and

    (c) he does not satisfy the conditions for entitlement to one or more of the payments or awards specified in Schedule 4 (other than by reason of a provision preventing receipt of overlapping benefits or by reason of a failure to satisfy the relevant contribution conditions).

(2) For the purposes of section 43(2)(a) of the Act, the prescribed amount shall be equal to the minimum amount prescribed in regulation 13(1) for the purposes of paragraph 7(1) of Schedule 1 to the Act.

Signed by authority of the Secretary of State for Social Security.

Alistair Burt
Parliamentary Under-Secretary of State,
Department of Social Security

20th July 1992

SCHEDULE 1

Regulations 7(1), (2) and 8

CALCULATION OF N AND M

PART I

EARNINGS

Chapter 1

Earnings of an employed earner

1.—(1) Subject to sub-paragraphs (2) and (3), "earnings" means in the case of employment as an employed earner, any remuneration or profit derived from that employment and includes—

(a) any bonus, commission, royalty or fee;

(b) any holiday pay except any payable more than 4 weeks after termination of the employment;

(c) any payment by way of a retainer;

(d) any payment made by the parent's employer in respect of any expenses not wholly, exclusively and necessarily incurred in the performance of the duties of the employment;

(e) any award of compensation made under section 68(2) or 71(2)(a) of the Employment Protection (Consolidation) Act 1978 (remedies and compensation for unfair dismissal);

(f) any such sum as is referred to in section 112 of the Contributions and Benefits Act (certain sums to be earnings for social security purposes);

(g) any statutory sick pay under Part I of the Social Security and Housing Benefits Act 1982 or statutory maternity pay under Part V of the Social Security Act 1986;

(h) any payment in lieu of notice and any compensation in respect of the absence or inadequacy of any such notice but only insofar as such payment or compensation represents loss of income;

   (i) any payment relating to a period of less than a year which is made in respect of the performance of duties as—

   (i) an auxiliary coastguard in respect of coast rescue activities;

   (ii) a part-time fireman in a fire brigade maintained in pursuance of the Fire Services Acts 1947 to 1959;

   (iii) a person engaged part-time in the manning or launching of a lifeboat;

   (iv) a member of any territorial or reserve force prescribed in Part I of Schedule 3 to the Social Security (Contributions) Regulations 1979;

(j) any payment made by a local authority to a member of that authority in respect of the performance of his duties as a member, other than any expenses wholly, exclusively and necessarily incurred in the performance of those duties.

(2) Earnings shall not include—

(a) any payment in respect of expenses wholly, exclusively and necessarily incurred in the performance of the duties of the employment;

(b) any occupational pension;

(c) any payment where—

    (i) the employment in respect of which it was made has ceased; and

    (ii) a period of the same length as the period by reference to which it was calculated has expired since that cessation but prior to the effective date;

(d) any advance of earnings or any loan made by an employer to an employee;

(e) any amount received from an employer during a period when the employee has withdrawn his services by reason of a trade dispute;

(f) any payment in kind;

(g) where, in any week or other period which falls within the period by reference to which earnings are calculated, earnings are received both in respect of a previous employment and in respect of a subsequent employment, the earnings in respect of the previous employment.

(3) The earnings to be taken into account for the purposes of calculating N and M shall be gross earnings less—

(a) any amount deducted from those earnings by way of—

    (i) income tax;

    (ii) primary Class 1 contributions under the Contributions and Benefits Act; and

(b) one half of any sums paid by the parent towards an occupational or personal pension scheme.

2.—(1) Subject to sub-paragraphs (2) to (4)—

(a) where a person is paid weekly, the amount of those earnings shall be determined by aggregating the amounts received in the 5 weeks ending with the relevant week and dividing by 5;

(b) where a person is paid monthly, the amount of those earnings shall be determined by aggregating the amounts received in the 2 months ending with the relevant week, multiplying the aggregate by 6 and dividing by 52;

(c) where a person is paid by reference to some other period, the amount of those earnings shall be determined by aggregating the amounts received in the 3 months ending with the relevant week, multiplying the aggregate by 4 and dividing by 52.

(2) Where a person's earnings include a bonus or commission which is paid during the period of 52 weeks ending with the relevant week and is paid separately from, or, in relation to a longer period than, the other earnings with which it is paid, the amount of that bonus or commission shall be determined by aggregating such payments received in the 52 weeks ending with the relevant week and dividing by 52.

(3) Subject to sub-paragraph (4), the amount of any earnings of a student shall be determined by aggregating the amount received in the year ending

with the relevant week and dividing by 52 or, where the person in question has been a student for less than a year, by aggregating the amount received in the period starting with his becoming a student and ending with the relevant week and dividing by the number of complete weeks in that period.

(4) Where a calculation would, but for this sub-paragraph, produce an amount which, in the opinion of the child support officer, does not accurately reflect the normal amount of the earnings of the person in question, such earnings, or any part of them, shall be calculated by reference to such other period as may, in the particular case, enable the normal weekly earnings of that person to be determined more accurately and for this purpose the child support officer shall have regard to—

(a) the earnings received, or due to be received, from any employment in which the person in question is engaged, has been engaged or is due to be engaged;

(b) the duration and pattern, or the expected duration and pattern, of any employment of that person.

Chapter 2

Earnings of a self-employed earner

3.—(1) Subject to sub-paragraphs (2) and (3) and to paragraph 4, "earnings" in the case of employment as a self-employed earner means the gross receipts of the employment including, where an allowance in the form of periodic payments is paid under section 2 of the Employment and Training Act 1973 or section 2 of the Enterprise and New Towns (Scotland) Act 1990 in respect of the relevant week for the purpose of assisting him in carrying on his business, the total of those payments made during the period by reference to which his earnings are determined under paragraph 5.

(2) Earnings shall not include—

(a) any allowance paid under either of those sections in respect of any part of the period by reference to which his earnings are determined under paragraph 5 if no part of that allowance is paid in respect of the relevant week;

(b) any income consisting of payments received for the provision of board and lodging accommodation unless such payments form the largest element of the recipient's income.

(3) There shall be deducted from the gross receipts referred to in sub-paragraph (1)—

(a) any expenses which are reasonably incurred and are wholly and exclusively defrayed for the purposes of the earner's business in the period by reference to which his earnings are determined under paragraph 5(1) or, where paragraph 5(2) applies, any such expenses relevant to the period there mentioned (whether or not defrayed in that period);

(b) any value added tax paid in the period by rererence to which earnings are determined in excess of value added tax received in that period;

(c) any amount in respect of income tax determined in accordance with sub-paragraph (5);

(d) any amount in respect of National Insurance contributions determined in accordance with sub-paragraph (6);

(e) one half of any premium paid in respect of a retirement annuity contract or a personal pension scheme.

(4) For the purposes of sub-paragraph (3)(a)—

  (a) such expenses include—

    (i) repayment of capital on any loan used for the replacement, in the course of business, of equipment or machinery, or the repair of an existing business asset except to the extent that any sum is payable under an insurance policy for its repair;

    (ii) any income expended in the repair of an existing business asset except to the extent that any sum is payable under an insurance policy for its repair;

    (iii) any payment of interest on a loan taken out for the purposes of the business;

  (b) such expenses do not include—

    (i) repayment of capital on any other loan taken out for the purposes of the business;

    (ii) any capital expenditure;

    (iii) the depreciation of any capital asset;

    (iv) any sum employed, or intended to be employed, in the setting up or expansion of the business;

    (v) any loss incurred before the beginning of the period by reference to which earnings are determined;

    (vi) any expenses incurred in providing business entertainment;

    (vii) any loss incurred in any other employment in which he is engaged as a self-employed earner.

(5) For the purposes of sub-paragraph (3)(c), the amount of income tax to be allowed against earnings shall be calculated as if those earnings, less any personal allowance applicable to the earner under Chapter 1 of Part VII of the Income and Corporation Taxes Act 1988 (Personal Relief) (or where the earnings are determined over a period of less than a year, a proportionate part of such relief), were assessable to income tax at the rates of tax applicable at the effective date.

(6) For the purposes of sub-paragraph (3)(d), the amount to be deducted in respect of National Insurance contributions shall be the total of—

  (a) the amount of Class 2 contributions (if any) payable under section 11(1) or, as the case may be, (4) of the Contributions and Benefits Act; and

  (b) the amount of Class 4 contributions (if any) payable under section 15(2) of that Act,

at the rates applicable at the effective date.

4. In a case where a person is self-employed as a childminder the amount of earnings referable to that employment shall be one-third of the gross receipts.

5.—(1) Subject to sub-paragraphs (2) and (3)—

(a) where a person has been a self-employed earner for 52 weeks or more including the relevant week. the amount of his earnings shall be determined by reference to the average of the earnings which he has received in the 52 weeks ending with the relevant week;

(b) where the person has been a self-employed earner for a period of less than 52 weeks including the relevant week, the amount of his earnings shall be determined by reference to the average of the earnings which he has received during that period.

(2) Where a person who is a self-employed earner provides in respect of the employment a profit and loss account and, where appropriate, a trading account or a balance sheet or both, and the profit and loss account is in respect of a period at least 6 months but not exceeding 15 months and that period terminates within the 12 months immediately preceding the effective date, the amount of his earnings shall be determined by reference to the average of the earnings over the period to which the profit and loss account relates and such earnings shall include receipts relevant to that period (whether or not received in that period).

(3) Where a calculation would, but for this sub-paragraph, produce an amount which, in the opinion of the child support officer, does not accurately reflect the normal amount of the earnings of the person in question, such earnings, or any part of them, shall be calculated by reference to such other period as may, in the particular case, enable the normal weekly earnings of that person to be determined more accurately and for this purpose the child support officer shall have regard to—

(a) the earnings received, or due to be received, from any employment in which the person in question is engaged, or has been engaged or is due to be engaged;

(b) the duration and pattern, or the expected duration and pattern, of any employment of that person.

(4) In sub-paragraph (2)—

(a) "balance sheet" means a statement of the financial position of the employment disclosing its assets, liabilities and capital at the end of the period in question;

(b) "profit and loss account" means a financial statement showing net profit or loss of the employment for the period in question; and

(c) "trading account" means a financial statement showing the revenue from sales, the cost of those sales and the gross profit arising during the period in question.

PART II

BENEFIT PAYMENTS

6.—(1) The benefit payments to be taken into account in calculating or estimating N and M shall be determined in accordance with this Part.

(2) "Benefit payments" means any benefit payments under the Contributions and Benefits Act except amounts to be disregarded by virtue of Schedule 2.

(3) The amount of any benefit payment to be taken into account shall be determined by reference to the rate of that benefit applicable at the effective date.

7.—(1)   Where a benefit payment under the Contributions and Benefits Act includes an adult or child dependency increase—

(a) if that benefit is payable to a parent, the income of that parent shall be calculated or estimated as if it did not include that amount;

(b) if that benefit is payable to some other person but includes an amount in respect of the parent, the income of the parent shall be calculated or estimated as if it included that amount.

(2) Subject to sub-paragraph (3), payments to a person by way of family credit shall be treated as the income of the parent who has qualified for them by his engagement in, and normal engagement in, remunerative work.

(3) Subject to sub-paragraphs (4) and (5), where family credit is payable and the amount which is payable has been calculated by reference either to the weekly earnings of the absent parent and another person or the parent with care and another person—

(a) if during the period which is used to calculate his earnings under paragraph 2 or, as the case may be, paragraph 5, the weekly earnings of that parent exceed those of the other person, the amount payable by way of family credit shall be treated as the income of that parent;

(b) if during that period the normal weekly earnings of that parent equal those of the other person, half of the amount payable by way of family credit shall be treated as the income of that parent; and

(c) if during that period the normal weekly earnings of that parent are less than those of that other person, the amount payable by way of family credit shall not be treated as the income of that parent.

(4) Where—

(a) family credit (calculated, as the case may be, by reference to the weekly earnings of the absent parent and another person or the parent with care and another person) is in payment; and

(b) not later than the effective date either or both the persons by reference to whose engagement and normal engagement in remunerative work that payment has been calculated has ceased to be so employed,

half of the amount payable by way of family credit shall be treated as the income of the parent in question.

(5) Where—

(a) family credit is in payment; and

(b) not later than the effective date the person or, if more than one, each of the persons by reference to whose engagement, and normal engagement, in remunerative work that payment has been calculated is no longer the partner of the person to whom that payment is made,

the payment in question shall only be treated as the income of the parent in question where he is in receipt of it.

PART III

OTHER INCOME

8. The amount of the other income to be taken into account in calculating or estimating N and M shall be the aggregate of the following amounts determined in accordance with this Part.

9. Any periodic payment of pension or other benefit under an occupational or personal pension scheme or a retirement annuity contract or other such scheme for the provision of income in retirement.

10. Any payment received on account of the provision of board and lodging which does not come within Part I of this Schedule.

11. Subject to regulation 7(3)(b) and paragraph 127 any payment to a student of—

(a) grant;

(b) an amount in respect of grant contribution;

(c) covenant income except to the extent that it has been taken into account under subparagraph (b);

(d) a student loan.

12. The income of a student shall not include any payment—

(a) intended to meet tuition fees or examination fees;

(b) intended to meet additional expenditure incurred by a disabled student in respect of his attendance on a course;

(c) intended to meet additional expenditure connected with term time residential study away from the student's educational establishment;

(d) on account of the student maintaining a home at a place other than that at which he resides during his course;

(e) intended to meet the cost of books, and equipment (other than special equipment) or, if not so intended, an amount equal to the amount allowed under regulation 38(2)(f) of the Family Credit (General) Regulations 1987 towards such costs;

(f) intended to meet travel expenses incurred as a result of his attendance on the course.

13. Any interest, dividend or other income derived from capital.

14. Any maintenance payments in respect of a parent.

15. Any other payments or other amounts received on a periodical basis which are not otherwise taken into account under Part I, II, IV or V of this Schedule.

16.—(1) Subject to sub-paragraphs (2) to (6) the amount of any income to which this Part applies shall be calculated or estimated—

(a) where it has been received in respect of the whole of the period of 26 weeks which ends at the end of the relevant week, by dividing such income received in that period by 26;

(b) where it has been received in respect of part of the period of 26 weeks which ends at the end of the relevant week, by dividing such income received in that period by the number of complete weeks in respect of which such income is received and for this purpose income shall be treated as received in respect of a week if it is received in respect of any day in the week in question.

(2) The amount of maintenance payments made in respect of a parent—

(a) where they are payable weekly and have been paid at the same amount in respect of each week in the period of 13 weeks which ends at the end of the relevant week, shall be the amount equal to one of those payments;

(b) in any other case, shall be the amount calculated by aggregating the total amount of those payments received in the period of 13 weeks which ends at the end of the relevant week and dividing by the number of weeks in that period in respect of which maintenance was due.

(3) In the case of a student—

(a) the amount of any grant and any amount paid in respect of grant contribution shall be calculated by apportioning it equally between the weeks in respect of which it is payable;

(b) the amount of any covenant income shall be calculated by dividing the amount payable in respect of a year by 52 (or, where such amount is payable in respect of a lesser period, by the number of complete weeks in that period) and, subject to sub-paragraph (4), deducting £5·00;

(c) the amount of any student loan shall be calculated by apportioning the loan equally between the weeks in respect of which it is payable and, subject to sub-paragraph (4), deducting £10·00.

(4) For the purposes of sub-paragraph (3)—

(a) not more than £5·00 shall be deducted under sub-paragraph (3)(b);

(b) not more than £10·00 in total shall be deducted under sub-paragraphs (3)(b) and (c).

(5) Where in respect of the period of 52 weeks which ends at the end of the relevant week a person is in receipt of interest, dividend or other income which has been produced by his capital, the amount of that income shall be calculated by dividing the aggregate of the income so received by 52.

(6) Where a calculation would, but for this sub-paragraph, produce an amount which, in the opinion of the child support officer, does not accurately reflect the normal amount of the other income of the person in question, such income, or any part of it, shall be calculated by reference to such other period as may, in the particular case, enable the other income of that person to be determined more accurately and for this purpose the child support officer shall have regard to the nature and pattern of receipt of such income.

PART IV

INCOME OF CHILD TREATED AS INCOME OF PARENT

17. The amount of any income of a child which is to be treated as the income of the parent in calculating or estimating N and M shall be the aggregate of the amounts determined in accordance with this Part.

18. Where a child has income which falls within the following paragraphs of this Part and that child is a member of the family of his parent (whether that child is a qualifying child in relation to that parent or not), the relevant income of that child shall be treated as that of his parent.

19. Where child support maintenance is being assessed for the support of only one qualifying child, the relevant income of that child shall be treated as that of the parent with care.

20. Where child support maintenance is being assessed to support more than one qualifying child, the relevant income of each of those children shall be treated as that of the parent with care to the extent that it does not exceed the aggregate of—

(a) the amount determined under—

   (i) regulation 3(1)(a) (calculation of AG) in relation to the child in question; and

   (ii) the total of any other amounts determined under regulation 3(1)(b) to (d) which are applicable in the case in question divided by the number of children for whom child support maintenance is being calculated,

   less the basic rate of child benefit (within the meaning of regulation 4) for the child in question; and

(b) three times the total of the amounts calculated under regulation 3(1)(a) (income support personal allowance for child or young person) in respect of that child and regulation 3(1)(c) (income support family premium).

21. Where child support maintenance is not being assessed for the support of the child whose income is being calculated or estimated, the relevant income of that child shall be treated as that of his parent to the extent that it does not exceed the amount determined under regulation 9(1)(g).

22. Where a benefit under the Contributions and Benefits Act includes an adult or child dependency increase in respect of a relevant child, the relevant income of that child shall be calculated or estimated as if it included that amount.

23. For the purposes of this Part, "the relevant income of a child" does not include—

(a) any earnings of the child in question;

(b) payments by an absent parent in respect of the child for whom maintenance is being assessed;

(c) where the class of persons who are capable of benefiting from a discretionary trust include the child in question, payments from that trust except in so far as they are made to provide for food, ordinary clothing and footwear, gas, electricity or fuel charges or housing costs; or

(d) any interest payable on arrears of child support maintenance for that child.

24. The amount of the income of a child which is treated as the income of the parent shall be determined in the same way as if such income were the income of the parent.

PART V

AMOUNTS TREATED AS THE INCOME OF A PARENT

25. The amounts which fall to be treated as income of the parent in calculating or estimating N and M shall include amounts to be determined in accordance with this Part.

26. Where a child support officer is satisfied—

(a) that a person has performed a service either—

(i) without receiving any remuneration in respect of it; or

(ii) for remuneration which is less than that normally paid for that service;

(b) that the service in question was for the benefit of—

(i) another person who is not a member of the same family as the person in question; or

(ii) a body which is neither a charity nor a voluntary organisation;

(c) that the service in question was performed for a person who, or as the case may be, a body which was able to pay remuneration at the normal rate for the service in question;

(d) that the principal purpose of the person undertaking the service without receiving any or adequate remuneration is to reduce his assessable income for the purposes of the Act; and

(e) that any remuneration foregone would have fallen to be taken into account as earnings,

the value of the remuneration foregone shall be estimated by a child support officer and an amount equal to the value so estimated shall be treated as income of the person who performed those services.

27. Subject to paragraphs 28 to 30, where the child support officer is satisfied that, otherwise than in the circumstances set out in paragraph 26, a person has intentionally deprived himself of—

(a) any income or capital which would otherwise be a source of income;

(b) any income or capital which it would be reasonable to expect would be secured by him,

with a view to reducing the amount of his assessable income, his net income shall include the amount estimated by a child support officer as representing the income which that person would have had if he had not deprived himself of or failed to secure that income, or as the case may be, that capital.

28. No amount shall be treated as income by virtue of paragraph 27 in relation to—

(a) one parent benefit;

(b) if the parent is a person to, or in respect of, whom income support is payable, unemployment benefit;

(c) a payment from a discretionary trust or a trust derived from a payment made in consequence of a personal injury.

29. Where an amount is included in the income of a person under paragraph 27 in respect of income which would become available to him on application, the amount included under that paragraph shall be included from the date on which it could be expected to be acquired.

30. Where a child support officer determines under paragraph 27 that a person has deprived himself of capital which would otherwise be a source of income, the amount of that capital shall be reduced at intervals of 52 weeks, starting with the week which falls 52 weeks after the first week in respect of which income from it is included in the calculation of the assessment in question, by an amount equal to the amount which the child support officer estimates would represent the income from that source in the immediately preceding period of 52 weeks.

31. Where a payment is made on behalf of a parent or a relevant child in respect of food, ordinary clothing or footwear, gas, electricity or fuel charges, housing costs or council tax, an amount equal to the amount which the child support officer estimates represents the value of that payment shall be treated as the income of the parent in question except to the extent that such amount is—

(a) disregarded under paragraph 38 of Schedule 2;

(b) a payment of school fees paid by or on behalf of someone other than the absent parent.

32. Where paragraph 26 applies the amount to be treated as the income of the parent shall be determined as if it were earnings from employment as an employed earner and in a case to which paragraph 27 or 31 applies the amount shall be determined as if it were other income to which Part III of this Schedule applies.

SCHEDULE 2   Regulations 7(2) and 8

AMOUNTS TO BE DISREGARDED WHEN CALCULATING OR ESTIMATING N and M

1. The amounts referred to in this Schedule are to be disregarded when calculating or estimating N and M (parent's net income).

2. An amount in respect of income tax applicable to the income in question where not otherwise allowed for under these Regulations.

3. Where a payment is made in a currency other than sterling, an amount equal to any banking charge or commission payable in converting that payment to sterling.

4. Any amount payable in a country outside the United Kingdom where there is a prohibition against the transfer to the United Kingdom of that amount.

5. Any compensation for personal injury and any payments from a trust fund set up for that purpose.

6. Any advance of earnings or any loan made by an employer to an employee.

7. Any payment by way of, or any reduction or discharge of liability resulting from entitlement to, housing benefit or council tax benefit.

8. Any disability living allowance, mobility supplement or any payment intended to compensate for the non-payment of any such allowance or supplement.

9. Any payment which is—
- (a) an attendance allowance under section 64 of the Contributions and Benefits Act;
- (b) an increase of disablement pension under section 104 or 105 of that Act (increases where constant attendance needed or for exceptionally severe disablement);
- (c) a payment made under regulations made in exercise of the power conferred by Schedule 8 to that Act (payments for pre-1948 cases);
- (d) an increase of an allowance payable in respect of constant attendance under that Schedule;
- (e) payable by virtue of articles 14, 15, 16, 43 or 44 of the Personal Injuries (Civilians) Scheme 1983 (allowances for constant attendance and exceptionally severe disablement and severe disablement occupational allowance) or any analogous payment; or
- (f) a payment based on the need for attendance which is paid as part of a war disablement pension.

10. Any payment under section 148 of the Contributions and Benefits Act (pensioners' Christmas bonus).

11. Any social fund payment within the meaning of Part VIII of the Contributions and Benefits Act.

12. Any payment made by the Secretary of State to compensate for the loss (in whole or in part) of entitlement to housing benefit.

13. Any payment made by the Secretary of State to compensate for loss of housing benefit supplement under regulation 19 of the Supplementary Benefit (Requirements) Regulations 1983.

14. Any payment made by the Secretary of State to compensate a person who was entitled to supplementary benefit in respect of a period ending immediately before 11 th April 1988 but who did not become entitled to income support in respect of a period beginning with that day.

15. Any concessionary payment made to compensate for the non-payment of income support, disability living allowance, or any payment to which paragraph 9 applies.

16. Any payments of child benefit to the extent that they do not exceed the basic rate of that benefit as defined in regulation 4.

17. Any payment made under regulations 9 to 11 or 13 of the Welfare Food Regulations 1988 (payments made in place of milk tokens or the supply of vitamins).

18. Subject to paragraph 20 and to the extent that it does not exceed £10·00—
- (a) war disablement pension or war widow's pension or a payment made to compensate for non-payment of such a pension;
- (b) a pension paid by the government of a country outside Great Britain and which either—
  - (i)   is analogous to a war disablement pension; or
  - (ii) is analogous to a war widow's pension.

19.—(1) Except where sub-paragraph (2) applies and subject to sub-paragraph (3) and paragraphs 20, 38 and 47, £10·00 of any charitable or voluntary payment made, or due to be made, at regular intervals.

(2) Subject to sub-paragraph (3) and paragraphs 38 and 47, any charitable or voluntary payment made or due to be made at regular intervals which is intended and used for an item other than food, ordinary clothing or footwear, gas, electricity or fuel charges, housing costs of any member of the family or the payment of council tax.

(3) Sub-paragraphs (1) and (2) shall not apply to a payment which is made by a person for the maintenance of any member of his family or of his former partner or of his children.

(4) For the purposes of sub-paragraph (1) where a number of charitable or voluntary payments fall to be taken into account they shall be treated as though they were one such payment.

20.—(1) Where, but for this paragraph, more than £10·00 would be disregarded under paragraphs 18 and 19(1) in respect of the same week, only £10·00 in aggregate shall be disregarded and where an amount falls to be deducted from the income of a student under paragraph 1 6(3)(b) or (c) of Schedule 1, that amount shall count as part of the £10·00 disregard allowed under this paragraph.

(2) Where any payment which is due to be paid in one week is paid in another week, subparagraph (1) and paragraphs 18 and 19(1) shall have effect as if that payment were received in the week in which it was due.

21. In the case of a person participating in arrangements for training made under section 2 of the Employment and Training Act 1973 or section 2 of the Enterprise and New Towns (Scotland) Act 1990 (functions in relation to training for employment etc.) or attending a course at an employment rehabilitation centre established under section 2 of the 1973 Act—

(a) any travelling expenses reimbursed to the person;

(b) any living away from home allowance under section 2(2)(d) of the 1973 Act or section 2(4)(c) of the 1990 Act;

(c) any training premium,

but this paragraph, except in so far as it relates to a payment mentioned in sub-paragraph (a), (b) or (c), does not apply to any part of any allowance under section 2(2)(d) of the 1973 Act or section 2(4)(c) of the 1990 Act.

22. Where a parent occupies a dwelling as his home and that dwelling is also occupied by a person, other than a non-dependant or a person who is provided with board and lodging accommodation, and that person is contractually liable to make payments in respect of his occupation of the dwelling to the parent, the amount or, as the case may be, the amounts specified in paragraph 19 of Schedule 2 to the Family Credit (General) Regulations 1987 which apply in his case, or, if he is not in receipt of family credit, the amounts which would have applied if he had been in receipt of that benefit.

23. Where a parent, who is not a self-employed earner, is in receipt of rent or any other money in respect of the use and occupation of property other than his home, that rent or other payment to the extent of any sums which that parent is liable to pay by way of—

(a) payments which would be treated as housing costs by paragraph 3 of Schedule 3 if that property were his home (exempt income: additional provisions relating to housing costs);

(b) council tax payable in respect of that property;

(c) water and sewerage charges payable in respect of that property.

24. Where a parent provides board and lodging accommodation in his home otherwise than as a self-employed earner—

(a) £20·00 of any payment for that accommodation made by the person to whom that accommodation is provided; and

(b) where any such payment exceeds £20·00, 50 per centum of the excess.

25. Any payment made to a person in respect of an adopted child who is a member of his family that is made in accordance with any regulations made under section 57A or pursuant to section 57A(6) of the Adoption Act 1976 (permitted allowances) or, as the case may be, section 51 of the Adoption (Scotland) Act 1978 (schemes for the payment of allowances to adopters)—

(a) where the child is not a child in respect of whom child support maintenance is being assessed, to the extent that it exceeds the amount referred to in regulation 9(1)(g)(i), reduced, as the case may be, under regulation 9(4);

(b) in any other case, to the extent that it does not exceed the amount of the income of a child which is treated as that of his parent by virtue of Part IV.

26. Where a local authority makes a payment in respect of the accommodation and maintenance of a child in pursuance of paragraph 15 of Schedule 1 to the Children Act 1989 (local authority contribution to child's maintenance) to the extent that it exceeds the amount referred to in regulation 9(1)(g)(i) (reduced, as the case may be, under regulation 9(4)).

27. Any payment received under a policy of insurance taken out to insure against the risk of being unable to maintain repayments on a loan taken out to acquire an interest in, or to meet the cost of repairs or improvements to, the parent's home and used to meet such repayments, to the extent that the payment received under that policy does not in any period exceed the total of—

(a) any interest payable on that loan;

(b) any capital repayable on that loan; and

(c) any premiums payable on that policy.

28. In the calculation of the income of the parent with care, any maintenance payments made by the absent parent in respect of his qualifying child.

29. Any payment made by a local authority to a person who is caring for a child under section 23(2)(a) of the Children Act 1989 (provision of accommodation and maintenance by a local authority for children whom the authority is looking after) or, as the case may be, section 21 of the Social Work (Scotland) Act 1968 or by a voluntary organisation under section 59(1)(a) of the Children Act 1989 (provision of accommodation by voluntary organisations) or by a care authority under regulation 9 of the Boarding Out and Fostering of Children (Scotland) Regulations 1985 (provision of accommodation and maintenance for children in care).

30. Any payment made by a health authority, local authority or voluntary organisation in respect of a person who is not normally a member of the household but is temporarily in the care of a member of it.

31. Any payment made by a local authority under section 17 or 24 of the Children Act 1989 or, as the case may be, section 12, 24 or 26 of the Social Work (Scotland) Act 1968 (local authorities' duty to promote welfare of children and powers to grant financial assistance to persons looked after, or in, or formerly in, their care).

32. Any resettlement benefit which is paid to the parent by virtue of regulation 3 of the Social Security (Hospital In-Patients) Amendment (No. 2) Regulations 1987 (transitional provisions).

33.—(1) Any payment or repayment made—

  (a) as respects England and Wales, under regulation 3, 5 or 8 of the National Health Service (Travelling Expenses and Remission of Charges) Regulations 1988 (travelling expenses and health service supplies);

  (b) as respects Scotland, under regulation 3, 5 or 8 of the National Health Service (Travelling Expenses and Remission of Charges) (Scotland) Regulations 1988 (travelling expenses and health service supplies).

(2) Any payment or repayment made by the Secretary of State for Health, the Secretary of State for Scotland or the Secretary of State for Wales which is analogous to a payment or repayment mentioned in sub-paragraph (1).

34. Any payment made (other than a training allowance), whether by the Secretary of State or any other person, under the Disabled Persons Employment Act 1944 or in accordance with arrangements made under section 2 of the Employment and Training Act 1973 to assist disabled persons to obtain or retain employment despite their disability.

35. Any contribution to the expenses of maintaining a household which is made by a nondependant member of that household.

36. Any sum in respect of a course of study attended by a child payable by virtue of regulations made under section 81 of the Education Act 1944 (assistance by means of scholarship or otherwise), or by virtue of section 2(1) of the Education Act 1962 (awards for courses of further education) or section 49 of the Education (Scotland) Act 1980 (power to assist persons to take advantage of educational facilities).

37. Where a person receives income under an annuity purchased with a loan which satisfies the following conditions—

  (a) that loan was made as part of a scheme under which not less than 90 per centum of the proceeds of the loan were applied to the purchase by the person to whom it was made of an annuity ending with his life or with the life of the survivor of two or more persons (in this paragraph referred to as "the annuitants") who include the person to whom the loan was made;

  (b) that the interest on the loan is payable by the person to whom it was made or by one of the annuitants;

  (c) that at the time the loan was made the person to whom it was made or each of the annuitants had attained the age of 65;

    (d) that the loan was secured on a dwelling in Great Britain and the person to whom the loan was made or one of the annuitants owns an estate or interest in that dwelling; and

    (e) that the person to whom the loan was made or one of the annuitants occupies the dwelling on which it was secured as his home at the time the interest is paid,

the amount, calculated on a weekly basis equal to—

        (i) where, or insofar as, section 26 of the Finance Act 1982 (deduction of tax from certain loan interest) applies to the payments of interest on the loan, the interest which is payable after the deduction of a sum equal to income tax on such payments at the basic rate for the year of assessment in which the payment of interest becomes due;

        (ii) in any other case the interest which is payable on the loan without deduction of such a sum.

38. Any payment of the description specified in paragraph 39 of Schedule 9 to the Income Support Regulations (disregard of payments made under certain trusts and disregard of certain other payments) and any income derived from the investment of such payments.

39. Any payment made to a juror or witness in respect of attendance at court other than compensation for loss of earnings or for loss of a benefit payable under the Contributions and Benefits Act.

40. Any special war widows' payment made under—

    (a) the Naval and Marine Pay and Pensions (Special War Widows Payment) Order 1990 made under section 3 of the Naval and Marine Pay and Pensions Act 1865;

    (b) the Royal Warrant dated 19th February 1990 amending the Schedule to the Army Pensions Warrant 1977;

    (c) the Queen's Order dated 26th February 1990 made under section 2 of the Air Force (Constitution) Act 191 7;

    (d) the Home Guard War Widows Special Payments Regulations 1990 made under section 151 of the Reserve Forces Act 1980;

    (e) the Orders dated 19th February 1990 amending Orders made on 12th December 1980 concerning the Ulster Defence Regiment made in each case under section 140 of the Reserve Forces Act 1980,

and any analogous payment by the Secretary of State for Defence to any person who is not a person entitled under the provisions mentioned in sub-paragraphs (a) to (e).

41. Any payment to a person as holder of the Victoria Cross or the George Cross or any analogous payment.

42. Any payment made either by the Secretary of State for the Home Department or by the Secretary of State for Scotland under a scheme established to assist relatives and other persons to visit persons in custody.

43. Any amount by way of a refund of income tax deducted from profits or emoluments chargeable to income tax under Schedule D or Schedule E.

44. Maintenance payments (whether paid under the Act or otherwise) insofar as they are not treated as income under Part III or IV.

45. Where following a divorce or separation—

(a) capital is divided between the parent and the person who was his partner before the divorce or separation; and

(b) that capital is intended to be used to acquire a new home for that parent or to acquire furnishings for a home of his,

income derived from the investment of that capital for one year following the date on which that capital became available to the parent.

46. Payments in kind.

47. Any payment made by the Joseph Rowntree Memorial Trust from money provided to it by the Secretary of State for Health for the purpose of maintaining a family fund for the benefit of severely handicapped children.

48. Any payment of expenses to a person who is—

(a) engaged by a charitable or voluntary body; or

(b) a volunteer,

he otherwise derives no remuneration or profit from the body or person paying those expenses.

49. In this Schedule—

"concessionary payment" means a payment made under arrangements made by the Secretary of State with the consent of the Treasury which is charged either to the National Insurance Fund or to a Departmental Expenditure Vote to which payments of benefit under the Contributions and Benefits Act are charged;

"health authority" means a health authority established under the National Health Service Act 1977 or the National Health Service (Scotland) Act 1978;

"mobility supplement" has the same meaning as in regulation 2(1) of the Income Support Regulations;

"war disablement pension" and "war widow" have the same meanings as in section 150(2) of the Contributions and Benefits Act.

SCHEDULE 3   Regulation 14

ELIGIBLE HOUSING COSTS

Eligible housing costs for the purposes of determining exempt income and protected income

1. Subject to the following provisions of this Schedule, the following payments in respect of the provision of a home shall be eligible to be taken into account as housing costs for the purposes of these Regulations—

(a) payments of, or by way of, rent;

(b) mortgage interest payments;

(c) interest payments under a hire purchase agreement to buy a home;

(d) interest payments on loans for repairs and improvements to the home;

(e) payments by way of ground rent or in Scotland, payments by way of feu duty;

(f) payments under a co-ownership scheme;

(g) payments in respect of, or in consequence of, the use and occupation of the home;

(h) where the home is a tent, payments in respect of the tent and the site on which it stands;

(i) payments in respect of a licence or permission to occupy the home (whether or not board is provided);

(j) payments by way of mesne profits or, in Scotland, violent profits;

(k) payments of, or by way of, service charges, the payment of which is a condition on which the right to occupy the home depends;

(l) payments under or relating to a tenancy or licence of a Crown tenant;

(m) mooring charges payable for a houseboat;

(n) where the home is a caravan or a mobile home, payments in respect of the site on which it stands;

(o) any contribution payable by a parent resident in an almshouse provided by a housing association which is either a charity of which particulars are entered in the register of charities established under section 4 of the Charities Act 1960 (register of charities) or an exempt charity within the meaning of that Act, which is a contribution towards the cost of maintaining that association's almshouses and essential services in them;

(p) payments under a rental purchase agreement, that is to say an agreement for the purchase of a home under which the whole or part of the purchase price is to be paid in more than one instalment and the completion of the purchase is deferred until the whole or a specified part of the purchase price has been paid;

(q) where, in Scotland, the home is situated on or pertains to a croft within the meaning of section 3(1) of the Crofters (Scotland) Act 1955, the payment in respect of the croft land;

(r) where the home is provided by an employer (whether under a condition or term in a contract of service or otherwise), payments to that employer in respect of the home, including payments made by the employer deducting the payment in question from the remuneration of the parent in question;

(s) payments analogous to those mentioned in this paragraph;

(t) payments in respect of a loan taken out to pay off another loan but only to the extent that it was incurred for that purpose and only to the extent to which the interest on that other loan would have been met under this paragraph.

Loans for repairs and improvements to the home

2. For the purposes of paragraph 1(d) "repairs and improvements" means major repairs necessary to maintain the fabric of the home and any of the following measures undertaken with a view to improving its fitness for occupation—

(a) installation of a fixed bath, shower, wash basin or lavatory, and necessary associated plumbing;

(b) damp proofing measures;

(c) provision or improvement of ventilation and natural lighting;

(d) provision of electric lighting and sockets;

(e) provision or improvement of drainage facilities;

(f) improvement of the structural condition of the home;

(g) improvements to the facilities for the storing, preparation and cooking of food;

(h) provision of heating, including central heating;

(i) provision of storage facilities for fuel and refuse;

(j) improvements to the insulation of the home;

(k) other improvements which the child support officer considers reasonable in the circumstances.

Exempt income: additional provisions relating to eligible housing costs

3.—(1) The additional provisions made by this paragraph shall have effect only for the purpose of calculating or estimating exempt income.

(2) Subject to sub-paragraph (6), where the home of an absent parent or, as the case may be, a parent with care, is subject to a mortgage or charge and that parent makes periodical payments to reduce the capital secured by that mortgage or charge of an amount provided for in accordance with the terms thereof, the amount of those payments shall be eligible to be taken into account as the housing costs of that parent.

(3) Subject to sub-paragraph (6), where the home of an absent parent or, as the case may be, a parent with care, is held under an agreement and certain payments made under that agreement are included as housing costs by virtue of paragraph 1 of this Schedule, the weekly amount of any other payments which are made in accordance with that agreement by the parent in order either—

(a) to reduce his liability under that agreement; or

(b) to acquire the home to which it relates,

shall also be eligible to be taken into account as housing costs.

(4) Where a policy of insurance has been obtained and retained for the purpose of discharging a mortgage or charge on the home of the parent in question, the amount of the premiums paid under that policy shall be eligible to be taken into account as a housing cost.

(5) Where a policy of insurance has been obtained and retained for the purpose of discharging a mortgage or charge on the home of the parent in question and also for the purpose of accruing profits on the maturity of the policy, the part of the premiums paid under that policy which are necessarily incurred for the purpose of discharging the mortgage or charge shall be eligible to be taken into account as a housing cost; and, where that part cannot be ascertained, 0.0277 per centum of the amount secured by the mortgage or charge shall be deemed to be the part which is eligible to be taken into account as a housing cost.

(6) For the purposes of sub-paragraphs (2) and (3), housing costs shall not include—

(a) any payment of arrears or payments in excess of those which are req uired to be made under or in respect of a mortgage, charge or agreement to which either of those sub-paragraphs relate;

(b) payments under any second or subsequent mortgage on the home to the extent that they are attributable to arrears or would otherwise not be eligible to be taken into account as housing costs;

(c) premiums payable in respect of any policy of insurance against loss caused by the destruction of or damage to any building or land.

Conditions relating to eligible housing costs

4.—(1) Subject to the following provisions of this paragraph the housing costs referred to in this Schedule shall be included as housing costs only where—

(a) they are incurred in relation to the parent's home;

(b) the parent or, if he is one of a family, he or a member of his family, is responsible for those costs; and

(c) the liability to meet those costs is to a person other than a member of the same household.

(2) For the purposes of sub-paragraph (1)(b) a parent shall be treated as responsible for housing costs where—

(a) because the person liable to meet those costs is not doing so, he has to meet those costs in order to continue to live in the home and either he was formerly the partner of the person liable, or he is some other person whom it is reasonable to treat as liable to meet those costs; or

(b) he pays a share of those costs in a case where—

(i)   he is living in a household with other persons;

(ii)   those other persons include persons who are not close relatives of his or his partner;

(iii) a person who is not such a close relative is responsible for those costs under the preceding provisions of this paragraph or has an equivalent responsibility for housing expenditure; and

(iv)   is reasonable in the circumstances to treat him as sharing that responsibility.

Accommodation also used for other purposes

5. Where amounts are payable in respect of accommodation which consists partly of residential accommodation and partly of other accommodation, only such proportion thereof as is attributable to residential accommodation shall be eligible to be taken into account as housing costs.

Ineligible service and fuel charges

6. Housing costs shall not include—

(a) where the costs are inclusive of ineligible service charges within the meaning of paragraph 1 of Schedule 1 to the Housing Benefit (General) Regulations 1987 (ineligible service charges), the amounts attributable to those ineligible service charges or, where that amount is not separated from or separately identified within the housing costs to be met under this paragraph, such part of the payments made in respect of those housing costs which are fairly attributable to the provision of those ineligible services having regard to the costs of comparable services;

(b) where the costs are inclusive of any of the items mentioned in paragraph 5(2) of Schedule 1 to the Housing Benefit (General) Regulations 1987 (payment in respect of fuel charges), the deductions prescribed in that paragraph unless the parent provides evidence on which the actual or approximate amount of the service charge for fuel may be estimated, in which case the estimated amount; and

(c) charges for water, sewerage or allied environmental services and where the amount of such charges is not separately identified, such part of the charges in question as is attributable to those services.

Interpretation

7. In this Schedule except where the context otherwise requires—

"close relative" means a parent, parent-in-law, son, son-in-law, daughter, daughter-in-law, step-parent, step-son, step-daughter, brother, sister, or the spouse of any of the preceding persons or, if that person is one of an unmarried couple, the other member of that couple;

"co-ownership scheme" means a scheme under which the dwelling is let by a housing association and the tenant, or his personal representative, will, under the terms of the tenancy agreement or of the agreement under which he became a member of the association, be entitled, on his ceasing to be a member and subject to any conditions stated in either agreement, to a sum calculated by reference directly or indirectly to the value of the dwelling;

"housing association" has the meaning assigned to it by section 1(1) of the Housing Association Act 1985

SCHEDULE 4   Regulation 26(1)(b)(i)

CASES WHERE CHILD SUPPORT MAINTENANCE IS NOT TO BE PAYABLE

The payments and awards specified for the purposes of regulation 26(1)(b)(i) are—

(a) the following payments under the Contributions and Benefits Act—

(i)   sickness benefit under section 31;

(ii)   invalidity pension under section 33;

(iii)   invalidity pension for widowers under section 34;

(iv)   maternity allowance under section 35;

(v)   invalidity pension for widows under section 40;

(vi)   attendance allowance under section 64;

(vii)   severe disablement allowance under section 68;

(viii) invalid care allowance under section 70;

(ix)   disability living allowance under section 71;

(x)   disablement benefit under section 103;

(xi)   disability working allowance under section 129;

(xii)   statutory sick pay within the meaning of section 151;

(xiii) statutory maternity pay within the meaning of section 164;

(b) awards in respect of disablement made under (or under provisions analogous to)—

(i)   the War Pensions (Coastguards) Scheme 1944;

(ii)   the War Pensions (Naval Auxiliary Personnel) Scheme 1964;

(iii)   the Pensions (Polish Forces) Scheme 1964;

(iv)   the War Pensions (Mercantile Marine) Scheme 1964;

(v)   the Royal Warrant of 21st December 1964 (service in the Home Guard before 1945);

(vi)   the Order by Her Majesty of 22nd December 1964 concerning pensions and other grants in respect of disablement or death due to service in the Home Guard after 27th April 1952;

(vii)   the Order by Her Majesty (Ulster Defence Regiment) of 4th January 1971;

(viii) the Personal Injuries (Civilians) Scheme 1983;

(ix)   the Naval, Military and Air Forces Etc. (Disablement and Death) Service Pensions Order 1983; and

(c) payments from the Independent Living Fund.

S. I. 1992 No. 1813

The Child Support (Maintenance Assessment Procedure) Regulations 1992)

Made — — — —   *20th July 1992*
Coming in to force   *5th April 1993*

ARRANGEMENT OF REGULATIONS

PART I
General

PART II
Applications for a maintenance assessment

PART III
Interim maintenance assessments

PART IV
Notifications following certain decisions by child support officers

PART V
Periodical reviews

PART VI
Reviews on a change of circumstances

PART VII
Reviews of a decision by a child support officer

PART VIII
Commencement and termination of maintenance assessments and maintenance periods

PART IX
Reduced benefit directions

PART X
Miscellaneous provisions

SCHEDULES

Whereas a draft of this instrument was laid before Parliament in accordance with section 52(2) of the Child Support Act 1991 and approved by a resolution of each House of Parliament:

Now, therefore, the Secretary of State for Social Security, in exercise of the powers conferred by sections 3(3), 5(3), 6(1), 12, 16, 17, 18, 42(3), 46(11), 51, 52(4), 54 and 55 of, and paragraphs 11, 14 and 16 of Schedule 1 to, the Child Support Act 1991 and of all other powers enabling him in that behalf hereby makes the following Regulations:

PART I
GENERAL

Citation, commencement and interpretation

1.—(1) These Regulations may be cited as the Child Support (Maintenance Assessment Procedure) Regulations 1992 and shall come into force on 5th April 1993.

(2) In these Regulations, unless the context otherwise requires

"the Act' means the Child Support Act 1991

"applicable amount" is to be construed in accordance with Part IV of the

Income Support Regulations;

"applicable amounts Schedule" means Schedule 2 to the Income Support Regulations;

"award period" means a period in respect of which an award of family credit or disability working allowance is made;

"balance of the reduction period" means, in relation to a direction that is or has been in force, the portion of the period specified in a direction in respect of which no reduction of relevant benefit has been made;

"benefit week", in relation to income support, has the same meaning as in the Income Support Regulations, and, in relation to family credit and disability working allowance, is to be construed in accordance with the Social Security (Claims and Payments) Regulations 1987;

"direction" means reduced benefit direction;

"disability working allowance" has the same meaning as in the Social Security Contributions and Benefits Act 1992;

"day to day care" has the same meaning as in the Maintenance Assessments and Special Cases Regulations;

"effective application" means any application that complies with theprovisions of regulation 2;

"effective date" means the date on which a maintenance assessment takes effect for the purposes of the Act;

"Income Support Regulations" means the Income Support (General) Regulations 1987;

"Information, Evidence and Disclosure Regulations" means the Child Support (Information, Evidence and Disclosure) Regulations 1992;

"Maintenance Assessments and Special Cases Regulations" means the Child Support (Maintenance Assessments and Special Cases) Regulations 1992;

"maintenance period" has the meaning prescribed in regulation 33;

"obligation imposed by section 6 of the Act" is to be construed in accordance with section 46(1) of the Act;

"parent with care" means a person who, in respect of the same child or children, is both a parent and a person with care;

"the parent concerned" means the parent with respect to whom a direction is given;

"protected income level" has the same meaning as in paragraph 6(6) of Schedule 1 to the Act;

"relevant benefit" means income support, family credit or disability working allowance;

"relevant person" means—

  (a) a person with care;

  (b) an absent parent;

  (c) a parent who is treated as an absent parent under regulation 20 of the Maintenance Assessments and Special Cases Regulations;

  (d) where the application for an assessment is made by a child under section 7 of the Act, that child,

in respect of whom a maintenance assessment has been applied for or is or has been in force.

(3) In these Regulations, references to a direction as being "in operation", "suspended", or "in force" shall be construed as follows

a direction is "in operation" if, by virtue of that direction, relevant benefit is currently being reduced;

a direction is "suspended" if either—

(a) after that direction has been given, relevant benefit ceases to be payable, or becomes payable at one of the rates indicated in regulation 40(3); or

(b) at the time that the direction is given, relevant benefit is payable at one of the rates indicated in regulation 40(3),

and these Regulations provide for relevant benefit payable from a later date to be reduced by virtue of the same direction;

a direction is "in force" if it is either in operation or is suspended, and cognate terms shall be construed accordingly.

(4) The provisions of Schedule 1 shall have effect to supplement the meaning of "child" in section 55 of the Act.

(5) The provisions of these Regulations shall have general application to cases prescribed in regulations 19 to 26 of the Maintenance Assessments and Special Cases Regulations as cases to be treated as special cases for the purposes of the Act, and the terms "absent parent" and "person with care" shall be construed accordingly.

(6) Except where express provision is made to the contrary, where, by any provision of the Act or of these Regulations—

(a) any document is given or sent to the Secretary of State, that document shall, subject to paragraph (7), be treated as having been so given or sent on the day it is received by the Secretary of State; and

(b) any document is given or sent to any person, that document shall, if sent by post to that person's last known or notified address, and subject to paragraph (8), be treated as having been given or sent on the second day after the day of posting, excluding any Sunday or any day which is a bank holiday in England, Wales, Scotland or Northern Ireland under the Banking and Financial Dealings Act 1971.

(7) Except where the provisions of regulation 8(6), 24(2), 29(3) or 31(6)(a) apply, the Secretary of State may treat a document given or sent to him as given or sent on such day, earlier than the day it was received by him, as he may determine, if he is satisfied that there was unavoidable delay in his receiving the document in question.

(8) Where, by any provision of the Act or of these Regulations, and in relation to a particular application, notice or notification—

(a) more than one document is required to be given or sent to a person, and more than one such document is sent by post to that person but not all the documents are posted on the same day; or

(b) documents are required to be given or sent to more than one person, and not all such documents are posted on the same day,

all those documents shall be treated as having been posted on the later or, as the case may be, the latest day of posting.

(9) In these Regulations, unless the context otherwise requires, a reference—
  (a) to a numbered Part is to the Part of these Regulations bearing that number;
  (b) to a numbered Schedule is to the Schedule to these Regulations bearing that number;
  (c) to a numbered regulation is to the regulation in these Regulations bearing that number;
  (d) in a regulation or Schedule to a numbered paragraph is to the paragraph in that regulation or Schedule bearing that number;
  (e) in a paragraph to a lettered or numbered sub-paragraph is to the sub-paragraph in that paragraph bearing that letter or number.

PART II

APPLICATIONS FOR A MAINTENANCE ASSESSMENT

Applications under section 4, 6 or 7 of the Act

2.—(1) Any person who applies for a maintenance assessment under section 4 or 7 of the Act shall do so on a form (a "maintenance application form") provided by the Secretary of State.

(2) Maintenance application forms provided by the Secretary of State under section 6 of the Act or under paragraph (1) shall be supplied without charge by such persons as the Secretary of State appoints or authorises for that purpose.

(3) A completed maintenance application form shall be given or sent to the Secretary of State.

(4) Subject to paragraph (5), an application for a maintenance assessment under the Act shall be an effective application if it is made on a maintenance application form and that form has been completed in accordance with the Secretary of State's instructions.

(5) Where an application is not effective under the provisions of paragraph (4), the Secretary of State may—
  (a) give or send the maintenance application form to the person who made the application, together, if he thinks appropriate, with a fresh maintenance application form, and request that the application be re-submitted so as to comply with the provisions of that paragraph; or
  (b) request the person who made the application to provide such additional information or evidence as the Secretary of State specifies,
and if a completed application form or, as the case may be, the additional information or evidence requested is received by the Secretary of State within 14 days of the date of his request, he shall treat the application as made on the date on which the earlier or earliest application would have been treated as made had it been effective under the provisions of paragraph (4).

(6) Subject to paragraph (7), a person who has made an effective application may amend his application by notice in writing to the Secretary of State at any time before a maintenance assessment is made.

(7) No amendment under paragraph (6) shall relate to any change of

circumstances arising after the effective date of a maintenance assessment resulting from an effective application .

Applications on the termination of a maintenance assessment

3.—(1) Where a maintenance assessment has been in force with respect to a person with care and a qualifying child and that person is replaced by another person with care, an application for a maintenance assessment with respect to that person with care and that qualifying child may for the purposes of regulation 30(2)(b)(ii) and subject to paragraph (3) be treated as having been received on a date earlier than that on which it was received.

(2) Where a maintenance assessment has been made in response to an application by a child under section 7 of the Act and either—

(a) a child support officer cancels that assessment following a request from that child; or

(b) that child ceases to be a child for the purposes of the Act,

any application for a maintenance assessment with respect to any other children who were qualifying children with respect to the earlier maintenance assessment may for the purposes of regulation 30(2)(b)(ii) and subject to paragraph (3) be treated as having been received on a date earlier than that on which it was received.

(3) No application for a maintenance assessment shall be treated as having been received under paragraph (1) or (2) on a date—

(a) more than 8 weeks earlier than the date on which the application was received; or

(b) on or before the first day of the maintenance period in which the earlier maintenance assessment ceased to have effect.

Multiple applications

4.—(1) The provisions of Schedule 2 shall apply in cases where there is more than one application for a maintenance assessment.

(2) The provisions of paragraphs 1, 2 and 3 of Schedule 2 relating to the treatment of two or more applications as a single application shall apply where no request is received for the Secretary of State to cease acting in relation to all but one of the applications.

(3) Where, under the provisions of paragraph 1, 2 or 3 of Schedule 2, two or more applications are to be treated as a single application, that application shall be treated as an application for a maintenance assessment to be made with respect to all of the qualifying children mentioned in the applications, and the effective date of that assessment shall be determined by reference to the earlier or earliest application.

Notice to other persons of an application for a maintenance assessment

5.—(1) Where an effective application for a maintenance assessment has been made the Secretary of State shall as soon as is reasonably practicable give notice in writing of that application to the relevant persons other than the applicant.

(2) The Secretary of State shall give or send to any person to whom notice

has been given under paragraph (1) a form (a "maintenance enquiry form") and a written request that the form be completed and returned to him for the purpose of enabling the application for the maintenance assessment to be proceeded with.

(3) Where the person to whom notice is being given under paragraph (1) is an absent parent, that notice shall specify the effective date of the maintenance assessment if one is to be made, and set out in general terms the provisions relating to interim maintenance assessments.

Response to notification of an application for a maintenance assessment

6.—(1) Any person who has received a maintenance enquiry form given or sent under regulation 5(2) shall complete that form in accordance with the Secretary of State's instructions and return it to the Secretary of State within 14 days of its having been given or sent.

(2) Subject to paragraph (3), a person who has returned a completed maintenance enquiry form may amend the information he has provided on that form at any time before a maintenance assessment is made by notifying the Secretary of State in writing of the amendments.

(3) No amendment under paragraph (2) shall relate to any change of circumstances arising after the effective date of any maintenance assessment made in response to the application in relation to which the maintenance enquiry form was given or sent.

Death of a qualifying child

7.—(1) Where the child support officer concerned is informed of the death of a qualifying child with respect to whom an application for a maintenance assessment has been made, he shall—

  (a) proceed with the application as if it had not been made with respect to that child if he has not yet made an assessment;
  (b) treat any assessment already made by him as not having been made if the relevant persons have not been notified of it and proceed with the application as if it had not been made with respect to that child.

(2) Where all of the qualifying children with respect to whom an application for a maintenance assessment has been made have died, and either the assessment has not been made or the relevant persons have not been notified of it, the child support officer shall treat the application as not having being made.

PART III

INTERIM MAINTENANCE ASSESSMENTS

Amount and duration of an interim maintenance assessment

8.—(1) Where a child support officer serves notice under section 12(4) of the Act of his intention to make an interim maintenance assessment, he shall not make the interim assessment before the end of a period of 14 days commencing with the date that notice was given or sent.

(2) The amount of child support maintenance fixed by an interim maintenance assessment shall be 1.5 multiplied by the amount of the maintenance requirement in respect of the qualifying child or qualifying children concerned

calculated in accordance with the provisions of paragraph 1 of Schedule 1 to the Act, and paragraphs 2 to 9 of that Schedule shall not apply to interim maintenance assessments.

(3) Where the provisions of regulation 30(2)(a) or (4) apply, the effective date of an interim maintenance assessment shall be such date, being not earlier than the first and not later than the seventh day following the expiry of the period of 14 days specified in paragraph (1), as falls on the same day of the week as the date specified in regulation 30(2)(a).

(4) Where a maintenance assessment is made after an interim maintenance assessment has been in force, child support maintenance calculated in accordance with Part I of Schedule 1 to the Act shall be payable in respect of the period preceding that during which the interim maintenance assessment was in force.

(5) The child support maintenance payable under the provisions of paragraph (4) shall be payable in respect of the period between the effective date of the assessment (or, where separate assessments are made for different periods under paragraph 15 of Schedule 1 to the Act, the effective date of the assessment in respect of the earliest such period) and the effective date of the interim maintenance assessment.

(6) Where a child support officer is satisfied that there was unavoidable delay by the absent parent in completing and returning a maintenance enquiry form under the provisions of regulation 6(1), or in providing information or evidence that is required by the Secretary of State for the determination of an application for a maintenance assessment, he may cancel an interim maintenance assessment which is in force.

(7) An interim maintenance assessment shall not be cancelled under paragraph (6) with effect from a date earlier than that on which the provisions of regulation 6(1) could have been complied with.

(8) Subject to paragraphs (6), (7) and (10), the child support maintenance payable in respect of any period in respect of which an interim maintenance assessment is in force shall not be adjusted following the making of a maintenance assessment.

(9) An interim maintenance assessment shall cease to have effect on the first day of the maintenance period during which the Secretary of State receives the information which enables a child support officer to make the maintenance assessment or assessments in relation to the same absent parent, person with care, and qualifying child or qualifying children, calculated in accordance with Part I of Schedule 1 to the Act.

(10) Where a maintenance assessment calculated in accordance with Part I of Schedule 1 to the Act is made following an interim maintenance assessment and the amount of child support maintenance payable under that assessment in respect of the period during which the interim maintenance assessment was in force is higher than the amount fixed by the interim maintenance assessment determined in accordance with paragraph (2), the amount of child support maintenance payable in respect of that period shall be that fixed by the maintenance assessment calculated in accordance with Part I of Schedule 1 to the Act.

(11) Subject to regulation 9(6), for the purposes of sections 17 and 18 of the Act a maintenance assessment shall not include an interim maintenance assessment.

(12) The provisions of regulations 29, 31, 32, 33(5) and 55 shall not apply to interim maintenance assessments.

Cancellation of an interim maintenance assessment

9.—(1) An absent parent with respect to whom an interim maintenance assessment is in force may apply to a child support officer for that interim assessment to be cancelled.

(2) Any application made under paragraph (1) shall be in writing, and shall include a statement of the grounds for the application.

(3) A child support officer who receives an application under the provisions of paragraph (1), shall—

   (a) decide whether the interim maintenance assessment is to be cancelled and, if so, the date with effect from which it is to be cancelled;

   (b) in any case where he does cancel an interim maintenance assessment, decide whether it is appropriate for a maintenance assessment to be made in accordance with the provisions of Part I of Schedule 1 to the Act;

   (c) in any case where he has decided that it is appropriate for a maintenance assessment to be made in accordance with the provisions of Part I of Schedule 1 to the Act, make that assessment.

(4) Where a child support officer has made a decision under paragraph (3), he shall immediately notify the applicant, so far as that is reasonably practicable, and shall give the reasons for his decision in writing.

(5) A notification under paragraph (4) shall include information as to the provisions of sections 18 and 20 of the Act and regulation 24(1) and, where an assessment is made in accordance with the provisions of Part I of Schedule 1 to the Act, the provisions of sections 16 and 17 of the Act.

(6) Where a child support officer has made a decision following an application under paragraph (1), the absent parent may apply to the Secretary of State for a review of that decision and, subject to the modification set out in paragraph (7), the provisions of section 18(5) to (8) of the Act shall apply to such a review.

(7) The modification referred to in paragraph (6) is that section 18(6) of the Act shall have effect as if for "the refusal, assessment or cancellation in question" there is substituted "the decision following an application under regulation 9(1) of the Child Support (Maintenance Assessment Procedure) Regulations 1992".

(8) Regulations 10, 11 and 25 shall apply to reviews under paragraph (6).

PART IV

NOTIFICATIONS FOLLOWING CERTAIN DECISIONS BY CHILD SUPPORT OFFICERS

Notification of a new or a fresh maintenance assessment

10.—(1) Where a child support officer makes a new or a fresh maintenance assessment following—

    (a) an application under section 4, 6 or 7 of the Act; or

    (b) a review under section 16,17,18 or 19 of the Act,

he shall immediately notify the relevant persons, so far as that is reasonably practicable, of the amount of the child support maintenance under that assessment.

    (2) A notification under paragraph (1) shall set out, in relation to the maintenance assessment in question—

    (a) the maintenance requirement;

    (b) the effective date of the assessment;

    (c) the absent parent's assessable income and, where relevant, his protected income level;

    (d) the assessable income of a parent with care;

    (e) details as to the minimum amount of child support maintenance payable by virtue of regulations made under paragraph 7 of Schedule 1 to the Act; and

    (f) details as to apportionment where a case is to be treated as a special case for the purposes of the Act under section 42 of the Act.

    (3) Except where a person gives written permission to the Secretary of State that the information, in relation to him, mentioned in sub-paragraphs (a) and (b) below may be conveyed to other persons, any document given or sent under the provisions of paragraph (1) or (2) shall not contain—

    (a) the address of any person other than the recipient of the document in question (other than the address of the office of the child support officer concerned) or any other information the use of which could reasonably be expected to lead to any such person being located;

    (b) any other information the use of which could reasonably be expected to lead to any person, other than a qualifying child or a relevant person, being identified.

    (4) A notification under paragraph (1) shall include information as to the following provisions—

    (a) where a new maintenance assessment is made following an application under the Act or a fresh maintenance assessment is made following a review under section 16 of the Act, sections 16, 17 and 18 of the Act;

    (b) where a fresh maintenance assessment is made following a review under section 17 of the Act, or following a review under section 19 of the Act where the child support officer conducting such a review is satisfied that if an application were to be made under section 17 of the Act it would be appropriate to make a fresh maintenance assessment, sections 16 and 18 of the Act;

    (c) where a fresh maintenance assessment is made following a review under section 18 of the Act, or following a review under section 19 of the Act where the child support officer conducting such a review is satisfied that if an application were to be made under section 18 of the Act, it would be appropriate to make a fresh maintenance assessment, sections 16, 17 and 20 of the Act.

Notification of a refusal to conduct a review

11.—(1) Where a child support officer refuses an application for a review under section 17 of the Act on the grounds set out in section 17(3) of the Act, or an application for a review under section 18 of the Act on the grounds set out in section 18(6) of the Act, he shall immediately notify the applicant, so far as that is reasonably practicable, and shall give the reasons for his refusal in writing.

(2) A notification under paragraph (1) shall include information as to the following provisions—

    (a) where the refusal is on the grounds set out in section 17(3) of the Act, sections 16 and 18 of the Act and regulations 24(1) and 31(7);

    (b) where the refusal is on the grounds set out in section 18(6) of the Act, sections 16,17 and 20 of the Act.

Notification of a refusal to make a new or a fresh maintenance assessment

12.—(1) Where a child support officer refuses an application for a maintenance assessment under the Act, or refuses to make a fresh assessment following a review under section 17 or 18 of the Act, he shall immediately notify the following persons, so far as that is reasonably practicable—

    (a) where an application for a maintenance assessment under section 4 or 6 of the Act is refused, the applicant;

    (b) where an application for a maintenance assessment under section 7 of the Act is refused, the applicant child and the other relevant persons who have been notified of the application;

    (c) where there is a refusal to make a fresh assessment following a review under section 17 or 18 of the Act, the relevant persons,

and shall give the reasons for his refusal in writing.

(2) A notification under paragraph (1) shall include information as to the following provisions—

    (a) where an application for a maintenance assessment under the Act is refused, section 18 of the Act and regulation 24(1);

    (b) where there is a refusal to make a fresh assessment following a review under section 17 of the Act, sections 16 and 18 of the Act and regulation 24(1);

    (c) where there is a refusal to make a fresh assessment following a review under section 18 of the Act, sections 16, 17 and 20 of the Act.

Notification of a refusal to cancel a maintenance assessment

13.—(1) Where a child support officer refuses a request under paragraph 16 of Schedule 1 to the Act for a maintenance assessment to be cancelled, or refuses to cancel a maintenance assessment following a review under section 18 of the Act, he shall immediately notify the following persons, so far as that is reasonably practicable—

    (a) where a request for a cancellation under paragraph 16 of Schedule 1 to the Act is refused, the applicant, or, as the case may be, the applicants;

    (b) where the cancellation of a maintenance assessment following a review under section 18 of the Act is refused, the relevant persons, and shall give the reasons for his refusal in writing.

(2) A notification under paragraph (1) shall include information as to the following provisions—

    (a) where a request for a cancellation under paragraph 16 of Schedule 1 to the Act is refused, sections 16 and 18 of the Act and regulation 24(1);

    (b) where the cancellation of a maintenance assessment following a review under section 18 of the Act is refused, sections 16, 17 and 20 of the Act.

Notification of a cancellation of a maintenance assessment

14.—(1) Where a child support officer cancels a maintenance assessment, he shall immediately notify the relevant persons, so far as that is reasonably practicable, and shall give the reasons for the cancellation in writing.

(2) A notification under paragraph (1) shall include information as to the provisions of section 18 of the Act and regulations 24(1) and 31(8).

Notification of a refusal to reinstate a cancelled maintenance assessment

15.—(1) Where a child support officer, following a review under section 18(3) of the Act, refuses to reinstate a maintenance assessment that has been cancelled, he shall immediately notify the relevant persons, so far as that is reasonably practicable, and shall give the reasons for his refusal in writing.

(2) A notification under paragraph (1) shall include information as to the provisions of section 20 of the Act.

Notification when an applicant under section 7 of the Act ceases to be a child

16.   Where a maintenance assessment has been made in response to an application by a child under section 7 of the Act and that child ceases to be a child for the purposes of the Act, a child support officer shall immediately notify, so far as that is reasonably practicable—

    (a) the other qualifying children over the age of 12 and the absent parent with respect to whom that maintenance assessment was made; and

    (b) the person with care.

PART V

PERIODICAL REVIEWS

Intervals between periodical reviews and notice of a periodical review

17.—(1) Subject to regulation 18(1), a maintenance assessment that has been in force for a period of 52 weeks shall be reviewed by a child support officer under section 16 of the Act.

(2) Where a review under section 17 of the Act results in a fresh maintenance assessment, the next review under the provisions of paragraph (1) shall be conducted when that fresh assessment has been in force for a period of 52 weeks.

(3) A child support officer may decide not to conduct a review under

paragraph (1) if a fresh maintenance assessment following such a review would cease to have effect within 28 days of the effective date of that fresh assessment.

(4) Before a child support officer conducts a review under section 16 of the Act, he shall give 14 days' notice of the proposed review to the relevant persons.

(5) Subject to paragraphs (6) and (7), a child support officer shall request every person to whom he is giving notice under paragraph (4) to provide, within 14 days, and in accordance with the provisions of regulations 2 and 3 of the Information, Evidence and Disclosure Regulations such information or evidence as to his current circumstances as may be specified.

(6) The provisions of paragraph (5) shall not apply in relation to any person to whom or in respect of whom income support is payable or to a person with care where income support is payable to or in respect of the absent parent.

(7) The provisions of paragraph (5) shall not apply in relation to a relevant person where—

    (a) a case is prescribed in regulation 22 or 23 of the Maintenance Assessments and Special Cases Regulations as a case to be treated as a special case for the purposes of the Act;

    (b) there has been a review under section 16 or 17 of the Act in relation to another maintenance assessment in force relating to that person;

    (c) the child support officer concerned has notified that person of the assessments following that review not earlier than 13 weeks prior to the date a review under section 16 of the Act is due under paragraph (1); and

    (d) the child support officer has no reason to believe that there has been a change in that person's circumstances.

Review under section 17 of the Act treated as a review under section 16 of the Act

18.—(1) Where, under the provisions of regulation 19(1), a child support officer gives notice of a review under section 17 of the Act, that notice is given or sent not earlier than 8 weeks prior to the next review, under the provisions of regulation 17(1), of the maintenance assessment in force, and the review under section 17 of the Act does not result in a fresh maintenance assessment by virtue of the provisions of regulation 20, 21 or 22, that review shall be treated as a review under section 16 of the Act, and the fresh assessment that would have been made but for the provisions of regulation 20, 21 or 22, as the case may be, shall be the assessment following that review.

(2) Where there is a fresh assessment under the provisions of paragraph (1), the next review under the provisions of regulation 17(1) shall be of that fresh assessment.

PART VI

REVIEWS ON A CHANGE OF CIRCUMSTANCES

Conduct of a review on a change of circumstances

19.—(1) Where a child support officer proposes to conduct a review under section 17 of the Act, he shall give 14 days' notice of the proposed review to the relevant persons.

(2) Subject to paragraphs (3) and (4), and except where the circumstances set out in regulation 17(7) apply, a child support officer proposing to conduct a review under section 17 of the Act shall request every person to whom he is giving notice under paragraph (1) to provide within 14 days, and in accordance with the provisions of regulations 2 and 3 of the Information, Evidence and Disclosure Regulations, such information or evidence as to his current circumstances as may be specified.

(3) The provisions of paragraph (2) shall not apply in relation to any person to whom or in respect of whom income support is payable.

(4) Where an application for a review under section 17 of the Act is made at the time that a review under section 16 of the Act is being conducted, the child support officer concerned may proceed with the review under section 17 of the Act notwithstanding that he has not complied with the provisions of paragraph (2) if in his opinion such compliance is not required in the particular circumstances of the case.

(5) Where a maintenance assessment is in force with respect to a parent with care and an absent parent in response to an application by the parent with care under section 6 of the Act, and the parent with care authorises the Secretary of State to take action under the Act to recover child support maintenance from that absent parent in relation to an additional child of whom she is a parent with care and he is an absent parent, that authorisation shall be treated by the Secretary of State as an application for a review under section 17 of the Act.

Fresh assessments following a review on a change of circumstances

20.—(1) Subject to paragraphs (2) and (3) and regulations 21 and 22, a child support officer who has completed a review under section 17 of the Act shall not make a fresh assessment if the difference between the amount of child support maintenance fixed by the assessment currently in force and the amount that would be fixed if a fresh assessment were to be made as a result of the review is less than £10.00 per week.

(2) Where a child support officer who has completed a review under section 17 of the Act determines that, were a fresh assessment to be made as a result of the review, the circumstances of the absent parent are such that the provisions of paragraph 6 of Schedule 1 to the Act would apply to that assessment, he shall not make a fresh assessment if the difference between the amount of child support maintenance fixed by the original assessment and the amount that would be fixed if a fresh assessment were to be made as a result of the review is less than £1.00 per week.

(3) Where a child support officer who has completed a review under section 17 of the Act determines that, were a fresh assessment to be made as a result of the review, the children in respect of whom that assessment would be made are not identical with the children in respect of whom the original assessment was made, he shall not make a fresh assessment if the difference between the amount of child support maintenance fixed by the original assessment and the amount that would be fixed if a fresh assessment were to be made as a result of the review is less than £1.00 per week.

Fresh assessments following a review on a change of circumstances: special case prescribed by regulation 22 of the Maintenance Assessments and Special Cases Regulations

21.—(1) The provisions of paragraphs (2) and (3) shall apply on a review under section 17 of the Act where a case is to be treated as a special case for the purposes of the Act by virtue of regulation 22 of the Maintenance Assessments and Special Cases Regulations.

(2) Where there is a change in the circumstances of the absent parent (whether or not there is also a change in the circumstances of one or more of the persons with care), a child support officer shall not make fresh assessments if the difference between the aggregate amount of child support maintenance fixed by the assessments currently in force and the aggregate amount that would be fixed if fresh assessments were to be made as a result of the review is less than £10.00 per week or, where the circumstances of the absent parent are such that the provisions of paragraph 6 of Schedule 1 to the Act would apply to those fresh assessments, that difference is less than £1.00 per week.

(3) Where there is a change in the circumstances of one or more of the persons with care but not in that of the absent parent, the provisions of regulation 20 shall apply in relation to each fresh assessment.

Fresh assessments following a review on a change of circumstances: special case prescribed by regulation 23 of the Maintenance Assessments and Special Cases Regulations

22.—(1) The provisions of paragraph (2) shall apply on a review under section 17 of the Act where a case is to be treated as a special case for the purposes of the Act by virtue of regulation 23 of the Maintenance Assessments and Special Cases Regulations.

(2) Where there is a change in the circumstances of the person with care or in the circumstances of one or more of the absent parents, the provisions of regulation 20 shall apply to each fresh assessment.

Reviews conducted under section 19 of the Act as if a review under section 17 of the Act had been applied for

23. The provisions of regulations 20, 21 and 22 shall apply to a review under section 19 of the Act which has been conducted as if an application for a review under section 17 of the Act had been made.

PART VII

REVIEWS OF A DECISION BY A CHILD SUPPORT OFFICER

Time limits for an application for a review of a decision by a child support officer

24.—(1) Subject to paragraph (2), the Secretary of State shall not refer any application for a review under section 18(1), (3) or (4) of the Act or under section 18 of the Act as extended by regulation 9(6) to a child support officer unless that application is received by the Secretary of State within 28 days of the date of notification to the applicant of the decision whose review he seeks.

(2) Where the Secretary of State receives an application for a review under section 18(1), (3) or (4) of the Act or under section 18 of the Act as extended by regulation 9(6) more than 28 days after the date of notification to the applicant of the decision whose review he seeks, the Secretary of State may refer that application to a child support officer if he is satisfied that there was unavoidable delay in making the application.

Notice of a review of a decision by a child support officer

25.—(1) Where on an application for a review under section 18 of the Act a child support officer proposes to conduct such a review, he shall give 14 days' notice of the proposed review to the relevant persons.

(2) A child support officer proposing to conduct a review under section 18 of the Act shall—

(a) send to the relevant persons the applicant's reasons for making the application for the review;

(b) where a maintenance assessment is in force, send to the relevant persons the information that was included, under the provisons of regulation 10(2), in the notification of that assessment made under the provisions of regulation 10(1);

(c) invite representations, either in person or in writing, from the relevant persons on any matter relating to the review and set out the provisions of paragraphs (3) to (6) in relation to such representations.

(3) Subject to paragraph (4), where the child support officer conducting the review does not within 14 days of the date on which notice of the review was given receive a request from a relevant person to make representations in person, or receives such a request and arranges for an appointment for such representations to be made but that appointment is not kept, he may complete the review in the absence of such representations from that person.

(4) Where the child support officer conducting the review is satisfied that there was good reason for failure to keep an appointment, he shall provide for a further opportunity for the making of representations by the relevant person concerned before he completes the review.

(5) Where the child support officer conducting the review does not receive written representations from a relevant person within 14 days of the date on which notice of the review was given, he may complete the review in the absence of written representations from that person.

(6) Except where a person gives written permission to the Secretary of State that the information, in relation to him, mentioned in sub-paragraphs (a) and (b) below may be conveyed to other persons, any document given or sent under the provisions of paragraph (1) or (2) shall not contain—

(a) the address of any person other than the recipient of the document in question (other than the address of the office of the child support officer concerned) or any other information the use of which could reasonably be expected to lead to any such person being located;

(b) any other information the use of which could reasonably be expected to lead to any person other than a qualifying child or relevant person being identified.

Procedure on a review of a decision by a child support officer

26.—(1) Where the Secretary of State has referred more than one application for a review to a child support officer under section 18 of the Act in relation to the same decision and that child support officer proposes to conduct a review but has not given notice under regulation 25(1), he shall give notice to the relevant persons under regulation 25(1) and shall conduct one review taking account of all the representations made and all the evidence before him.

(2) Where the child support officer conducting a review under section 18 of the Act has given notice under regulation 25(1) and has a further application referred to him by the Secretary of State in relation to the same decision before he has completed his review, he shall notify the person who has made that further application that he is already conducting a review of that decision and that he will take into account the information contained in that application.

Review following an application under section 18(1)(b) of the Act

27.   Where a child support officer has completed a review following an application for a review under section 18(1)(b) of the Act, regulations 20 to 22 shall apply in relation to any fresh assessment following that review.

Reviews conducted under section 19 of the Act as if a review under section 18(1)(b) of the Act had been applied for

28.   The provisions of regulation 27 shall apply to a review under section 19 of the Act which has been conducted as if an application for a review under section 18(1)(b) of the Act had been made.

Extension of provisions of section 18(2) of the Act

29.—(1) The provisions of section 18(2) of the Act shall apply where a maintenance assessment has been in force but is no longer in force if the condition specified in paragraph (2) is satisfied.

(2) The condition mentioned in paragraph (1) is that, subject to paragraph (3), the application for a review under section 18(2) of the Act as extended by this regulation is received by the Secretary of State within 28 days of the date of notification to the applicant of the maintenance assessment whose review he seeks.

(3) Where the Secretary of State receives such an application more than 28 days after the date of notification to the applicant of the maintenance assessment whose review he seeks, the Secretary of State may refer that application to a child support officer if he is satisfied that there was unavoidable delay.

PART VIII

COMMENCEMENT AND TERMINATION OF MAINTENANCE ASSESSMENTS AND MAINTENANCE PERIODS

Effective dates of new maintenance assessments

30.—(1) Subject to regulation 8(3), the effective date of a new maintenance assessment following an application under section 4, 6 or 7 of the Act shall be the date determined in accordance with paragraphs (2) to (4).

(2) Where no maintenance assessment is in force with respect to the person with care and absent parent, the effective date of a new assessment shall be—

   (a) the date a maintenance enquiry form is given or sent to an absent parent in a case where the application for a maintenance assessment is made by a person with care or by a child under section 7 of the Act; or

   (b) the date an effective maintenance application form is received by the Secretary of State in a case where the application for a maintenance assessment—

      (i)   is made by an absent parent; or

      (ii) is an application in relation to which the provisions of regulation 3 have been applied.

(3) The provisions of regulation 1(6)(b) shall not apply to paragraph (2)(a).

(4) Where a child support officer is satisfied that an absent parent has deliberately avoided receipt of a maintenance enquiry form, he may determine the date on which the form would have been given or sent but for such avoidance, and that date shall be the relevant date for the purposes of paragraph (2)(a).

Effective dates of maintenance assessments following a review under sections 16 to 19 of the Act

31.—(1) Where a fresh maintenance assessment is made following a review under section 16 of the Act, the effective date of that assessment shall be 52 weeks after the effective date of the previous assessment.

(2) Subject to paragraph (4), where an application is made under section 17 of the Act for a review of a maintenance assessment in force, and a fresh maintenance assessment is made in accordance with the provisions of regulation 20, 21 or 22, the effective date of that assessment shall be the first day of the maintenance period in which the application is received.

(3) Where a case falls within regulation 18(1), the effective date of the fresh assessment shall be the first day of the maintenance period in which the assessment is made.

(4) Where an application is made under section 17 of the Act for a review of a maintenance assessment in force following the death of a qualifying child and a fresh maintenance assessment is made in accordance with the provisions of regulation 20, 21 or 22, the effective date of that assessment shall be the first day of the maintenance period during the course of which that child died.

(5) Where, following a review under section 18(1)(a) of the Act, a maintenance assessment is made following a refusal to make a maintenance assessment, the effective date of that assessment shall be the effective date of the assessment that would have been made if the application for a maintenance assessment had not been refused.

(6) Subject to paragraphs (7), (10) and (11), where an application is made under section 18(2) of the Act for a review of a maintenance assessment in force, the effective date of a fresh assessment (if one is made) following such a review shall be—

   (a) where the application is received by the Secretary of State within 28 days of the date of notification of that assessment, or on a later date but the Secretary of State is satisfied that there was unavoidable delay, the effective date as determined on the review;

(b) subject to sub-paragraph (a), where the application is received by the Secretary of State later than 28 days after the date of notification of that assessment, the first day of the maintenance period in which the application is received.

(7) Where an application is made under section 18(1)(b) of the Act for a review of a refusal of an application under section 17 of the Act for the review of a maintenance assessment which is in force, the effective date of a fresh maintenance assessment (if one is made) shall be the date determined under paragraph (2).

(8) Where, following a review under section 18(3) of the Act, a cancelled maintenance assessment is reinstated, the effective date of the reinstated assessment shall be the date on which the cancelled assessment ceased to have effect.

(9) Where there has been a misrepresentation or failure to disclose a material fact on the part of the person with care or absent parent in connection with an application for a maintenance assessment under the Act, or a review under section 16 or 17 of the Act, and that misrepresentation or failure has resulted in an incorrect assessment or a series of incorrect assessments, the effective date of a fresh assessment (or of a fresh assessment in relation to the earliest relevant period) following discovery of the misrepresentation or failure shall be the effective date of the incorrect assessment or the first incorrect assessment, as the case may be.

(10) Where a fresh maintenance assessment is made on a review under section 18 or 19 of the Act by reason of an assessment having been made in ignorance of a material fact or having been based on a mistake as to a material fact and that ignorance or mistake, as the case may be, is attributable to an operational or administrative error on the part of the Secretary of State or of a child support officer, the effective date of that fresh assessment shall be the effective date of the assessment that has been reviewed.

(11) Subject to paragraphs (9), (10), (12), (13) and (14), where a fresh maintenance assessment is made under section 19 of the Act, the effective date of the assessment shall be the first day of the maintenance period in which the assessment is made.

(12) Where a fresh maintenance assessment is made under section 19 of the Act following the death of a qualifying child, the effective date of that assessment shall be the first day of the maintenance period during which that child died.

(13) Where a child support officer on a review under section18 or 19 of the Act is satisfied that a maintenance assessment which is or has been in force is defective by reason of a mistake as to the effective date of that assessment, the effective date of a fresh assessment shall be that determined in accordance with regulation 30 or in accordance with paragraphs (1) to (12), as the case may be.

(14) Where a child support officer on a review under section 19 of the Act is satisfied that if an application were to be made under section 18 of the Act

it would be appropriate to make a fresh maintenance assessment, and does so, the effective date of that fresh assessment shall be determined in accordance with paragraphs (5) to (8).

Cancellation of a maintenance assessment

32. Where a child support officer cancels a maintenance assessment under paragraph 16(2) or (3) of Schedule 1 to the Act, the assessment shall cease to have effect from the date of receipt of the request for the cancellation of the assessment or from such later date as the child support officer may determine.

Maintenance periods

33.—(1) The child support maintenance payable under a maintenance assessment shall be calculated at a weekly rate and be in respect of successive maintenance periods, each such period being a period of 7 days.

(2) Subject to paragraph (6), the first maintenance period shall commence on the effective date of the first maintenance assessment, and each succeeding maintenance period shall commence on the day immediately following the last day of the preceding maintenance period.

(3) The maintenance periods in relation to a fresh maintenance assessment following a review under section 16, 17, 18 or 19 of the Act shall coincide with the maintenance periods in relation to the earlier assessment, had it continued in force, and the first maintenance period in relation to a fresh assessment shall commence on the day following the last day of the last maintenance period in relation to the earlier assessment.

(4) The amount of child support maintenance payable in respect of a maintenance period which includes the effective date of a fresh maintenance assessment shall be the amount of maintenance payable under that fresh assessment.

(5) The amount of child support maintenance payable in respect of a maintenance period during the course of which a cancelled maintenance assessment ceases to have effect shall be the amount of maintenance payable under that assessment.

(6) Where a case is to be treated as a special case for the purposes of the Act by virtue of regulation 22 of the Maintenance Assessments and Special Cases Regulations (multiple applications relating to an absent parent) and an application is made by a person with care in relation to an absent parent where there is already a maintenance assessment in force in relation to that absent parent and a different person with care, the maintenance periods in relation to an assessment made in response to that application shall coincide with the maintenance periods in relation to the earlier maintenance assessment, and the first such period shall commence not later than 7 days after the date of notification to the relevant persons of the later maintenance assessment.

PART IX
REDUCED BENEFIT DIRECTIONS

Prescription of disability working allowance for the purposes of section 6 of the Act

34. Disability working allowance shall be a benefit of a prescribed kind for the purposes of section 6 of the Act.

Periods for compliance with obligations imposed by section 6 of the Act

35.—(1) Where the Secretary of State considers that a parent has failed to comply with an obligation imposed by section 6 of the Act he shall serve written notice on that parent that, unless she complies with that obligation, he intends to refer the case to a child support officer for the child support officer to take action under section 46 of the Act if the child support officer considers such action to be appropriate.

(2) The Secretary of State shall not refer a case to a child support officer prior to the expiry of a period of 6 weeks from the date he serves notice under paragraph (1) on the parent in question, and the notice shall contain a statement to that effect.

(3) Where the Secretary of State refers a case to a child support officer and the child support officer serves written notice on a parent under section 46(2) of the Act, the period to be specified in that notice shall be 14 days.

Amount of and period of reduction of relevant benefit under a reduced benefit direction

36.—(1) The reduction in the amount payable by way of a relevant benefit to, or in respect of, the parent concerned and the period of such reduction by virtue of a direction shall be determined in accordance with paragraphs (2) to (9).

(2) Subject to paragraph (6) and regulations 37, 33(7) and 40, there shall be a reduction for a period of 26 weeks from the day specified in the direction under the provisions of section 46(9) of the Act in respect of each such week equal to

$$0.2 \times B$$

where B is an amount equal to the weekly amount, in relation to the week in question, specified in column (2) of paragraph 1(1)(e) of the applicable amounts Schedule.

(3) Subject to paragraph (6) and regulations 37, 38(7) and 40, at the end of the period specified in paragraph (2) there shall be a reduction from the day immediately succeeding the last day of that period for a period of 52 weeks of an amount in respect of each such week equal to

$$0.1 \times B$$

where B has the same meaning as in paragraph (2).

(4) Subject to paragraph (5), a direction shall come into operation on the first day of the second benefit week following the review, carried out by the adjudication officer in consequence of the direction, of the relevant benefit that is payable.

(5) Where the relevant benefit is income support and the provisions of regulation 26(2) of the Social Security (Claims and Payments) Regulations 1987 (deferment of payment of different amount of income support) apply, a direction shall come into operation on such later date as may be determined by the Secretary of State in accordance with those provisions.

(6) Where the benefit payable is income support and there is a change in the benefit week whilst a direction is in operation, the periods of the reduc-

tions specified in paragraphs (2) and (3) shall be—
- (a) where the reduction is that specified in paragraph (2), a period greater than 25 weeks but less than 26 weeks;
- (b) where the reduction is that specified in paragraph (3), a period greater than 51 weeks but less than 52 weeks,

and ending on the last day of the last benefit week falling entirely within the period of 26 weeks specified in paragraph (2), or the period of 52 weeks specified in paragraph (3), as the case may be.

(7) Where the weekly amount specified in column (2) of paragraph 1(1)(e) of the applicable amounts Schedule changes on a day when a direction is in operation, the amount of the reduction of the relevant benefit shall be changed—
- (a) where the benefit is income support, from the first day of the first benefit week to commence for the parent concerned on or after the day that weekly amount changes;
- (b) where the benefit is family credit or disability working allowance, from the first day of the next award period of that benefit for the parent concerned commencing on or after the day that weekly amount changes.

(8) Only one direction in relation to a parent shall he in force at any one time.

(9) Where a direction has been in operation for the aggregate of the periods specified in paragraphs (2) and (3) ("the full period"), no further direction shall be given with respect to the same parent on account of that parent's failure to comply with the obligations imposed by section 6 of the Act in relation to any child in relation to whom the direction that has been in operation for the full period was given.

Modification of reduction under a reduced benefit direction to preserve minimum entitlement to relevant benefit

37. Where in respect of any benefit week the amount of the relevant benefit that would be payable after it has been reduced following a direction would, but for this regulation, be nil or less than the minimum amount of that benefit that is payable as determined—
- (a) in the case of income support, by regulation 26(4) of the Social Security (Claims and Payments) Regulations 1987;
- (b) in the case of family credit and disability working allowance, by regulation 27(2) of those Regulations,

the amount of that reduction shall be decreased to such extent as to raise the amount of that benefit to the minimum amount that is payable.

Suspension of a reduced benefit direction when relevant benefit ceases to be payable

38.—(1) Where relevant benefit ceases to be payable to, or in respect of, the parent concerned at a time when a direction is in operation, that direction shall, subject to paragraph (2), be suspended for a period of 52 weeks from the date the relevant benefit has ceased to be payable.

(2) Where a direction has been suspended for a period of 52 weeks and no

relevant benefit is payable at the end of that period, it shall cease to be in force.

(3) Where a direction is suspended and relevant benefit again becomes payable to or in respect of the parent concerned, the amount payable by way of that benefit shall, subject to regulations 40, 41 and 42, be reduced in accordance with that direction for the balance of the reduction period.

(4) The amount or, as the case may be, amounts of the reduction to be made during the balance of the reduction period shall be determined in accordance with regulation 36(2) and (3).

(5) No reduction in the amount of benefit under paragraph (3) shall be made before the expiry of a period of 14 days from service of the notice specified in paragraph (6), and the provisions of regulation 36(4) shall apply as to the date when the direction again comes into operation.

(6) Where relevant benefit again becomes payable to or in respect of a parent with respect to whom a direction is suspended she shall be notified in writing by a child support officer that the amount of relevant benefit paid to or in respect of her will again be reduced, in accordance with the provisions of paragraph (3), if she continues to fail to comply with the obligations imposed by section 6 of the Act.

(7) Where a direction has ceased to be in force by virtue of the provisions of paragraph (2), a further direction in respect of the same parent given on account of that parent's failure to comply with the obligations imposed by section 6 of the Act in relation to one or more of the same qualifying children shall, unless it also ceases to be in force by virtue of the provisions of paragraph (2), be in operation for the balance of the reduction period relating to the direction that has ceased to be in force, and the provisions of paragraph (4) shall apply to it.

Reduced benefit direction where family credit or disability working allowance is payable and income support becomes payable

39.—(1) Where a direction is in operation in respect of a parent to whom or in respect of whom family credit or disability working allowance is payable, and income support becomes payable to or in respect of that parent, income support shall become a relevant benefit for the purposes of that direction, and the amount payable by way of income support shall be reduced in accordance with that direction for the balance of the reduction period.

(2) The amount or, as the case may be, the amounts of the reduction to be made during the balance of the reduction period shall be determined in accordance with regulation 36(2) and (3).

Suspension of a reduced benefit direction when a modified applicable amount is payable

40.—(1) Where a direction is given or is in operation at a time when income support is payable to or in respect of the parent concerned but her applicable amount falls to be calculated under the provisions mentioned in paragraph (3), that direction shall be suspended for so long as the applicable amount falls to be calculated under the provisions mentioned in that paragraph, or 52 weeks, whichever period is the shorter.

(2) Where a case falls within paragraph (1) and a direction has been suspended for a period of 52 weeks, it shall cease to be in force.

(3) The provisions of paragraph (1) shall apply where the applicable amount in relation to the parent concerned falls to be calculated under—

(a) regulation 19 of and Schedule 4 to the Income Support Regulations (applicable amounts for persons in residential care and nursing homes);

(b) regulation 21 of and paragraphs 1 to 3 of Schedule 7 to the Income Support Regulations (patients);

(c) regulation 21 of and paragraphs 10B, IOC, IOD and 13 of Schedule 7 to the Income Support Regulations (persons in residential accommodation).

Termination of a reduced benefit direction following compliance with obligations imposed by section 6 of the Act

41.—(1) Where a parent with care with respect to whom a direction is in force complies with the obligations imposed by section 6 of the Act, that direction shall cease to be in force on the date determined in accordance with paragraph (2) or (3), as the case may be.

(2) Where the direction is in operation, it shall cease to be in force on the last day of the benefit week during the course of which the parent concerned complied with the obligations imposed by section 6 of the Act.

(3) Where the direction is suspended, it shall cease to be in force on the date on which the parent concerned complied with the obligations imposed by section 6 of the Act.

Review of a reduced benefit direction

42.—(1) Where a parent with care with respect to whom a direction is in force gives the Secretary of State reasons—

(a) additional to any reasons given by her in response to the notice served on her under section 46(2) of the Act for having failed to comply with the obligations imposed by section 6 of the Act; or

(b) as to why she should no longer be required to comply with the obligations imposed by section 6 of the Act,

the Secretary of State shall refer the matter to a child support officer who shall conduct a review of the direction ("a review") to determine whether the direction is to continue or is to cease to be in force.

(2) Where a parent with care with respect to whom a direction is in force gives a child support officer reasons of the kind mentioned in paragraph (1), a child support officer shall conduct a review to determine whether the direction is to continue or is to cease to be in force.

(3) A review shall not be carried out by the child support officer who gave the direction with respect to the parent concerned.

(4) Where the child support officer who is conducting a review considers that the parent concerned is no longer to be required to comply with the obligations imposed by section 6 of the Act, the direction shall cease to be in force on the date determined in accordance with paragraph (5) or (6), as the case may be.

(5) Where the direction is in operation, it shall cease to be in force on the last day of the benefit week during the course of which the parent concerned

gave the reasons specified in paragraph (1).

(6) Where the direction is suspended, it shall cease to be in force on the date on which the parent concerned gave the reasons specified in paragraph (1).

(7) The provisions of section 20 of the Act shall apply in relation to a decision of a child support officer following a review.

(8) A child support officer shall on completing a review immediately notify the parent concerned of his decision, so far as that is reasonably practicable, and shall give the reasons for his decision in writing.

(9) A notification under paragraph (8) shall include information as to the provisions of section 20 of the Act.

Termination of a reduced benefit direction where a maintenance assessment is made following an application by a child under section 7 of the Act

43. Where a qualifying child of a parent with respect to whom a direction is in force applies for a maintenance assessment to be made with respect to him under section 7 of the Act, and an assessment is made in response to that application in respect of all of the qualifying children in relation to whom the parent concerned failed to comply with the obligations imposed by section 6 of the Act, that direction shall cease to be in force from the date determined in accordance with regulation 45.

Termination of a reduced benefit direction where a maintenance assessment is made following an application by an absent parent under section 4 of the Act

44. Where—

(a) an absent parent applies for a maintenance assessment to be made under section 4 of the Act with respect to all of his qualifying children in relation to whom the other parent of those children is a person with care;

(b) a direction is in force with respect to that other parent following her failure to comply with the obligations imposed by section 6 of the Act in relation to those qualifying children; and

(c) an assessment is made in response to that application by the absent parent for a maintenance assessment,

that direction shall cease to be in force on the date determined in accordance with regulation 45.

Date from which a reduced benefit direction ceases to be in force following a termination under regulation 43 or 44

45.—(1) The date a direction ceases to be in force under the provisions of regulation 43 or 44 shall be determined in accordance with paragraphs (2) and (3).

(2) Where the direction is in operation, it shall cease to be in force on the last day of the benefit week during the course of which the Secretary of State is supplied with the information that enables a child support officer to make the assessment.

(3) Where the direction is suspended, it shall cease to be in force on the date on which the Secretary of State is supplied with the information that enables

a child support officer to make the assessment.

Cancellation of a reduced benefit direction in cases of error

46. Where a child support officer is satisfied that a direction was given as a result of an error on the part of the Secretary of State or a child support officer, or though not given as a result of such an error has not subsequently ceased to be in force as a result of such an error, the child support officer shall cancel the direction and it shall be treated as not having been given, or as having ceased to be in force on the date it would have ceased to be in force if that error had not been made, as the case may be.

Reduced benefit directions where there is an additional qualifying child

47.—(1) Where a direction is in operation or would be in operation but for the provisions of regulation 40 and a child support officer gives a further direction with respect to the same parent on account of that parent failing to comply with the obligations imposed by section 6 of the Act in relation to an additional qualifying child of whom she is a person with care, the earlier direction shall cease to be in force on the last day of the benefit week preceding the benefit week on the first day of which, in accordance with the provisions of regulation 36(4), the further direction comes into operation, or would come into operation but for the provisions of regulation 40.

(2) Where a further direction comes into operation in a case falling within paragraph (1), the provisions of regulation 36 shall apply to it.

(3) Where a direction has ceased to be in force by virtue of regulation 38(2) and a child support officer gives a direction with respect to the same parent on account of that paren's failure to comply with the obligations imposed by section 6 of the Act in relation to an additional qualifying child, no further direction shall be given with respect to that parent on account of her failure to comply with the obligations imposed by section 6 of the Act in relation to one or more children in relation to whom the direction that has ceased to be in force by virtue of regulation 38(2) was given.

(4) Where a case falls within paragraph (1) or (3) and the further direction, but for the provisions of this paragraph would cease to be in force by virtue of the provisions of regulation 41 or 42, but the earlier direction would not have ceased to be in force by virtue of the provisions of those regulations, the later direction shall continue in force for a period ("the extended period") calculated in accordance with the provisions of paragraph (5) and the reduction of relevant benefit shall be determined in accordance with paragraphs (6) and (7).

(5) The extended period for the purposes of paragraph (4) shall be

$$(78 - F - S) \text{ weeks}$$

where—

> F is the number of weeks for which the earlier direction was in operation; and
> S is the number of weeks for which the later direction has been in operation.

(6) Where the extended period calculated in accordance with paragraph (5) is greater than 52 weeks, there shall be a reduction of relevant benefit in

respect of the number of weeks in excess of 52 determined in accordance with regulation 36(2), and a reduction of relevant benefit in respect of the remaining 52 weeks determined in accordance with regulation 36(3).

(7) Where the extended period calculated in accordance with paragraph (5) is equal to or less than 52 weeks, there shall be a reduction of relevant benefit in respect of that period determined in accordance with regulation 36(3).

(8) In this regulation "an additional qualifying child" means a qualifying child of whom the parent concerned is a person with care and who was either not such a qualifying child at the time the earlier direction was given or had not been born at the time the earlier direction was given.

Suspension and termination of a reduced benefit direction where the sole qualifying child ceases to be a child or where the parent concerned ceases to be a person with care

48.—(1) Where, whilst a direction is in operation—

   (a) there is, in relation to that direction, only one qualifying child, and that child ceases to be a child within the meaning of the Act; or

   (b) the parent concerned ceases to be a person with care,

the direction shall be suspended from the last day of the benefit week during the course of which the child ceases to be a child within the meaning of the Act, or the parent concerned ceases to be a person with care, as the case may be.

(2) Where, under the provisions of paragraph (1), a direction has been suspended for a period of 52 weeks and no relevant benefit is payable at that time, it shall cease to be in force.

(3) If during the period specified in paragraph (1) the former child again becomes a child within the meaning of the Act or the parent concerned again becomes a person with care and relevant benefit is payable to or in respect of that parent, a reduction in the amount of that benefit shall be made in accordance with the provisions of paragraphs (3) to (7) of regulation 38.

Notice of termination of a reduced benefit direction

49.—(1) Where a direction ceases to be in force under the provisions of regulations 41 to 44 or 46 to 48, or is suspended under the provisions of regulation 48, a child support officer shall serve notice of such termination or suspension, as the case may be, on the adjudication officer and shall specify the date on which the direction ceases to be in force or is suspended, as the case may be.

(2) Any notice served under paragraph (1) shall set out the reasons why the direction has ceased to be in force or has been suspended.

(3) The parent concerned shall be served with a copy of any notice served under paragraph (1) .

Rounding provisions

50. Where any calculation made under this Part of these Regulations results in a fraction of a penny, that fraction shall be treated as a penny if it exceeds one half, and shall otherwise be disregarded.

PART X

MISCELLANEOUS PROVISIONS

Persons who are not persons with care

51.—(1) For the purposes of the Act the following categories of person shall not be persons with care—

(a) a local authority;

(b) a person with whom a child who is looked after by a local authority is placed by that authority under the provisions of the Children Act 1989,

(c) in Scotland, a person with whom a child is boarded out by a local authority under the provisions of section 21 of the Social Work (Scotland) Act 1968.

(2) In paragraph (1) above "local authority" means, in relation to England and Wales, the council of a county, a metropolitan district, a London Borough or the Common Council of the City of London and, in relation to Scotland, a regional council or an islands council; "a child who is looked after by a local authority" has the same meaning as in section 22 of the Children Act 1989.

Terminations of maintenance assessments

52.—(1) Where the Secretary of State is satisfied that a question arises as to whether a maintenance assessment has ceased to have effect under the provisions of paragraph 16(1)(a) to (d) of Schedule 1 to the Act, he shall refer that question (a "termination question") to a child support officer.

(2) Where a child support officer has made a decision on a termination question (a "termination decision") he shall immediately notify the following persons of his decision, so far as that is reasonably practicable—

(a) in a case falling within paragraph 16(1)(a) of Schedule 1 to the Act, the surviving relevant persons;

(b) in a case falling within paragraph 16(1)(b), (c) or (d) of Schedule 1 to the Act, the relevant persons.

(3) Any notification under paragraph (2) shall give the reasons for the termination decision made, include information as to the provisions of section 18 of the Act, and explain the provisions of paragraph (4).

(4) The persons specified in paragraph (2) may apply to the Secretary of State for a review of a termination decision as if it were a case falling within section 18 of the Act and, subject to the modifications set out in paragraph (5), section 18(5) to (9) and (11) of the Act shall apply to such a review.

(5) The modifications referred to in paragraph (4) are—

(a) section 18(6) of the Act shall have effect as if for "the refusal, assessment or cancellation" there is substituted "the termination decision";

(b) section 18(9) of the Act shall have effect as if for "a maintenance assessment or (as the case may be) a fresh maintenance assessment" there is substituted "a different termination decision".

(6) The provisions of regulation 24 as to time limits for an application for a review of a decision by a child support officer shall apply to reviews under paragraph (4).

(7) Where a child support officer has completed a review of a termination decision he shall immediately notify the persons specified in paragraph (2), so far as that is reasonably·practicable, of the review decision, give the reasons for that decision in writing, and notify them of the provisions of section 20 of the Act.

(8) Where a case falls within regulation 19 of the Maintenance Assessments and Special Cases Regulations and both absent parents have made an application for a maintenance assessment under section 4 of the Act, the Secretary of State shall be under the duty imposed by section 4(6) of the Act only if both absent parents have, under section 4(5) of the Act, requested the Secretary of State to cease acting under section 4 of the Act.

Authorisation of representative

53.—(1) A person may authorise a representative, whether or not legally qualified, to receive notices and other documents on his behalf and to act on his behalf in relation to the making of applications and the supply of information under any provision of the Act or these Regulations.

(2) Where a person has authorised a representative for the purposes of paragraph (1) who is not legally qualified, he shall confirm that authorisation in writing to the Secretary of State.

Correction of accidental errors in decisions

54.—(1) Subject to regulation 56, accidental errors in any decision or record of a decision may at any time be corrected by a child support officer and a correction made to, or to the record of, a decision shall be deemed to be part of the decision or of that record.

(2) A child support officer who has made a correction under the provisions of paragraph (1) shall immediately notify the persons who were notified of the decision that has been corrected, so far as that is reasonably practicable.

Setting aside of decisions on certain grounds

55.—(1) Subject to paragraph (7) and regulation 56, on an application made by a relevant person, a decision may be set aside by a child support officer on the grounds that the interests of justice so require, and in particular that a relevant document in relation to that decision was not sent to, or was not received at an appropriate time by the person making the application or his representative or was sent but not received at an appropriate time by the child support officer who gave the decision.

(2) Any application made under paragraph (1) shall be in writing, shall include a statement of the grounds for the application, and shall be made by giving or sending it to the Secretary of State within 28 days of the date of notification of the decision in question.

(3) Where an application to set aside a decision is being considered by a child support officer under paragraph (1), he shall notify the relevant persons other than the applicant of the application and they shall be given 14 days to make representations as to that appllcation.

(4) The provisions of regulation 25(6) shall apply to notifications under paragraph (5).

(5) A child support officer who has made a determination on an application to set aside a decision shall immediately notify the relevant persons, so far as that is reasonably practicable, and shall give the reasons for his determination in writing.

(6) For the purposes of determining an application to set aside a decision under this regulation, there shall be disregarded regulation 1(6)(b) and any provision in any enactment or instrument to the effect that any notice or other document required or authorised to be given or sent to any person shall be deemed to have been given or sent if it was sent by post to that person's last known or notified address.

(7) The provisions of paragraphs (1) to (6) shall not apply to any document given or sent under any provision of Part IX.

Provisions common to regulations 54 and 55

56.—(1) In determining whether the time limits specified in regulation 17, 19, 24 or 25 have been complied with, there shall be disregarded any day falling before the day on which notification is given of a correction made to, or to the record of, a decision made under regulation 54 or on which notification is given that a decision shall not be set aside following an application made under regulation 55, as the case may be.

(2) The power to correct errors under regulation 54 or set aside decisions under regulation 55 shall not be taken to limit any other powers to correct errors or set aside decisions that are exercisable apart from these Regulations.

Signed by authority of the Secretary of State for Social Security.

Alisair Burt
Parliamentary Under-Secretary of State,
Department of Social Security

20th July 1992

SCHEDULE 1

Regulation 1(4)

MEANING OF "CHILD" FOR THE PURPOSES OF THE ACT

Persons of 16 or 17 years of age who are not in full-time non-advanced education

1.—(1) Subject to sub-paragraph (3), the conditions which must be satisfied for a person to be a child within section 55(1)(c) of the Act are—

(a) the person is registered for work or for training under youth training with—

    (i)   the Department of Employment;

    (ii) the Ministry of Defence;

    (iii) in England and Wales, a local education authority within the meaning of the Education Acts 1944 to 1992;

    (iv) in Scotland, an education authority within the meaning of section 135(1) of the Education (Scotland) Act 1980 (interpretation); or

    (v) for the purposes of applying Council Regulation (EEC) No. 1408/71, any corresponding body in another member State;

(b) the person is not engaged in remunerative work, other than work of a temporary nature that is due to cease before the end of the extension period which applies in the case of that person;

(c) the extension period which applies in the case of that person has not expired; and

(d) immediately before the extension period begins, the person is a child for the purposes of the Act without regard to this paragraph.

(2) For the purposes of paragraphs (b), (c) and (d) of sub-paragraph (1), the extension period—

(a) begins on the first day of the week in which the person would no longer be a child for the purposes of the Act but for this paragraph; and

(b) where a person ceases to fall within section 55(1)(a) of the Act or within paragraph 5—

    (i)   on or after the first Monday in September, but before the first Monday in January of the following year, ends on the last day of the week which falls immediately before the week which includes the first Monday in January in that year;

    (ii) on or after the first Monday in January but before the Monday following Easter Monday in that year, ends on the last day of the week which falls 12 weeks after the week which includes the first Monday in January in that year;

    (iii) at any other time of the year, ends on the last day of the week which falls 12 weeks after the week which includes the Monday following Easter Monday in that year.

(3) A person shall not be a child for the purposes of the Act under this paragraph if—

(a) he is engaged in training under youth training; or

(b) he is entitled to income support.

Meaning of "advanced education" for the purposes of section 55 of the Act

2. For the purposes of section 55 of the Act "advanced education" means education of the following description—

(a) a course in preparation for a degree, a Diploma of Higher Education, a higher national diploma, a higher national diploma or higher national certificate of the Business and Technician Education Council or the Scottish Vocational Education Council or a teaching qualification; or

(b) any other course which is of a standard above that of an ordinary national diploma, a national diploma or national certificate of the Business and Technician Education Council or the Scottish Vocational Education Council, the advanced level of the General Certificate of Education, a Scottish certificate of education (higher level) or a Scottish certificate of sixth year studies.

Circumstances in which education is to be treated as full-time education

3. For the purposes of section 55 of the Act education shall be treated as being full-time if it is received by a person attending a course of education at a recognised educational establishment and the time spent receiving instruction or tuition, undertaking supervised study, examination or practical work or taking part in any exercise, experiment or project for which provision is made in the curriculum of the course, exceeds 12 hours per week, so however that in calculating the time spent in pursuit of the course, no account shall be taken of time occupied by meal breaks or spent on unsupervised study, whether undertaken on or off the premises of the educational establishment.

Interruption of full-time education

4.—(1) Subject to sub-paragraph (2), in determining whether a person falls within section 55(1)(b) of the Act no account shall be taken of a period (whether beginning before or after the person concerned attains age 16) of up to 6 months of any interruption to the extent to which it is accepted that the interruption is attributable to a cause which is reasonable in the particular circumstances of the case; and where the interruption or its continuance is attributable to the illness or disability of mind or body of the person concerned, the period of 6 months may be extended for such further period as a child support officer considers reasonable in the particular circumstances of the case.

(2) The provisions of sub-paragraph (1) shall not apply to any period of interruption of a person's full-time education which is likely to be followed immediately or which is followed immediately by a period during which—

(a) provision is made for the training of that person, and for an allowance to be payable to that person, under youth training; or

(b) he is receiving education by virtue of his employment or of any office held by him.

Circumstances in which a person who has ceased to receive full-time education is to be treated as continuing to fall within section 55(1) of the Act

5.—(1) Subject to sub-paragraphs (2) and (5), a person who has ceased to receive full-time education (which is not advanced education) shall, if—

(a) he is under the age of 16 when he so ceases, from the date on which he attains that age; or

(b) he is 16 or over when he so ceases, from the date on which he so ceases,

be treated as continuing to fall within section 55(1) of the Act up to and including the week including the terminal date or if he attains the age of 19 on or before that date up to and including the week including the last Monday before he attains that age.

(2) In the case of a person specified in sub-paragraph (1)(a) or (b) who had not attained the upper limit of compulsory school age when he ceased to receive full-time education, the terminal date in his case shall be that specified in paragraph (a), (b) or (c) of sub-paragraph (3), whichever next follows the date on which he would have attained that age.

(3) In this paragraph the "terminal date" means—

(a) the first Monday in January; or

(b) the Monday following Easter Monday; or

(c) the first Monday in September,

whichever first occurs after the date on which the person's said education ceased.

(4) In this paragraph "compulsory school age" means—

(a) in England and Wales, compulsory school age as determined in accordance with section 9 of the Education Act 1962;

(b) in Scotland. school age as determined in accordance with sections 31 and 33 of the Education (Scotland) Act 1980.

(5) A person shall not be treated as continuing to fall within section 55(1) of the Act under this paragraph if he is engaged in remunerative work, other than work of a temporary nature that is due to cease before the terminal date.

(6) Subject to sub-paragraphs (5) and (8), a person whose name was entered as a candidate for any external examination in connection with full-time education (which is not advanced education), which he was receiving at that time, shall so long as his name continued to be so entered before ceasing to receive such education be treated as continuing to fall within section 55(1) of the Act for any week in the period specified in sub-paragraph (7).

(7) Subject to sub-paragraph (13), the period specified tor the purposes of sub-paragraph (6) is the period beginning with the date when that person ceased to receive such education ending with—

(a) whichever of the dates in sub-paragraph (3) first occurs after the conclusion of the examination (or the last of them, if there are more than one); or

(b) the expiry of the week which includes the last Monday before his 19th birthday, whichever is the earlier.

(8) The period specifed in sub-paragraph (7) shall, in the case of a person who has not attained the age of 16 when he so ceased, begin with the date on which he attained that age.

Interpretation

6.   In this Schedule—

"Education Acts 1944 to 1992" has the meaning prescribed in section 94(2) of the Further and Higher Education Act 1992;

"remunerative work" means work of not less than 24 hours a week—

    (a) in respect of which payment is made; or

    (b) which is done in expectation of payment;

"week" means a period of 7 days beginning with a Monday;

"youth training" means—

    (a) arrangements made under section 2 of the Employment and Training Act 1973 (functions of the Secretary of State) or section 2 of the Enterprise and New Towns (Scotland) Act 1990;

    (b) arrangements made by the Secretary of State for persons enlisted in Her Majesty's forces for any special term of service specified in regulations made under section 2 of the Armed Forces Act 1966 (power of Defence Council to make regulations as to engagement of persons in regular forces); or

    (c) for the purposes of the application of Council Regulation (EEC) No. 1408/71, any corresponding provisions operated in another member State,

for purposes which include the training of persons who, at the beginning of their training, are under the age of 18.

SCHEDULE 2   Regulation 4

MULTIPLE APPLICATIONS

No maintenance assessment in force: more than one application for a maintenance assessment by the same person under section 4 or 6 or under sections 4 and 6 of the Act

1.—(1) Where a person makes an effective application for a maintenance assessment under section 4 or 6 of the Act and, before that assessment is made, makes a subsequent effective application under that section with respect to the same absent parent or person with care, as the case may be, those applications shall be treated as a single application.

(2) Where a parent with care makes an effective application for a maintenance assessment—

    (a) under section 4 of the Act; or

    (b) under section 6 of the Act,

and, before that assessment is made, makes a subsequent effective application—

    (c) in a case falling within paragraph (a), under section 6 of the Act; or

    (d) in a case falling within paragraph (b), under section 4 of the Act,

with respect to the same absent parent, those applications shall, if the parent with care does not cease to fall within section 6(1) of the Act, be treated as a single application under section 6 of the Act, and shall otherwise be treated as a single application under section 4 of the Act.

No maintenance assessment in force: more than one application by a child under section 7 of the Act

2. Where a child makes an effective application for a maintenance assessment under section 7 of the Act and, before that assessment is made, makes a subsequent effective application under that section with respect to the same person with care and absent parent, both applications shall be treated as a single application for a maintenance assessment.

No maintenance assessment in force: applications by different persons for a maintenance assessment

3.—(1) Where the Secretary of State receives more than one effective application for a maintenance assessment with respect to the same person with care and absent parent, he shall refer each such application to a child support officer and, if no maintenance assessment has been made in relation to any of the applications, the child support officer shall determine which application he shall proceed with in accordance with sub-paragraphs (2) to (11).

(2) Where there is an application by a person with care under section 4 or 6 of the Act and an application by an absent parent under section 4 of the Act, the child support officer shall proceed with the application of the person with care.

(3) Where there is an application for a maintenance assessment by a qualifying child under section 7 of the Act and a subsequent application is made with respect to that child by a person who is, with respect to that child, a person with care or an absent parent, the child support officer shall proceed with the application of that person with care or absent parent, as the case may be.

(4) Where, in a case falling within sub-paragraph (3), there is more than one subsequent application, the child support officer shall apply the provisions of sub-paragraph (2), (8), (9) or (11), as is appropriate in the circumstances of the case, to determine which application he shall proceed with.

(5) Where there is an application for a maintenance assessment by more than one qualifying child under section 7 of the Act in relation to the same person with care and absent parent, the child support officer shall proceed with the application of the elder or, as the case may be, eldest of the qualifying children.

(6) Where a case is to be treated as a special case for the purposes of the Act under regulation 19 of the Maintenance Assessments and Special Cases Regulations (both parents are absent) and an effective application is received from each absent parent, the child support officer shall proceed with both applications, treating them as a single application for a maintenance assessment.

(7) Where, under the provisions of regulation 20 of the Maintenance Assessments and Special Cases Regulations (persons treated as absent parents), two

persons are to be treated as absent parents and an effective application is received from each such person, the child support officer shall proceed with both applications, treating them as a single application for a maintenance assessment.

(8) Where there is an application under section 6 of the Act by a parent with care and an application under section 4 of the Act by another person with care who has parental responsibility for (or, in Scotland, parental rights over) the qualifying child or qualifying children with respect to whom the application under section 6 of the Act was made, the child support officer shall proceed with the application under section 6 of the Act by the parent with care.

(9) Where—

(a) more than one person with care makes an application for a maintenance assessment under section 4 of the Act in respect of the same qualifying child or qualifying children (whether or not any of those applications is also in respect of other qualifying children);

(b) each such person has parental responsibility for (or, in Scotland, parental rights over) that child or children; and

(c) under the provisions of regulation 20 of the Maintenance Assessments and Special Cases Regulations one of those persons is to be treated as an absent parent,

the child support officer shall proceed with the application of the person who does not fall to be treated as an absent parent under the provisions of regulation 20 of those Regulations.

(10) Where, in a case falling within sub-paragraph (9), there is more than one person who does not fall to be treated as an absent parent under the provisions of regulation 20 of those Regulations, the child support officer shall apply the provisions of paragraph (11) to determine which application he shall proceed with.

(11) Where—

(a) more than one person with care makes an application for a maintenance assessment under section 4 of the Act in respect of the same qualifying child or qualifying children (whether or not any of those applications is also in respect of other qualifying children); and

(b) either—

(i) none of those persons has parental responsibility for (or, in Scotland, parental rights over) that child or children; or

(ii) the case falls within sub-paragraph (9)(b) but the child support officer has not been able to determine which application he is to proceed with under the provisions of sub-paragraph (9),

the child support officer shall proceed with the application of the principal provider of day to day care, as determined in accordance with sub-paragraph (12).

(12) Where—

(a) the applications are in respect of one qualifying child, the application of that person with care with whom the child spends the greater or, as the case may be, the greatest proportion of his time;

(b) the applications are in respect of more than one qualifying child, the application of that person with care with whom the children spend the greater or, as the case may be, the greatest proportion of their time, taking account of the time each qualifying child spends with each of the persons with care in question;

(c) the child support officer cannot determine which application he is to proceed with under paragraph (a) or (b), and child benefit is paid in respect of the qualifying child or qualifying children to one but not any other of the applicants, the application of the applicant to whom child benefit is paid;

(d) the child support officer cannot determine which application he is to proceed with under paragraph (a), (b) or (c), the application of that applicant who in the opinion of the child support officer is the principal provider of day to day care for the child or children in question.

(13) Subject to sub-paragraph (14) , where, in any case falling within sub-paragraphs (2) to (11), the applications are not in respect of identical qualifying children, the application that the child support officer is to proceed with as determined by those paragraphs shall be treated as an application with respect to all of the qualifying children with respect to whom the applications were made.

(14) Where the child support officer is satisfied that the same person with care does not provide the principal day to day care for all of the qualifying children with respect to whom an assessment would but for the provisions of this paragraph be made under sub-paragraph (13), he shall make separate assessments in relation to each person with care providing such principal day to day care.

Maintenance assessment in force: subsequent application for a maintenance assessment with respect to the same persons

4. Where a maintenance assessment is in force and a subsequent application is made under the same section of the Act for an assessment with respect to the same person with care, absent parent, and qualifying child or qualifying children as those with respect to whom the assessment in force has been made, that application shall not be proceeded with unless the Secretary of State treats that application as an application for a review under section 17 of the Act.

Maintenance assessment in force: subsequent application for a maintenance assessment under section 6 of the Act

5. Where a maintenance assessment is in force following an application under section 4 or 7 of the Act and the person with care makes an application under section 6 of the Act, any maintenance assessment made in response to that application shall replace the assessment currently in force.

Maintenance assessment in force: subsequent application for a maintenance assessment in respect of additional children

6.—(1) Where a maintenance assessment made in response to an application by an absent parent under section 4 of the Act is in force and that assessment is not in respect of all of his children who are in the care of the person with care with respect to whom that assessment has been made, all assessment made in response to an application by that person with care under section 4 of the Act with respect to—

    (a) the children in respect of whom the assessment currently in force was made; and

    (b) the additional child or, as the case may be, one or more of the additional children in that person's care who are children of that absent parent,

shall replace the assessment currently in force.

    (2) Where—

    (a) a maintenance assessment made in response to an application by an absent parent or a person with care under section 4 of the Act is in force;

    (b) that assessment is not in respect of all of the children of the absent parent who are in the care of the person with respect to whom that assessment has been made; and

    (c) the absent parent makes a subsequent application in respect of all additional qualifying child or additional qualifying children of his in the care of the same person,

that application shall be treated as an application for a maintenance assessment in respect of all of the qualifying children concerned, and the assessment made shall replace the assessment currently in force.

    (3) Where a maintenance assessment made in response to an application by a child under section 7 of the Act is in force and the person with care of that child makes an application for a maintenance assessment under section 4 of the Act in respect of that child and all other children of the absent parent who are in her care, that assessment shall replace the assessment currently in force.

S.I. 1992 No. 1816

The   Child   Support   (Arrears,   Interest   and   Adjustment   of Maintenance Assessments) Regulations 1992

Made — — — — *20th July 1992*

Coming into force *5th April 1993*

ARRANGEMENT OF REGULATIONS

PART I

General

PART II

Arrears of child support maintenance and interest on arrears

PART III

Attribution of payments and adjustment of the amount payable under a maintenance assessment

PART IV

Miscellaneous

Whereas a draft of this instrument was laid before Parliament in accordance with section 52(2) of the Child Support Act 1991 and approved by a resolution of each House of Parliament:

Now therefore, the Secretary of State for Social Security, in exercise of the powers conferred by sections 41, 51, 52(4) and 54 of the Child Support Act 1 991 and of all other powers enabling him in that behalf hereby makes the following Regulations:

PART I

GENERAL

Citation, commencement and interpretation

1.—(1) These Regulations may be cited as the Child Support (Arrears, Interest and Adjustment of Maintenance Assessments) Regulations 1992 and shall come into force on 5th April 1993.

(2) In these Regulations, unless the context otherwise requires—
"absent parent" includes a person treated as an absent parent by virtue of regulation 20 of the Maintenance Assessments and Special Cases Regulations;

   "the Act" means the Child Support Act 1991;

   "arrears" means arrears of child support maintenance;

   "arrears of child support maintenance" is to be construed in accordance with section 41 (1) and (2) of the Act;

   "arrears notice"has the meaning prescribed in regulation 2;

   "due date" has the meaning prescribed in regulation 3;

   "Maintenance Assessments and Special Cases Regulations" means the Child Support (Maintenance Assessments and Special Cases) Regulations 1992;

   "Maintenance Assessment Procedure Regulations" means the Child Support (Maintenance Assessment Procedure) Regulations 1992;

   "parent with care" means a person who, in respect of the same child or children, is both a parent and a person with care;

   "relevant person" has the same meaning as in the Maintenance Assessment Procedure Regulations.

(3) In these Regulations, unless the context otherwise requires, a reference—

   (a) to a numbered regulation is to the regulation in these Regulations bearing that number;

   (b) in a regulation to a numbered paragraph is to the paragraph in that regulation bearing that number;

   (c) in a paragraph to a lettered or numbered sub-paragraph is to the sub-paragraph in that paragraph bearing that letter or number.

PART II

ARREARS OF CHILD SUPPORT MAINTENANCE AND INTEREST ON ARREARS

Applicability of provisions as to arrears and interest and arrears notices

2.—(1) The provisions of paragraphs (2) to (4) and regulations 3 to 9 shall apply where—

(a) a case falls within section 41(1) of the Act; and

(b) the Secretary of State is arranging for the collection of child support maintenance under section 29 of the Act.

(2) Where the Secretary of State is considering taking action with regard to a case falling within paragraph (1), he shall serve a notice (an "arrears notice") on the absent parent.

(3) An arrears notice shall—

(a) itemize the payments of child support maintenance due and not paid;

(b) set out in general terms the provisions as to arrears and interest contained in this regulation and regulations 3 to 9; and

(c) request the absent parent to make payment of all outstanding arrears.

(4) Where an arrears notice has been served under paragraph (2), no duty to serve a further notice under that paragraph shall arise in relation to further arrears unless those further arrears have arisen after an intervening continuous period of not less than 12 weeks during the course of which all payments of child support maintenance due from the absent parent have been paid on time in accordance with regulations made under section 29 of the Act.

Liability to make payments of interest with respect to arrears

3.—(1) Subject to paragraph (2) and regulations 4 and 5, interest shall be payable with respect to any amount of child support maintenance due in accordance with a maintenance assessment and not paid by the date specified by the Secretary of State in accordance with regulations made under section 29 of the Act (the "due date"), and shall be payable in respect of the period commencing on that day and terminating on the date that amount is paid.

(2) Subject to paragraph (3), interest with respect to arrears shall only be payable if the Secretary of State has served an arrears notice in relation to those arrears, and shall not be payable in respect of any period terminating on a date earlier than 14 days prior to the date the arrears notice is served on the absent parent.

(3) Where the Secretary of State has served an arrears notice, the provisions of paragraph (2) shall not apply in relation to further arrears unless the conditions mentioned in regulation 2(4) are satisfied.

(4) Subject to paragraph (6), where, following a review under section 18 or 19 of the Act or an appeal under section 20 of the Act, a fresh maintenance assessment is made with retrospective effect, interest in respect of the

relevant retrospective period shall be payable with respect to the arrears calculated by reference to that fresh assessment.

(5) The provisions of paragraph (4) shall apply to a fresh assessment following a review under section 18 or 19 of the Act or an appeal under section 20 of the Act prior to any adjustment of that assessment under the provisions of regulation 10.

(6) For the purposes of paragraph (4), where the review under section 18 or 19 of the Act or an appeal under section 20 of the Act results in an increased assessment, andarrears in relation to that assessment arise, no interest shall be payable with respect to the arrears relating to the additional maintenance payable under that assessment in respect of any period prior to the date the absent parent is notified of the increased assessment.

Circumstances in which no liability to pay interest arises

4.—(1) An absent parent shall not be liable to make payments of interest with respect to arrears in respect of any period if the conditions set out in paragraph (2) are satisfied in relation to that period.

(2) The conditions referred to in paragraph (1) are—

(a) the absent parent did not know, and could not reasonably have been expected to know, of the existence of the arrears; or

(b) the arrears have arisen solely in consequence of an operational or administrative error on the part of the Secretary of State or a child support officer.

Payment of arrears by agreement

5.—(1) The Secretary of State may at any time enter into an agreement in writing with an absent parent (an "arrears agreement") for the absent parent to pay all outstanding arrears.

(2) An arrears agreement shall specify the dates on which the payments of arrears shall be made and the amount to be paid on each such date.

(3) If an arrears agreement is entered into within 28 days of the due date, and the terms of that agreement are adhered to by the absent parent, there shall be no liability to make payments of interest under the provisions of regulation 3 with respect to the arrears in relation to which the arrears agreement was entered into.

(4) If an arrears agreement is entered into later than 28 days after the due date and the terms of that agreement are adhered to by the absent parent, there shall, with respect to the arrears in relation to which that agreement was entered into, be no liability to make payments of interest in respect of any period commencing on the date that agreement was entered into.

(5) The Secretary of State may at any time enter into a further arrears agreement with the absent parent in relation to all arrears then outstanding.

(6) Where the terms of any arrears agreement are not adhered to by an absent parent, interest shall be payable with respect to arrears in accordance with the provisions of regulation 3.

(7) It shall be an implied term of any arrears agreement that any payment of child support maintenance that becomes due whilst that agreement is in force shall be made by the due date.

Rate of interest and calculation of interest

6.—(1) The rate of interest payable where liability to pay interest under regulation 3 arises shall be one per centum per annum above the median base rate prevailing from time to time calculated on a daily basis.

(2) Interest shall be payable only with respect to arrears of child support maintenance and shall not be payable with respect to any interest that has already become due.

(3) For the purposes of paragraph (1)—

  (a) the median base rate, in relation to a year or part of a year, is the base rate quoted by the reference banks; or, if different base rates are quoted, the rate which, when the base rate quoted by each bank is ranked in a descending sequence of seven, is fourth in the sequence;

  (b) the reference banks are the seven largest institutions—

    (i)   authorised by the Bank of England under the Banking Act 1987, and

    (ii) incorporated in and carrying on a deposit-taking business within the United Kingdom,

  which quote a base rate in sterling; and

  (c) the size of an institution is to be determined by reference to its total consolidated gross assets in sterling, as shown in its audited end-year accounts last published.

(4) In paragraph (3)(c), the reference to the consolidated gross assets of an institution is a reference to the consolidated gross assets of that institution together with any subsidiary (within the meaning of section 736 of the Companies Act 1985).

Receipt and retention of interest paid

7.—(1) Payments of interest with respect to arrears shall be made in accordance with regulations under section 29 of the Act as though they were payments of child support maintenance payable in accordance with a maintenance assessment, and shall be made within 14 days of being demanded by the Secretary of State.

(2) Subject to paragraph (3), where the Secretary of State has been authorised to recover child support maintenance under section 6 of the Act and income support is paid to or in respect of the parent with care, interest with respect to arrears relating to the period during which income support is paid shall be payable to the Secretary of State and may be retained by him.

(3) Where a case falls within paragraph (2), but the Secretary of State considers that, if the absent parent had made payments of child support maintenance due from him in accordance with that assessment, the parent with care would not have been entitled to income support, any interest shall be payable to the parent with care.

(4) Where the child support maintenance payable under a maintenance assessment is payable to more than one person, any interest in respect of arrears under that assessment shall be apportioned in the same ratio as the child support maintenance that is payable, and the provisions of paragraphs (1) to (3) shall apply to each amount of interest so apportioned.

Retention of recovered arrears of child support maintenance by the Secretary of State

8. Where the Secretary of State recovers arrears from an absent parent and income support is paid to or in respect of the person with care, the Secretary of State may retain such amount of those arrears as is equal to the difference between the amount of income support that was paid to or in respect of the person with care and the amount of income support that he is satisfied would have been paid had the absent parent paid the child support maintenance due in accordance with the maintenance assessment in force by the due dates.

PART III

ATTRIBUTION OF PAYMENTS AND ADJUSTMENT OF THE AMOUNT PAYABLE UNDER A MAINTENANCE ASSESSMENT

Attribution of payments

9. Where a maintenance assessment is or has been in force and there are arrears of child support maintenance, the Secretary of State may attribute any payment of child support maintenance made by an absent parent to child support maintenance due as he thinks fit.

Adjustment of the amount payable under a maintenance assessment

10.—(1) Where a new or a fresh maintenance assessment has retrospective effect, the amount payable under that assessment may be adjusted by a child support officer for the purpose of taking account of the retrospective effect of the assessment by such amount as, subject to the provisions of paragraph (4), he considers appropriate in the circumstances of the case.

(2) Subject to paragraph (3), where the payments of child support maintenance have been over-payments or under-payments, the amount payable under a maintenance assessment may be adjusted by a child support officer for the purpose of taking account of such over-payments or under-payments by such amount as, subject to the provisions of paragraph (5), he considers appropriate in the circumstances of the case.

(3) The provisions of paragraph (2) shall not apply to any case falling within section 41 of the Act.

(4) Where a case falls within paragraph (1), the child support officer shall—

    (a) in the case of a new assessment, not increase the amount payable under that assessment by an amount greater than 1.5 multiplied by that assessment;

(b) in the case of a fresh assessment, not adjust the amount payable under that assessment by an amount greater than 1.5 multiplied by the difference between the amount payable under the earlier assessment and the amount payable under the fresh assessment.

(5) Where a case falls within paragraph (2), the child support officer shall not adjust the amount payable under a maintenance assessment by an amount greater than 1.5 multiplied by the mean over-payment or the mean under-payment, as the case may be.

(6) For the purposes of paragraph (5), the mean over-payment or the mean underpayment shall be the total net over-payment or the total net under-payment divided by the number of occasions on which, in respect of the period being taken into acount for the purposes of paragraph (2), there have been over-payments or, as the case may be, under-payments of child support maintenance.

PART IV

MISCELLANEOUS

Notifications following an adjustment under the provisions of regulation 10

11.—(1) Where a child support officer has, under the provisions of regulation 10, adjusted the amount payable under a maintenance assessment, he shall immediately notify the relevant persons, so far as that is reasonably practicable, of the amount and period of the adjustment, and the amount payable during the period of the adjustment.

(2) A notification under paragraph (1) shall include information as to the provisions of regulation 12(1) and regulation 13(1) in so far as it relates to time limits for an application for a review under regulation 12(1).

Review of adjustments under regulation 10 or of the calculation of arrears or interest

12.—(1) Where the amount payable under a maintenance assessment has been adjusted under the provisions of regulation 10, a relevant person may apply to the Secretary of State for a review of that adjustment as if it were a case falling within section 18 of the Act and, subject to the modifications set out in paragraph (2), section 18(5) to (9) and (11) of the Act shall apply to such a review.

(2) The modifications referred to in paragraph (1) are—

(a) section 18(6) of the Act shall have effect as if for "the refusal, assessment or cancellation in question" there is substituted "the adjustment of the amount payable under regulation 10 of the Child Support (Arrears, Interest and Adjustment of Maintenance Assessments) Regulations 1992";

(b) section 18(9) of the Act shall have effect as if for "a maintenance assessment or (as the case may be) a fresh maintenance assessment"

there is substituted "a revised adjustment of the amount payable
under regulation 10 of the Child Support (Arrears, Interest and
Adjustment of Maintenance Assessments) Regulations 1992".

(3) Where there has been a calculation of arrears due under a maintenance
assessmentor a calculation of the interest payable with respect to arrears, a
relevant person may apply to the Secretary of State for a review of that
calculation as if it were a case falling within section 18 of the Act and, subject
to the modifications set out in paragraph (4), section 18(5) to (9) and (11) of
the Act shall apply to such a review.

(4) The modifications referred to in paragraph (3) are—

    (a) section 18(6) of the Act shall have effect as if—

        (i)   for "the refusal, assessment or cancellation in question" there is
substituted "the calculation of arrears due under a maintenance
assessment or the calculation of the interest payable with respect
to arrears";

       (ii) after "law" in paragraph (c) there is inserted—
            "   or

           (d) involved an arithmetical error";

    (b) section 18(9) of the Act shall have effect as if for "a maintenance
assessment or (as the case may be) a fresh maintenance assessment" there is substituted "a fresh calculation of the arrears due
under a maintenance assessment or a fresh calculation of the
interest payable with respect to arrears".

(5) Where the amount payable under a maintenance assessment has been
adjusted under the provisions of regulation 10 a child support officer may
revise that adjustment if he is satisfied that one or more of the circumstances
set out in paragraphs (a) to (c) of section 19(1) of the Act apply to that
adjustment.

(6) Where there has been a calculation of the arrears due under a maintenance assessment or a calculation of interest payable with a respect to
arrears, a child support officer may re-calculate the arrears or the interest if
he is satisfied that one or more of the circumstances set out in paragraphs (a)
to (c) of section 19(1) of the Act apply or that there has been an arithmetical
error in the calculation.

Procedure and notifications on applications and reviews under regulation 12

13.—(1) The provisions of regulations 24 to 26 of the Maintenance Assessment Procedure Regulations shall apply to an application for a review under
regulation 12(1) or (3).

(2) Where a child support officer refuses an application for a review under
regulation 12(1) or (3) on the grounds set out in section 18(6) of the Act (as
applied by regulation 12), he shall immediately notify the applicant, so far as
that is reasonably practicable, and shall give the reasons for his refusal in
writing.

(3) Where a child support officer adjusts the amount payable under a maintenance assessment following a review under regulation 12(1) or (5), he shall immediately notify the relevant persons, so far as that is reasonably practicable, of the amount and period of the adjustment, and the amount payable during the period of adjustment.

(4) Where a child support officer refuses to adjust the amount payable under a maintenance assessment following a review under regulation 12(1) he shall immediately notify the relevant persons, so far as that is reasonably practicable, of the refusal, and shall give the reasons for his refusal in writing.

(5) Where a child support officer has conducted a review under regulation 12(3), or has revised the calculation of the arrears due or the interest payable with respect to arrears following a review under regulation 12(6), he shall immediately notify the relevant persons, so far as that is reasonably practicable, of his decision.

(6) A notification under paragraphs (2) to (5) shall include information as to the provisions of section 20 of the Act.

Non-disclosure of information to third parties

14. The provisions of regulation 10(3) of the Maintenance Assessment Procedure Regulations shall apply to any document given or sent under the provisions of regulation 11 or 13.

Applicability of regulations 1(6) and 53 to 56 of the Maintenance Assessment Procedure Regulations

15. Regulations 1(6) and 53 to 56 of the Maintenance Assessment Procedure Regulations shall apply to the provisions of these Regulations.

Signed by authority of the Secretary of State for Social Security.

Alistair Burt
Parliamentary Under-Secretary of State,
Department of Social Security

20th July 1992

S.I. 1992 No. 1989

**The Child Support (Collection and Enforcement)
Regulations 1992**

Made — — — —   *17th August 1992*
Laid before Parliament   *26th August 1992*
Coming into force   *5th April 1993*

ARRANGEMENT OF REGULATIONS

PART I
General

1. Citation, commencement and interpretation

PART 11
Collection of child support maintenance

2. Payment of child support maintenance
3. Method of payment
4. Interval of payment
5. Transmission of payments
6. Representations about payment arrangements
7. Notice to liable person as to requirements about payment

PART III
Deduction from earnings orders

8. Interpretation of this Part
9. Deduction from earnings orders
10. Normal deduction rate
11. Protected earnings rate
12. Amount to be deducted by employer
13. Employer to notify liable person of deduction
14. Payment by employer to Secretary of State
15. Information to be provided by liable person
16. Duty of employers and others to notify Secretary of State
17. Requirement to review deduction from earnings orders
18. Power to vary deduction from earnings orders
19. Compliance with deduction from earnings orders as varied
20. Discharge of deduction from earnings orders
21. Lapse of deduction from earnings orders
22. Appeals against deduction from earnings orders
23. Crown employment
24. Priority as between orders
25. Offences

PART IV

Liability orders

SCHEDULES

The Secretary of State for Social Security, in exercise of the powers conferred by sections 29(2) and (3), 31(8), 32(1) to (5) and (7) to (9), 34(1), 35(2), (7) and (8). 39(1), (3) and (4), 40(4), (8) and (11), 51, 52 and 54 of the Child Support Act 1991 and of all other powers enabling him in that behalf, hereby makes the following Regulations:

PART I

GENERAL

Citation, commencement and interpretation

1.—(1) These Regulations may be cited as the Child Support (Collection and Enforcement) Regulations 1992 and shall come into force on 5th April 1993.

(2) In these Regulations "the Act" means the Child Support Act 1991.

(3) Where under any provision of the Act or of these Regulations—

    (a) any document or notice is given or sent to the Secretary of State, it shall be treated as having been given or sent on the day it is received by the Secretary of State; and

    (b) any document or notice is given or sent to any other person, it shall, if sent by post to that person's last known or notified address, be treated as having been given or sent on the second day after the day of posting, excluding any Sunday or any day which is a bank holiday under the Banking and Financial Dealings Act 1971.

(4) In these Regulations. unless the context otherwise requires, a reference—

    (a) to a numbered Part is to the Part of these Regulations bearing that number;

    (b) to a numbered regulation is to the regulation in these Regulations bearing that number;

(c) in a regulation to a numbered or lettered paragraph or sub-paragraph is to the paragraph or sub-paragraph in that regulation bearing that number or letter;

(d) in a paragraph to a lettered or numbered sub-paragraph is to the sub-paragraph in that paragraph bearing that letter or number;

(e) to a numbered Schedule is to the Schedule to these Regulations bearing that number.

PART II
COLLECTION OF CHILD SUPPORT MAINTENANCE

Payment of child support maintenance

2.—(1) Where a maintenance assessment has been made under the Act and the case is one to which section 29 of the Act applies, the Secretary of State may specify that payments of child support maintenance shall be made by the liable person—

(a) to the person caring for the child or children in question or, where an application has been made under section 7 of the Act, to the child who made the application;

(b) to. or through, the Secretary of State; or

(c) to, or through, such other person as the Secretary of State may, from time to time, specify.

(2) In paragraph (1) and in the rest of this Part, "liable person" means a person liable to make payments of child support maintenance.

Method of payment

3.—(1) Payments of child support maintenance shall be made by the liable person by whichever of the following methods the Secretary of State specifies as being appropriate in the circumstances—

(a) by standing order;

(b) by any other method which requires one person to give his authority for payments to be made from an account of his to an account of another's on specific dates during the period for which the authority is in force and without the need for any further authority from him;

(c) by an arrangement whereby one person gives his authority for payments to be made from an account of his or on his behalf to another person or to an account of that other person;

(d) by cheque or postal order;

(e) in cash.

(2) The Secretary of State may direct a liable person to take all reasonable steps to open an account from which payments under the maintenance assessment may be made in accordance with the method of payment specified under paragraph (1).

Interval of payment

4.—(1) The Secretary of State shall specify the day and interval by reference to which payments of child support maintenance are to be made by the liable person and may from time to time vary such day or interval.

(2) In specifying the day and interval of payment the Secretary of State shall have regard to all the circumstances and in particular to—

    (a) the needs of the person entitled to receive payment and the day and interval by reference to which any other income is normally received by that person;

    (b) the day and interval by reference to which the liable person's income is normally received; and

    (c) any period necessary to enable the clearance of cheques or otherwise necessary to enable the transmission of payments to the person entitled to receive them.

Transmission of payments

5.—(1) Payments of child support maintenance made through the Secretary of State or other specified person shall be transmitted to the person entitled to receive them in whichever of the following ways the Secretary of State specifies as being appropriate in the circumstances—

    (a) by a transfer of credit to an account nominated by the person entitled to receive the payments;

    (b) by cheque, girocheque or other payable order;

    (c) in cash.

(2) The Secretary of State shall specify the interval by reference to which the payments referred to in paragraph (1) are to be transmitted to the person entitled to receive them.

(3) The interval referred to in paragraph (2) may differ from the interval referred to in regulation 4 and may from time to time be varied by the Secretary of State.

(4) In specifying the interval for transmission of payments the Secretary of State shall have regard to all the circumstances and in particular to—

    (a) the needs of the person entitled to receive payment and the interval by reference to which any other income is normally received by that person;

    (b) any period necessary to enable the clearance of cheques or otherwise necessary to enable the transmission of payments to the person entitled to receive them.

Representations about payment arrangements

6. The Secretary of State shall insofar as is reasonably practicable provide the liable person and the person entitled to receive the payments of child support maintenance with an opportunity to make representations with regard to the matters referred to in regulations 2 to 5 and the Secretary of State shall have regard to those representations in exercising his powers under those regulations.

Notice to liable person as to requirements about payment

7.—(1) The Secretary of State shall send the liable person a notice stating—

    (a) the amount of child support maintenance payable;

    (b) to whom it is to be paid;

(c) the method of payment; and

(d) the day and interval by reference to which payments are to be made.

(2) A notice under paragraph (1) shall be sent to the liable person as soon as is reasonably practicable after—

(a) the making of a maintenance assessment, and

(b) after any change in the requirements referred to in any previous such notice.

PART III

DEDUCTION FROM EARNINGS ORDERS

Interpretation of this Part

8.—(1) For the purposes of this Part—

"disposable income"' means the amount determined under regulation 12(1) of the Child Support (Maintenance Assessments and Special Cases) Regulations 1992;

"earnings" shall be construed in accordance with paragraphs (3) and (4);

"exempt income" means the amount determined under regulation 9 of the Child Support (Maintenance Assessments and Special Cases) Regulations 1992;

"net earnings" shall be construed in accordance with paragraph (5);

"normal deduction rate" means the rate specified in a deduction from earnings order (expressed as a sum of money per week, month or other period) at which deductions are to be made from the liable person's net earnings;

"pay-day" in relation to a liable person means an occasion on which earnings are paid to him or the day on which such earnings would normally fall to be paid;

"prescribed minimum amount" means the minimum amount prescribed in regulation 13 of the Child Support (Maintenance Assessments and Special Cases) Regulations 1992;

"protected earnings rate" means thc level of earnings specified in a deduction from earnings order (expressed as a sum of money per week, month or other period) below which deductions of child support maintenance shall not be made for the purposes of this Part;

"protected income level" means the level of protected income determined in accordance with regulation 11 of the Child Support (Maintenance Assessments and Special Cases) Regulations 1992.

(2) For the purposes of this Part the relationship of employer and employee shall be treated as subsisting between two persons if one of them, as a principal and not as a servant or agent, pays to the other any sum defined as earnings under paragraph (1) and "employment", "employer" and "employee" shall be construed accordingly.

(3) Subject to paragraph (4), "earnings" are any sums payable to a person—

(a) by way of wages or salary (including any fees, bonus, commission, overtime pay or other emoluments payable in addition to wages or salary or payable under a contract of service);

(b) by way of pension (including an annuity in respect of past service, whether or not rendered to the person paying the annuity, and including periodical payments by way of compensation for the loss, abolition or relinquishment, or diminution in the emoluments, of any office or employment);

(c) by way of statutory sick pay.

(4) "Earnings" shall not include—

(a) sums payable by any public department of the Government of Northern Ireland or of a territory outside the United Kingdom;

(b) pay or allowances payable to the liable person as a member of Her Majesty's forces;

(c) pension allowances or benefit payable under any enactment relating to social security;

(d) pension or allowances payable in respect of disablement or disability;

(e) guaranteed minimum pension within the meaning of the Social Security Pensions Act 1975.

(5) "Net earnings" means the residue of earnings after deduction of—

(a) income tax;

(b) primary class I contributions under Part I of the Contributions and Benefits Act 1992;

(c) amounts deductible by way of contributions to a superannuation scheme which provides for the payment of annuities or lumps sums—

  (i) to the employee on his retirement at a specificd age or on becoming incapacitated at some earlier age; or

  (ii) on his death or otherwise, to his personal representative widow relatives or dependants.

Deduction from earnings orders

9. A deduction from earnings order shall specify—

(a) the name and address of the liable person;

(b) the name of the employer at whom it is directed;

(c) where known the liable person's place of work the nature of his work and any works or pay number:

(d) the normal deduction rate;

(e) the protected earnings rate;

(f) the address to which amounts deducted from earnings are to be sent.

Normal deduction rate

10.—(1) The period by reference to which the normal deduction rate is set shall be the period by reference to which the liable person's earnings are normally paid or if none, such other period as the Sceretary of State may specify.

(2) The Secretary of State in specifying the normal deduction rate shall not include any amount in respect of arrears or interest if at the date of making of the current assessment—

(a) the liable person's disposable income was below the level specified in paragraph (3); or

(b) the deduction of such an amount from the liable person's disposable income would have reduced his disposable income below the level specified in paragraph (3).

(3) The level referred to in paragraph (2) is the liable person's protected income level less the prescribed minimum amount.

Protected earnings rate

11.—(1) The period by reference to which the protected earnings rate is set shall be the same as the period by reference to which the normal deduction rate is set under regulation 10(1).

(2) The amount to be specified as the protected earnings rate in respect of any period shall be an amount equal to the liable person's exempt income in respect of that period as calculated at the date of the current assessment.

Amount to be deducted by employer

12.—(1) Subject to the provisions of this regulation an employer who has been served with a copy of a deduction from earnings order in respect of a liable person in his employment shall each pay-day make a deduction from the net earnings of that liable person of an amount equal to the normal deduction rate.

(2) Where the deduction of the normal deduction rate would reduce the liable person's net earnings below the protected earnings rate the employer shall deduct only such amount as will leave the liable person with net earnings equal to the protected earnings rate.

(3) Where the liable person receives a payment of earnings at an interval greater or lesser than the interval specified in relation to the normal deduction rate and the protected earnings rate ("the specified interval") the employer shall for the purpose of such payments take as the normal deduction rate and the protected earnings rate such amounts (to the nearest whole penny) as are in the same proportion to the interval since the last pay-day as the normal deduction rate and the protected earnings rate bear to the specified interval.

(4) Where on any pay-day the employer fails to deduct an amount due under the deduction from earnings order or deducts an amount less than the amount of the normal deduction rate the shortfall shall subject to the operation of paragraph (2) be deducted in addition to the normal deduction rate at the next available pay-day or days.

(5) Where on any pay-day the liable person's net earnings are less than his protected earnings rate the amount of the difference shall be carried forward to his next pay-day and treated as part of his protected earnings in respect of that pay-day.

(6) Where on any pay-day an employer makes a deduction from the earnings of a liable person in accordance with the deduction from earnings order he may also deduct an amount not exceeding £1 in respect of his administrative costs and such deduction for administrative costs may be made notwithstanding that it may reduce the liable person's net earnings below the protected earnings rate.

Employer to notify liable person of deduction

13.—(1) An employer making a deduction from earnings for the purposes of this Part shall notify the liable person in writing of the amount of the deduction including any amount deducted for administrative costs under regulation 12(6).

(2) Such notification shall be given not later than the pay-day on which the deduction is made or, where that is impracticable, not later than the following pay-day.

Payment by employer to Secretary of state

14.—(1) Amounts deducted by an employer under a deduction from earnings order (other than any administrative costs deducted under regulation 12(6)) shall be paid to the Secretary of State by the 19th day of the month following the month in which the deduction is made.

(2) Such payment may be made—
(a) by cheque;
(b) by automated credit transfer; or
(c) by such other method as the Secretary of State may specify.

Information to be provided by liable person

15.—(1) The Secretary of State may in relation to the making or operation of a deduction from earnings order require the liable person to provide the following details—
(a) the name and address of his employer;
(b) the amount of his earnings and anticipated earnings;
(c) his place of work the nature of his work and any works or pay number;
and it shall be the duty of the liable person to comply with any such requirement within 7 days of being given written notice to that effect.

(2) A liable person in respect of whom a deduction from earnings order is in force shall notify the Secretary of State in writing within 7 days of every occasion on which he leaves employment or becomes employed or re-employed.

Duty of employers and others to notify Secretary of State

16.—(1) Where a deduction from earnings order is served on a person on the assumption that he is the employer of a liable person but the liable person to whom the order relates is not in his employment, the person on whom the order was served shall notify the Secretary of State of that fact in writing, at the address specified in the order, within 10 days of the date of service on him of the order.

(2) Where an employer is required to operate a deduction from earnings order and the liable person to whom the order relates ceases to be in his employment the employer shall notify the Secretary of State of that fact in writing, at the address specified in the order, within 10 days of the liable person ceasing to be in his employment.

(3) Where an employer becomes aware that a deduction from earnings order is in force in relation to a person who is an employee of his he shall, within 7 days of the date on which he becomes aware, notify the Secretary of State of that fact in writing at the address specified in the order.

Requirement to review deduction from earnings orders

17.— The Secretary of State shall review a deduction from earnings order in the following circumstances—
- (a) where there is a change in the amount of the maintenance assessment;
- (b) where any arrears and interest on arrears payable under the order are paid off.

Power to vary deduction from earnings orders

18.—(1) The Secretary of State may (whether on a review under regulation 17 or otherwise) vary a deduction from earnings order so as to—
- (a) include any amount which may be included in such an order or exclude or decrease any such amount;
- (b) substitute a subsequent employer for the employer at whom the order was previously directed.

(2) The Secretary of State shall serve a copy of any deduction from earnings order, as varied, on the liable person's employer and on the liable person.

Compliance with deduction from earnings order as varied

19.—(1) Where a deduction from earnings order has been varied and a copy of the order as varied has been served on the liable person's employer it shall, subject to paragraph (2), be the duty of the employer to comply with the order as varied.

(2) The employer shall not be under any liability for non-compliance with the order, as varied, before the end of the period of 7 days beginning with the date on which a copy of the order, as varied, was served on him.

Discharge of deduction from earnings orders

20.—(1) The Secretary of State may discharge a deduction from earnings order where—
- (a) no further payments under it are due; or
- (b) it appears to him that the order is ineffective or that some other way of securing that payments are made would be more effective.

(2) The Secretary of State shall give written notice of the discharge of the deduction from earnings order to the liable person and to the liable person's employer.

Lapse of deduction from earnings orders

21.—(1) A deduction from earnings order shall lapse (except in relation to any deductions made or to be made in respect of the employment not yet paid to the Secretary of State) where the employer at whom it is directed ceases to have the liable person in his employment.

(2) The order shall lapse from the pay-day coinciding with, or, if none, the pay-day following, the termination of the employment.

(3) A deduction from earnings order which has lapsed under this regulation shall nonetheless be treated as remaining in force for the purposes of regulations 15 and 24.

(4) Where a deduction from earnings order has lapsed under paragraph (1) and the liable person recommences employment (whether with the same or another employer), the order may be revived from such date as may be specified by the Secretary of State.

(5) Where a deduction from earnings order is revived under paragraph (4), the Secretary of State shall give written notice of that fact to, and serve a copy of the notice on, the liable person and the liable person's employer.

(6) Where an order is revived under paragraph (4), no amount shall be carried forward under regulation 12(4) or (5) from a time prior to the revival of the order.

Appeals against deduction from earnings orders

22.—(1) A liable person in respect of whom a deduction from earnings order has been made may appeal to the magistrates court, or in Scotland the sheriff, having jurisdiction in the area in which he resides.

(2) Any appeal shall—
   (a) be by way of complaint for an order or, in Scotland, by way of application:
   (b) be made within 28 days of the date on which the matter appealed against arose.

(3) An appeal may be made only on one or both of the following grounds—

   (a) that the deduction from earnings order is defective;
   (b) that the payments in question do not constitute earnings.

(4) Where the court or, as the case may be, the sheriff is satisfied that the appeal should be allowed the court. or sheriff, may—
   (a) quash the deduction from earnings order; or
   (b) specify which, if any, of the payments in question do not constitute earnings.

Crown employment

23. Where a liable person is in the employment of the Crown and a deduction from earnings order is made in respect of him then for the purposes of this Part—
   (a) the chief officer for the time being of the Department, office or other body in which the liable person is employed shall he treated as having

the liable person in his employment (any transfer of the liable person from one Department, office or body to another being treated as a change of employment); and

(b) any earnings paid by the Crown or a minister of thc Crown, or out of the public revenue of the United Kingdom, shall be treated as paid by that chief officer.

Priority as between orders

24.—(1) Where an employer would, but for this paragraph, be obliged, on any payday, to make deductions under two or more deduction from earnings orders he shall—

(a) deal with the orders according to the respective dates on which they were made, disregarding any later order until an earlier one has been dealt with;

(b) deal with any later order as if the earnings to which it relates were the residue of the liable person's earnings after the making of any deduction to comply with any earlier order.

(2) Where an employer would, but for this paragraph, be obliged to comply with one or more deduction from earnings orders and one or more attachment of earnings orders he shall—

(a) in the case of an attachment of earnings order which was made either wholly or in part in respect of the payment of a judgment debt or payments under an administration order, deal first with the deduction from earnings order or orders and thereafter with the attachment of earnings order as if the earnings to which it relates were the residue of the liable person's earnings after the making of deductions to comply with the deduction from earnings order or orders;

(b) in the case of any other attachment of earnings order, deal with the orders according to the respective dates on which they were made in like manner as under paragraph (1).

"Attachment of earnings order" in this paragraph means an order made under the Attachment of Earnings Act 1971 or under regulation 32 of the Community Charge (Administration and Enforcement) Regulations 1989.

(3) Paragraph (2) does not apply to Scotland.

(4) In Scotland, where an employer would, but for this paragraph, be obliged to comply with one or more deduction from earnings orders and one or more diligences against earnings he shall deal first with the deduction from earnings order or orders and thereafter with the diligence against earnings as if the earnings to which the diligence relates were the residue of the liable person's earnings after the making of deductions to comply with the deduction from earnings order or orders.

Offences

25. The following regulations are designated for the purposes of section 32(8) of the Act (offences relating to deduction from earnings orders)—

(a) regulation 15(1) and (2);
(b) regulation 16(1), (2) and (3);
(c) regulation 19(1)

PART IV
LIABILITY ORDERS

Extent of this Part

26. This Part, except regulation 29(2), does not apply to Scotland.

Notice of intention to apply for a liability order

27.—(1) The Secretary of State shall give the liable person at least 7 days notice of his intention to apply for a liability order under section 33(2) of the Act.

(2) Such notice shall set out the amount of child support maintenance which it is claimed has become payable by the liable person and has not been paid and the amount of any interest in respect of arrears payable under section 41(3) of the Act .

(3) Payment by the liable person of any part of the amounts referred to in paragraph (2) shall not require the giving of a further notice under paragraph (1) prior to the making of the application.

Application for a liability order

28.—(1) An application for a liability order shall be by way of complaint for an order to the magistrates' court having jurisdiction in the area in which the liable person resides.

(2) An application under paragraph (1) may not be instituted more than 6 years after the day on which payment of the amount in question became due.

(3) A warrant shall not be issued under section (2) of the Magistrates' Courts Act 1980 in any proccedings under this regulation.

Liability orders

29.—(1) A liability order shall be made in the form prescribed in Schedule 1.

(2) A liability order made by a court in England or Wales or any corresponding order made by a court in Northern Ireland may be enforced in Scotland as if it had been made by the sheriff.

(3) A liability order made by the sheriff in Scotland or any corresponding order made by a court in Northern Ireland may, subject to paragraph (4), be enforced in England and Wales as if it had been made by a magistrates' court in England and Wales.

(4) A liability order made by the sheriff in Scotland or corresponding order made by a court in Northern Ireland shall not be enforced in England or Wales unless registered in accordance with the provisions of Part I of the Maintenance Orders Act 1950 and for this purpose—

    (a) a liability order made by the sheriff in Scotland shall be treated as if it were a decree to which section 16(2)(b) of that Act applies (decree for payment of aliment);

    (b) a corresponding order made by a court in Northern Ireland shall be treated as if it were an order to which section 16(2)(c) of that Act applies (order for alimony, maintenance or other payments).

Enforcement of liability orders by distress

30.—(1) A distress made pursuant to section 3(1) of the Act may be made anywhere in England and Wales.

(2) The person levying distress on behalf of the Secretry of State shall carry with him the written authorisation of the Secretary of State, which he shall show to the liable person if so requested, and he shall hand to the liable person or leave at the premises where the distress is levied—

    (a) copies of this regulation, regultion 31 and Schedule 2;

    (b) a memorandum setting out the amount which is the appropriate amount for the purposes of section 3(2) of the Act;

    (c) a memorandum setting out details of any arrangement entered into regarding the taking of possession of the goods distrained; and

    (d) a notice setting out the liable person's rights of appeal under regulation 1 giving the Secretary of State's address for the purposes of any appeal.

(3) A distress shall not be deemed unlawful on account of any defect or want of form in the liability order.

(4) If, before any goods are seized, the approprite amount (including charges arising up to the time of the payment or tender) is paid or tendered to the Secretary of State, the Secretary of State shall accept the amount and the levy shall not be proceeded with.

(5) Where the Secretary of State has seized goods of the liable person in pursuance of the distress, but before sale of those goods the appropriate amount (including charges arising up to the time of the payment or tender) is paid or tendered to the Secretary of State, the Secretary of State shall accept the amount, the sale shall not be proceeded with and the goods shall be made available for collection by the liable person.

Appeals in connection with distress

31.—(1) A person aggrieved by the levy of, or an attempt to levy, a distress may appeal to the magistrates' court having jurisdiction in the area in which he resides.

(2) The appeal shall be by way of complaint for an order.

(3) If the court is satisfied that the levy was irregular it may—

(a) order the goods distrained to be discharged if they are in the possession of the Secretary of State;

(b) order an award of compensation in respect of any goods distrained and sold of an amount equal to the amount which, in the opinion of the court, would be awarded by way of Special damages in respect of the goods if proceedings under section 3(6) of the Act were brought in trespass or otherwise in connection with the irregularity.

(4) If the court is satisfied that an attempted levy was irregular, it may by order require the Secretary of State to desist from levying in the manner giving rise to the irregularity.

Charges connected with distress

32. Schedule 2 shall have effect for the purpose of determining the amounts in respect of charges in connection with the distress for the purposes of section 35(2)(b) of the Act.

Application for warrant of commitment

33.—(1) For the purposes of enabling an inquiry to be made under section 40 of the Act as to the liable person's conduct and means a justice of the peace having jurisdiction for the area in which the liable person resides may—

(a) issue a summons to him to appear before a magistrates' court and (if he does not obey the summons) issue a warrant for his arrest; or

(b) issue a warrant for his arrest without issuing a summons.

(2) In any proceedings under section 40 of the Act a statement in writing to the effect that wages of any amount have been paid to the liable person during any period purporting to be signed by or on behalf of his employer, shall be evidence of the facts there stated.

(3) Where an application under section 40 of the Act has been made but no warrant of commitment is issued or term of imprisonment fixed the application may be renewed on the ground that the circumstances of the liable person have changed.

Warrant of commitment

34.—(1) A warrant of commitment shall be in the form specified in Schedule 3 or in a form to the like effect.

(2) The amount to be included in the warrant under section 40(4)(a)(ii) of the Act in respect of costs shall be such amount as in the view of the court is equal to the costs reasonably incurred by the Secretary of State in respect of the costs of commitment.

(3) A warrant issued under section 40 of the Act may be executed anywhere in England and Wales by any person to whom it is directed or by any constable acting within his police area.

(4) A warrant may be executed by a constable notwithstanding that it is not in his possession at the time but such warrant shall on the demand of the person arrested be shown to him as soon as possible.

(5) Where after the issue of a warrant, part-payment of the amount stated in it is made the period of imprisonment shall be reduced proportionately so that for the period of imprisonment specified in the warrant there shall be substituted a period of imprisonment of such number of days as bears the same proportion to the number of days specified in the warrant as the amount remaining unpaid under the warrant bears to the amount specified in the warrant.

(6) Where the part-payment is of such an amount as would under paragraph (5) reduce the period of imprisonment to such number of days as have already been served (or would be so served in the course of the day of payment), the period of imprisonment shall be reduced to the period already served plus one day.

Signed by authority of the Secretary of State for Social Security.

Ann Widdecombe
Parliamentary Under-Secretary of State,
17th August 1992 Department of Social Security

SCHEDULE 1

Regulation 29(1)

LIABILITY ORDER PRESCRIBED FORM

Section 33 of the Child Support Act 1991 and regulation 29(1) of the Child Support (Collection and Enforcement) Regulations 1992

. . . . Magistrates' Court

Date:

Defendant:

Address:

On the complaint of the Secretary of State for Social Security that the sums specified below are due from the defendant under the Child Support Act 1991 and Part IV of the Child Support (Collection and Enforcement) Regulations 1992 and are outstanding it is adjudged that the defendant is liable to pay the aggregate amount specified below.

Sum payalbe and outstanding   – child support maintenance
– interest
– other periodical payments
  collected by virtue of
  section 30 of the Child
  Support Act 1991

Aggregate amount in respect of which the liability order is made:

Justice of the Peace

[*or* by order of the Court
Clerk of the Court]

SCHEDULE 2

Regulation 32

CHARGES CONNECTED WITH DISTRESS

1. The sum in respect of charges connected with the distress which may be aggregated under section 35(2)(b) of the Act shall be set out in the following Table—

(1) *Matter connected with distress*	(2) *Charge*
A	For making a visit to premises with a view to levying distress (whether the levy is made or not):	Reasonable costs and fees incurred, but not exceeding an amount which, when aggregated with charges under this head for any previous visits made with a view to levying distress in relation to an amount in respect of which the liability order concerned was made, is not greater than the relevant amount calculated under paragraph 2(1) with respect to the visit.
B	For levying distress:	An amount (if any) which, when aggregated with charges under head A for any visits made with a view to levying distress in relation to an amount in respect of which the liability order concerned was made, is equal to the relevant amount calculated under paragraph 2(1) with respect to the levy.
C	For the removal and storage of goods for the purposes of sale:	Reasonable costs and fees incurred.
D	For the possession of goods as described in paragraph 2(3)—	
	(i) for close possession (the person in possession on behalf of the Secretary of State to provide his own board):	£4.50 per day.
	(ii) for walking possession:	45p per day.
E	For appraisement of an item distrained, at the request in writing of the liable person:	Reasonable fees and expenses of the broker appraising.
F	For other expenses of, and commission on, a sale by auction—	
	(i) where the sale is held on the auctioneer's premises:	The auctioneer's commission fee and out-of-pocket expenses (but not exceeding in aggregate 15 per cent. of the sum realised), together with reasonable costs and fees incurred in respect of advertising.
	(ii) where the sale is held on the liable person's premises:	The auctioneer's commission fee (but not exceeding 7½ per cent. of the sum realised), together with the auctioneer's out-of-pocket expenses and reasonable costs and fees incurred in respect of advertising.
G	For other expenses incurred in connection with a proposed sale where there is no buyer in relation to it:	Reasonable costs and fees incurred.

2.—(1) In heads A and B of the Table to paragraph 1, "the relevant amount" with respect to a visit or a levy means—

(a) where the sum due at the time of the visit or of the levy (as the case may be) does not exceed £100, £12.50;

(b) where the sum due at the time of the visit or of the levy (as the case may be) exceeds £100, $12\frac{1}{2}$ per cent. on the first £100 of the sum due, 4 per cent. on the next £400, $2\frac{1}{2}$ per cent. on the next £1,500, 1 per cent. on the next £8,000 and $\frac{1}{4}$ per cent. on any additional sum;

and the sum due at any time for these purposes means so much of the amount in respect of which the liability order concerned was made as is outstanding at the time.

(2) Where a charge has arisen under head B with respect to an amount no further charge may be aggregated under heads A or B in respect of that amount.

(3) The Secretary of State takes close or walking possession of goods for the purposes of head D of the Table to paragraph 1 if he takes such possession in pursuance of an agreement which is made at the time that the distress is levied and which (without prejudice to such other terms as may be agreed) is expressed to the effect that in consideration of the Secretary of State not immediately removing the goods distrained upon from the premises occupied by the liable person and delaying the sale of the goods the Secretary of State may remove and sell the goods after a later specified date if the liable person has not by then paid the amount distrained for (including charges under this Schedule); and the Secretary of State is in close possession of goods on any day for these purposes if during the greater part of the day a person is left on the premises in physical possession of the goods on behalf of the Secretary of State under such an agreement.

3.—(1) Where the calculation under this Schedule of a percentage of a sum results in an amount containing a fraction of a pound that fraction shall be reckoned as a whole pound.

(2) In the case of dispute as to any charge under this Schedule the amount of the charge shall be taxed .

(3) Such a taxation shall be carried out by the district judge of the county court for the district in which the distress is or is intended to be levied and he may give such directions as to the costs of the taxation as he thinks fit; and any such costs directed to be paid by the liable person to the Secretary of State shall be added to the sum which may be aggregated under section 35(2) of the Act .

(4) References in the Table in paragraph 1 to costs, fees and expenses include references to amounts payable by way of value added tax with respect to the supply of goods or services to which the costs fees and expenses relate.

SCHEDULE 3

Regulation 34(1)

FORM OF WARRANT OF COMMITMENT

Section 40 of the Child Support Act 1991 and regulation 34(1) of the Child Support (Collection and Enforcement) Regulations 1992

. . . . .Magistrates' Court

Date:

Liable Person:

Address:

A liability order ("the order") was made against the liable person by the [   ] Magistrates' Court on [   ] under section 33 of the Child Support Act 1991 ("the Act") in respect of an amount of [   ].

The court is satisfied—

    (i)   that the Secretary of State sought under section 3 of the Act to levy by distress the amount then outstanding in respect of which the order was made:

[and/or]

        that the Secretary of State sought under section 3 of the Act to recover through the [   ] County Court by means of [garnishee proceedings] or [a charging order] the amount then outstanding in respect of which the order was made;

    (ii) that such amount or any portion of it remains unpaid; and

    (iii) having inquired in the liable person's presence as to his means and as to whether there has been [wilful refusal] or [culpable neglect] on his part, the court is of the opinion that there has been [wilful refusal] or [culpable neglect] on his part.

The decision of the court is that the liable person be [committed to prison] [detained] for [   ] unless the aggregate amount mentioned below in respect of which this warrant is made is sooner paid.*

This warrant is made in respect of—

Amount outstanding (including any interest costs and charges):

Costs of commitment of the Secretary of State:

Aggregate amount:

And you *[name of person or persons to whom warrant is directed]* are hereby required to take the liable person and convey him to *[name of prison or place of detention]* and there deliver him to the [governor] [officer in charge] thereof; and you the [governor] [officer in charge], to receive the liable person into your custody and keep him for *[period of imprisonment]* from the date of his arrest under this warrant or until he be sooner discharged in due course of law

Justice of the Peace
[*or* by order of the Court
Clerk of the Court].

Note: The period of imprisonment will be reduced as provided by regulation 34(5) and (6) of the Child Support (Collection and Enforcement) Regulations 1992 if part-payment is made of the aggregate amount.

S.I. 1992 No. 1812

The Child Support (Information, Evidence and Disclosure) Regulations 1992

Made — — — —	*20th July 1992*
Coming into force	*5th April 1993*

ARRANGEMENT OF REGULATIONS

PART I
General

1. Citation, commencement and interpretation.

PART II
Furnishing of information or evidence

2. Persons under a duty to furnish information or evidence.
3. Purposes for which information or evidence may be required.
4. Information from an appropriate authority in connection with housing benefit or council tax benefit.
5. Time within which information or evidence is to be furnished.
6. Continuing duty of persons with care.
7. Powers of inspectors in relation to Crown residences.

PART III

Disclosure of information

8. Disclosure of information to a court or tribunal.
9. Disclosure of information to an appropriate authority for use in the exercise of housing benefit or council tax benefit functions.
10. Disclosure of information to the Secretary of State.
11. Employment to which section 50 of the Act applies.

Whereas a draft of this instrument was laid before Parliament in accordance with section 52(2) of the Child Support Act 1991 and approved by a resolution of each House of Parliament:

Now, therefore, the Secretary of State for Social Security, in exercise of the powers conferred by sections 4(4), 6(9), 7(5), 14(1) and (3), 50(5), 51, 54 and 57 of, and paragraphs 16(10) of Schedule1 to and 2(4) of Schedule 2 to, the Child Support Act 1991, and of all other powers enabling him in that behalf hereby makes the following Regulations:

PART I

GENERAL

Citation, commencement and interpretation
1.—(1) These Regulations may be cited as the Child Support (Information, Evidence and Disclosure) Regulations 1992 and shall come into force on 5th April 1993.

(2) In these Regulations, unless the context otherwise requires
"the Act" means the Child Support Act 1991;
"appropriate authority" means—
  (a) in relation to housing benefit, the housing or local authority concerned; and
  (b) in relation to council tax benefit, the billing authority or, in Scotland, the levying authority;
"local authority" means, in relation to England and Wales, the council of a county, a metropolitan district, a London Borough or the Common Council of the City of London and, in relation to Scotland, a regional council or an islands council;
"Maintenance Assessments and Special Cases Regulations" means the Child Support (Maintenance Assessments and Special Cases) Regulations 1992;
"Maintenance Assessment Procedure Regulations" means the Child Support (Maintenance Assessment Procedure) Regulations 1992;
"parent with care" means a person who, in respect of the same child or children, is both a parent and a person with care;
"related proceeding" means proceedings in which a relevant court order was or is being sought;
"relevant court order" means—
  (a) an order as to periodical or capital provision or as to variation of property rights made under an enactment specified in paragraphs (a) to (e) of section 8(11) of the Act or prescribed under section 8(11)(f) of the Act in relation to a qualifying child or a relevant person; or
  (b) an order under Part II of the Children Act 1989 (Orders With Respect To Children In Family Proceedings) in relation to a qualifying child or, in Scotland, an order under section 3 of the Law Reform (Parent and Child) (Scotland) Act 1986 or a decree of declarator under section 7 of that Act in relation to a qualifying child;
"relevant person" means—
  (a) a person with care;
  (b) an absent parent;
  (c) a parent who is treated as an absent parent under regulation 20 of the Maintenance Assessments and Special Cases Regulations;
  (d) where the application for an assessment is made by a child under section 7 of the Act, that child,
in respect of whom a maintenance assessment has been applied for or is or has been in force.

(3) In these Regulations, unless the context otherwise requires, a reference—

    (a) to a numbered regulation is to the regulation in these Regulations bearing that number;

    (b) in a regulation to a numbered paragraph is to the paragraph in that regulation bearing that number;

    (c) in a paragraph to a lettered or numbered sub-paragraph is to the sub-paragraph in that paragraph bearing that letter or number.

PART I

FURNISHING OF INFORMATION OR EVIDENCE

Persons under a duty to furnish information or evidence

2.—(1) Where an application for a maintenance assessment has been made under the Act, a person falling within a category listed in paragraph (2) shall, subject to the restrictions specified in that paragraph, furnish such information or evidence as is required by the Secretary of State and which is needed to enable a determination to be made in relation to one or more of the matters listed in regulation 3(1), and the person concerned has that information or evidence in his possession or can reasonably be expected to acquire that information or evidence.

(2) The persons who may be required to furnish information or evidence, and the matter or matters with respect to which such information or evidence may be required, are as follows—

    (a) the relevant persons, with respect to the matters listed in regulation 3(1);

    (b) a person who is alleged to be a parent of a child with respect to whom an application for a maintenance assessment has been made who denies that he is one of that child's parents, with respect to the matters listed in sub-paragraphs (b) and (d) of regulation 3(1);

    (c) the current or recent employer of the absent parent or the parent with care in relation to whom an application for a maintenance assessment has been made, with respect to the matters listed in sub-paragraphs (d), (e), (f), (h) and (j) of regulation 3(1);

    (d) the local authority in whose area a person falling within a category listed in sub-paragraphs (a) and (b) above resides or has resided, with respect to the matter listed in sub-paragraph (a) of regulation 3(1);

    (e) a person specified in paragraph (3) below, in any case where, in relation to the qualifying child or qualifying children or the absent parent—

        (i) there is or has been a relevant court order; or

        (ii) there have been, or are pending, related proceedings before a court,

    with respect to the matters listed in sub-paragraphs (g), (h) and (k) of regulation 3(1).

(3) The persons who may be required to furnish information or evidence in relation to a relevant court order or related proceedings under the provisions of paragraph (2)(e) are—

(a) in England and Wales—
   (i)   in relation to the High Court, the senior district judge of the principal registry of the Family Division or, where proceedings were instituted in a district registry, the district judge;
   (ii) in relation to a county court, the proper officer of that court within the meaning of Order 1, Rule 3 of the County Court Rules 1981;
   (iii) in relation to a magistrates' court, the clerk to the justices of that court;
(b) in Scotland—
   (i)   in relation to the Court of Session, the Deputy Principal Clerk of Session;
   (ii) in relation to a sheriff court, the sheriff clerk.

Purposes for which information or evidence may be required

3.— (1) The Secretary of State may require information or evidence under the provisions of regulation 2 only if that information or evidence is needed to enable—
   (a) a decision to be made as to whether, in relation to an application for a maintenance assessment, there exists a qualifying child, an absent parent and a person with care;
   (b) a decision to be made as to whether a child support officer has jurisdiction to make a maintenance assessment under section 44 of the Act;
   (c) a decision to be made, where more than one application has been made, as to which application is to be proceeded with;
   (d) an absent parent to be identified;
   (e) an absent parent to be traced;
   (f) the amount of child support maintenance payable by an absent parent to be assessed;
   (g) the amount payable under a relevant court order to be ascertained;
   (h) the amounts specified in sub-paragraphs (f) and (g) to be recovered from an absent parent;
   (i) the amount of interest payable with respect to arrears of child support maintenance to be determined;
   (j) the amount specified in sub-paragraph (i) to be recovered from an absent parent;
   (k) any related proceedings to be identified.
   (2) The information or evidence to be furnished in accordance with regulation 2 may in particular include information and evidence as to—
   (a) the habitual residence of the person with care, the absent parent and any child in respect of whom an application for a maintenance assessment has been made;
   (b) the name and address of the person with care and of the absent parent, their marital status, and the relationship of the person with

care to any child in respect of whom the application for a maintenance assessment has been made;

(c) the name, address and date of birth of any such child, that child's marital status, and any education that child is undergoing;

(d) the persons who have parental responsibility for (or, in Scotland, parental rights over) any qualifying child where there is more than one person with care;

(e) the time spent by a qualifying child in respect of whom an application for a maintenance assessment has been made with each person with care, where there is more than one such person;

(f) the matters relevant for determining, in a case falling within section 26 of the Act (disputes about parentage), whether that case falls within one of the Cases set out in subsection (2) of that section, and if it does not, the matters relevant for determining the parentage of a child whose parentage is in dispute;

(g) the name and address of any current or recent employer of an absent parent or a parent with care, and the gross earnings and the deductions from those earnings deriving from each employment;

(h) the address from which an absent parent or parent with care who is self-employed carries on his trade or business, the trading name, and the gross receipts and expenses and other outgoings of the trade or business;

(i) any other income of an absent parent and a parent with care;

(j) any income, other than earnings, of a qualifying child;

(k) amounts payable and paid under a relevant court order or a maintenance agreement;

(l) the persons living in the same household as the absent parent or living in the same household as the parent with care, their relationship to the absent parent or the parent with care, as the case may be, and to each other, and, in the case of the children of any such party, the dates of birth of those children;

(m) the matters set out in sub-paragraphs (g) and (h) in relation to the persons specified in sub-paragraph (1) other than any children living in the same household as the absent parent or the parent with care, as the case may be;

(n) income other than earnings of the persons living in the same household as the absent parent or the parent with care;

(o) benefits related to disability that the absent parent, parent with care and other persons living in the same household as the absent parent or the parent with care are entitled to or would be entitled to if certain conditions were satisfied;

(p) the housing costs to be taken into account for the purposes of determining assessable or disposable income;

(q) the identifying details of any bank, building society or similar account held in the name of the absent parent or the person with care, and statements relating to any such account;

(r) the matters relevant for determining whether—

    (i)   a maintenance assessment has ceased to have effect or should be cancelled under the provisions of paragraph 16 of Schedule 1 to the Act;

    (ii) a person is a child within the meaning of section 55 of the Act.

Information from an appropriate authority in connection with housing benefit or council tax benefit

4. For the purposes of paragraph 2 of Schedule 2 to the Act, "relevant information" means—

    (a) information as to the amount of housing costs of an absent parent or person with care which are treated as eligible rent for housing benefit purposes, and the entitlement to housing benefit at the date the Secretary of State gives a direction under paragraph 2(2) of that Schedule;

    (b) information as to the amount of council tax payable by an absent parent or person with care, and as to the entitlement to council tax benefit at the date the Secretary of State gives a direction under paragraph 2(2) of that Schedule.

Time within which information or evidence is to be furnished

5. Subject to the provisions of regulations 2(5), 6(1), 17(5) and 19(2) of the Maintenance Assessment Procedure Regulations, any information or evidence furnished in accordance with regulations 2 and 3 shall be furnished as soon as is reasonably practicable in the particular circumstances of the case.

Continuing duty of persons with care

6. Where a person with care with respect to whom a maintenance assessment has been made believes that, by virtue of section 44 or 55 of, or paragraph 16 of Schedule 1 to, the Act, the assessment has ceased to have effect or should be cancelled, she shall, as soon as is reasonably practicable, inform the Secretary of State of that belief, and of the reasons for it, and shall provide such other information as the Secretary of State may reasonably require, with a view to assisting the Secretary of State or a child support officer in determining whether the assessment has ceased to have effect, or should be cancelled.

Powers of inspectors in relation to Crown residences

7. Subject to Her Majesty not being in residence, an inspector appointed under section 15 of the Act may enter any Crown premises for the purpose of exercising any powers conferred on him by that section.

PART III

DISCLOSURE OF INFORMATION

Disclosure of information to a court or tribunal

8. The Secretary of State or a child support officer may disclose any information held by them for the purposes of the Act to—

(a) a court;

(b) any tribunal or other body or person mentioned in the Act;

(c) any tribunal established under the benefit Acts,

where such disclosure is made for the purposes of any proceedings before any of those bodies relating to this Act or to the benefit Acts.

Disclosure of information to an appropriate authority for use in the exercise of housing benefit or council tax benefit functions

9. The Secretary of State or a child support officer may disclose information held by him for the purposes of the Act to, and as required by, an appropriate authority for use in the exercise of its functions relating to housing benefit or council tax benefit.

Disclosure of information to the Secretary of State

10. A child support officer may disclose any information held by him for the purposes of the Act to, and as required by, the Secretary of State for use in connection with the functions of the Secretary of State under any of the benefit Acts.

Employment to which section 50 of the Act applies

11. For the purposes of section 50 of the Act (unauthorised disclosure of information) the following kinds of employment are prescribed in addition to those specified in paragraphs (a) to (e) of section 50(5)—

(a) the Comptroller and Auditor General;

(b) the Parliamentary Commissioner for Administration;

(c) the Health Service Commissioner for England;

(d) the Health Service Commissioner for Wales;

(e) the Health Service Commissioner for Scotland;

(f) any member of the staff of the National Audit Office;

(g) any other person who carries out the administrative work of that Office, or who provides, or is employed in the provision of, services to it;

(h) any officer of any of the Commissioners referred to in paragraphs (b) to (e) above; and

(i) any person who provides, or is employed in the provision of, services to the Department of Social Security.

Signed by authority of the Secretary of State for Social Security.

Alistair Burt
Parliamentary Under-Secretary of State,
20th July 1992 Department of Social Security

S. I. 1992 No. 2643

The Child Support (Collection and Enforcement of Other Forms of Maintenance) Regulations 1992

Made — — — —	*26th October 1992*
Laid before Parliament	*29th October 1992*
Coming into force	*5th April 1993*

The Secretary of State for Social Security, in exercise of the powers conferred upon him by sections 30(1), (4) and (5), 51 and 54 of the Child Support Act 1991, and of all other powers enabling him in that behalf, hereby makes the following Regulations:

Citation, commencement and interpretation

1.—(1) These Regulations may be cited as the Child Support (Collection and Enforcement of Other Forms of Maintenance) Regulations 1992 and shall come into force on 5th April 1993.

(2) In these Regulations—

"the Act " means the Child Support Act 1991;

"child of the family" has the same meaning as in the Matrimonial Causes Act 1973 or, in Scotland, the Family Law (Scotland) Act 1985; and

"periodical payments" includes secured periodical payments.

Periodical payments and categories of person prescribed for the purposes of section 30 of the Act

2. The following periodical payments and categories of persons are prescribed for the purposes of section 30(1) of the Act—

(a) payments under a maintenance order made in relation to a child in accordance with the provisions of section 8(6) (periodical payments in addition to child support maintenance), 8(7) (periodical payments to meet expenses incurred in connection with the provision of instruction or training) or 8(8) of the Act (periodical payments to meet expenses attributable to disability);

(b) any periodical payments under a maintenance order which are payable to or for the benefit of a spouse or former spouse who is the person with care of a child who is a qualifying child in respect of whom a child support maintenance assessment is in force in accordance with which the Secretary of State has arranged for the collection of child support maintenance under section 29 of the Act; and

(c) any periodical payments under a maintenance order payable to or for the benefit of a former child of the family of the person against whom the order is made, that child having his home with the person with care.

Collection and enforcement—England and Wales

3. In relation to England and Wales, sections 29(2) and (3) and 31 to 40 of the Act, and any regulations made under those sections, shall apply for the purpose of enabling the Secretary of State to enforce any obligation to pay any amount which he is authorised to collect under section 30 of the Act, with the modification that any reference in those sections or regulations to child support maintenance shall be read as a reference to any of the periodical payments mentioned in regulation 2 above, and any reference to a main-tenance assessment shall be read as a reference to any of the maintenance orders mentioned in that regulation.

Collection and enforcement—Scotland

4. In relation to Scotland, for the purpose of enforcing any obligation to pay any amount which the Secretary of State is authorised to collect under section 30 of the Act—

   (a) the Secretary of State may bring any proceedings and take any other steps (other than diligence against earnings) which could have been brought or taken by or on behalf of the person to whom the periodical payments are payable; and

   (b) sections 29(2) and (3), 31 and 32 of the Act, and any regulations made under those sections, shall apply, with the modification that any reference in those sections or regulations to child support maintenance shall be read as a reference to any of the periodical payments men-tioned in regulation 2 above, and any reference to a maintenance assessment shall be read as a reference to any of the maintenance orders mentioned in that regulation.

Collection and enforcement—supplementary

5. Nothing in Regulations 3 or 4 applies to any periodical payment which falls due before the date specified by the Secretary of State by a notice in writing to the absent parent that he is arranging for those payments to be collected, and that date shall be not earlier than the date the notice is given.

Signed by authority of the Secretary of State for Social Security.

Alistair Burt
Parliamentary Under-Secretary of State,
Department of Social Security

26th October 1992

S.I. 1992 No. 2645

The Child Support (Maintenance Arrangements and Jurisdiction) Regulations 1992

Made — — — —	*26th October 1992*
Laid before Parliament	*29th October 1992*
Coming into force	*5th April 1993*

The Secretary of State for Social Security, in exercise of the powers conferred upon him by sections 8(11), 10(1), (2) and (4), 44(3), 51, 52(4) and 54 of, and paragraph 11 of Schedule 1 to, the Child Support Act 1991 and of all other powers enabling him in that behalf hereby makes the following Regulations:

Citation, commencement and interpretation

1.—(1) These Regulations may be cited as the Child Support (Maintenance Arrangements and Jurisdiction) Regulations 1992 and shall come into force on 5th April 1993.

(2) In these Regulations—

"the Act" means the Child Support Act 1991;

"Maintenance Assessments and Special Cases Regulations" means the Child Support (Maintenance Assessments and Special Cases) Regulations 1992;

"effective date" means the date on which a maintenance assessment takes effect for the purposes of the Act;

"maintenance order" has the meaning given in section 8(11) of the Act.

(3) In these Regulations, unless the context otherwise requires, a reference—

- (a) to a numbered regulation is to the regulation in these Regulations bearing that number;
- (b) in a regulation to a numbered paragraph is to the paragraph in that regulation bearing that number;
- (c) in a paragraph to a lettered or numbered sub-paragraph is to the sub-paragraph in that paragraph bearing that letter or number.

Prescription of enactment for the purposes of section 8(11) of the Act

2. The Affiliation Proceedings Act 1957 is prescribed for the purposes of section 8(11) of the Act.

Relationship between maintenance assessments and certain court orders

3.—(1) Orders made under the following enactments are of a kind prescribed for the purposes of section 10(1) of the Act—

- (a) the Affiliation Proceedings Act 1957;
- (b) Part II of the Matrimonial Causes Act 1973;

(c) the Domestic Proceedings and Magistrates' Courts Act 1978;

(d) Part III of the Matrimonial and Family Proceedings Act 1 984;

(e) the Family Law (Scotland) Act 1985;

(f) Schedule1 to the Children Act 1989.

(2) Subject to paragraphs (3) and (4), where a maintenance assessment is made with respect to—

(a) all of the children with respect to whom an order falling within paragraph (1) is in force; or

(b) one or more but not all of the children with respect to whom an order falling within paragraph (1) is in force and where the amount payable under the order to or for the benefit of each child is separately specified,

that order shall, so far as it relates to the making or securing of periodical payments to or for the benefit of the children with respect to whom the maintenance assessment has been made, cease to have effect.

(3) The provisions of paragraph (2) shall not apply where a maintenance order has been made in accordance with section 8(7) or (8) of the Act.

(4) In Scotland, where—

(a) an order has ceased to have effect by virtue of the provisions of paragraph (2) to the extent specified in that paragraph; and

(b) a child support officer no longer has jurisdiction to make a maintenance assessment with respect to a child with respect to whom the order ceased to have effect,

that order shall, so far as it relates to that child, again have effect from the date a child support officer no longer has jurisdiction to make a maintenance assessment with respect to that child.

(5) Where a maintenance assessment is made with respect to children with respect to whom an order falling within paragraph (1) is in force, the effective date of that assessment shall be two days after the assessment is made.

(6) Where the provisions of paragraph (2) apply to an order, that part of the order to which those provisions apply shall cease to have effect from the effective date of the maintenance assessment.

Relationship between maintenance assessments and certain agreements

4.—(1) Maintenance agreements within the meaning of section 9(1) of the Act are agreements of a kind prescribed for the purposes of section 10(2) of the Act.

(2) Where a maintenance assessment is made with respect to—

(a) all of the children with respect to whom an agreement falling within paragraph (1) is in force; or

(b) one or more but not all of the children with respect to whom an agreement falling within paragraph (1) is in force and where the amount payable under the agreement to or for the benefit of each child is separately specified,

that agreement shall, so far as it relates to the making or securing of periodical payments to or for the benefit of the children with respect to whom the maintenance assessment has been made, become unenforceable from the effective date of the assessment.

(3) Where an agreement becomes unenforceable under the provisions of paragraph (2) to the extent specified in that paragraph, it shall remain unenforceable in relation to a particular child until such date as a child support officer no longer has jurisdiction to make a maintenance assessment with respect to that child.

Notifications by child support officers

5.—(1) Where a child support officer is aware that an order of a kind prescribed in paragraph (2) is in force and considers that the making of a maintenance assessment has affected, or is likely to affect, that order, he shall notify the persons prescribed in paragraph (3) in respect of whom that maintenance assessment is in force, and the persons prescribed in paragraph (4) holding office in the court where the order in question was made or subsequently registered, of the assessment and its effective date.

(2) The prescribed orders are those made under an enactment mentioned in regulation 3(1).

(3) The prescribed persons in respect of whom the maintenance assessment is in force are—

(a) a person with care;

(b) an absent parent;

(c) a person who is treated as an absent parent under regulation 20 of the Maintenance Assessments and Special Cases Regulations;

(d) a child who has made an application for a maintenance assessment under section 7 of the Act.

(4) The prescribed person holding office in the court where the order in question was made or subsequently registered is—

(a) in England and Wales—

   (i)   in relation to the High Court, the senior district judge of the principal registry of the Family Division or, where proceedings were instituted in a district registry, the district judge;

   (ii) in relation to a county court, the proper officer of that court within the meaning of Order 1, Rule 3 of the County Court Rules 1981;

   (iii) in relation to a magistrates' court, the clerk to the justices of that court;

(b) in Scotland—

   (i)   in relation to the Court of Session, the Deputy Principal Clerk of Session;

   (ii) in relation to a sheriff court, the sheriff clerk.

Notification by the court

6.—(1) Where a court is aware that a maintenance assessment is in force and makes an order mentioned in regulation 3(1) which it considers has affected, or is likely to affect, that assessment, the person prescribed in paragraph (2) shall notify the Secretary of State to that effect.

(2) The prescribed person is the person holding the office specified below in the court where the order in question was made or subsequently registered—

(a) in England and Wales—

  (i) in relation to the High Court, the senior district judge of the principal registry of the Family Division or, where proceedings were instituted in a district registry, the district judge;

  (ii) in relation to a county court, the proper officer of that court within the meaning of Order 1, Rule 3 of the County Court Rules 1981;

  (iii) in relation to a magistrates' court, the clerk to the justices of that court;

(b) in Scotland—

  (i) in relation to the Court of Session, the Deputy Principal Clerk of Session;

  (ii) in relation to a sheriff court, the sheriff clerk.

Cancellation of a maintenance assessment on grounds of lack of jurisdiction

7.—(1) Where—

(a) a person with care;

(b) an absent parent; or

(c) a qualifying child

with respect to whom a maintenance assessment is in force ceases to be habitually resident in the United Kingdom, a child support officer shall cancel that assessment.

(2) Where the person with care is not an individual, paragraph (1) shall apply as if subparagraph (a) were omitted.

(3) Where a child support officer cancels a maintenance assessment under paragraph (1) or by virtue of paragraph (2), the assessment shall cease to have effect from the date that the child support officer determines is the date on which—

(a) where paragraph (1) applies, the person with care, absent parent or qualifying child; or

(b) where paragraph (2) applies, the absent parent or qualifying child

with respect to whom the assessment was made ceases to be habitually resident in the United Kingdom.

Maintenance assessments and maintenance orders made in error

8.—(1) Where—

(a) at the time that a mainenance assessment with respect to a qualifying child was made a maintenance order was in force with respect to that child;

(b) the absent parent has made payments of child support maintenance due under that assessment; and

(c) the child support officer cancels that assessment on the grounds that it was made in error, the payments of child support maintenance shall be treated as payments under the maintenance order and that order shall be treated as having continued in force.

(2) Where—

(a) at the time that a maintenance order with respect to a qualifying child was made a maintenance assessment was in force with respect to that child;

(b) the absent parent has made payments of maintenance due under that order; and

(c) the maintenance order is revoked by the court on the grounds that it was made in error,

the payments under the maintenance order shall be treated as payments of child support maintenance and the maintenance assessment shall be treated as not having been cancelled.

Signed by authority of the Secretary of State for Social Security.

Alistair Burt
Parliamentary Under-Secretary of State,
Department of Social Security

26th October 1992

S. I. 1992 No. 2644 (C.83)

The Child Support Act 1991 (Commencement No.3 and Transitional Provisions) Order 1992

Made — — — —   *26th October 1992*

The Secretary of State for Social Security, in exercise of the powers conferred upon him by section 58(2) to (6) of the Child Support Act 1991, hereby makes the following Order:

Citation

1. This Order may be cited as the Child Support Act 1991 (Commencement No.3 and Transitional Provisions) Order 1992.

Date appointed for the coming into force of certain provisions of the Child Support Act 1991

2 Subject to the following provisions of this Order, the date appointed for the coming into force of all the provisions of the Child Support Act 1991, in so far as they are not already in force, except sections 19(3), 30(2), 34(2), 37(2) and (3) and 58(12), is 5th April 1993.

Transitional Provisions

3. The transitional provisions set out in the Schedule to this Order shall have effect.

Signed by authority of the Secretary of State for Social Security.

Alistair Burt
Parliamentary Under-Secretary of State,
Department of Social Security

26th October 1992

SCHEDULE
Article 3

PART I

PHASED TAKE-ON OF CASES

1. In this Part of this Schedule—

"the Act" means the Child Support Act 1991;

"benefit" means income support, family credit, or disability working allowance under Part VII of the Social Security Contributions and Benefits Act 1992, or any other benefit prescribed under section 6(1) of the Act (applications by persons receiving benefit); and

"transitional period" means the period beginning with 5th April 1993 and ending with 6th April 1997.

2. Subject to paragraph 4 below, during the transitional period no application under section 4 of the Act (applications for child support maintenance) in relation to a qualifying child or any qualifying children may be made at any time when—

(a) there is in force a maintenance order or maintenance agreement in respect of that qualifying child or those qualifying children and the absent parent, or there is pending before any court an application for such a maintenance order; or

(b) benefit is being paid to a parent of that child or those children.

3. Subject to paragraph 4 below, during the transitional period no application under section 7 of the Act (right of child in Scotland to apply for assessment) may be made by a qualifying child at any time when there is in force a maintenance order or maintenance agreement in respect of that child and the absent parent, or there is pending before any court an application for such a maintenance order.

4.—(1) Paragraphs 2 and 3 above do not apply to an application made—

(a) in that part of the transitional period beginning with 8th April 1996, if the surname of the person with care begins with any of the letters A to D inclusive;

(b) in that part of the transitional period beginning with 1st July 1996, if the surname of the person with care begins with any of the letters E to K inclusive;

(c) in that part of the transitional period beginning with 7th October 1996, if the surname of the person with care begins with any of the letters L to R inclusive; and

(d) in that part of the transitional period beginning with 6th January 1997, if the surname of the person with care begins with any of the letters S to Z inclusive.

(2) Where paragraph 2 or 3 applies to a case because there is pending before a court an application for a maintenance order, and that application was made before 5th April 1993, those paragraphs shall not prevent the making of an application for a maintenance assessment under section 4 or,

as the case may be, section 7 of the Act; but in such a case section 8(3) of the Act shall not have effect until such an application is actually made.

5. For so long as paragraph 2 or 3 above operates in a case so as to prevent an application being made under section 4 of the Act or, as the case may be, section 7 of the Act, and no application has been made under section 6 of the Act, then in relation to that case section 8(3) of the Act (role of the courts with respect to maintenance orders) shall be modified so as to have effect as if the word "vary" was omitted.

PART II

MODIFICATION   OF   MAINTENANCE   ASSESSMENT   IN   CERTAIN
CASES

6. In this Part of this Schedule
"the Act" means the Child Support Act 1991;
"formula amount" means the amount of child support maintenance that would, but for the provisions of this Part of this Schedule, be payable under an original assessment, or any fresh assessment made during the period specified in paragraph 8 consequent on a review under section 17, 18 or 19 of the Act;
"the Maintenance Assessment Procedure Regulations" means the Child Support (Maintenance Assessment Procedure) Regulations 1992;
"modified amount" means an amount which is £20 greater than the aggregate weekly amount which was payable under the orders, agreements or arrangements mentioned in paragraph 7(1)(a) below; and
"original assessment" means a maintenance assessment made in respect of a qualifying child where no previous such assessment has been made or, where the assessment is made in respect of more than one child, where no previous such assessment has been made in respect of any of those children .

7.—(1) Subject to sub-paragraph (2), the provisions of this Part of this Schedule apply to cases where—

(a) on 4th April 1993 there is in force, in respect of all the qualifying children in respect of whom an application for a maintenance assessment is made under the Act and the absent parent concerned, one or more—

    (i)   maintenance orders;

    (ii)   orders under section 151 of the Army Act 1955 (deductions from pay for maintenance of wife or child) or section 151 of the Air Force Act 1955 (deductions from pay for maintenance of wife or child) or arrangements corresponding to such an order and made under Article 1(b) or 3 of the Naval and Marine Pay and Pensions (Deductions for Maintenance) Order 1959; or

    (iii)   maintenance agreements (being agreements which are made or evidenced in writing); and

(b) the absent parent is responsible for maintaining a child or children residing with him other than the child or children in respect of whom the application is made; and

(c) the formula amount is not more than £60; and

(d) the formula amount exceeds the aggregate weekly amount which was payable under the orders, agreements or arrangements mentioned in sub-paragraph (a) above by more than £20 a week.

(2) Nothing in this Part of this Schedule applies to an interim maintenance assessment made under section 12 of the Act.

8. In a case to which this Part of this Schedule applies, the amount payable under an original assessment, or any fresh assessment made consequent on a review under section 17, 18 or 19 of the Act, during the period of one year beginning with the date on which the original assessment takes effect or, if shorter, until any of the conditions specified in paragraph 7(1) is no longer satisfied, shall, instead of being the formula amount, be the modified amount.

9. For the purpose of determining the aggregate weekly amount payable under the orders, agreements or arrangements mentioned in paragraph 7(1)(a) above any payments in kind and any payments made to a third party on behalf of or for the benefit of the qualifying child or qualifying children or the person with care shall be disregarded.

10. If, in making a maintenance assessment, a child support officer has applied the provisions of this Part of this Schedule, regulation 10(2) of the Maintenance Assessment Procedure Regulations shall have effect as if there was added at the end

"(g) the aggregate weekly amount which was payable under the orders, agreements or arrangements specified in paragraph 7(1)(a) of the Schedule to the Child Support Act 1991 (Commencement No.3 and Transitional Provisions) Order 1992 (modification of maintenance assessment in certain cases).".

11. The first review of an original assessment under section 16 of the Act (periodical reviews) shall be conducted on the basis that the amount payable under the assessment immediately before the review takes place was the formula amount.

12.—(1) The provisions of the following sub-paragraphs shall apply where there is a review of a previous assessment under section 17 of the Act (reviews on change of circumstances) at any time when the amount payable under that assessment is the modified amount.

(2) Where the child support officer determines that, were a fresh assessment to be made as a result of the review, the amount payable under it (disregarding the provisions of this Part of this Schedule) (in this paragraph called "the reviewed formula amount") would be—

(a) more than the formula amount, the amount of child support maintenance payable shall be the modified amount plus the difference between the formula amount and the reviewed formula amount;

(b) less than the formula amount but more than the modified amount, the amount of child support maintenance payable shall be the modified amount;

   (c) less than the modified amount, the amount of child support maintenance payable shall be the reviewed formula amount.

   (3) The child support officer shall, in determining the reviewed formula amount, apply the provisions of regulations 20 to 22 of the Maintenance Assessment Procedure Regulations.

S. I 1992 No. 3094

The Child Support Fees Regulations 1992

Made — — — —	*1992*
Coming into force	*5th April 1993*

Whereas a draft of this instrument was laid before Parliament in accordance with section 52(2) of the Child Support Act 1991 and approved by a resolution of each House of Parliament:

Now, therefore, the Secretary of State for Social Security, in exercise of the powers conferred by sections 47, 52(4) and 54 of the Child Support Act 1991 and of all other powers enabling him in that behalf hereby makes the following Regulations:

Citation, commencement and interpretation

1. —(1) These Regulations may be cited as the Child Support Fees Regulations 1992 and shall come into force on 5th April 1993.

(2) In these Regulations, unless the context otherwise requires—

"the Act" means the Child Support Act 1991;

"assessable income" means income calculated in accordance with paragraph 5 of Schedule 1 to the Act;

"assessment fee" means a fee in respect of the assessment of child support maintenance;

"collection fee" means a fee in respect of the Secretary of State arranging for the collection of child support maintenance which becomes due, in accordance with a maintenance assessment, after that fee becomes payable, and (if necessary) arranging for the enforcement of the obligation to pay that child support maintenance in accordance with that assessment;

"Maintenance Assessment Procedure Regulations" means the Child Support (Maintenance Assessment Procedure) Regulations 1992;

"parent with care" means a person who, in respect of the same child or children, is both a parent and a person with care.

(3) In these Regulations, unless the context otherwise requires, a reference—

   (a) to a numbered regulation is to the regulation in these Regulations bearing that number;
   (b) in a regulation to a numbered paragraph is to the paragraph in that regulation bearing that number;
   (c) in a paragraph to a lettered or numbered sub-paragraph is to the sub-paragraph in that paragraph bearing that letter or number.

Circumstances when fees are payable

2. Where a maintenance assessment is made following an application under section 4, 6 or 7 of the Act fees shall be payable to the Secretary of State in accordance with regulations 3 and 4.

Liability to pay fees

3.—(1) Subject to the provisions of paragraphs (4) and (5), where a maintenance assessment is in force the following persons shall be liable to pay fees, in accordance with the provisions of regulation 4—

(a) where an application has been made under section 4 or 7 of the Act—

    (i)   the person with care if he is a parent with care; and

    (ii) the absent parent with respect to whom the assessment was made;

(b) where an application has been made under section 6 of the Act and the parent with care remains within section 6(1) of the Act, the absent parent with respect to whom the assessment was made.

(2) In a case falling within paragraph (1)(a), the fees payable shall be the assessment fee and, where the Secretary of State exercises his powers under section 4(2) or 7(3) of the Act, the collection fee.

(3) In a case falling within paragraph (1)(b), the fees payable shall be the assessment fee and the collection fee.

(4) Where—

(a) an application has been made under section 6 of the Act; and

(b) the parent with care no longer falls within section 6(1) of the Act but has not requested the Secretary of State to cease taking action under section 6 of the Act,

the case shall for the purposes of paragraph (1) be treated as if the application had been made under section 4 of the Act.

(5) No fees shall be payable by the following categories of person—

(a) any person to or in respect of whom income support, family credit or disability working allowance under Part VII of the Social Security Contributions and Benefits Act 1992 is paid;

(b) any person under the age of 16 or under the age of 19 and receiving full-time education which is not advanced education;

(c) any person whose assessable income is nil;

(d) an absent parent to whom the provisions of paragraph 6 of Schedule 1 to the Act (protected income) apply.

(6) The provisions of paragraph (5) shall—

(a) be applied in relation to any occasion when a liability to pay fees under the provisions of regulation 4 would otherwise arise; and

(b) have no effect on the fees payable by any other person.

(7) For the purposes of paragraph (5)(b), " advanced education" has the same meaning as in paragraph 2 of Schedule1 to the Maintenance Assessment Procedure Regulations (meaning of "child" for the purposes of the Act), and education is to be treated as fulltime education if it satisfies the conditions set out in paragraph 3 of that Schedule.

Fees

4.—(1) The first assessment fee shall become payable on the date a maintenance assessment is made following an application under section 4, 6 or 7 of the Act and an assessment fee shall thereafter become payable on each anniversary of that date.

(2) The first collection fee shall become payable on the date the Secretary of State arranges for the collection of child support maintenance and a collection fee shall thereafter become payable on the date the assessment fee becomes payable.

(3) Subject to paragraphs (4) and (6)—

  (a) the assessment fee shall be £44 00;

  (b) the collection fee shall be £34 00.

(4) Where the first collection fee becomes payable on a date ("the first collection date") later than the date the first assessment fee becomes payable or an anniversary of that date, the amount of that fee shall be an amount equal to the collection fee specified in paragraph (3) above, multiplied by the number of complete weeks between the first collection date and the date the assessment fee next becomes payable, and divided by 52.

(5) The provisions of this regulation in relation to collection fees shall apply where there has been an earlier period, which has terminated, during which collection fees were payable and the Secretary of State again arranges for the collection of child support maintenance, and references to "the first collection fee" shall be construed accordingly.

(6) No additional assessment fees or collection fees shall be payable by a person with respect to whom more than one maintenance assessment is in force.

(7) Where a liability to pay assessment fees or collection fees under these Regulations arises, the fees shall become due on the fourteenth day after the date the fee invoice is given or sent by the Secretary of State.

(8) If a fee invoice is sent by post to a person's last known or notified address, it shall, for the purposes of paragraph (7), be treated as having been given or sent on the second day after the day of posting, excluding any Sunday or any day which is a bank holiday in England, Wales, Scotland or Northern Ireland under the Banking and Financial Dealings Act 1971.

Signed by authority of the Secretary of State for Social Security.

Parliamentary Under-Secretary of State,
Department of Social Security

1992

S. I. 1992 No. 2641

The Child Support Appeal Tribunals (Procedure) Regulations 1992

Made — — — —	*26th October 1992*
Laid before Parliament	*29th October 1992*
Coming into force	*5th April 1993*

ARRANGEMENT OF REGULATIONS

The Secretary of State for Social Security, in exercise of the powers conferred by sections 21(2) and (3) and 51(1) of the Child Support Act 1991 and of all other powers enabling him in that behalf, after consultation with the Council on Tribunals in accordance with section 8 of the Tribunals and Inquiries Act 1992, hereby makes the following Regulations:

Citation, commencement and interpretation

1.—(1) These Regulations may be cited as the Child Support Appeal Tribunals (Procedure) Regulations 1992 and shall come into force on 5th April 1993.

(2) In these Regulations, unless the context otherwise requires:—
"absent parent" has the meaning assigned to it in section 3(2) of the Act;
"the Act" means the Child Support Act 1991;
"Central Office" means the Central Office of Child Support Appeal Tribunals at Anchorage Two, Anchorage Quay, Salford Quays, Manchester, M5 2YN;
"chairman", subject to paragraph (3), means a person nominated under paragraph 3 of Schedule 3 to the Act and includes the President and any full-time chairman;
"clerk to the tribunal" means a person appointed under paragraph 6 of Schedule 3 to the Act;

"Commissioner" means the Chief or any other Child Support Commissioner appointed under section 22 of the Act;

"full-time chairman" means a regional or other full-time chairman of a child support appeal tribunal appointed under paragraph 4 of Schedule 3 to the Act;

"party to the proceedings" means—

(a) the person with care;

(b) the absent parent;

(c) any child who has made an application for a maintenance assessment under section 7 of the Act;

(d) the child support officer;

(e) any other person, who on an application made by him, appears to the chairman of the tribunal to be interested in the proceedings;

"person with care" has the meaning assigned to it by section 3(3) of the Act;

"President" has the meaning assigned to it in paragraph 1(1) of Schedule 3 to ths Act;

"proceedings" means proceedings on an appeal or application to which these Regulations apply; and

"tribunal" means a child support appeal tribunal constituted in accordance with section 21 of the Act.

(3) Unless otherwise provided, where by these Regulations anything is required to be done by, or any power is conferred on, a chairman, then—

(a) if that thing is to be done or the power is to be exercised at the hearing of an appeal or application, it shall be done or exercised by the chairman of the tribunal hearing the appeal or application; and

(b) otherwise, shall be done or exercised by a person who is eligible to be nominated to act as a chairman of a child support appeal tribunal under paragraph 3(2) of Schedule 3 to the Act.

(4) In these Regulations, unless the context otherwise requires, a reference—

(a) to a numbered regulation is to the regulation in these Regulations bearing that number; and

(b) in a regulation to a numbered paragraph is to the paragraph in that regulation bearing that number.

Service of notices or documents

2.—(1) Where by any provision of the Act or of these Regulations any notice or other document is required to be given or sent to the clerk to the tribunal that notice or document shall be treated as having been so given or sent on the day that it is received by the clerk to the tribunal.

(2) Where by any provision of the Act or of these Regulations any notice or other document is required to be given or sent to any person other than the clerk to the tribunal that notice or document shall, if sent by post to that person's last known address, be treated as having been given or sent on the day that it was posted.

Making an appeal or application and time limits

3.—(1) An appeal to a tribunal under section 20(1) of the Act or an application to a tribunal to set aside its decision under regulation 15 shall be by notice in writing signed by the person making it or by his representative where it appears to a chairman that he was unable to sign personally, or by a barrister, advocate or solicitor on his behalf.

(2) The notice shall be made or given by sending or delivering it to the clerk to the tribunal at the Central Office.

(3) An appeal under section 20(1) of the Act shall be brought within the period of 28 days beginning with the date on which notification of the decision in question was given or sent to the appellant.

(4) An application under regulation 15 shall be made within the period of 3 months beginning· with the date when a copy of the record of the decision was given or sent to the applicant.

(5) In paragraphs (6) and (7) "the specified time" means the time specified in paragraph (3) or, as the case may be, paragraph (4).

(6) When an appeal or application is made after the specified time has expired, that time may for special reasons be extended by the chairman to the date of the making of the appeal or application.

(7) Any appeal or application made after the specified time has expired which does not include an application for an extension of time shall be deemed to include such an application, and if it appears to a chairman that an application for an extension of time does not state reasons for the appeal or application being made after the specified time the chairman may before determining it give the person making the application for an extension of time a reasonable opportunity to provide reasons.

(8) An application for an extension of time which has been refused may not be rcncwcd, but any chairman may set aside a refusal if it appears to him just to do so on any of the grounds set out in regulation 15(1).

(9) In the case of an appeal the notice shall contain sufficient particulars of the decision under appeal to enable that decision to be identified.

(10) Any notice of appeal or application other than an application for an extension of time shall state the grounds on which it is made.

(11) If it appears to a chairman that the notice of appeal does not enable the decision under appeal to be identified or that the notice of appeal or application does not state the grounds on which it is made the chairman may direct the person making it to provide such particulars as the chairman may reasonably require.

Lack of jurisdiction

4. When a chairman is satisfied that the tribunal does not have jurisdiction to entertain a purported appeal he may make a declaration to that effect and such declaration shall dispose of the purported appeal.

Directions

5. At any stage of the proceedings a chairman may either of his own motion or on a written application made to the clerk to the tribunal by any party to the proceedings give such directions as he may consider necessary or desirable for the just, effective and efficient conduct of the proceedings and may direct any party to provide such further particulars or to produce such documents as may reasonably be required.

Striking out of proceedings

6.—(1) Subject to paragraph (2), a chairman may, either of his own motion or on the application of any party to the proceedings, order that the appeal or application be struck out because of the failure of the appellant or applicant to comply with a direction under regulation 3(11) or 5 or to reply to an enquiry from the clerk to the tribunal about his availability to attend a hearing.

(2) Before making an order under paragraph (1) the chairman shall send notice to the person against whom it is proposed that any such order should be made and any other party to the proceedings giving each of them a reasonable opportunity to show cause why such an order should not be made.

(3) The chairman may, on application by any party to the proceedings made not later than one year beginning with the date of the order made under paragraph (1), give leave to reinstate any appeal or application which has been struck out in accordance with that order.

Withdrawal of appeals and applications

7.—(1) Any appeal to a tribunal may be withdrawn by the person making the appeal—
   (a) at a hearing with the leave of the chairman; or
   (b) at any other time, by giving written notice of intention to withdraw to the clerk to the tribunal and either
      (i) with the consent in writing of every other party to the proceedings; or
      (ii) with the leave of the chairman after every other party to the proceedings has had a reasonable opportunity to make representations.

(2) A person who has made an application to a tribunal to set aside their decision under regulation 15 may withdraw it at any time before the application is determined by giving written notice of withdrawal to the clerk to the tribunal.

Postponement

8.—(1) Where a person to whom notice of a hearing has been given wishes to request a postponement of that hearing he shall give notice in writing to the clerk to the tribunal stating his reasons for the request and a chairman may grant or refuse the request as he thinks fit.

(2) A chairman may of his own motion at any time before the beginning of the hearing postpone the hearing.

Representation of parties to the proceedings

9. Any party to the proceedings may be accompanied and (whether or not the party himself attends) may be represented by another person whether having a professional qualification or not, and for the purposes of any proceedings any such representative shall have all the rights and powers to which the person represented is entitled under these Regulations, except that a representative who is not a barrister, advocate or solicitor shall not have the power to sign the notice of appeal or application.

Summoning of witnesses

10.—(1) A chairman may by summons or, in Scotland, citation require any person in Great Britain to attend as a witness at a hearing of an appeal or application at such time and place as shall be specified in the summons or citation and, subject to paragraph (2), at the hearing to answer any question or produce any documents in his custody or under his control which relate to any matter in question in the appeal or application, but—

    (a) no person shall be required to attend in obedience to such a summons or citation unless he has been given at least 10 days' notice of the hearing or, if less than 10 days' notice is given, he has informed the tribunal that he accepts that notice as sufficient; and

    (b) no person shall be required to attend and give evidence or to produce any document in obedience to such a summons or citation unless the necessary expenses of attendance are paid or tendered to him.

(2) No person shall be compelled to give any evidence or produce any document or other material that he could not be compelled to give or produce on a trial of an action in a court of law in that part of Great Britain where the hearing takes place.

(3) In exercising the powers conferred by this regulation, the chairman shall take into account the need to protect any matter that relates to intimate personal or financial circumstances, is commercially sensitive, consists of information communicated or obtained in confidence or concerns national security.

(4) Every summons or citation issued under this regulation shall contain a statement to the effect that the person in question may apply in writing to a chairman to vary or set aside the summons or citation.

Hearings

11.—(1) A tribunal shall hold an oral hearing of every appeal, and may hold an oral hearing of an application, and subject to the provisions of the Act and of these Regulations the procedure in connection with the hearing shall be such as the chairman shall determine.

(2) Not less than 10 days' notice (beginning with the day on which it is given and ending on the day before the hearing) of the time and place of any hearing shall be given to every party to the proceedings, and if such notice

has not been given to a person to whom it should have been given under the provisions of this paragraph the hearing may proceed only with the consent of that person.

(3) At any hearing any party to the proceedings shall be entitled to be present and be heard.

(4) Any person entitled to be heard at a hearing may address the tribunal, give evidence, call witnesses and put questions directly to any other party to the proceedings, to any representative of the child support officer or to any other person called as a witness.

(5) A tribunal may require any witness to give evidence on oath or affirmation and for that purpose there may be administered an oath or affirmation in due form.

(6) If a party to the proceedings to whom notice has been given under paragraph (2) fails to appear at the hearing the tribunal may, having regard to all the circumstances including any explanation offered for the absence, proceed with the appeal notwithstanding his absence or give such directions with a view to the determination of the appeal as it may think proper.

(7) Any hearing before the tribunal shall be in private unless the chairman directs that the hearing, or part of it, shall be in public.

(8) The following persons shall also be entitled to be present at a hearing even though it is in private—

(a) the President, any full-time chairman and the clerk to the tribunal;

(b) any person undergoing training as a chairman or other member of the tribunal or as a clerk to the tribunal;

(c) any person acting on behalf of the President in the training or supervision of clerks to tribunals;

(d) a member of the Council on Tribunals or of the Scottish Committee of the Council;

(e) any person undergoing training as a child support officer or as the representative of a child support officer and any person acting on behalf of the Chief Child Support Officer or the Secretary of State in the training or supervision of child support officers or representafives of child support officers or in the monitoring of standards of adjudication by child support officers;

(f) with leave of the chairman and the consent of every party to the proceedings actually present, any other person.

(9) For the purposes of arriving at its decision a tribunal shall, and for the purposes of discussing any question of procedure may, notwithstanding anything contained in these Regulations, order all persons to withdraw from the sitting of the tribunal other than the members of the tribunal, any of the persons mentioned in sub-paragraphs (a), (b) and (d) of paragraph (8) and, with the leave of the chairman and if no party to the proceedings actually present objects, any of the persons mentioned in sub-paragraphs (c) and (f) of that paragraph.

(10) None of the persons mentioned in paragraph (8) shall take any part in the hearing or (where entitled or permitted to remain) in the deliberations of the tribunal.

Adjourmnents

12.—(1) A hearing may be adjourned by the tribunal at any time on the application of any party to the proceedings or of its own motion.

(2) Where a hearing has been adjourned and it is not practicable, or would cause undue delay, for it to be resumed before a tribunal consisting of the same members, the appeal or application shall be heard by a tribunal none of the members of which was a member of the original tribunal and the proceedings shall be by way of a complete rehearing of the case.

Decisions

13.—(1) A decision of the tribunal may be taken by a majority.

(2) The chairman shall—

  (a) record in writing the decision of the tribunal;

  (b) include in the record of every decision a statement of the reasons for it, the findings of the tribunal on questions of fact material to the decision and the terms of any direction given under section 20(4) of the Act; and

  (c) if a decision is not unanimous, record a statement that one of the members dissented and the reasons given by him for so dissenting.

(3) As soon as may be practicable after the decision of the tribunal a copy of the record of the decision made in accordance with this regulation shall be sent to every party to the proceedings who shall also be informed of the conditions governing appeals to a Commissioner.

(4) If a child support officer to whom a case is referred by the Secretary of State under section 20(3) of the Act (procedure following a successful appeal) is uncertain, having regard to the terms of the decision and of any directions contained in it, how he should deal with the case, he may apply to the tribunal or another tribunal for directions or further directions, and the tribunal may give such directions or further directions as it thinks fit.

(5) Upon receiving an application from a child support officer under paragraph (4) the clerk to the tribunal shall send a copy of it to all the other parties to the case, and the tribunal shall not give any directions or further directions on the application until those other parties have had a reasonable opportunity of making representations on it.

Corrections

14.—(1) Subject to regulation 16 (provisions common to regulations 14 and 15) accidental errors (whether of omission or commission) in any decision or record of any decision may at any time be corrected by the tribunal who gave the decision or by another tribunal.

(2) A correction made to a decision or to the record of a decision shall be deemed to be part of the decision or of the record thereof and written notice of it shall be given as soon as practicable to every party to the proceedings.

Setting aside

15.—(1) Subject to regulation 16 (provisions common to regulations 14 and 15) on an application made by a party to the proceedings a decision may be set aside by the tribunal who gave the decision or by another tribunal in a case where it appears just to do so on the grounds that—

(a) a document relating to the proceedings in which the decision was given was not sent to, or was not received at an appropriate time by, a party to the proceedings or the party's representative or was not received at an appropriate time by the tribunal who gave the decision;

(b) a party to the proceedings in which the decision was given or the party's representative was not present at the hearing notice of which had been given under regulation 11(2); or

(c) there has been some other procedural irregularity or mishap.

(2) An application under this regulation shall be made in accordance with regulation 3.

(3) Where an application to set aside a decision is made under paragraph (1) every party to the proceedings shall be sent a copy of the application and shall be afforded a reasonable opportunity of making representations on it before the application is decided.

(4) Notice in writing of a decision on an application to set aside a decision shall be given to every party to the proceedings as soon as may be practicable and the notice shall contain a statement giving the reasons for the decision.

(5) For the purpose of deciding an application to set aside a decision under these Regulations there shall be disregarded regulation 2 and any provision in any enactment or instrument to the effect that any notice or other document required or authorised to be given or sent to any person shall be deemed to have been given or sent if it was sent by post to the person's last known address.

Provisions common to regulations 14 and 15

16.—(1) In calculating time under regulation 2(1) of the Child Support Commissioners (Procedure) Regulations 1992 (applications for leave to appeal to a Commissioner) there shall be disregarded any day falling before the day on which notice was given of a correction of a decision or record thereof pursuant to regulation 14 or on which notice is given of a decision that a prior decision shall not be set aside following an application made under regulation 15, as the case may be.

(2) Notwithstanding anything contained in these Regulations, there shall be no appeal against a correction made under regulation 14, or a refusal to make such a correction, or against a decision given under regulation 15.

(3) Nothing in these Regulations shall be construed as derogating from any power to correct errors or set aside decisions which is exercisable apart from these Regulations.

Confidentiality

17.—(1) No information such as is mentioned in paragraph (2), and which has been provided for the purposes of any proceedings to which these Regulations apply, shall be disclosed except with the written consent of the person to whom the information relates.

(2) The information referred to in paragraph (1) is—

    (a) any address, other than the address of the Central Office and the place where the oral hearing is to be held; and

    (b) any other information the use of which could reasonably be expected to lead to a person being located.

Signed by authority of the Secretary of State for Social Security.

Alistair Burt
Parliamentary Under-Secretary of State,
Department of Social Security

26th October 1992

S. I. 1992 No. 2640

The Child Support Commissioners (Procedure) Regulations 1992

Made — — — —   *26th October 1992*
Laid before Parliament   *29th October 1992*
Coming into force   *5th April 1993*

ARRANGEMENT OF REGULATIONS

PART I

Introduction

1. Citation, commencement and interpretation

PART II

Applications for leave to appeal and appeals to a Commissioner

2. Application to the chairman of an appeal tribunal or to a Commissioner for leave to appeal to a Commissioner
3. Notice of application for leave to appeal to a Commissioner
4. Determination of applications for leave to appeal
5. Notice of appeal
6. Time limit for appealing
7. Directions on notice of appeal
8. Acknowledgement of a notice of appeal and notification to each respondent
9. Secretary of State as respondent to an appeal

PART III

General Procedure

10. Other directions
11. Requests for oral hearings
12. Representation at an oral hearing
13. Oral hearings
14. Summoning of witnesses
15. Postponement and adjournment
16. Withdrawal of applications for leave to appeal and appeals
17. Irregularities

PART IV

Decisions

18. Determinations and decisions of a Commissioner
19. Correction of accidental errors in decisions

PART V

Miscellaneous and Supplementary

The Lord Chancellor, in exercise of the powers conferred by sections 22(3), 24(6) and (7),and 25(2), (3) and (5) of the Child Support Act 1991 and of all other powers enabling him in that behalf, after consultation with the Lord Advocate and, in accordance with section 8 of the Tribunals and Inquiries Act 1992, with the Council on Tribunals, hereby makes the following Regulations:

PART I

INTRODUCTION

Citation, commencement and interpretation

1.—(1) These Regulations may be cited as the Child Support Commissioners (Procedure) Regulations 1992 and shall come into force on 5th April 1993.

(2) In these Regulations, unless the context otherwise requires—

"the Act" means the Child Support Act 1991;

"appeal tribunal" means a child support appeal tribunal;

"the chairman", for the purposes of regulations 2 and 3, means—

(i)   the person who was the chairman of the appeal tribunal which gave the decision against which leave to appeal is being sought; or

(ii) where the application for leave to appeal to a Commissioner was dealt with under regulation 2(2), the chairman who dealt with the application;

"Chief Commissioner" means the Chief Child Support Commissioner appointed under section 22(1) of the Act;

"Commissioner" means the Chief or any other Child Support Commissioner appointed under section 22(1) of the Act and includes a Tribunal of Commissioners constituted under paragraph 5 of Schedule 4 to the Act;

"proceedings" means any proceedings before a Commissioner, whether by way of an application for leave to appeal to, or from, a Commissioner, or by way of an appeal or otherwise;

"respondent" means any person, other than the applicant or appellant, who participated as a party to the proceedings before the appeal tribunal, and any other person who, pursuant to a direction given under regulation 7(1)(a), is served with notice of the appeal; and

"summons" in relation to Scotland, means "citation" and regulation 14 shall be construed accordingly.

(3)   In these Regulations, unless the context otherwise requires, a reference—

(a) to a numbered regulation is to the regulation in these Regulations bearing that number;

(b) in a regulation to a numbered paragraph is to the paragraph in that regulation bearing that number;

(c) in a paragraph to a lettered sub-paragraph is to the sub-paragraph in that paragraph bearing that letter.

PART II

APPLICATIONS FOR LEAVE TO APPEAL AND APPEALS TO A COMMISSIONER

Application to the chairman of an appeal tribunal or to a Commissioner for leave to appeal to a Commissioner

2.—(1) An application for leave to appeal to a Commissioner from the decision of an appeal tribunal shall be made—

(a) in the case of an application to the chairman of an appeal tribunal, within the period of 3 months beginning with the date on which notice of the decision of the tribunal was given or sent to the applicant; or

(b) in the case of an application to a Commissioner, within the period of 42 days beginning with the date on which notice of the refusal of leave to appeal by the chairman of the appeal tribunal was given or sent to the applicant.

(2) Where in any case it is impracticable, or it would be likely to cause undue delay for an application for leave to appeal against a decision of an appeal tribunal to be determined by the person who was the chairman of that tribunal, that application shall be determined by any other person qualified under paragraph 3 of Schedule 3 to the Act to act as a chairman of appeal tribunals.

(3) Subject to paragraph (4), an application may be made to a Commissioner for leave to appeal against a decision of an appeal tribunal only where the applicant has been refused leave to appeal by the chairman of the appeal tribunal.

(4) Where there has been a failure to apply to the chairman of the tribunal, either within the time specified in paragraph (1)(a) or at all, an application for leave to appeal may be made to a Commissioner who may, if for special reasons he thinks fit, accept and proceed to consider and determine the application.

(5) A Commissioner may accept and proceed to consider and determine an application for leave to appeal under paragraph (3) notwithstanding that the period specified for making the application has expired if for special reasons he thinks fit.

Notice of application for leave to appeal to a Commissioner

3.—(1) An application for leave to appeal shall be brought by a notice in writing to the clerk to the tribunal at the Central Office of Child Support Appeal Tribunals at Anchorage Two, Anchorage Quay, Salford Quays, Manchester, M5 2YN or, as the case may be, to a Commissioner, and shall contain—

(a) the name and address of the applicant;

(b) the grounds on which the applicant intends to rely;

(c) an address for service of notices and other documents on the applicant; and

(d) where the applicant is to be represented by a person who is not a barrister, advocate or solicitor, the written authority of the applicant for that person to represent him,

and the notice shall have annexed to it a copy of the decision against which leave to appeal is being sought.

(2) In the case of an application for leave to appeal to a Commissioner made to a Commissioner where the applicant has been refused leave to appeal by the chairman of an appeal tribunal the notice shall also have annexed to it a copy of the decision refusing leave to appeal, and shall state the date on which the applicant was given notice of the refusal of leave.

(3) Where the applicant has failed to apply within the time specified in regulation 2(1)(a) or, as the case may be, 2(1)(b) for leave to appeal, the notice of application for leave to appeal shall, in addition to complying with paragraph (1), state the grounds relied upon for seeking acceptance of the application notwithstanding that the relevant period has expired.

(4) In a case where the application for leave to appeal is made by a child support officer he shall send a copy of the application to each person who was a party to the proceedings before the appeal tribunal, and in any other case the clerk to the tribunal or, as the case may be, the Office of the Commissioner shall send a copy of the application to each person, other than the applicant, who was such a party.

(5) An applicant for leave to appeal to a Commissioner may at any time before the application is determined withdraw it by giving written notice of withdrawal to the clerk to the tribunal or, as the case may be, to the Commissioner.

Determination of applications for leave to appeal

4.—(1) The determination of an application for leave to appeal to a Commissioner made to the chairman of an appeal tribunal shall be recorded in writing by the chairman and a copy of the determination shall be sent by the clerk to the tribunal to the applicant and every other person to whom notice of the application was given under regulation 3(4).

(2) Unless a Commissioner directs to the contrary, where a Commissioner grants leave to appeal on an application made in accordance with regulation 3, notice of appeal shall be deemed to have been duly given on the date when notice of the determination was given to the applicant and the notice of application shall be deemed to be a notice of appeal duly served under regulation 5.

(3) If on consideration of an application for leave to appeal to him from the decision of an appeal tribunal the Commissioner grants leave he may, with the consent of the applicant and each respondent, treat the application as an appeal and determine any question arising on the application as though it were a question arising on an appeal.

Notice of appeal

5.—(1) Subject to regulation 4(2), an appeal shall be brought by a notice to a Commissioner containing—
- (a) the name and address of the appellant;
- (b) the date on which leave to appeal was granted;
- (c) the grounds on which the appellant intends to rely;
- (d) an address for service of notices and other documents on the appellant, and the notice shall have annexed to it a copy of the determination granting leave to appeal and a copy of the decision against which leave to appeal has been granted.

Time limit for appealing

6.—(1) Subject to paragraph (2), a notice of appeal shall not be valid unless it is served on a Commissioner within 42 days of the date on which the applicant was given notice in writing that leave to appeal had been granted.

(2) A Commissioner may accept a notice of appeal served after the expiry of the period prescribed by paragraph (1) if for special reasons he thinks fit.

Directions on notice of appeal

7.—(1) As soon as practicable after the receipt of a notice of appeal a Commissioner shall give such directions as appear to him to be necessary, specifying—
- (a) the parties who are to be respondents to the appeal; and
- (b) the order in which and the time within which any party is to be allowed to make written observations on the appeal or on the observations made by any other party.

(2) If in any case two or more persons who were parties to the proceedings before the appeal tribunal give notice of appeal to a Commissioner, a Commissioner shall direct which one of them is to be treated as the appellant, and thereafter, but without prejudice to any rights or powers conferred on appellants by the Act or these Regulations, any other person who has given notice of appeal shall be treated as a respondent.

(3) Subject to regulation 23(2)(b), the time specified in directions given under paragraph (1)(b) as being the time within which written observations are to be made shall be not less than 30 days beginning with the day on which the notice of the appeal or, as the case may be, the observations were sent to the party concerned.

Acknowledgement of a notice of appeal and notification to each respondent

8. There shall be sent by the office of the Child Support Commissioners—
  (a) to the appellant, an acknowledgement of the receipt of the notice of appeal; and
  (b) to each respondent, a copy of the notice of appeal.

Secretary of State as respondent to an appeal

9. The Secretary of State may at any time apply to a Commissioner for leave to intervene in an appeal pending before a Commissioner, and if such leave is granted the Secretary of State shall thereafter be treated as a respondent to that appeal.

PART III

GENERAL PROCEDURE

Other directions

10.—(1) Where it appears to a Commissioner that an application or appeal which is made to him gives insufficient particulars to enable the question at issue to be determined, he may direct the party making the application or appeal or any respondent to furnish such further particulars as may reasonably be required.

(2) At any stage of the proceedings a Commissioner may, either of his own motion or on application, give such directions or further directions as he may consider necessary or desirable for the efficient and effective despatch of the proceedings.

(3) Without prejudice to the provisions of paragraph (2), a Commissioner may direct any party to any proceedings before him to make such written

observations as may seem to him necessary to enable the question at issue to be determined.

(4) An application under paragraph (2) shall be made in writing to a Commissioner and shall set out the direction which the applicant is seeking to have made and the grounds for the application.

(5) Unless a Commissioner otherwise determines, an application made pursuant to paragraph (2) shall be copied by the office of the Child Support Commissioners to the other parties.

(6) The powers to give directions conferred by paragraphs (2) and (3) include power to revoke or vary any such direction.

Requests for oral hearings

11.—(1) Subject to paragraphs (2) and (3), a Commissioner may determine an application for leave to appeal or an appeal without an oral hearing.

(2) Where in any proceedings before a Commissioner a request is made by any party for an oral hearing the Commissioner shall grant the request unless, after considering all the circumstances of the case and the reasons put forward in the request for the hearing, he is satisfied that the application or appeal can properly be determined without a hearing, in which event he may proceed to determine the case without a hearing and he shall in writing either before giving his deterrnination or decision, or in it, inform the person making the request that it has been refused.

(3) A Commissioner may of his own motion at any stage, if he is satisfied that an oral hearing is desirable, direct such a hearing.

Representation at an oral hearing

12. At any oral hearing a party may conduct his case himself (with assistance from any person if he wishes) or be represented by any person whom he may appoint for the purpose.

Oral hearings

13.—(1) This regulation applies to any oral hearing to which these Regulations apply.

(2) Reasonable notice (being not less than 10 days beginning with the day on which notice is given and ending on the day before the hearing of the case is to take place) of the time and place of any oral hearing before a Commissioner shall be given to the parties by the office of the Child Support Commissioners.

(3) If any party to whom notice of an oral hearing has been given in accordance with these Regulations should fail to appear at the hearing, the Commissioner may, having regard to all the circumstances including any explanation offered for the absence, proceed with the case notwithstanding that party's absence, or may give such directions with a view to the determination of the case as he thinks fit.

(4) Any oral hearing before a Commissioner shall be in public except where the Commissioner for special reasons directs otherwise, in which case the hearing or any part thereof shall be in private.

(5) Where a Commissioner holds an oral hearing the applicant or appellant and every respondent shall be entitled to be present and be heard.

(6) Any person entitled to be heard at an oral hearing may—

    (a) address the Commissioner;

    (b) with the leave of the Commissioner but not otherwise, give evidence, call witnesses and put questions directly to any other person called as a witness.

(7) Nothing in these Regulations shall prevent a member of the Council on Tribunals or of the Scottish Committee of the Council in his capacity as such from being present at an oral hearing before a Commissioner notwithstanding that the hearing is not in public.

Summoning of witnesses

14.—(1) Subject to paragraph (2), a Commissioner may summon any person to attend as a witness at an oral hearing, at such time and place as may be specified in the summons, to answer any questions or produce any documents in his custody or under his control which relate to any matter in question in the proceedings.

(2) No person shall be required to attend in obedience to a summons under paragraph (1) unless he has been given at least 7 days' notice of the hearing or, if less than 7 days, has informed the Commissioner that he accepts such notice as he has been given.

(3) A Commissioner may upon the application of a person summoned under this regulation set the summons aside.

(4) A Commissioner may require any witness to give evidence on oath and for that purpose there may be administered an oath in due form.

Postponement and adjournment

15.—(1) A Commissioner may, either of his own motion or on an application by any party to the proceedings, postpone an oral hearing.

(2) An oral hearing, once commenced, may be adjourned by the Commissioner at any time either on the application of any party to the proceedings or of his own motion.

Withdrawal of applications for leave to appeal and appeals

16.—(1) At any time before it is determined, an application to a Commissioner for leave to appeal against a decision of an appeal tribunal may be withdrawn by the applicant by giving written notice to a Commissioner of his intention to do so.

(2) At any time before the decision is made, an appeal to a Commissioner may, with the leave of a Commissioner, be withdrawn by the appellant.

(3) A Commissioner may, on application by the party concerned, give leave to reinstate any application or appeal which has been withdrawn in accordance with paragraphs (1) and (2) and, on giving leave, he may make such directions as to the future conduct of the proceedings as he thinks fit.

Irregularities

17. Any irregularity resulting from failure to comply with the requirements of these Regulations before a Commissioner has determined the application or appeal shall not by itself invalidate any proceedings, and the Commissioner, before reaching his decision may waive the irregularity or take such steps as he thinks fit to remedy the irregularity whether by amendment of any document, or the giving of any notice or directions or otherwise.

PART IV

DECISIONS

Determinations and decisions of a Commissioner

18.—(1) The determination of a Commissioner on an application for leave to appeal shall be in writing and signed by him.

(2) The decision of a Commissioner on an appeal shall be in writing and signed by him and, except in respect of a decision made with the consent of the parties, he shall record the reasons.

(3) A copy of the determination or decision and any reasons shall be sent to the parties by the office of the Child Support Commissioners.

(4) Without prejudice to paragraphs (2) and (3), a Commissioner may announce his determination or decision at the conclusion of an oral hearing.

(5) When giving his decision on an application or appeal, whether in writing or orally, a Commissioner shall omit any reference to the surname of any child to whom the appeal relates and any other information which would be likely, whether directly or indirectly, to identify that child.

Correction of accidental errors in decisions

19.—(1) Subject to regulation 21, accidental errors in any decision or record of a decision may at any time be corrected by the Commissioner who gave the decision.

(2) A correction made to, or to the record of, a decision shall become part of the decision or record thereof and written notice thereof shall be given by the office of the Child Support Commissioners to any party to whom notice of the decision had previously been given.

Setting aside of decisions on certain grounds

20.—(1) Subject to the following provisions of this regulation and regulation 21, on an application made by any party a decision may be set aside by the Commissioner who gave the decision in a case where it appears just to do so on the ground that

    (a) a document relating to the proceedings was not sent to, or was not received at an appropriate time by, a party or his representative, or was not received at an appropriate time by the Commissioner; or

    (b) a party or his representative had not been present at an oral hearing which had been held in the course of the proceedings; or

    (c) there has been some other procedural irregularity or mishap.

(2) An application under this regulation shall be made in writing to a Commissioner within 30 days from the date on which notice in writing of the decision was given by the office of the Child Support Commissioners to the party making the application.

(3) Where an application to set aside a decision is made under paragraph (1), each party shall be sent by the office of the Child Support Commissioners a copy of the application and shall be afforded a reasonable opportunity of making representations on it before the application is determined.

(4) Notice in writing of a determination of an application to set aside a decision shall be given by the office of the Child Support Commissioners to each party and shall contain a statement giving the reasons for the determination.

Provisions common to regulations 19 and 20

21.—(1) In regulations 19 and 20 the word "decision" shall include determinations of applications for leave to appeal as well as decisions on appeals.

(2) Subject to a direction by a Commissioner to the contrary, in calculating any time for applying for leave to appeal against a Commissioner's decision there shall be disregarded any day falling before the day on which notice was given of a correction of a decision or the record thereof pursuant to regulation 19 or on which notice was given of a determination that a decision shall not be set aside under regulation 20, as the case may be.

(3) There shall be no appeal against a correction or a refusal to correct under regulation 19 or a determination given under regulation 20.

(4) If it is impracticable or likely to cause undue delay for a decision or record of a decision to be dealt with pursuant to regulation 19 or 20 by the Commissioner who gave the decision, the Chief Commissioner or another Commissioner may deal with the matter.

PART V

MISCELLANEOUS AND SUPPLEMENTARY

Confidentiality

22.—(1) No information such as is mentioned in paragraph (2), and which has been furnished for the purposes of any proceedings to which these Regulations apply, shall be disclosed except with the written consent of the person to whom the information relates.

(2) The information mentioned in paragraph (1) is—

   (a) the address, other than the address of the office of the Commissioner concerned and the place where the oral hearing (if any) is to be held; and

   (b) any other information the use of which could reasonably be expected to lead to a person being located.

General powers of a Commissioner

23.—(1) Subject to the provisions of these Regulations, and without prejudice to regulations 7 and 10, a Commissioner may adopt such procedure in relation to any proceedings before him as he sees fit.

(2) A Commissioner may, if he thinks fit—

   (a) subject to regulations 2(5) and 6(2), extend the time specified by or under these Regulations for doing any act, notwithstanding that the time specified may have expired;

   (b) abridge the time so specified; or

   (c) expedite the proceedings in such manner as he thinks fit.

(3) Subject to paragraph (4), a Commissioner may, if he thinks fit, either on the application of a party or of his own motion, strike out for want of prosecution any application for leave to appeal or any appeal.

(4) Before making an order under paragraph (3), the Commissioner shall send notice to the party against whom it is proposed that it shall be made giving him an opportunity to show cause why it should not be made.

(5) A Commissioner may, on application by the party concerned, give leave to reinstate any application or appeal which has been struck out in accordance with paragraph (3) and, on giving leave, he may make such directions as to the future conduct of the proceedings as he thinks fit.

(6) Nothing in these Regulations shall be construed as derogating from any other power which is exercisable apart from these Regulations.

Manner of and time for service of notices, etc.

24.—(1) Any notice or other document required or authorised to be given or sent to any party under the provisions of these Regulations shall be deemed to have been given or sent if it was sent by post properly addressed and pre-paid to that party at his ordinary or last notified address.

(2) Any notice or other document given, sent or served by post shall be deemed to have been given on the day on which it was posted.

(3) Any notice or other document required to be given, sent or submitted to or served on a Commissioner—

    (a) shall be given, sent or submitted to an office of the Child Support Commissloners;

    (b) shall be deemed to have been given, sent or submitted if it was sent by post properly addressed and pre-paid to an office of the Child Support Commissloners.

Application to a Commissioner for leave to appeal to the Courts

25.—(1) A person who was a party to the proceedings in which the original decision or appeal decision was given (both of those expressions having the meaning assigned to them by section 25 of the Act) may appoint any person for the purpose of making an application for leave to appeal under section 25 of the Act.

(2) An application to a Commissioner under section 25 of the Act for leave to appeal against a decision of a Commissioner shall be made in writing and shall be made within 3 months from the date on which the applicant was given written notice of the decision.

(3) In a case where the Chief Commissioner considers that it is impracticable, or would be likely to cause undue delay, for such an application to be determined by the Commissioner who decided the case, that application shall be determined—

    (a) where the decision was a decision of an individual Commissioner, by the Chief Commissioner or a Commissioner selected by the Chief Commissioner; and

    (b) where the decision was a decision of a Tribunal of Commissioners, by a differently constituted Tribunal of Commissioners selected by the Chief Commissioner.

(4) If the office of Chief Commissioner is vacant, or if the Chief Commissioner is unable to act, paragraph (3) shall have effect as if the expression "the

Chief Commissioner" referred to such other of the Commissioners as may have been nominated to act for the purpose either by the Chief Commissioner or, if he has not made such a nomination, by the Lord Chancellor.

(5) Regulations 16(1) and 16(3) shall apply to applications to a Commissioner for leave to appeal from a Commissioner as they do to the proceedings therein set out.

26th October 1992   *Mackay of Clashfern, C.*

S.I. 1993 No. (L.) DRAFT

The High Court (Distribution of Business) Order 1993

Made — — — —	*199*
Laid before Parliament	*199*
Coming into force	*5th April 1993*

The Lord Chancellor, in exercise of the powers conferred on him by section 61(3)(a) and (c) of the Supreme Court Act 1981, hereby makes the following order:

1. This order may be cited as the High Court (Distribution of Business) Order 1993 and shall come into force on 5th April 1993.

2. There shall be assigned to the Family Division all proceedings in the High Court under the Child Support Act 1991.

3. In consequence of the provision made by article 2, paragraph 3 of Schedule 1 to the Supreme Court Act 1981 shall be amended by the insertion, after sub-paragraph (g), of the following:—

"(h) all proceedings under the Child Support Act 1991.".

Dated ,C

S.I. 1993 No. (L.) DRAFT

The Children (Allocation of Proceedings) (Amendment) Order 1993

Made — — — —   *199*
Laid before Parliament   *199*
Coming into force   *5th April 1993*

The Lord Chancellor, in exercise of the powers conferred on him by section 92(9) and (10) of, and Part I of Schedule 11 to, the Children Act 1989 hereby makes the following order:—

Title and commencement

1. This order may be cited as the Children (Allocation of Proceedings) (Amendment) Order 1993 and shall come into force on 5th April 1993.

2. The Children (Allocation of Proceedings) Order 1991 shall be amended in accordance with the following provisions of this Order and, in those provisions, a reference to an article by number alone shall be construed as a reference to an article so numbered in the said Order of 1991.

Child Support Act 1991

3. In article 3, at the end of paragraph (1) there shall be inserted the following:

"(s) section 27(1) of the Child Support Act 1991 (declaration of parentage);

(t) section 20 of the Child Support Act 1991 (appeals) where the proceedings are to be dealt with in accordance with the Child Support Appeals (Jurisdiction of Courts) Order 1992.".

4. In articles 6, 10, 12 and 13—

(a) after the number of the article there shall be inserted "(1)";

(b) for the words "under the Act or under the Adoption Act 1976" there shall be substituted the words "to which this article applies"; and

(c) at the end there shall be inserted the following:—

"(2) This article applies to proceedings—

(a) under the Act;

(b) under the Adoption Act 1976;

(c) of the kind mentioned in sub-paragraph (s) or (t) of article 3(1).".

Miscellaneous amendments

5. In articles 3(3) and 4(1), for the words "made to" there shall be substituted the words "commenced in".

6. In article 4(4), for the word "made" there shall be substituted the word "commenced".

7. In articles 14 and 18(1), for the words "commenced in" wherever they appear there shall be substituted the words "made to".

8. In article 20, for the word "commenced" there shall be substituted the words "made to".

Dated   ,C

S.I. 1993 No. (L.) DRAFT

The Child Support Appeals (Jurisdiction of Courts) Order 1993

Made — — — —	*199*
Laid before Parliament	*199*
Coming into force	*5th April 1993*

The Lord Chancellor, in exercise of the powers conferred on him by section 45(1) and (7) of the Child Support Act 1991 hereby makes the following order:—

Title, commencement and interpretation

1. This order may be cited as the Child Support Appeals (Jurisdiction of Courts) Order 1993 and shall come into force on 5th April 1993.

Parentage appeals to be made to courts

2. An appeal under section 20 shall be made to a court instead of to a child support appeal tribunal in the circumstances mentioned in article 3.

3. The circumstances are that—

(a) the decision against which the appeal is to be brought was made on the basis that a particular person (whether the applicant or some other person) either was, or was not, a parent of a child in question, and

(b) the ground of the appeal will be that the decision should not have been made on that basis.

Modification of section 20(2)-(4) in relation to appeals to courts

4. In relation to an appeal which is to be made to a court in accordance with this Order, the reference to the chairman of a child support appeal tribunal in section 20(2) shall be construed as a reference to the court.

5. In relation to an appeal which has been made to a court in accordance with this Order, the references to the tribunal in section 20(3) and (4) shall each be construed as a reference to the court.

Dated   ,C

S. I. 1993 No. (L.) DRAFT

The Child Maintenance (Written Agreements) Order 1993

Made — — — —	*199*
Laid before Parliament	*199*
Coming into force	*5th April 1993*

The Lord Chancellor, in exercise of the powers conferred on him by section 8(5) of the Child Support Act 1991, hereby makes the following order:—

1. This order may be cited as the Child Maintenance (Written Agreements) Order 1993 and shall come into force on 5th April 1993.

2. Section 8 shall not prevent a court from exercising any power which it has to make a maintenance order in relation to a child in any circumstances in which paragraphs (a) and (b) of section 8(5) apply.

Dated   ,C

S. I. 1993 No. DRAFT

The Children (Admissibility of Hearsay Evidence) Order 1993

Made — — — —   *199*
Laid before Parliament   *199*
Coming into force   *5th April 1993*

The Lord Chancellor, in exercise of the powers conferred on him by section 96(3) of the Children Act 1989, hereby makes the following order:—

Citation and Commencement

1. This order may be cited as the Children (Admissibility of Hearsay Evidence) Order 1993 and shall come into force on 5th April 1993.

Admissibility of hearsay evidence

2. In—
  (a) civil proceedings before the High Court or a county court; and
  (b) (i)   family proceedings, and
      (ii)   civil proceedings under the Child Support Act 1991 in a magistrates' court,
evidence given in connection with the upbringing, maintenance or welfare of a child shall be admissible notwithstanding any rule of law relating to hearsay.

Revocation

3. The Children (Admissibility of Hearsay Evidence) Order 1991 is hereby revoked.

Dated   ,C

S.I. 1993 No. (L.) DRAFT

The Maintenance Orders (Backdating) Order 1993

Made — — — —   *1992*
Laid before Parliament   *1992*
Coming into force   *5th April 1993*

The Lord Chancellor, in exercise of the powers conferred on him by section 58(7) of the Child Support Act 1991, hereby makes the following Order:—

Citation and Commencement

1. This Order may be cited as the Maintenance Orders (Backdating) Order 1993 and shall come into force on 5th April 1993.

Backdating of certain court orders

2. The amendments set out in the Schedule to this Order (which extend the powers of courts to backdate certain orders in circumstances relating to the operation of the Child Support Act 1991) shall have effect.

Dated   ,C.

SCHEDULE 1   Article 2
AMENDMENT OF PROVISIONS RELATING TO THE BACK-DATING OF CERTAIN COURT ORDERS

Matrimonial Causes Act 1973

1. In section 29(2) of the Matrimonial Causes Act 1973 (duration of continuing financial provision orders in favour of children), after the words "any later date" there shall be inserted the words "or a date ascertained in accordance with subsection (5) or (6) below".

2. After section 29(4) of that Act there shall be inserted—

"(5) Where—

(a) a maintenance assessment is in force with respect to a child; and

(b) an application is made under Part II of this Act for a periodical payments or secured periodical payments order in favour of that child—

(i)   in accordance with section 8 of the Child Support Act 1991, and

(ii) before the end of the period of 6 months beginning with the date on which the maintenance assessment was made,

the term to be specified in any such order made on that application may begin with the date on which any qualifying maintenance assessment took effect or any later date.

(6) For the purposes of subsection (5) above, the following are qualifying maintenance assessments—

(a) the maintenance assessment that is in force; and

(b) any previous maintenance assessment that was in force with respect to the child concerned if—

(i)   it was made before the end of the period of 6 months beginning with the date on which the application mentioned in subsection (5)(b) above was made, and

(ii) since it was made, successive maintenance assessments have been continuously in force with respect to the child concerned.

(7) Where—

(a) a maintenance assessment ceases to have effect or is cancelled by or under any provision of the Child Support Act 1991; and

(b) an application is made, before the end of the period of 6 months beginning with the relevant date, for a periodical payments or secured periodical payments order in favour of a child with respect to whom that maintenance assessment was in force immediately before it ceased to have effect or was cancelled,

the term to be specified in any such order made on that application may begin with the date on which that maintenance assessment ceased to have effect or, as the case may be, the date with effect from which it was cancelled, or any later date.

(8) In subsection (7)(b) above,—

(a) where the maintenance assessment ceased to have effect, the relevant date is the date on which it so ceased; and

(b) where the maintenance assessment was cancelled, the relevant date is the later of—

    (i) the date on which the person who cancelled it did so, and

    (ii) the date from which the cancellation first had effect."

3. After section 31(10) of that Act (effective date of variation of certain orders for financial relief) there shall be inserted—

"(11) Where—

(a) a periodical payments or secured periodical payments order in favour of more than one child ("the order") is in force;

(b) the order requires payments specified in it to be made to or for the benefit of more than one child without apportioning those payments between them;

(c) a maintenance assessment ("the assessment") is made with respect to one or more, but not all, of the children with respect to whom those payments are to be made; and

(d) an application is made, before the end of the period of 6 months beginning with the date on which the assessment was made, for the variation or discharge of the order,

the court may, in exercise of its powers under this section to vary or discharge the order, direct that the variation or discharge shall take effect from the date on which the assessment took effect or any later date.

(12) Where—

(a) an order ("the child order") of a kind prescribed for the purposes of section 10(1) of the Child Support Act 1991 is affected by a maintenance assessment;

(b) on the date on which the child order became so affected there was in force a periodical payments or secured periodical payments order ("the spousal order") in favour of a party to a marriage having the care of the child in whose favour the child order was made; and

(c) an application is made, before the end of the period of 6 months beginning with the date on which the maintenance assessment was made, for the spousal order to be varied or discharged,

the court may, in exercise of its powers under this section to vary or discharge the spousal order, direct that the variation or discharge shall take effect from the date on which the child order became so affected or any later date.

(13) For the purposes of subsection (12) above, an order is affected if it ceases to have effect or is modified by or under section 10 of the Child Support Act 1991.

(14) Subsections (11) and (12) above are without prejudice to any other power of the court to direct that the variation of discharge of an order under this section shall take effect from a date earlier than that on which the order for variation or discharge was made."

4. In section 52(1) of that Act (interpretation), after the definition of "education" there shall be inserted—

""maintenance assessment" has the same meaning as in has in the Child Support Act 1991 by virtue of section 54 of that Act as read with any regulations in force under that section."

Domestic Proceedings and Magistrates' Courts Act 1978

5. In section 5(2) of the Domestic Proceedings and Magistrates' Courts Act 1978 (duration of orders for financial provision for children), after the words "any later date" there shall be inserted the words "or a date ascertained in accordance with subsection (5) or (6) below.".

6. After section 5(4) of that Act there shall be inserted—

"(5) Where—

    (a) a maintenance assessment is in force with respect to a child; and

    (b) an application is made for an order under section 2(1)(c) of this Act

        (i) in accordance with section 8 of the Child Support Act 1991; and

        (ii) before the end of the period of 6 months beginning with the date on which the maintenance assessment was made,

the term to be specified in any such order, or in any interim order under section 19, made on that application, may begin with the date on which any qualifying maintenance assessment took effect or any later date.

(6) For the purposes of subsection (5) above, the following are qualifying maintenance assessments—

    (a) the maintenance assessment that is in force; and

    (b) any previous maintenance assessment that was in force with respect to the child concerned if—

        (i) it was made before the end of the period of 6 months beginning with the on which the application mentioned in subsection (5)(b) above was made, and

        (ii) since it was made, successive maintenance assessments have been continuously in force with respect to the child concerned.

(7) Where—

    (a) a maintenance assessment ceases to have effect or is cancelled by or under any provision of the Child Support Act 1991; and

    (b) an application is made, before the end of the period of 6 months beginning with the relevant date, for an order under section 2(1)(c) of this Act in relation to a child with respect to whom that maintenance assessment was in force immediately before it ceased to have effect or was cancelled,

the term to be specified in any such order, or in any interim order under section 19 of this Act, made on that application, may begin with the date on which that maintenance assessment ceased to have effect or, as the case may be, the date with effect from which it was cancelled, or any later date.

(8) In subsection (7)(b) above,—

    (a) where the maintenance assessment ceased to have effect, the relevant date is the date on which it so ceased; and

    (b) where the maintenance assessment was cancelled, the relevant date is the later of—

        (i) the date on which the person who cancelled it did so, and

        (ii) the date from which the cancellation first had effect."

7. In section 19(3) of that Act (duration of interim orders), for the words ",not being" there shall be substituted the words "except that, subject to section 5(5) and (6) of this Act, the date shall not be".

8. In section 20(9) of that Act (effective date of variation of orders for periodical payments), for the words ",not being" there shall be substituted "except that, subject to subsections (9A) and (9B) below, the date shall not be".

9. After section 20(9) of that Act there shall be inserted—

"(9A) Where—

   (a) there is in force an order ("the order")—

      (i) under section 2(1)(c) of this Act,

      (ii) under section 6(1) of this Act making provision of a kind mentioned in paragraph (c) of section 6(2) of this Act (regardless of whether it makes provision of any other kind mentioned in that paragraph),

      (iii) under section 7(2)(b) of this Act, or

      (iv) which is an interim maintenance order under which the payments are to be made to a child or to the applicant for the benefit of a child;

   (b) the order requires payments specified in it to be made to or for the benefit of more than one child without apportioning those payments between them;

   (c) a maintenance assessment ("the assessment") is made with respect to one or more, but not all, of the children with respect to whom those payments are to be made; and

   (d) an application is made, before the end of the period of 6 months beginning with the date on which the assessment was made, for the variation or revocation of the order,

the court may, in exercise of its powers under this section to vary or revoke the order, direct that the variation or revocation shall take effect from the date on which the assessment took effect or any later date.

(9B) Where—

   (a) an order ("the child order") of a kind prescribed for the purposes of section 10(1) of the Child Support Act 1991 is affected by a maintenance assessment;

   (b) on the date on which the child order became so affected there was in force an order ("the spousal order")—

      (i) under section 2(1)(a) of this Act,

      (ii) under section 6(1) of this Act making provision of a kind mentioned in section 6(2)(a) of this Act (regardless of whether it makes provision of any other kind mentioned in that paragraph),

      (iii) under section 7(2)(a) of this Act, or

      (iv) which is an interim maintenance order under which the payments are to be made to the applicant (otherwise than for the benefit of a child); and

   (c) an application is made, before the end of the period of 6 months

beginning with the date on which the maintenance assessment was made, for the spousal order to be varied or revoked,
the court may, in exercise of its powers under this section to vary or revoke the spousal order, direct that the variation or revocation shall take effect from the date on which the child order became so affected or any later date.

(9C) For the purposes of subsection (9B) above, an order is affected if it ceases to have effect or is modified by or under section 10 of the Child Support Act 1991."

10. In section 88 of that Act (interpretation), after the definition of "magistrates' court maintenance order" there shall be inserted—
"maintenance assessment" has the same meaning as in has in the Child Support Act 1991 by virtue of section 54 of that Act as read with any regulations in force under that section."

Children Act 1989

11. In paragraph 3(1) of Schedule 1 to the Children Act 1989 (duration of orders for financial relief), after the words "any later date" there shall be inserted "or a date ascertained in accordance with sub-paragraph (5) or (6)".

12. After paragraph 3(4) of that Schedule there shall be inserted—
"(5) Where—
  (a) a maintenance assessment is in force with respect to a child; and
  (b) an application is made for an order under paragraph 1(2)(a) or (b) of this Schedule for periodical payments in favour of that child—
      (i) in accordance with section 8 of the Child Support Act 1991, and
      (ii) before the end of the period of 6 months beginning with the date on which the maintenance assessment was made,
the term to be specified in any such order, or in any interim order under paragraph 9, made on that application may begin with the date on which any qualifying maintenance assessment took effect or any later date.

(6) For the purposes of subsection (5) above, the following are qualifying maintenance assessments—
  (a) the maintenance assessment that is in force; and
  (b) any previous maintenance assessment that was in force with respect to the child concerned if—
      (i) it was made before the end of the period of 6 months beginning with the date on which the application mentioned in paragraph (5)(b) above was made, and
      (ii) since it was made, successive maintenance assessments have been continuously in force with respect to the child concerned.

(7) Where—
  (a) a maintenance assessment ceases to have effect or is cancelled by or under any provision of the Child Support Act 1991, and
  (b) an application is made, before the end of the period of 6 months beginning with the relevant date, for an order for periodical payments under paragraph 1(2)(a) or (b) in favour of a child with respect to

whom that maintenance assessment was in force immediately before it ceased to have effect or was cancelled,
the term to be specified in any such order, or in any interim order under paragraph 9, made on that application may begin with the date on which that maintenance assessment ceased to have effect or, as the case may be, the date with effect from which it was cancelled, or any later date.

(8) In sub-paragraph (7)(b),—

(a) where the maintenance assessment ceased to have effect, the relevant date is the date on which it so ceased; and

(b) where the maintenance assessment was cancelled, the relevant date is the later of—

(i) the date on which the person who cancelled it did so, and

(ii) the date from which the cancellation first had effect."

13. In paragraph 6(3) of that Schedule (effective date of variation of orders for periodical payments), for the words ",not being" there shall be substituted "except that, subject to subparagraph (9), the date shall not be".

14. After paragraph 6(8) of that Schedule, there shall be inserted—

"(9) Where—

(a) an order under paragraph 1(2)(a) or (b) for the making or securing of periodical payments in favour of more than one child ("the order") is in force;

(b) the order requires payments specified in it to be made to or for the benefit of more than one child without apportioning those payments between them;

(c) a maintenance assessment ("the assessment") is made with respect to one or more, but not all, of the children with respect to whom those payments are to be made; and

(d) an application is made, before the end of the period of 6 months beginning with the date on which the assessment was made, for the variation or discharge of the order,

the court may, in exercise of its powers under paragraph 1 to vary or discharge the order, direct that the variation or discharge shall take effect from the date on which the assessment took effect or any later date."

15. In paragraph 9(2) of that Schedule (effective date of interim orders) for the words ",not being" there shall be substituted "except that, subject to paragraph 3(5) and (6), the date shall not be".

16. After paragraph 16(2) of that Schedule (interpretation), there shall be inserted—

"(3) In this Schedule, "maintenance assessment" has the same meaning as in has in the Child Support Act 1991 by virtue of section 54 of that Act as read with any regulations in force under that section."

SCHEDULE 2

DEFINITION OF FAMILY PROCEEDINGS

Magistrates' Courts Act 1980

In section 65(1) of the Magistrates' Courts Act 1980 (meaning of family proccedings), the following paragraph shall be inserted after paragraph (n)—

"(o) section 20 (so far as it provides, by virtue of an order under section 45, for appeals to be made to a court) or section 27 of the Child Support Act 1991;".

S.I. 1993 No. (L.) DRAFT

The Family Proceedings (Amendment No. 3) Rules 1993

Made — — — —	*1992*
Laid before Parliament	*1992*
Coming into force	*5th April 1993*

We, the authority having power under section 40(1) of the Matrimonial and Family Proceedings Act 1984 to make rules of court for the purposes of family proceedings in the High Court and county courts, in the exercise of the powers conferred by the said section 40, and of all other powers enabling us in that behalf, hereby make the following rules:

1. These rules may be cited as the Family Proceedings (Amendment No.3) Rules 1993 and shall come into force on 5th April 1993.

2. The Family Proceedings Rules 1991 shall be amended in accordance with the following provisions of these Rules and, in those provisions, any reference to a rule or Appendix by number alone shall be construed as a reference to the rule or Appendix so numbered in the said Rules of 1991.

3. In rule 1.2(1), after the definition of "the Act of 1989" there shall be inserted the words "the Act of 1991" means the Child Support Act 1991;"

4. After rule 3.20 there shall be inserted the following:—

"Application under section 27 of Act of 1991 for declaration of parentage

3.21—(1) Rule 4.6 shall apply to an application under section 27 of the Act of 1991 as it applies to an application under the Act of 1989.

(2) Where an application under section 27 of the Act of 1991 (reference to court for declaration of parentage) has been transferred to the High Court or a county court the court may give such directions as it thinks proper with regard to the conduct of the proceedings.

(3) Without prejudice to the generality of paragraph (1), the court may, in particular, direct that the proceedings shall proceed as if they had been commenced by originating summons or originating application and that any document served or other thing done while the proceedings were pending in another court, including a magistrates' court, shall be treated for such purposes as may be specified in the direction as if it had been such document or other thing, being a document or other thing provided for by the rules of court applicable in the court to which the proceedings have been transferred, as may be specified in the direction and had been served or done pursuant to any such rule.

(4) The district judge shall, as soon as practicable after a transfer of a kind mentioned in paragraph (2) has occurred, consider what directions to give under paragraph (2), and, without prejudice to the generality of paragraph (1), he may give directions for the holding of a pre-trial hearing to determine what further directions, if any, should be given.

(5) The application may be heard and determined by a district judge.

Appeal under section 20 of Act of 1991 from decision of child support officer

3.22—(1) Rule 4.6 shall apply to an appeal under section 20 of the Act of 1991 (appeals against certain decisions of child support officers) as it applies to an application under the Act of 1989.

(2) Where an appeal under section 20 of the Act of 1991 (appeals against certain decisions of child support officers) is transferred to the High Court or a county court, Rule 3.21(2), (3) and (4) shall apply to the appeal as it applies to an application under section 27 of the Act of 1991.

Appeal from Child Support Commissioner

3.23—(1) This rule shall apply to any appeal to the Court of Appeal under section 25 of the Act of 1991 (Appeal from Child Support Commissioner on question of law).

(2) Where leave to appeal is granted by the Commissioner, the notice of appeal must be served within 6 weeks from the date on which notice of the grant was given in writing to the appellant.

(3) Where leave to appeal is granted by the Court of Appeal upon an application made within 6 weeks of the date on which notice of the Commissioner's refusal of leave to appeal was given in writing to the appellant, the notice of appeal must be served—

(a) before the end of the said period of 6 weeks; or

(b) within 7 days after the date on which leave is granted.

5. After rule 10.21 there shall be inserted the following:—

"Disclosure of information under the Act of 1991

10.21A. Where the Secretary of State requires a person mentioned in regulation 2(2) or (3)(a) of the Child Support (Information, Evidence and Disclosure) Regulations 1992 to furnish information or evidence for a purpose mentioned in regulation 3(1) of those Regulations, nothing in rules 10.20 (inspection etc of documents in court) or 10.21 (disclosure of addresses) shall prevent that person from furnishing the information or evidence sought.

6. After rule 10.23 there shall be inserted the following:—

"Applications for relief which is precluded by Act of 1991

10.24—(1) Where an application is made for an order which, in the opinion of the proper officer or the district judge, the court would be prevented from making by section 8 or 9 of the Act of 1991, he may send a notice in Form M34 to the applicant.

(2) Where a notice is sent under paragraph (1), no requirement of these rules, except for those of this rule, as to the service of the application by the proper officer or as to any other procedural step to follow the making of an application of the type in question, shall apply unless and until the court directs that they shall apply or that they shall apply to such extent and subject to such modifications as may be specified in the direction.

(3) Where an applicant who has been sent a notice under paragraph (1) informs the proper officer in writing, within 14 days of the date of the notice, that he wishes to persist with his application, the proper officer shall refer the matter to the district judge for action in accordance with paragraph (4).

(4) Where the matter is referred to the district judge under paragraph (3), he shall—

 (a) where the notice under paragraph (1) had been completed by the proper officer, act in accordance with paragraph (5) or (7); and

 (b) where that notice had been completed by a district judge, act in accordance with paragraph (7).

(5) Where the district judge acts in accordance with this paragraph he shall consider the matter himself, without holding a hearing and, if he forms the opinion that the court would be prevented by section 8 or 9 of the Act of 1991 from making the order sought by the application, he shall send a notice in Form M35 to the applicant.

(6) Where an applicant who has been sent a notice under paragraph (5) informs the proper officer in writing, within 5 days of the date of the notice, that he wishes a hearing to be held in relation to the matter, the district judge shall act in accordance with paragraph (7).

(7) Where the district judge acts in accordance with this paragraph, he shall give such directions as he considers appropriate for the matter to be heard and determined by the court and, without prejudice to the generality of the foregoing, such directions may provide for the hearing to be ex parte.

(8) Where directions are given under paragraph (7), the proper officer shall inform the applicant of the directions and, in relation to the other parties,—

 (a) send them a copy of the application;

 (b) where the hearing is to be ex parte, inform them briefly—

  (i) of the nature and effect of the notice under this rule,

  (ii) that the matter is being resolved ex parte, and

  (iii) that they will be informed of the result in due course; and

 (c) where the hearing is to be inter partes, inform them of—

  (i) the circumstances which led to the directions being given, and

  (ii) the directions.

(9) Where a notice has been sent under paragraph (1) or (5) and the proper officer is not informed under paragraph (3) or (6), as the case may be, the application shall be treated as having been withdrawn.

(10) Where the matter is heard pursuant to directions under paragraph (7) and the court determines that the court would be prevented by section 8 or 9 of the Act of 1991 from making the order sought by the application, he shall dismiss the application.

(11) Where the court dismisses an application under this rule it shall give its reasons in writing, copies of which shall be sent to the parties by the proper officer.

(12) In this rule, 'the matter' means the question whether the making of an order in the terms sought by the application would be prevented by section 8 or 9 of the Act of 1991.

Modification of rule 10.24 where an application relates to more than one child

10.25—(1) Where, on an application for a single order in respect of more than one child, a notice is sent under rule 10.24(1), the applicant may inform the proper officer, under paragraph (3) of that rule, that he wishes to persist with his application in relation only to some of the children with respect to whom the notice related, in which case he shall specify the children in question.

(2) Where an application is made for a single order in respect of more than one child and, in the opinion of the proper officer or the district judge, the court would be prevented by section 8 or 9 of the Act of 1991 from making an order of the type sought only in respect of one or more, but not all, of the children with respect to whom the application was made, any notice under rule 10.24(1) or (5) shall specify the children with respect to whom that opinion is held and, where such a specification is made in a notice under rule 10.24(1)—

(a) paragraph (2) of that rule shall not apply;

(b) the application shall, until the contrary is directed under sub-paragraph (d) of this paragraph, be treated as if it related only to such children as were not specified in that notice;

(c) the proper officer shall, when he sends copies of the application to the respondents under any provision of these rules, attach a copy of the notice under rule 10.24(1) and a notice informing the respondents of the effect of sub-paragraph (b) of this paragraph;

(d) where, under rule 10.24, it is determined that the court would not be prevented, by section 8 or 9 of the Act of 1991, from making an order in relation to one or more of any children who had been specified in the notice under paragraph (1), the court shall direct that the application be treated as if it related to those children as well as to the child or children in relation to whom the proceedings had been proceeding, and it may give such directions as it considers appropriate for the conduct of the proceedings in consequence of that direction;

(e) rule 10.24(9) shall, where it applies, cause the application to be treated, not as having been withdrawn, but as having been made in relation only to the children who were not specified in the notice; and

    (f) rule 10.24(10) shall, where it applies, empower the court only to direct that the application shall proceed as if it had been made in relation only to the children who were not specified in the notice.

(3) Where a specification has been made under paragraph (1) or (2), "the matter" shall, in rule 10.24, be construed as meaning the question whether the application should be treated as not relating to all or some of the children that have been so specified.

Modification of rule 10.24 in relation to non-free-standing applications

10.26 Where a notice, except one containing a specification under rule 10.25(2), is sent under rule 10.24(1) in respect of an application which is contained in a petition or other document ("the document") which contains material extrinsic to the application—

    (a) the document shall, until the contrary is directed under sub-paragraph (c) of this rule, be treated as if did not contain the application in respect of which the notice was served;

    (b) the proper officer shall, when he sends copies of the document to the respondents under any provision of these rules, attach a copy of the notice under rule 10.24(1) and a notice informing the respondents of the effect of sub-paragraph (a) of this paragraph; and

    (c) it is determined, under rule 10.24, that the court would not be prevented, by section 8 or 9 of the Act of 1991, from making the order sought by the application, the court shall direct that the document shall be treated as if it contained the application, and it may give such directions as it considers appropriate for the conduct of the proceedings in consequence of that direction.".

7. In the list of forms at the beginning of Appendix 1, after the entry relating to M33 there shall be inserted the following:—

    "M34 Notice under rule 10.24(1)

    M35 Notice under rule 10.24(5)".

8. In Appendix 1, after Form M33 there shall be inserted the forms set out in Schedule 1 to these Rules.

9. In Appendix 1, the forms set out in Schedule 2 to these Rules shall be substituted for forms M11, M19, M21 and CHA13 and 14.

10. In Appendix 2, after paragraph 1(i), the following shall be inserted—

    "(ia) whether or not there have been any applications under the Act of 1991 for a maintenance assessment in respect of any child of the family and if so

        (i)   the date of any such application and, if available,

        (ii) the relevant National Insurance number, and

        (iii) details of the assessment made;".

Income Support Statutory Material

The statutory provisions governing the various Income Support premiums are to be found in Schedule 2 to the Income Support (General) Regulations 1987 [SI 1987/1967] and are as follows (the numbering refers to the Paragraph numbers of that schedule):

Lone parent premium

8. The condition is that the claimant is a member of a family but has no partner.

Disability premium

11. The condition is that
  (a) where the claimant is a single claimant or a lone parent, he is aged less than 60 and the additional condition specified in Paragraph 12 is satisfied, or
  (b) where the claimant has a partner, either
    (i) the claimant is aged less than 60 and the additional condition specified in Paragraph 12(1)(a) or (b) is satisfied by him, or
    (ii) his partner is aged less than 60 and the additional condition specified in Paragraph 12(1)(a) is satisfied by his partner.

Additional condition for the ... disability premium

12.—(1) Subject to sub-paragraph (2) and Paragraph 7 the additional condition referred to in Paragraph... 11 is that either
  (a) the claimant or, as the case may be, his partner
    (i) is in receipt of one or more of the following benefits: attendance allowance, mobility allowance, mobility supplement, invalidity pension under Section 15 of the Social Security Act, or severe disablement allowance under Section 36 of that Act, or

(ii) is provided by the Secretary of State with an invalid carriage or other vehicle under Section 5(2) of the National Health Service Act 1977 (other services) or, in Scotland, under Section 46 of the National Health Service (Scotland) Act 1978 (provision of vehicles) or receives payments by way of grant from the Secretary of State under Paragraph 2 of Schedule 2 to that 1977 Act (additional provisions as to vehicles) or, in Scotland, under that Section 46, or

(iii) is registered as blind in a register compiled by a local authority under Section 29 of the National Assistance Act 1948 (welfare services) or, in Scotland, has been certified as blind and in consequence he is registered as blind in a register maintained by or on behalf of a regional or islands council, or

(b) the claimant is and has, in respect of a period of not less than 28 weeks, been treated as having been incapable of work for the purposes of one or more of the provisions of the Social Security Act or Part I of the Social Security and Housing Benefits Act 1982 or, if he was in Northern Ireland for the whole or part of that period, was treated as having been incapable of work for the purposes of one or more of the comparable Northern Irish provisions, or

(c) the claimant or, as the case may be, his partner was in receipt of either

(i) mobility allowance or invalidity pension under Section 15 of the Social Security Act when entitlement to that benefit ceased solely on account of the maximum age for its payment being reached and the claimant has since remained continuously entitled to Income Support and, if the mobility allowance or invalidity pension was payable to his partner, the partner is still alive, or

(ii) except where Paragraph 1(a), (b), (c)(ii) or (d)(ii) of Schedule 7 (patients) applies, attendance allowance which is no longer in payment solely on account of the claimant or, as the case may be, his partner having undergone or having been treated as under-going treatment for a period of more than 4 weeks by virtue of Regulation 5 of the Social Security (Attendance Allowance) (No. 2) Regulations 1975, and, ...the disability premium has been applica-ble to the claimant or his partner.

(2) For the purposes of sub-paragraph (1)(a)(iii), a person who has ceased to be registered as blind on regaining his eyesight shall nevertheless be treated as blind and as satisfying the additional condition set out in that sub-paragraph for a period of 28 weeks following the date on which he ceased to be so registered.

(3) For the purposes of sub-paragraph (1)(b), once the disability premium is applicable to a claimant by virtue of his satisfying the condition specified in that provision, if he then ceases, for a period of 8 weeks or less, to be treated as incapable of work for the purposes of the provisions specified in that provision he shall, on again becoming so incapable of

work, immediately thereafter be treated as satisfying the condition in sub-paragraph (1)(b).

Severe disability premium

13.—(1) The condition is that the claimant is a severely disabled person.

(2) For the purposes of sub-paragraph (1), a claimant shall be treated as being a severely disabled person if, and only if

(a) in the case of a single claimant or a lone parent

    (i)   he is in receipt of attendance allowance, and

    (ii) subject to sub-paragraph (3), he has no non-dependants aged 18 or over residing with him, and

    (iii) no-one is in receipt of an invalid care allowance under Section 37 of the Social Security Act in respect of caring for him,

(b) if he has a partner

    (i)   he is in receipt of attendance allowance, and

    (ii) his partner is also in receipt of such an allowance or, if he is a member of a polygamous marriage, all the partners of that marriage are in receipt thereof, and

    (iii) subject to sub-paragraph (3), he has no-non-dependants aged 18 or over residing with him,

and, either there is someone in receipt of an invalid care allowance in respect of caring for only one of the couple or, in the case of a polygamous marriage, for one or more but not all the partners of the marriage, or, as the case may be, there is no one in receipt of such an allowance in respect of caring for either member of the couple or any partner of the polygamous marriage.

(3) For the purposes of sub-paragraph (2)(a)(ii) and (2)(b)(iii) no account shall be taken of

(a) a person receiving attendance allowance, or

(b) a person to whom Regulation 3(3) (non-dependants) applies, or

(c) subject to sub-paragraph (4), a person who joins the claimant's household for the first time in order to care for the claimant or his partner and immediately before so joining the claimant or his partner was treated as a severely disabled person.

(4) Sub-paragraph (3)(c) shall apply only for the first 12 weeks following the date on which the person to whom that provision applies first joins the claimant's household.

Disabled child premium

14. The condition is that a child or young person for whom the claimant or a partner of his is responsible and who is a member of the claimant's household

(a) [not relevant]

(b) is in receipt of attendance allowance or mobility allowance or both or is no longer in receipt of that allowance because he is a patient provided that the child or young person continues to be a member of the family, or

(c) is blind or treated as blind within the meaning of Paragraph 12(1)(a)(iii) and (2).

Carer premium

14ZA (1) The condition is that the claimant or his partner is, or both of them are, in receipt of invalid care allowance under Section 37 of the Social Security Act.

(2) If a claimant or his partner, or both of them, would be in receipt of invalid care allowance but for the provisions of the Social Security (Overlapping Benefits) Regulations 1979, where

(a) the claim for that allowance was made on or after 1st October 1990, and

(b) the person or persons in respect of whose care the allowance has been claimed remains or remain in receipt of attendance allowance,

he or his partner, or both of them, as the case may be, shall be treated for the purposes of sub-paragraph (1) as being in receipt of invalid care allowance.

Family premium

This is not dealt with within Schedule 2 but in Regulation 17(c) of the Income Support (General) Regulations 1987 which provides that the condition of entitlement is

"(where the claimant) is a member of a family of which at least one member is a child or young person"

By Regulation 14 of those Regulations a "young person" is defined as a person aged 16, 17 or 18 who is treated as a child for the purposes of Section 2 of the Child Benefit Act 1975 (i.e. still in full-time education up to A level or its equivalent).

APPENDIX 3

Social security rates 1993/4

All rates are weekly rates unless otherwise shown. Figures correct at time of going to press.

ATTENDANCE ALLOWANCE
higher rate	44.90
lower rate	30.00

CHILD BENEFIT
only, elder or eldest for whom child benefit is payable	10.00
each subsequent child	8.10

CHILD'S SPECIAL ALLOWANCE
see note on Child Dependency Increase	10.95

COUNCIL TAX BENEFIT
Personal allowances
single	
18 to 24	34.80
25 or over	44.00
lone parent - 18 or over	44.00
couple - one or both over 18	69.00
dependent children	
under 11	15.05
11 to 15	22.15
16 to 17	26.45
18	34.80

Premiums
family	9.65
lone parent	10.95
pensioner	
single	17.30
couple	26.25
pensioner (enhanced)	
single	19.30
couple	29.00
pensioner (higher)	
single	23.55
couple	33.70

disability
single	18.45
couple	26.45

severe disability
single	33.70
couple (one qualifies)	33.70
couple (both qualify)	67.40
disabled child	18.45
carer	11.95

Allowance for personal expenses for claimants in hospital
higher rate	14.05
lower rate	11.20

Non-dependant deductions
aged 18 or over and in remunerative work
-gross income: £105.00 or more	2.00
-gross income: up to £104.99	1.00
others, aged 18 or over	1.00

Alternative maximum Council Tax Benefit
second adult on Income Support	25%

second adult's gross income:
-up to £105	15%
-£105.01 to £135	7.5%

Capital
upper limit	16000.00
amount disregarded	3000.00
child's limit	3000.00

Tariff income
£1 for every complete £250 or part thereof between amount of capital
disregarded and capital upper limit

Earnings disregards
where disability premium awarded	15.00
various specified employments	15.00
lone parent	25.00
where the claimant has a partner	10.00
single claimant	5.00
where carer premium awarded	15.00

Other income disregards
maintenance disregard	15.00
war disablement pension and war widow's pension	10.00
voluntary and charitable payments	10.00
student loan	10.00
student's covenanted income	5.00
income from boarders:	
disregard the fixed amount (£20) plus 50% of the balance of the charge	20.00

Expenses for subtenants
furnished or unfurnished	4.00
where heating is included, additional	8.60

DEPENDENCY INCREASES
Adult Dependency Increases
For spouse or person looking after children, with:–
retirement pension on own insurance, invalidity pension, unemployability supplement and, if beneficiary over pension age, unemployment benefit	33.70
non-contributory retirement pension, invalid care allowance and severe disablement allowance	20.15

sickness benefit if beneficiary over pension age	32.30
unemployment benefit	27.55
maternity allowance/sickness benefit	26.40

Child Dependency Increases
For each child, with:–
retirement pension, widow's benefit, invalidity benefit, invalid care allowance,   10.95
severe disablement allowance, higher rate industrial death benefit,
unemployability supplement and sickness/unemployment benefit if
beneficiary over pension age

NB -The Overlapping Benefits Regulations provide for the rate of child dependency increases, guardian's allowance and child special allowance to be adjusted where the increase or allowance is payable for the eldest eligible child for whom child benefit is also payable. The weekly rate of the increase or allowance is reduced by the differential (less the 75p derived from the Oct 1991 increase in child benefit) between the rate of child benefit pay for the oldest eligible child and that payable for a subsequent child. This gives a rate of £9.80.

DISABILITY LIVING ALLOWANCE
Care Component

Highest	44.90
Middle	30.00
Lowest	11.95

Mobility Component

Higher	31.40
Lower	11.95

DISABILITY WORKING ALLOWANCE
Adult allowance

Single people	43.95
Couples/Lone Parents	60.95

Child allowance

under 11	10.75
11 to 15	17.85
16 to 17	22.20
18	31.00

Applicable amount (ie taper threshold)

Single People	41.40
Couples/Lone Parents	69.00

Capital

upper limit	16000.00
amount disregarded	3000.00
child's limit	3000.00

Tariff income
£1 for every complete £250 or part thereof between amount of capital
disregarded and capital upper limit

Disregards

maintenance disregard	15.00
war disablement pension and war widow's pension	10.00
voluntary and charitable payments	10.00
student loan	10.00
student's covenanted income	5.00
income from boarders:	
disregard the fixed amount (£20) plus 50% of the balance of the charge	20.00

Expenses for subtenants

furnished or unfurnished	4.00
where heating is included, additional	8.60

EARNINGS RULES
Invalid Care Allowance	50.00
Unemployment Benefit (daily rate)	2.00
Unemployment Benefit (maximum weekly amount)	56.00
Therapeutic earnings limit	42.00
Industrial injuries unemployability supplement permitted earnings level (annual amount)	2184.00
War pensioners' unemployability supplement permitted earnings level (annual amount)	2184.00

Adult dependency increases with
sickness benefit where claimant is
(a) under pension age	26.40
(b) over pension age	32.30
maternity allowance	26.40

unemployment benefit where claimant is
(a) under pension age	27.55
(b) over pension age	33.70

retirement pension, invalidity pension, severe disablement allowance, unemployability supplement where dependant
(a) is living with claimant	44.65
(b) still qualifies for the tapered earnings rule	45.09

retirement pension, invalidity benefit and unemployability supplement where dependant not living with claimant	33.70
severe disablement allowance where dependant not living with claimant	20.15
invalid care allowance	20.15

Child dependency increases
level at which CDIs payable with long-term benefits are affected by earnings of claimant's spouse or partner
for first child	120.00
for each subsequent child	16.00

FAMILY CREDIT
Adult credit	42.50

Child credit
under 11	10.75
11 to 15	17.85
16 to 17	22.20
18	31.00

Applicable amount (ie taper threshold)	69.00

Capital
upper limit	8000.00
amount disregarded	3000.00
child's limit	3000.00

Tariff income
£1 for every complete £250 or part thereof between amount of capital disregarded and capital upper limit

Disregards
maintenance disregard	15.00
war disablement pension and war widow's pension	10.00
voluntary and charitable payments	10.00
student loan	10.00
student's covenanted income	5.00
income from boarders:	
disregard the fixed amount (£20) plus 50% of the balance of the charge	20.00

Expenses for subtenants
  furnished or unfurnished   4.00
  where heating is included, additional   8.60

GUARDIAN'S ALLOWANCE
see note on Child Dependency Increase   10.95

HOSPITAL DOWNRATING
20% rate   11.20
40% rate   22.40

HOUSING BENEFIT
Personal allowances
  single
  16 to 24   34.80
  25 or over   44.00

  lone parent
  under 18   34.80
  18 or over   44.00

  couple
  both under 18   52.40
  one or both over 18   69.00

  dependent children
  under 11   15.05
  11 to 15   22.15
  16 to 17   26.45
  18   34.80

Premiums
  family   9.65

  lone parent   10.95

  pensioner
  single   17.30
  couple   26.25

  pensioner (enhanced)
  single   19.30
  couple   29.00

  pensioner (higher)
  single   23.55
  couple   33.70

  disability
  single   18.45
  couple   26.45

  severe disability
  single   33.70
  couple (one qualifies)   33.70
  couple (both qualify)   67.40

  disabled child   18.45

  carer   11.95

Allowance for personal expenses for claimants in hospital
  higher rate   14.05
  lower rate   11.20

Non-dependant deductions rent rebates and allowances
  aged 25 and over, in receipt of Income Support
  aged 18 or over, not in work or
  – gross income under £70   4.00
  – gross income: £70 to £104.99   8.00
  – gross income: £105 to £134.99   12.00
  – gross income: £135 or more   21.00

Service charges for fuel
  heating   8.60
  hot water   1.05
  lighting   .70
  cooking   1.05

Amount ineligible for meals
  three or more meals a day
  single claimant   15.75
  each person in family aged 16 or over   15.75
  each child under 16   7.95

  less than three meals a day
  single claimant   10.45
  each person in family aged 16 or over   10.45
  each child under 16   5.25

  breakfast only - claimant and each member of family   1.90

Capital
  upper limit   16000.00
  amount disregarded   3000.00
  child's limit   3000.00

Tariff income
£1 for every complete £250 or part thereof between amount of capital
disregarded and capital upper limit

Earnings disregards
  where disability premium awarded   15.00
  various specified employments   15.00
  lone parent – not in receipt of IS   25.00
  where the claimant has a partner   10.00
  single claimant   5.00
  where carer premium awarded   15.00

Other income disregards
  maintenance disregard   15.00
  war disablement pension and war widow's pension   10.00
  voluntary and charitable payments   10.00
  student loan   10.00
  student's covenanted income   5.00
  income from boarders:
  disregard the fixed amount (£20) plus 50% of the balance of the charge   20.00

Expenses for subtenants
  furnished or unfurnished   4.00
  where heating is included, additional   8.60

INCOME SUPPORT
Personal allowances
  single
  under 18 - usual rate   26.45
  under 18 - higher rate payable in specific circumstances   34.80
  18 to 24   34.80
  25 or over   44.00

lone parent
under 18 - usual rate   26.45
under 18 - higher rate payable in specific circumstances   34.80
18 or over   44.00

couple
both under 18   52.40
one or both over 18   69.00

dependent children
under 11   15.05
11 to 15   22.15
16 to 17   26.45
18   34.80

Premiums
family   9.65

lone parent   4.90

pensioner
single   17.30
couple   26.25

pensioner (enhanced)
single   19.30
couple   29.00

pensioner (higher)
single   23.55
couple   33.70

disability
single   18.45
couple   26.45

severe disability
single   33.70
couple (one qualifies)   33.70
couple (both qualify)   67.40

disabled child   18.45

carer   11.95

Maximum amounts for accommodation and meals in

residential care homes
old age   185.00
very dependent elderly   215.00
mental disorder (not handicap)   195.00
drug/alchohol dependence   195.00
mental handicap   225.00
physical disablement
(a) (under pension age)   255.00
(b) (over pension age)   185.00
others   185.00
maximum Greater London increase   25.00

nursing homes
mental disorder (not handicap)   280.00
drug/alchohol dependence   280.00
mental handicap   285.00
terminal illness   280.00
physical disablement
(a) (under pension age)   315.00
(b) (over pension age)   280.00
others (including elderly)   280.00
maximum Greater London increase   35.00

Amounts for meals where these cannot be purchased within the
accommodation
(Daily Rate)
    breakfast   1.10
    midday meal   1.55
    evening meal   1.55

Reduction in benefit for strikers   23.50

Capital
    upper limit   8000.00
    amount disregarded   3000.00
    child's limit   3000.00

Tariff income
£1 for every complete £250 or part thereof between amount of capital
disregarded and capital upper limit

Disregards
    standard earnings   5.00
    higher earnings   15.00
    war disablement pension and war widow's pension   10.00
    voluntary and charitable payments   10.00
    student loan   10.00
    student's covenanted income   5.00
    income from boarders:
    disregard the fixed amount (£20) plus 50% of the balance of the charge   20.00

Expenses for subtenants
    furnished or unfurnished   4.00
    where heating is included, additional   8.60

INDUSTRIAL DEATH BENEFIT
Widow's pension
    higher rate   56.10
    lower rate   16.83

INDUSTRIAL DISABLEMENT PENSION
18 and over, or under 18 with dependants
    100%   91.60
    90%   82.44
    80%   73.28
    70%   64.12
    60%   54.96
    50%   45.80
    40%   36.64
    30%   27.48
    20%   18.32

Under 18
    100%   56.10
    90%   50.49
    80%   44.88
    70%   39.27
    60%   33.66
    50%   28.05
    40%   22.44
    30%   16.83
    20%   11.22

Maximum life gratuity (lump sum)   6080.00

Unemployability Supplement	56.10
plus where appropriate an increase for early incapacity	
higher rate	11.95
middle rate	7.50
lower rate	3.75
Maximum reduced earnings allowance	36.64
Maximum retirement allowance	9.16
Constant attendance allowance	
exceptional rate	73.40
intermediate rate	55.05
normal maximum rate	36.70
part-time rate	18.35
Exceptionally severe disablement allowance	36.70
INVALID CARE ALLOWANCE	33.70
INVALIDITY BENEFIT	
Invalidity pension	56.10
Invalidity allowance	
higher rate	11.95
middle rate	7.50
lower rate	3.75
MATERNITY ALLOWANCE	43.75
ONE PARENT BENEFIT	6.05
PNEUMOCONIOSIS, BYSSINOSIS, WORKMEN'S COMPENSATION (SUPPLEMENTATION) AND OTHER SCHEMES	
Total disablement allowance and major incapacity allowance (maximum)	91.60
Partial disablement allowance	33.70
Unemployability supplement	56.10
plus where appropriate increases for early incapacity	
higher rate	11.95
middle rate	7.50
lower rate	3.75
Constant attendance allowance	
exceptional rate	73.40
intermediate rate	55.05
normal maximum rate	36.70
part-time rate	18.35
Exceptionally severe disablement allowance	36.70
Lesser incapacity allowance	
maximum rate of allowance	33.70
based on loss of earnings over	44.90
RETIREMENT PENSION	
Category A or B	56.10
Category B (lower) – husband's insurance	33.70
Category C or D – non-contributory	33.70
Category C (lower) – non-contributory	20.15

Additional pension

Increments to basic and additional pension, contracted out deductions (from pre April 1988 increase by 3.6% earnings) and graduated retirement benefit	Increase by 3.6%
Contracted out deductions (CODS) and increments to CODS (from post April 1988 earnings)	(3% paid by scheme, RPI minus 3% by state)

Graduated retirement benefit (unit) (pence)	7.35
Addition at age 80	.25

SEVERE DISABLEMENT ALLOWANCE

Basic rate	33.70

Age-related addition (from Dec 90)

Higher rate	11.95
Middle rate	7.50
Lower rate	3.75

SICKNESS BENEFIT

Over pension age	53.80
Under pension age	42.70

SOCIAL FUND

Maternity payment	100.00

Capital limit

aged under 60	500.00
aged 60 and over	1000.00

STATUTORY MATERNITY PAY

Earnings threshold	56.00
Lower rate	47.95

STATUTORY SICK PAY

Earnings threshold	56.00
Standard rate threshold	195.00
Lower rate	46.95
Standard rate	52.50

UNEMPLOYMENT BENEFIT

Over pension age	56.10
Under pension age	44.65
Occupational pension abatement	35.00

WAR PENSIONS

Disablement pension (100% rates)

private or equivalent	92.20
non-commissioned officer	93.00
officer (£ per annum)	5081.00

NB: Under the further package of changes, which are to be discussed with the Central Advisory Committee on War Pensions the rates would be:

private or equivalent	97.20
officer (£ per annum)	5072.00

Age allowances

40% – 50%	6.50
over 50% but not over 70%	10.00
over 70% but not over 90%	14.30
over 90%	20.00

Disablement gratuity
(base figures for calc purposes only)
   specified minor injury   6080.00
   unspecified minor injury   3344.00

Unemployability allowance
   personal   59.55
   adult dependency increase   33.70
   a. increase for first child   9.80
   b. increase for subsequent children   10.95

Invalidity allowance
   higher rate   11.95
   middle rate   7.50
   lower rate   3.75

Constant attendance allowance
   exceptional rate   73.40
   intermediate rate   55.05
   normal maximum rate   36.70
   part-time rate   18.35

Comforts allowance
   higher rate   15.70
   lower rate   7.85

Mobility supplement   34.90

Allowance for lowered standard of occupation (maximum)   36.64

Exceptionally severe disablement allowance   36.70

Severe disablement occupational allowance   18.35

Clothing allowance (£ per annum)
   higher rate   124.00
   lower rate   79.00

Education allowance (£ per annum) (max)   120.00

War widow's pension (private)
   widow   72.90
   childless widow under 40   16.83
   age allowance
   (a) age 65 to 69   8.35
   (b) age 70 to 79   16.10
   (c) age 80 and over   23.95
   children's allowance
   a. increase for first child (adjusted for child benefit increase)   13.85
   b. increase for subsequent children   15.00

Orphan's pension
   a. increase for first child (adjusted for child benefit increase)   15.45
   b. increase for subsequent children   16.60

Unmarried dependant living as spouse (max)   70.85

Rent allowance (maximum)   27.75

Adult orphan's pension (maximum)   56.10

Widower's pension (maximum)   72.90

WIDOW'S BENEFIT
Widow's payment (lump sum)   1000.00

Widowed mother's allowance   56.10

Widow's pension
  standard rate
  age-related   56.10
    age 54 (49)   52.17
    53 (48)   48.25
    52 (47)   44.32
    51 (46)   40.39
    50 (45)   36.47
    49 (44)   32.54
    48 (43)   28.61
    47 (42)   24.68
    46 (41)   20.76
    45 (40)   16.83

Note: For deaths occurring before 11 April 1988 refer to age-points shown in brackets.

NATIONAL INSURANCE

CLASS 1 EARNINGS LIMITS, EARNINGS BRACKETS AND CLASS 2, CLASS 3 AND CLASS 4 LIMITS AND CONTRIBUTIONS

		1992–93	1993–94
Class 1	Lower earnings limit	£54 a week	£56 a week
	Boundaries of earnings brackets	£90 a week	£95 a week
	for employees contribution	£135 a week	£140 a week
		£190 a week	£195 a week
	Upper earnings limit	£405 a week	£420 a week
Class 2	Flat rate contribution	£5.35 a week	£5.55 a week
	Small earnings exception	£3,030 a year	£3,140 a year
Class 3	Flat rate contribution	£5.25 a week	£5.45 a week
Class 4	Lower profits limit	£6,120 a year	£6,340 a year
	Upper profits limit	£21,060 a year	£21,840 a year
	Contribution rate	6.3%	6.3%

RATES OF CLASS 1 CONTRIBUTIONS FOR 1993–94

Weekly earnings	Primary contribution (employee)		Reduced rate for married women and widow optants %	Secondary contribution (employer)	
	Standard rate				
	Not contracted-out rate %	Contracted-out rate %		Not contracted-out rate[†] %	Contracted-out rate %
£56.00–£94.99	2% of £56 PLUS 9% of that part of earnings which exceeds £56 but does not exceed £420	2% of £56 PLUS 7.2% of that part of earnings which exceeds £56 but does not exceed £420	3.85% of earnings up to £420	4.6	1.6
£95.00–£139.99				6.6	3.6
£140.00–£194.99				8.6	5.6
£195.00–and over				10.4	7.4

[†]Rates apply to all earnings

˙The contracted-out rate applies to that portion of earnings between the lower and upper earnings limits (£56 and £420 respectively). Employers' contributions on earnings below the lower limit and above the upper limit, are assessed at the not contracted-out rate.

APPENDIX 4

The application of the requirement to co-operate: C.S.A. policy guidelines

INTRODUCTION

These guidelines discuss the issues that should be taken into account by staff acting for the Secretary of State when they consider whether or not a parent with care who is on Income Support, Family Credit or Disability Working Allowance has good cause for refusing to co-operate with the Child Support Agency in seeking maintenance for her child or children. The guidelines have been prepared on behalf of the Secretary of State and will be embodied in the Agency's operational guidance to staff. Separate adjudication guidance to child support officers will be issued by the Chief Child Support Officer (CCSO).

All examples are illustrative and do not represent an exhaustive list of circumstances which might arise. Each case must be dealt with on its own merits.

Throughout, the Parent With Care is referred to as female and the Absent Parent as male. This is for convenience only and it must be remembered that the requirement to co-operate applies to both male and female Parents With Care.

THE REQUIREMENT TO CO-OPERATE

1. Section 6(1) of the Child Support Act 1991 requires the parent with the care of a child whose other parent is an absent parent to authorise the Secretary of State to take action under the Act if she is in receipt of, or claims, Income Support, Family Credit or any other prescribed benefit, if the Secretary of State requires her to give him that authorisation. Disability Working Allowance was prescribed in Regulation 34 of the Child Support Maintenance Assessment and Procedures (MAP) Regulations 1992. Section 6 of the Act will also apply if a claim for these benefits is made or paid in respect of the parent with care (PWC), for example if the claim is made by her partner. Section 6 of the Act applies solely to

413

parents with care. It does not apply to other people such as grandparents or other relations, or guardians, who apply for the above benefits and have the care of a child whose parent or parents are living elsewhere.

2. A parent with care who is under the age of 16 or over 16 but still classed as a child for IS purposes (ie still at school) will not be required by the Secretary of State to authorise action, even if a benefit is being claimed for her and her child by someone else. When a PWC claims benefit in her own right, however, the requirement to co-operate will apply.

3. The requirement to co-operate will be waived if there are reasonable grounds for believing that there would be a risk of the parent with care, or any child living with her, suffering harm or "undue distress" as a result of authorising the Secretary of State to take action (section 6(2) of the Act).

4. The test of harm or undue distress is not given a technical definition and the expression is therefore to be understood in accordance with ordinary English usage. The dictionary definition of these terms indicates that "harm" means to hurt, injure or damage; and "undue distress" means excessive, unjustifiable or disproportionate strain, pressure, anguish or pain. Case law from the Child Support Commissioners will, of course, assist in interpreting these words in the context of the Child Support Act.

5. A claimant, or the partner of a claimant, to Income Support, Family Credit and Disability Working Allowance, who is a PWC under the terms of the Act, will be asked to complete a maintenance application form (MAF) which will ask for details of the name and date of birth of the absent parent and for other information about him. If she does not wish to give this information, she will be asked to seek an interview with a Child Support Agency (CSA) official. Under section 46 of the Act, if the parent fails to comply with the requirement to co-operate or fails to give reasons why she should not comply with it, a child support officer may serve written notice requiring her to comply or to give reasons for not doing so.

The following general sequence of events will apply:
— parent or parent's partner claims benefit (or is already in receipt of benefit);
— a MAF is sent out by the Benefits Agency (BA) or CSA for completion (the benefit claim is dealt with separately and is not dependent on the return of the MAF);
— the MAF is returned with absent parent details uncompleted or incomplete, or the MAF is not returned;
— the PWC is asked to attend an interview or is visited at home or work if necessary;
either
— the PWC shows good cause why she should withhold details of the absent parent and no further action need be taken under Section 6 of the Act;
— or the PWC fails to show good reason why she should withhold details

of the absent parent, or fails to attend for interview;
— in this latter case, a letter is sent to her on behalf of the Secretary of State to tell her that she has not shown good reason for failing to co-operate;
— the parent has six weeks in which to consider her position and make further representations;
— if, at the end of this six weeks, the PWC has either not co-operated or has failed to show good reason for not co-operating, the case is referred to a CSO who will consider the case afresh. The CSO will write again to the PWC, if he considers she does not have good reason for failure to co-operate, to give her a further 14 days in which to comply with the requirement to co-operate or to give good reason not to do so;
— after this 14 day period, if, after careful consideration, the CSO is satisfied there is no reason to waive the requirement to co-operate, the CSO may issue a reduced benefit direction and send a copy to the PWC.

6. PWCs have a right to ask for a reconsideration of the Secretary of State decision but cannot appeal against it. They have a right to appeal against the decision of the CSO.

7. This steer sets out the matters to be considered by the interviewing officer acting on behalf of the Secretary of State. There are several important points which should be borne in mind:
— the welfare of any children living with the PWC must be considered;
— the PWC has a right to be believed unless what she says is inherently contradictory or implausible;
— a reduced benefit direction is a strong sanction and will have an important impact on the income of a PWC;
— a reduced benefit direction should not be counted in any benefit savings statistics.

8. Wherever possible, the interview should not take place in the presence of a child who is old enough to understand what is being discussed.

Incomplete evidence

9. If the MAF is returned with insufficient information to enable the absent parent (AP) to be traced, the PWC should be asked whether she can provide the necessary information. A PWC who has known an AP for some time can, of course, be expected to know more about him than a PWC who had only a short relationship. A PWC who has only a small amount of information about the AP should be encouraged to provide it.

10. If the PWC has given as much information as she can, even if it is not enough to trace the AP, she has complied with the requirement to co-operate. She may re-apply for maintenance at any time she gets more information.

Failure to return the MAF

11. Any failure to return the MAF should be followed up. At this point, some PWCs may make it clear they do not want to fill in the form.

PWC refuses to co-operate

12. The PWC should be made aware of a number of important points:
— the CSA exists to help her obtain maintenance;
— she need not see the AP;
— the AP will not be given her address, or even information about the town she lives in;
— the CSA will collect maintenance for her;
— paying maintenance does not give the AP the right to contact (formerly called access) with the child;
— she may want more flexibility in her life in future, and maintenance will help give her that flexibility;
— getting maintenance should increase her income if she starts work and gets family credit or DWA or moves off benefit altogether;
— £15 of maintenance is ignored when family credit, DWA, housing benefit and council tax benefit is claimed.

PWC still refuses to co-operate

13. In spite of knowing the advantages to her the PWC may still refuse to co-operate. Consideration then needs to be given to whether the PWC and/or any children living with her (including children who are not those of the AP) would be at risk of harm or undue distress if she were required to co-operate in seeking maintenance. The interview to discuss this must be handled with care and sensitivity – many PWCs will be genuinely distressed about having to discuss the circumstances surrounding a former relationship. It will, however, be necessary to obtain enough information to enable a decision to be made about the case. The question of whether the PWC will need to produce evidence to support what she says will depend on the circumstances of the case. Evidence will not always be available, and a claim of good cause not to co-operate should not fail simply because evidence is not provided. It must again be stressed that the PWC has a right to be believed unless what she says is inherently contradictory or implausible.

14. It is neither possible nor desirable to draw up a definitive list of the circumstances in which it would be reasonable to conclude that a PWC had good cause not to co-operate in seeking maintenance but the following guidelines apply to indicative circumstances.

PWC fears violence

15. The PWC's account of her reasons for fearing violence will need to be obtained. Where the AP has a history of violence to the PWC or her children, it may be relatively easier to reach a decision; but the PWC's fear of violence may be reasonable even where there is no history of it.

PWC a rape victim

16. Where a PWC says she has been a victim of rape by the AP interviews must be handled with the utmost tact and sympathy, though the circumstances will need to be established. It should be remembered that, even when rape has occurred, there may be circumstances in which the PWC feels that the AP should not be freed from the responsibility to provide support for the child particularly if she is reassured that the CSA will act on her behalf and that her address will not be revealed.

Sexual abuse

17. A PWC may decline to co-operate in seeking maintenance because the AP has sexually abused one of her children. This is a subject which many PWCs will find extremely distressing, and questioning should be conducted with great care and sensitivity. The PWC should be urged to report the matter to the police if she has not done so. Even when sexual abuse has occurred, there may be circumstances in which the PWC nevertheless decides that the AP should not be freed from his responsibility to provide support for his child, particularly if she is reassured that the CSA will act on her behalf, and will not reveal her address to the AP.

Child conceived as a result of sexual abuse (including incest)

18. If the PWC says that she does not wish to name the father because the child was conceived as the result of sexual abuse or incest, the interview must be handled with extreme tact and care, although the PWC's account of events must be obtained and a judgement made on the consistency and plausibility of what she says. Again, there may be circumstances in which the PWC nevertheless decides that maintenance should be pursued.

Other circumstances

19. There are a number of other circumstances in which the PWC will say that she or her children would suffer harm or undue distress, where there may be less of a prima facie case that this would be so. The extent to which harm or undue distress would result in a particular set of circumstances will vary from case to case and it will be for the interviewing officer to decide in the light of the facts whether (s)he considers that there is a risk of harm or undue distress. The situations described below are not exhaustive and each case must be considered individually.

Fear that the AP will want to see the child

20. Some PWCs will be afraid that, if the AP is required to pay them maintenance, he will demand to see the child. Sometimes the PWC may be concerned that it will be disruptive to the child to see the AP, and sometimes she herself will wish to sever all links with the AP.

21. It is important that PWCs are made aware that questions of contact (formerly known as access) are entirely separate from issues of maintenance. Many PWCs and APs are known to link the two but it is important to stress that both the parents are responsible for maintaining the child, subject to their financial circumstances. This responsibility is not removed because an AP no longer sees, or has never seen, the child.

22. A belief that an approach to an AP would result in demands for contact should not, on its own, normally be sufficient to enable a PWC to succeed in a claim that harm or undue distress would be caused by pursuing maintenance. If an AP subsequently sought contact, it would be for the courts to decide, on the merits of the case, whether it was in the child's interests for contact to be allowed. In all cases, the court would have the best interests of the child as its primary consideration and would take into account whether, for example, the AP had had regular contact with the child in the past.

PWC wishes to sever links with the AP

23.   The PWC's wish to sever links with the AP should not normally provide grounds for her to succeed in a claim of harm or undue distress. There would normally need to be additional factors before the requirement to co-operate would be waived. The PWC should be reminded that the CSA will not disclose her address to the AP.

No recent contact with the AP

24. PWCs who have older children who have no contact with the AP may refuse to co-operate because it would cause them or their children undue distress to re-open any degree of contact after a lengthy period. Again, there would normally need to be additional factors before the requirement to co-operate would be waived.

25. In many cases, the child need never know about the maintenance application. The PWC should be reminded that the CSA will not tell the AP her address and that, if the AP then wants contact with the child, the matter would be for the courts, who would have regard to the child's best interests.

PWC wishes to protect the AP

26.   Sometimes, a PWC will wish to protect an AP, most usually because he is living in a stable relationship with someone else who is unaware of the child he shares with the PWC. There may also be cases where the PWC wishes to protect the identity of an AP who is a prominent or well known person. It would be unusual for this situation to justify a claim that co-

operating would cause undue distress to the PWC or her children, unless there are other relevant circumstances. The PWC should be reminded that the CSA will act as a buffer between her and the AP and that the CSA's contact with the AP will be on a confidential basis. The fact that payment of maintenance may be awkward for the AP is not in itself a reason to waive the requirement to co-operate.

Juvenile PWCs

27. Where the PWC is under 16, or is over 16 but still classed as a child for IS purposes (ie she is still at school), she and her child will feature on someone else's benefit claim. In these cases, although Section 6 of the Act still applies, the Secretary of State will waive the requirement to co-operate until she applies for benefit on her own account.

Juvenile AP

28. A PWC who is required to co-operate must do so even if the AP is aged under 16 (or was at the time that the child was conceived). For the purposes of any interview, an AP under 16 years must be accompanied by an adult, to safeguard his position.

29. In the case of juvenile PWCs and APs there is a risk that one of the parents has committed a criminal offence. An older PWC, for example, may be reluctant to name a juvenile AP out of fear that a criminal prosecution might be brought against her. A PWC who was underage when her child was conceived may also fear that by naming the AP she might make him open to prosecution. Disclosure of information is covered by section 50 of the Child Support Act and in the Child Support (Information, Evidence and Disclosure) Regulations 1992. Other than in the most exceptional circumstances, information obtained by the Child Support Agency will not be passed to the police.

30. It is unlikely that these circumstances, on their own, will be sufficient to justify a refusal to co-operate.

Artificial insemination

31. Where a married woman has conceived as a result of artificial insemination (AI), it is usual for her husband to accept the child as his own either through formal adoption or by registering the birth. Indeed, a husband who does not oppose AI is treated in law as the father of the resulting child. The husband or former husband is, therefore, normally the AP in these cases and is the person from whom maintenance would be sought.

32. It is a licensing condition for centres which provide AI by anonymous donor that a woman shall not be provided with treatment unless account has been taken of the welfare of any child who may be born as a result of the treatment, including the child's need for a father. They are also required to consider the prospective mother's ability to meet the child's needs. Careful enquiries are made. It is uncommon for AI by anonymous donor to be provided for an unmarried woman. Any unmarried PWC who says that her child was conceived as a result of AI should be asked to provide evidence. If AI by anonymous donor is confirmed, there is legally no known father of the child and no further action should be taken. Where the PWC has made her own private arrangements for artificial insemination without involving a treatment centre, the man concerned is the child's father and should be named unless the PWC can show that there are reasons why harm or undue distress would result.

Test tube and donor births

33. Where a third person has been involved in donating ova or sperm for a test tube birth, the couple to whom the child is born normally accept the child as their own, again by adoption or by registering the birth. As with AI, where the husband did not oppose the treatment he is treated in law as the father.

34. As with AI, it is very rare for an unmarried woman to obtain a test tube birth. Evidence should be requested when a PWC says her child was conceived in this way.

PWC wanted the child: AP did not

35. A PWC may say that she deliberately set out to conceive a child with no intention of involving the AP in her decision to have a child or in its upbringing. She may have had no intention of pursuing a relationship with the father. On its own, this is not an acceptable reason for not co-operating with the CSA. Both parents are responsible for their children.

36. Some PWCs may have gone on to have a child after the AP made it clear he would prefer the PWC to have an abortion. Again, without other factors, this is unlikely to provide grounds for waiving the requirement to co-operate.

Naming unlikely fathers

37. There may be some instances where the PWC names as the AP someone who, the balance of probability suggests, is unlikely to be the AP. Examples might include entertainment or sports personalities or other well-known individuals.

38. Although the allegation may seem improbable, sufficient detail should be obtained of the circumstances to enable a judgement to be made about its validity.

39. If the claim is judged to be improbable, the PWC may have good cause not to name the real AP. She should be reminded of the advantages to her of getting maintenance, and encouraged to be open with the CSA about her real fears.

A voluntary arrangement exists

40. The PWC may not wish to co-operate because she considers she already has a satisfactory voluntary arrangement with the AP and does not wish to disturb it. Under the Child Support Act, where the Secretary of State requires her to co-operate she should do so unless this would cause harm or undue distress. The disturbance of a voluntary agreement would not, on its own, be sufficient to justify a claim of harm or undue distress.

PWC is mentally ill or handicapped

41. Where a PWC is suffering from mental distress or learning disability which prevents her from understanding what is required, or leads her to seem unco-operative, officials should treat her with patience and sensitivity. She may have given as much information as she can at this time. Alternatively, there may be an appointee who is able to help.

Other situations

42. Other circumstances may arise. In each case the facts must be established and the case judged on its merits.

Reaching a decision

43. Interviewing officers must start from the supposition that the PWC is telling the truth. Their decision that harm or undue distress would not be caused by pursuing maintenance could lead to the loss to the PWC of a significant amount of income: such a decision should be reached only after very careful thought and a full record needs to be kept of the PWC's account and the officer's reasons for not accepting her argument. The officer's reasons will be considered, along with any other evidence, by the child support officer in reaching a final decision about whether or not the PWC has shown good cause for not co-operating.

Index

Glossary of abbreviations

MR   The maintenance requirement

AG   The aggregate of the Income Support allowances and premiums applicable to the person with care

Q1   The aggregate of the Income Support allowances for the children used when calculating AG

Q2   The Income Support family premium

CB   The total child benefit payable, less any one parent benefit

BE   The basic element of child maintenance

AE   The additional element of child maintenance

A   The assessable income of the absent parent

C   The assessable income of the person with care

N   The net income of the absent parent

E   The exempt income of the absent parent

M   The net income of the parent with care

F   The exempt income of the parent with care

T   The maintenance payable under Special Case 2